D0938861

Cambridge Studies in Historical Geography 2

THE HISTORICAL GEOGRAPHY OF SCOTLAND SINCE 1707

Cambridge Studies in Historical Geography

Series editors:
ALAN R. H. BAKER   J. B. HARLEY   DAVID WARD

Cambridge Studies in Historical Geography encourages exploration of the philosophies, methodologies and techniques of historical geography and publishes the results of new research within all branches of the subject. It endeavours to secure the marriage of traditional scholarship with innovative approaches to problems and to sources, aiming in this way to provide a focus for the discipline and to contribute towards its development. The series is an international forum for publication in historical geography which also promotes contact with workers in cognate disciplines.

1 Period and place: research methods in historical geography. *Edited by* A. R. H. BAKER *and* M. BILLINGE.

2 The historical geography of Scotland since 1707: geographical aspects of modernisation DAVID TURNOCK.

3 Historical understanding in geography: An idealist approach LEONARD T. GUELKE.

THE HISTORICAL GEOGRAPHY OF SCOTLAND SINCE 1707

Geographical aspects of modernisation

DAVID TURNOCK

Reader in Geography, University of Leicester

CAMBRIDGE UNIVERSITY PRESS

CAMBRIDGE

LONDON   NEW YORK   NEW ROCHELLE

MELBOURNE   SYDNEY

Published by the Press Syndicate of the University of Cambridge
The Pitt Building, Trumpington Street, Cambridge CB2 1RP
32 East 57th Street, New York, NY 10022, USA
296 Beaconsfield Parade, Middle Park, Melbourne 3206, Australia

First published 1982

Printed in Great Britain at
The Pitman Press, Bath

Library of Congress catalogue card number: 82-1175

British Library Cataloguing in Publication Data

Turnock, David
The historical geography of Scotland since 1707.
—(Cambridge studies in historical geography; 2)
1. Scotland—Geography, Historical
I. Title
911'.411   G141

ISBN 0 521 24453 6

FOR GRAHAM

Contents

List of figures   *page* viii
List of tables   x
Acknowledgements   xi

1   Introduction   1
2   Scotland before 1707   12

Scotland from 1707 to 1821
3   General review   37
4   Agricultural improvement   66
5   The planned village movement   82
6   The whisky industry   97

Scotland from 1821 to 1914
7   General review   111
8   Glasgow and the Clyde   153
9   The iron and steel industry   167
10 Crofting in north Scotland   179

Scotland since 1914
11 General review   195
12 Planning for the Central Belt   233
13 Forestry   246
14 Island perspectives   262

15 Conclusion   278

Appendix   289
Notes   295
Bibliography   337
Index   340

List of figures

1.1 Administrative regions and study areas   10

4.1 Expansion of settlement in Glenlivet (Moray) and adjacent areas after 1750   72

4.2 Agricultural improvement in the Central Belt c. 1790   75

4.3 Agricultural improvement in the Outer Regions c. 1790   77

5.1 Industrial development in the Central Belt c. 1790   86

5.2 Industry and commerce in the Grampian and Highland regions c. 1790   92

6.1 Whisky distilleries 1798 and 1887   101

7.1 Distribution of population 1871   112

7.2 Population in the Central Belt 1871 by parishes   114–15

7.3 Population growth 1801–1901 and 1901–71   117

7.4 Agriculture in Strathclyde 1911   126

7.5 Sporting valuations in part of north Scotland 1871–1969   130

7.6 Transport and commerce in the Grampian and Highland regions c. 1840   132

7.7 Shetland fishing industry since the late eighteenth century   134

7.8 West-Central Scotland: development of railways and iron-works   137

7.9 Railway and steamer networks c. 1910   142

7.10 Nineteenth-century Glasgow industry correlated with the railway system   144

7.11 Lead mining at Wanlockhead: aspects of development from 1700   146

7.12 Large nucleated settlements 1891   147

7.13 Diffusion of electricity and gas supplies   149

10.1 Drimnin estate (Lochaber) 1978   181

10.2 Landholdings and settlement in Ardnamurchan and Morvern (Lochaber) in the late nineteenth century   185

10.3 Smallholdings in the Outer Regions 1870–1971   190

11.1 Aspects of regional policy since 1945   199
11.2 Farm classification for the Outer Regions 1969   208
11.3 Arable land in the Grampian and Highland regions 1871 and
      1967   210
11.4 Road density in the Central Belt 1953   220
11.5 Distribution of population 1971   224
13.1 Woodlands in the Grampian and Highland regions in 1914 by
      parishes   248–9
13.2 Forestry Commission plantations in the Outer Regions 1975   252
13.3 Local forestry studies: changes in the woodland area since
      1900   254
14.1 Island population 1871–1971   264
14.2 Population of Westray (Orkney) 1871–1976   268
14.3 Lighthouses in the west Highlands and Islands 1978   274

List of tables

1.1 Population data 1801–1971   8
1.2 Population in burghs 1851–1971   9
3.1 Population data 1755–1801   40
3.2 Linen production 1730–1820   55
3.3 Largest burghal parishes 1755 and 1821   64
3.4 Distribution of the largest burghal parishes 1755 and 1821   65
6.1 Distillery capacities 1798–1833   104
7.1 Distribution of settlements 1871 by settlement size groups   113
7.2 Population trends 1871–91 by settlement type   113
7.3 Classification of parishes 1871   116
7.4 Aspects of agriculture in Strathclyde 1911   127
7.5 Sporting valuations in part of north Scotland 1971–1969   131
7.6 Largest towns and cities 1891 and 1971   151
7.7 Distribution of the largest towns and cities 1891 and 1971   152
10.1 Agricultural holdings 1871–1969   189
11.1 Advance factory floorspace 1960–79   198
11.2 Employment in manufacturing 1950–74   200–1
11.3 Fisheries 1938–78   216
11.4 Herring fishing 1948–78   217
11.5 Electricity power station capacities 1948–78   222–3
11.6 Population change 1871–1971 by settlement size groups   226–7
11.7 Growth of large settlements 1891–1971   228
11.8 Population change 1961–71 by settlement size groups   230–1
12.1 Central Clydeside Conurbation 1801–1971   243
13.1 Afforestation 1920–79   247
13.2 Forestry Commission activity in Scotland 1945–73   250
14.1 Island population 1871–1971   265

Acknowledgements

This work is the outcome of many interesting years of research on the geography of Scotland spent on both sides of the border. It would be wrong to deny that the unique aspects of the humanised landscape have always been a major source of inspiration and that this modest contribution arises from a conviction that the sparsity of publications on Scotland's historical geography stands in inverse relation to the intrinsic interest of this topic. Nevertheless it is possible to show that the Scottish experience with modernisation exemplifies many of the general principles that have been advanced in different branches of social science. The distinctive qualities of the Scottish scene have emerged in no small way through the researches of countless geographers and historians. Careful referencing of their contributions, without which this book would be impossible, is a most pleasureable duty. I am also greatly obliged to many people in Scotland for their help over the years with my own field studies particularly in the Grampian and Highland regions. But I owe particular thanks to Professor J. B. Caird of Dundee and Dr J. R. Coull of Aberdeen, and two former colleagues now deceased, Mr H. A. Moisley and Professor A. C. O'Dell, for encouraging my interest in the early stages. The broader context of ideas on modernisation and regional development owes much to Professor M. Gaskin of Aberdeen and also to the editors of the series, Dr A. R. H. Baker and Dr J. B. Harley, both of whom provided valuable advice on the introductory and concluding sections. Useful information was provided by public bodies in Scotland and in many cases the references to sources for maps and tables represent supply of data over and above what is readily available in annual reports and similar publications. Production of the book also rests heavily on the cartographic skills of Katie Moore and Ruth Rowell and the secretarial assistance of Susan Haywood and Jean Smith. My family have supported me steadfastly over the years and sacrificed a number of conventional holiday pursuits in consequence. Furthermore my wife has given me invaluable help over many aspects of production.

1

Introduction

In view of a recent pronouncement that 'the production of a major summary of Scottish historical geography must lie a long way in the future' this book may well appear to constitute a dangerous and presumptuous literary adventure.[1] The arguments for caution are well founded since much early documentary material has been lost, and with the sparsity of cartographic evidence of any kind before the great eighteenth-century military survey by General Roy there is a formidable contrast in the quality and availability of source material for the periods before and after c. 1750. Furthermore, the limited effort made by historical geographers working on Scottish topics has been made still less effective in terms of potential for a general synthesis by a tendency to concentrate on a rather limited range of issues. Studies of rural settlement evolution are certainly hampered by a lack of continuity, arising from the particularly radical changes made at the time of the improving movement, but there seems little justification for the strange neglect of urban, industrial and transport themes where promising early studies have not been developed.[2] The lack of diversification cannot be attributed entirely to the absence of data, because economic historians have made very substantial contributions in this neglected area over the last ten years.[3] The imbalance in Scottish historical geography is all the more unsatisfactory because there are very few general reviews. Back in 1913 W. R. Kermack wrote the first and, so far, the only *Historical Geography of Scotland*, but this publication is significant only in the use of the term 'historical geography' because it was written as a 'geography behind history' and has very little potential as a stimulus for a modern version.[4]

The inter-war period produced a number of substantial papers, and saw the appearance of the first major regional monograph, A. C. O'Dell's *Historical geography of the Shetland Islands*.[5] But it is perhaps indicative of prevailing views on the relevance of different branches of geography that Professor A. G. Ogilvie should envisage no substantial role for historical geography, where interest was apparently to be restricted largely to anthropology and the study of place names.[6] Nevertheless, contemporary research did enable an important historical element to appear in modern text books on Scotland, most notably in the British Association handbooks for Aberdeen, Dundee and Glasgow.[7] But it should not be overlooked that in 1962 A. C. O'Dell and K. Walton published their *Highlands and Islands of Scotland*, which included a very strong historical dimension on what was in fact a review of the whole of northern Scotland, including the Grampian region as well as the Highlands proper.[8] Many of the illustrations attempted to map for the first time some of the basic source materials for Scottish historical geography, and such maps generally covered the whole of Scotland. A descriptive landscape approach which characterised much of this work was extended to the whole of the country by R. Millman in 1975, in a belated attempt to involve Scotland in the type of research which W. G. Hoskins had long been advocating in England.[9] Two further books subsequently appeared which provide a more analytical approach to urban and rural areas. I. H. Adams acknowledges inspiration from Hoskins, but gives considerable emphasis to processes of change in *The making of Urban Scotland*, while M. L. Parry and T. R. Slater, editors of *The making of the Scottish countryside*, claim no such descent although their authors are similarly concerned with the processes, both evolutionary and revolutionary, of landscape change.[10]

   This text represents a complementary effort to these two recent publications, although it had a longer gestation period. It is motivated by the belief that, despite the lack of any definitive appeal in this transitionary stage, it is educationally desirable to offer tentative overall assessment as a stimulus to both teaching and research. Urban and rural environments are covered, but there is no attempt to cover the whole time span of human settlement, and emphasis on the period since the union of 1707 should make the viability of the project rather less uncertain. Since 'there have been virtually no attempts to present a composite picture of the geography of a past period' the general examination of three periods, 1707–1821, 1821–1914, and 1914 to the present, in addition to a review of events leading up to 1707, involves some originality.[11] A further innovation arises through the presentation of three special studies for each of the major periods. These essays are meant to add depth where the accumulation of research makes an overall assessment particularly appropriate at this time. As far as possible these studies avoid the major topics of previous works, but they have been selected to provide the best overall balance and to reveal something of the spatial intricacies of Scotland's growth over the last two hundred and fifty years. Further, although the project is conceived fundamentally as an empirical study in regional development, with decision-making examined as far as possible in the context of individual behaviour and broader values or ideologies, some concluding assessments are offered to integrate the work with concepts of modernisation and development in the social sciences. Some of the more relevant ideas are therefore summarised here.

The task of placing the empirical work in a context of general ideas is complicated by the impressionistic nature of most models concerned with change through space and time. Various concepts of heuristic value have been outlined, but few have been tied to specific criteria and quantitative indicators which allow for testing against empirical research. Broadly it may be claimed that this work deals with the *modernisation* of Scotland, involving the change from a traditional, largely subsistence economy to one that is highly integrated with a wider trading system. A key role in this process was played by a modernisation elite which advocated new organisational forms and implemented necessary measures through its political power, combined perhaps with some charisma and personality.[12] K. W. Deutsch has referred to 'social mobilisation' as the process by which the old society is broken down so that people become available for new patterns of activity.[13] However the criteria used to indicate the transition to modernity cannot evidently be laid down as a discrete set of factors against which all societies can be measured. The level of modernisation has been shown to vary according to the values selected and although the debate has been largely related to the relevance of western values in the Third World there is the possibility that certain apparently 'recalcitrant' areas within western countries may be considered backward because of distinctive features in their routes to modernisation.[14] A further issue involves the relationship between modernisation and *development*. If modernisation is simply the increasing integration of a region into the world capitalist economy then it may take place on a colonial basis with external control of resources, leading to an emphasis on primary activities without corresponding attention to the secondary and tertiary sectors and the urbanisation which growth of these activities normally implies. Real development then involves the systematic increase in the total economic resources of society so as to bring out fundamental improvements in material and social welfare. Once again the distinction seems most significant for developing countries with their background as 'modern colonial societies', but it may also be of some relevance in considering Scotland's adaptation to the stimulus of union, both as regards the country as a whole and its constituent regions.[15]

One obvious source of stimulation is W. W. Rostow's model for the stages of economic growth, in the full context of political and social forces.[16] *Traditional* societies based on pre-Newtonian attitudes to the physical world (with men not disposed to believe that the world was systematically capable of manipulation) could not foster scientific research or take full advantage of progress in technology made elsewhere. Hence the *preconditions* for rapid economic development had to include a fundamental change in attitudes such as was evident in Western Europe in the late seventeenth century. Such a ferment of ideas, coupled with due attention to agriculture, education and public works (infrastructure or social overhead capital investment) may then be associated with a *take-off* where growth becomes the normal state of affairs. 'During the take-off new industries expand rapidly, yielding profits a large proportion of which are reinvested in new plant; and these new industries in turn stimulate through their rapidly expanding requirements for factory workers, the services to support them and for other manufactured goods.'[17] The initial emphasis on a relatively narrow complex of industry and technology gives way to a diversified range of activities, and thereby in *maturity* the economy 'demonstrates the capacity to move beyond the original industries which powered its take-off and to absorb and apply efficiently over a very wide range of its resources . . . the most advanced fruits of modern technology'.[18] Finally comes the stage of *high mass consumption* with emphasis on consumer durables and services, and more resources diverted to social welfare as the extension of modern technology ceases to be the overriding objective. The Rostow formula has encountered some criticism, and it is clear that quantification is much more feasible through an aggregate view that is perhaps more appropriate to a mature economy than one undergoing take-off. It may also be unwise to envisage a clear sequential pattern of change and allow instead for considerable overlap, especially between the take-off and the preconditions for it. Yet the existence of propulsive industries can hardly be denied, and the significance of ideological backing for change (through various non-economic preconditions) to maximise what is technically and physically possible is well-established.[19] It is therefore useful to examine the eighteenth and nineteenth centuries in Scotland to see how the nation participated in the take-off which has been traced in Britain to the end of the eighteenth century when a mechanised factory-based textile industry emerged.[20]

The preoccupation with the state as a whole as the unit for the study of economic growth leaves aside the inevitable spatial restriction of rapid growth. It can by no means be assumed that Scotland's regional economy will show dynamic tendencies and stand as a microcosm of the United Kingdom's performance. It is evident that before the take-off England and Wales had reached a high level of integration. In this achievement E. A. Wrigley emphasises the invigorating role of towns through their services and transport links, which 'helped to liberate more fully the productive capacity of the countryside' and therefore to invalidate the notion of a parasitic town.[21] More specifically he underlines the importance of London as a 'potent engine' working for change between 1650 and 1750. The largest city in Europe in 1801, London created a demand for food and fuel which in itself brought about a modernisation of agriculture and mining as well as improvements in communications.[22] In addition, for example, London merchants dealing in meat, fruit and poultry took an increasing interest in the conditions of production and put both capital and expertise into production, thereby accelerating the transformation of English agriculture.[23] Scotland's leading city was much smaller. In 1755 the 64,800 people in the Edinburgh area constituted only 5.1 per cent of the total population of Scotland, and in 1821, when 162,000 were resident in the parishes which eventually made up the city of Glasgow, they accounted for only 7.8 per cent of Scotland's population. London's 900,000 in 1801 was equivalent to 10.8 per cent of the population of England. Thus there was a possibility that Scotland would react passively to union. English textiles might flood the northern market and English merchants might outclass their Scottish rivals on the Atlantic routes, leaving the principal benefits to Scottish farmers who would have assured entry to the London food market with their cattle. It must therefore be considered how far Scotland was able to respond actively to the union and contribute through her own propulsive industries to the take-off and maturity of the British economy.

However, a region is unlikely to respond uniformly to an external stimulus for growth, and a call has recently been made for a general theoretical context of regional development which would allow understanding of how the geography of a region evolves as development proceeds.[24] In an area which is being opened up to modernisation it is argued that there is an initial *pre-industrial* phase (covering the traditional and preconditional phases in Rostow's scheme) when the emphasis is placed on primary industry. The spatial pattern of the resource area will consist of dispersed farms and small nucleated service centres which are wholly dependent on the needs of the primary sector. Initially manufactures will be imported, but as the economy develops into the second *industrial* phase (covering Rostow's take-off and maturity) import-replacing manufacturing industries begin to grow in the main port where local and imported raw materials can most efficiently be assembled and from which all parts of the regional market can be reached. Some primary processing of farm products may also develop in the inland service centres. Eventually the growth of the regional market allows the manufacturing in the port city to take advantage of economies of scale to the point where it may begin to export some of its output. Increased trade will place greater demands on service industries which will also expand on account of the improvement in living standards associated with the growth of the economy. At the same time, the better-placed inland centres will have become towns and acquired a considerable importance for manufacturing, which now becomes a major element in the regional economy. The final *post-industrial* stage of high mass consumption sees further expansion of manufacturing and services and the perfection of the central place hierarchy which assures continuity between the small communities still engaged in primary production and the port city. If the organisation of the primary sector is continuously modified, by labour shedding and farm amalgamation, so that *per capita* incomes increase, then the people working in the resource sector will secure incomes comparable with those secured elsewhere. But if the process of adjustment in the once dominant primary industry is frustrated by a reluctance to migrate (which could in part be caused by poor information flows resulting from inadequate attention by government to transport and education), then serious 'problem area' situations are likely to arise. The new reality of resource area dependence on distant urban centres with mature economies based on manufacturing will induce a traumatic readjustment marked by heavy depopulation and a continuous run-down in local services.

This approach has been applied to South Wales where coal is the important primary activity.[25] Particularly in the eastern part, a clear geographical distinction is seen between the resource areas of the coalfield and the service centre to the south, located off the coalfield. By 1913 the resource industries dominated the regional economy, but the southern service centres had acquired some industry as the ports engaged in flour milling and making confectionery for local markets. A decline in the demand for coal after the First World War meant a labour surplus that might have been absorbed by the growth of manufacturing industries serving local and extra-regional markets. But virtually no activity of this kind developed, so there was high unemployment and heavy out-migration. However, after the Second World War the growth of manufacturing did take place, encouraged by government regional policy. The trend towards manufacturing has increased to such an extent that this sector employs more than twice as many people as the basic industries of coal-mining, steel and tinplate production. Services are also becoming more important and employ over half the total labour force. And the change in structure has spatial implications because the manufacturing and services are most important in the southern centres, which have also benefited from rationalisation of public sector services. Thus the coalfield settlements are now faced with a difficult process of adjustment similar to the challenge that faced the whole region in the inter-war period.

The regional development model provides a framework for the analysis of change in a particular area and a useful vehicle for the integration of specific evolutionary themes such as central place structure, transport networks, industrial patterns and population distribution. It is also useful in reducing the five Rostow stages to three phases which should be easier to identify at the regional level. The discussion on Scotland will therefore look broadly at industrial progress in relation to the take-off and maturity which Rostow has recognised for the British economy as a whole, thereby avoiding the question of how far a region can experience an autonomous take-off. But there remains the problem of classification for resource industries like coal and iron. The application to South Wales seems questionable in the sense that the basically pre-industrial phase of primary production should be tied in with coal mining and iron production, as resource industries. Any form of manufacturing implies a degree of sophistication in the economy and it should be the significance for wage levels, urbanisation, education skills and technology that is decisive for classification rather than use of local materials. Moreover the significance of coal for manufacturing industry under nineteenth-century technology suggests a link with the second (industrial) stage rather than with the first. Assessment for Scotland will therefore follow from these assumptions.

For patterns within regions, the model and its elaboration in a region of the UK is helpful in emphasising the polarisation of growth on a port city which will tend to emerge whether or not there is active or passive adjustment. There will be the inevitable centre/periphery or core/fringe contrasts emerging, as 'backwash effects' draw population and investment resources to the central area of the region where secondary (manufacturing) and tertiary (service) functions can best be concentrated.[26] It is also useful in underlining the possibility that areas of primary industry may find adjustment difficult. Relations between centre and periphery may become so antagonistic as to produce a dual economy situation. 'Society must provide a socially and geographically fluid medium to accommodate ceaseless change in the relative worth of occupations and locations as the blend and amounts of goods and services required change through time.'[27] In the western world sweeping migration and rapid occupational change have been characteristics of the last two centuries, but there may be resistance in certain areas where 'more viscous communities' create duality as 'a back country of traditionally organised subsistence farmers surrounds limited commercialised areas dependent on foreign trade for markets'.[28] Such peripheries may not respond quickly to the diffusion of innovation from the centre, and government may be obliged to implement special programmes of economic assistance to improve living standards.

The socio-political aspects of centre–periphery relations are also worth considering. Centre formation can be regarded as a non-spatial concept, which refers to a central value system tending to find wide acceptance in a modern society. The values and beliefs of the centre gradually extend over the peripheral societies as an agreed basis for government, and the country becomes a fully integrated political unit.[29] However, these ideas may be transformed on to a spatial basis with the dominant social class related to a leading territory which then interacts with the periphery and seeks to

Table 1.1. *Population data 1801–1971*

Region	Population (thousands) in						Percentage change 1801–1971
	1801	1851	1901	1951	1961	1971	
Islands	68.5	98.5	103.0	76.2	69.2	64.3	−6.2
Highlands	250.0	318.2	274.3	234.3	230.6	241.1	−3.5
Grampian	211.9	339.2	448.4	451.1	440.4	438.6	107.0
Tayside	214.7	333.0	399.5	396.2	397.8	397.6	85.2
North	745.1	1,088.8	1,255.2	1,157.8	1,138.0	1,141.6	53.2
Borders	79.9	110.5	120.0	109.1	102.2	98.5	23.3
Dumfries & Galloway	106.7	164.6	144.6	148.0	146.4	143.2	34.2
South	186.6	275.1	264.7	257.1	248.7	241.7	29.5
Outer Regions	931.8	1,363.9	1,519.9	1,415.0	1,386.6	1,383.3	48.5
East-Central	335.3	589.7	983.9	1,230.5	1,275.5	1,335.8	298.4
West-Central	341.3	945.1	1,998.3	2,450.9	2,517.2	2,509.9	635.2
Central Belt	676.7	1,534.8	2,982.2	3,681.5	3,792.7	3,845.6	468.3
Scotland	1,608.4	2,898.7	4,502.1	5,096.4	5,179.3	5,229.0	225.1

Source: Census of Scotland

incorporate it within the prevailing value system. For the centre to survive territorially there must be an adequate degree of social and cultural homogeneity, otherwise regional centres may emerge as 'counter-centres' and invalidate the idea of a single political unit.[30] A clash of values between rival centres may well provoke military conflict, particularly when the strategic implications are ominous. But *modern* institutions should develop as far as possible to absorb conflict with the periphery and 'insofar as the modernisation of the central political institutions takes place before that of the periphery, without at the same time blocking the incorporation of the periphery, the greater the propensity for sustained development'.[31] The relevance of these issues to Scotland lies in the conflict between the Highlands and Lowlands which has sometimes made the unity of Scotland a purely nominal one. It may be anticipated that the values of the centre would encounter resistance in the peripheral areas, and that new political structures would be needed to assimilate the provinces and to introduce a pluralistic society. Any imposition of alien values, coupled with the emergence of a dual-economy (as described above), would constitute 'internal colonialism', an oppressive economic and political system with centre and periphery respectively displaying high levels of dominance and dependence.[32] So it is a fundamental assumption of this work that development will reveal core–periphery problems. The limited resources of the northern and southern extremities of Scotland, emphasised by the relative inaccessibility of the northwest mainland and islands, makes the anticipation of highly polarised growth in the Central Belt all the more justified.

Perception of broad regional variations arising from slow and uneven

Table 1.2. *Population of Burghs 1851–1971[a]*

	1851[b]		1901		1951[c]		1961[c]		1971[c]	
	A	B	A	B	A	B	A	B	A	B
Islands	10.8	11.0	14.6	14.2	16.3	21.4	16.9	24.4	17.5	27.2
Highlands	55.4	17.4	78.4	28.6	92.2	39.4	96.9	42.0	107.3	44.5
Grampian	140.5	41.2	249.9	55.6	288.7	63.9	291.8	66.2	293.2	66.7
Tayside	168.9	52.3	292.3	73.1	302.6	76.3	308.9	77.6	314.0	79.0
North	375.6	34.8	635.2	51.8	699.8	60.4	714.5	62.8	732.0	64.1
Borders	35.4	32.0	60.0	50.0	60.0	55.0	57.6	56.4	59.8	60.6
Dumfries & Galloway	46.4	28.2	54.4	37.6	65.3	44.1	67.0	45.8	70.3	49.1
South	81.8	29.7	114.4	43.2	125.3	48.7	124.6	50.1	130.1	53.8
Outer Regions	457.4	33.8	749.6	50.3	825.1	58.3	839.1	60.5	862.1	62.3
East-Central	361.4	61.3	713.3	72.5	900.9	73.2	933.6	73.2	967.3	72.4
West-Central	635.6	67.3	1,451.6	72.6	1,914.8	78.1	1,996.4	79.3	1,997.9	79.6
Central Belt	997.0	64.7	2,164.9	72.6	2,185.7	76.5	2,930.0	77.2	2,965.2	77.1
Scotland	1,454.4	50.2	2.914.5	65.2	3,640.8	71.4	3,769.1	72.9	3,827.3	73.2

A Total urban population (thousands)
B Percentage of the total population
[a] Includes New Towns and former Counties of Cities
[b] Includes estimates for burghs created in the decade 1851–61. Also where there are boundary differences between different categories of burgh, e.g. Municipal, Parliamentary and Police, the one with the highest population is normally selected.
[c] Adjustments are made in respect of boundary changes between 1951 and 1971

Source: Census of Scotland

diffusion of innovations thus becomes all important and contrasts must be examined on a quantitative basis wherever possible. Therefore to complement the three periods of study a regional system is adopted to identify the core and periphery of Scotland (Central Belt and Outer Regions) and each component is divided into a group of sub-regions which provide a realistic base for discussion and data analysis (Tables 1.1 and 1.2). There is no suggestion that the regions proposed are entirely satisfactory: given the many different topics investigated and the changes in functional relationships through time. Ten were considered the maximum for convenience and the present official administrative regions were used as a base (Figure 1.1).[33]

Some problems arose where data are compiled by combining figures for groups of pre-1975 counties. The reckoning of the county of Bute with Highland, Moray with Grampian, Midlothian and Stirling with East Central does not create serious difficulty, but the allocation of the whole of Perthshire to Tayside introduces recognisable distortion. Furthermore the inclusion of the Outer Hebrides in the counties of Inverness and Ross & Cromarty makes it impossible to separate the island authorities in certain cases, and the Highland region is therefore enlarged in such instances. Except where there are no satisfactory alternatives to the old counties, as in the case of Ayrshire and Lanarkshire, the modern administrative regions

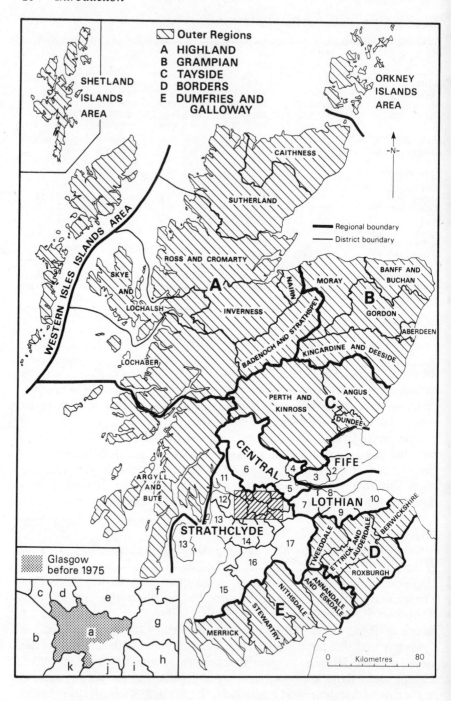

Outer Regions
A HIGHLAND
B GRAMPIAN
C TAYSIDE
D BORDERS
E DUMFRIES AND
 GALLOWAY

SHETLAND
ISLANDS
AREA

ORKNEY
ISLANDS
AREA

-N-

CAITHNESS

SUTHERLAND

Regional boundary
District boundary

WESTERN ISLES ISLANDS AREA

ROSS AND CROMARTY

SKYE
AND
LOCHALSH

A

NAIRN

MORAY

BANFF AND
BUCHAN

INVERNESS

GORDON

ABERDEEN

BADENOCH AND STRATHSPEY

KINCARDINE AND DEESIDE

B

LOCHABER

PERTH AND
KINROSS

KINROSS

ANGUS

C

DUNDEE

1

CENTRAL

6

4

3

2

FIFE

ARGYLL
AND
BUTE

11

5

8

7

LOTHIAN

10

12

9

BERWICKSHIRE

13

STRATHCLYDE

14

17

TWEEDDALE

ETTRICK AND LAUDERDALE

D

13

ROXBURGH

16

NITHSDALE

ANNANDALE AND ESKDALE

15

E

MERRICK

STEWARTRY

0　Kilometres　80

Glasgow
before 1975

c

d

e

f

b

a

g

k

j

i

h

are used in locational references. Finally it should be added that in terms of regional planning concepts (including growth pole theory) the whole of Scotland constitutes the region; the major divisions are merely sub-regions. But because of Scotland's claims to be a nation and the inelegance of the term 'sub-regions', the terms county and region are preferred, although this can cause confusion when models of regional development are being considered.

Figure 1.1. Administrative regions and study areas

Key for districts in the Central Belt:

1. North East Fife	2. Kirkaldy
3. Dunfermline	4. Clackmannan
5. Falkirk	6. Stirling
7. West Lothian	8. City of Edinburgh
9. Midlothian	10. East Lothian
11. Dumbarton	12. Inverclyde
13. Cunninghame	14. Kilmarnock & Loudoun
15. Kyle & Carrick	16. Cumnock & Doon Valley
17. Lanark	

a. City of Glasgow	b. Renfrew
c. Clydebank	d. Bearsden & Milngavie
e. Bishopbriggs & Kirkintilloch	f. Cumbernauld
g. Monklands	h. Motherwell
i. Hamilton	j. East Kilbride
k. Eastwood	

Note: On all the relevant maps the Argyll & Bute district is separated from the rest of Strathclyde region by a regional boundary to emphasise its inclusion in the Highlands for the purposes of this book

2

Scotland before 1707

This chapter examines the development of Scotland as an independent state strong enough to withstand external pressures for a unified Britain until the beginning of the eighteenth century. The emergence of the idea of a separate state in north Britain remains somewhat mysterious. Most conventional explanations seem inadequate.However, there is no doubt about Scotland's resolve to defend her independence through the introduction of a feudal system on the Anglo-Norman model. The modernisation of government was essential for survival although the price was a heavy one, not simply in terms of conflict with England but equally as a result of debilitating strife within Scotland due to the regional problem of Highland separatism. The growth of industry and commercial agriculture was inevitably stunted by these harsh strategic realities; yet there is evidence of an accelerating rhythm of growth in the seventeenth century. The border and lowlands were peaceful and social change was creating a climate where economic expansion was accepted, except in the Highlands where traditional values could still be asserted through military activity.

The formation of Scotland

About a thousand years after the Romans had first built Hadrian's Wall, the southern boundary of a northern state was drawn along the river Tweed as the result of the battle of Carham (Berwickshire) in 1018. This line, which eventually became the accepted boundary between England and Scotland, remained unstable for centuries. The whole area between the Forth–Clyde line in the north and the Tees in the south became a zone of bitter contention with the struggles of the two states mirrored by the feuds of local families, in whose hands lay much of the responsibility for administering the border. Undoubtedly there were stronger forces and potentials on the southern side of the border, and although English power based in London became greatly attenuated in the border region, the capacity to intervene in the far north is brought out clearly by Edward III's assault on Aberdeen in 1336. Scotland's resistance is however legendary; and it is this consistently inspired defence of a state idea that is so puzzling.

The *Picti* referred to in Roman chronicles may not have been regarded as members of a culturally and politically coherent community. Although there is no convincing case for supposing fundamental differences, there is nevertheless much uncertainty.[1] Studies of the prehistoric period fail to present any clear consensus over the routes used in the diffusion of new cultures and in the numerical strength of new arrivals as against the indigenous inhabitants.[2] There is also doubt over the extent of cultural and ethnic variations in different parts of the area that became 'Scotland', for even so compelling a contrast as the one which is displayed in fortification techniques between the Iron Age hill forts of the mainland and the contemporary broch towers of Caithness and the North Isles has not been convincingly impressed into the cultural mosaic.[3] The enigma spills over into the Roman period because the conquest of Western Europe in general, and the spasmodic advances made north of Hadrian's Wall in particular, may have contributed to what some commentators have seen as a confrontation between the land power of the mainland and the sea power of the islands. For it is clear that Scotland was well settled and while the closeness of settlements, along with their altitudinal range, average size and orientations over vegetation and soil type has obviously changed over the years there do not appear to have been extensive empty areas. Certainly the islands were extremely active in the Neolithic period, in view of the burial sites marked by megalithic tombs (and the 'village' of Skara Brae). And while the Iron Age brochs have been subject to various interpretations there is no doubt that, like the *duns* of the Hebrides, they indicate a substantial colonisation in terms of both numbers and abilities.[4] The interesting speculation of a Roman advance northwards through the Scottish mainland supported by the naval expertise of the broch builders remains largely conjectural. And thus the argument that a precedent for a separate state in the northern-most part of Britain lay in the combination of a Pictish people and Roman aloofness, symbolised by the wall, cannot be entirely dismissed as a product of hindsight.

The cultural contrasts within medieval Scotland are beyond doubt, for the Picts were left undisturbed after the Roman withdrawal for a compara-tively short time. The third and fourth centuries saw the arrival of the *Scotti* from Ireland and their takeover of the southwest Highlands to form the principality of Dalriada where Dunadd eventually emerged as the political centre.[5] At the same time Anglian settlement penetrated the southeast and the kingdom of Northumbria then extended over both sides of the 'frontier'. Although the record of the Picts in the Dark Ages is very fragmentary it would appear that their informal political structures were overhauled and a formerly loose collection of provinces gained stronger central control from a seat of government at the head of the Tay. Such a 'core area' had previously stimulated a degree of coherence in the limited context of south Pictland, in distinction to the northern section, beyond the Mounth, that was grouped around a 'rival' core area round the inner Moray Firth.[6] The Angles were now defeated at Nectansmere near Forfar (Angus) in 685 and the Scots were temporarily overcome, once Pictish successional problems had been resolved, in fighting near Perth in 728/9.

The Vikings introduce a further element into the picture.[7] It was Scandinavian pressure, first noticed in 794, but felt more gravely along Strathearn (Perth and Kinross) in 839, that stimulated the union of Picts and Scots in 842/3, under the Scottish King Kenneth MacAlpin. The gaelic culture of the Scots, reinforced by the rudimentary Christianity disseminated by Columba and his followers after 563, was now embraced by the Picts who in their turn contributed to the union the strategically important lands in eastern Scotland and an apparent preference for a matrilinear descent which enabled the royal stem to be nourished by strong blood from without. With bases around the Firth of Tay at Abernethy, Dunkeld and Scone the new state of Alba or Scotia was well-placed in the ensuing struggle with the Britons of Strathclyde and the Angles of Northumbria for control of the whole Central Belt. Strathclyde was weakened by the attack of Danes based in Ireland, which included the sacking of the capital at Dumbarton in 870, while Scandinavian activity also succeeded in dividing into two halves a Northumbria already weakened by the anarchy of internal dissension. Formal annexation was unnecessary as long as English power was constrained by the Scandinavian occupation in the south but a renewal of English pressure in the late tenth century brought a vigorous response. As a result of Malcolm II's victory at Carham the frontier was pushed from the Lammermuirs to the Tweed (to include Berwick, whose woollen trade made it the most important town in Scotland) and in 1034 the union with Strathclyde enabled Duncan to become the ruler of a united Scotland.

In a pioneer paper on the historical geography of Scotland W. R. Kermack stressed the importance of ethnicity and territory in the emergence and preservation of the nation state. The forces that derive from physiological and climatic conditions and which 'together shape mysteriously a nation's individuality' work on the ethnic qualities that are already present.[8] At the same time these forces can only work effectively, if at all, where there is a suitable territorial basis affording 'an entity of geographic conditions to whose influence the inhabitants may be subjected and at the same time afford the national individuality opportunity for undisturbed development'. However, it is difficult to present a convincing case along these lines. Ignoring the achievements of the Picts he says that Ireland contributed 'the first impulse towards unity and the development of a cultured national life'.[9] But the goidelic speech introduced by the Scots was complemented by the Teutonic influence of the English language which eventually found its way even into the Highlands. The territorial approach is equally unconvincing for although the frontier line extending east from Solway is relatively short and crosses sparsely populated hill country for much of its length there is no compelling advantage in terms of ease of administration or fortification (apart from the river section in the east) such as might be perceived in the case of the Roman wall. One must conclude that the frontier which emerged represented basically what was acceptable to England, giving her control of the Tyne valley and of the eastern plain until pinched out by high ground north of the Tweed.[10] Berwick was a particular bone of contention and was finally lost to England in 1482. Equally there was a formidable challenge to any centralising government in north Britain in extending any form of infrastructure over rugged and broken terrain. The routes extending northwards from the Central Belt across Rannoch Moor to the Great Glen and by Badenoch to Inverness were hardly feasible for the movement of large armies and emphasis was necessarily placed on the east coast route, with the option of reaching Moray by the Angus glens, Deeside and Donside in preference to the still longer journey through Aberdeen. To reach the southern Highlands the main route ran westwards from Stirling through to Crianlarich and Dalmally to reach either Crinan (where Dunadd was situated) or the Sound of Mull.

All studies of Scottish affairs refer to the distinction between 'Highland' and 'Lowland'. It is one that has a physical significance through the mountainous nature of much of the land north of the Central Belt with movement inhibited by ill-drained moorland and, at the northern and western extremities, pronounced insularity. But it has a greater significance when allied with the cultural divisions. It has been shown that the 'core area' plays an important role in the territorial growth of a state: it is a fertile zone strategically placed to sustain a drive for outward expansion. Clearly East-Central Scotland achieved this status, evident in the context of Pictland and also Alba, as Kenneth MacAlpin transferred his religious centre from the island of Iona on the Atlantic seaboard. The core area of Strathclyde lost its status after the union in 1034 and no separatist force has sought to regain it, but the core areas in the Highlands (mid-Argyll and the Moray Firth, originally associated with Dalriada and North Pictland respectively), did remain active and thereby posed a serious threat to the survival of Scotland as a nation state. The convention of treating the Highlands as a special case has probably been used to excess, and the regional character of other parts of the country has been rather overlooked in consequence, but the basic justification in terms of strategic and cultural issues is evident enough.

Arguably therefore the question is not one of demonstrating some convincing ethnic and territorial base for Scottish independence but rather of accounting for this condition in spite of the many difficulties that inhibited an effective unity. Some emphasis may be placed on the nature of the Scandinavian assault on Britain. External pressure forced the union of 843 but also prevented an English invasion from forestalling any consolidation of this early movement. Thus Mackie argues that 'the success of the invaders in England delayed for almost a century and a half the advance of English power against the north' while in Scotland the Norse people 'adapted their own institutions to local conditions and contributed to the population a strain of competent and adventurous blood'.[11] The Norwegians, however, controlled substantial parts of Scotland at the height of their power. In the eleventh century Thorfinn the Mighty held a great sea empire centred on Birsay in Orkney and extending to Caithness, Shetland and Sutherland as well as the Hebrides.[12] Although this peripheral power did not destroy the young state of Scotland it nevertheless complicated the consolidation process and contributed to the spirit of resistance to feudalism in the Gaelic areas. It was not until the Norse defeat at Largs in 1263 that the Hebrides were placed under Scottish rule, while Orkney and Shetland were retained even longer, until 1469.[13] Thus while the Norse may have provided a stimulus to consolidation of the Scottish mainland and simultaneously neutralised the other external influence (England) the explanation cannot rest solely with them. G. Donaldson has recently accepted that the matter is fundamentally enigmatic. He suggests that the different groups 'adopted as their heritage the history and mythology of the original Scots who had come as Irish invaders': the acceptance of a single history made one nation.[14] As regards the persistence of this sense of identity after the introduction of a feudal system, imposed with the help of incoming families who formed an alien elite, Donaldson says that 'no doubt the persistence of some native institutions despite all southern innovations had something to do with it and no doubt the retention by the monarchy of its ancient trappings contributed too', yet the full explanation must remain mysterious.

Administration: the role of the royal burghs

The development of an adequate administration and the extension of central control over the provinces were serious problems that had to be overcome. A direct succession was introduced in 1034 and under the House of Canmore the essentially Celtic monarchy gradually evolved towards the feudal state, on the lines of the English model. A seat of government emerged at Dunfermline, the favourite royal residence of Malcolm III (1058–83), but even at this time Edinburgh's rock fortress, guarded by precipitous slopes on three sides, was of ecclesiastical and military significance. During the reign of David I (1124–53) the castle there became the place of custody for the king's treasure and records of government. Moreover an Augustinian abbey was founded and alongside grew up the associated burgh of Canongate which, along with the castle and the 'new burgh', formed the three burghs of the old town. Edinburgh does not appear to have been formally regarded as capital of Scotland and much early town development took place in Fife, an area less exposed to English attack. Yet Edinburgh's fine defensive site close to the Forth and its nodal position in relation to routes across the border from the south assured its importance. The first Scottish university was founded at St Andrews in 1412 and the see of St Andrews was erected as an archbishopric in 1472.[15] The growing trade in wool, hides and skins, dried herring and salmon increased the importance of a group of royal burghs in Fife. Yet it was Edinburgh, graced by Holyrood Palace, that was the principal burgh of Scotland in 1482.[16] However, while various towns could enjoy prestige there was no doubt that the core area of medieval Scotland lay in East-Central Scotland: a region with adequate agricultural potential, good access by land and sea and enclosed by the high ground of the Campsies, Ochils and Lammermuirs (with heavily guarded 'gateways' at Perth to the north, Stirling in the west and Edinburgh to the south).

The extension of effective control over the provinces was a serious problem that was not properly solved until the eighteenth century, when the resources of the whole of Britain became available to eliminate separatist military forces. In the early twelfth century only the land between the Forth and Spey was under the king's direct control. During the reign of David I a feudal system was introduced with heavy reliance on an Anglo-Norman aristocracy.[17] There must have been a significant migration, some of it associated with commercial development that brought English blood into the towns, yet W. R. Kermack is probably right in seeing 'no reason to believe that the victory of English speech and civilisation was the result of any considerable admixture of English blood with the pre-existing population'.[18] Scotland's independence continued to be upheld by a population that was fundamentally of non-English racial origin. Yet there must have been a bitter confrontation between rival sets of cultures and values and given the actual circumstances of Scotland's progress to independence it was inevitable that the clearing of 'Celtic ways' from the Lowlands would assure their persistence in the Highlands. And at the same time the whole feudal movement, a package of measures to provide an efficient and effective chain of command from the sovereign to each individual, with reciprocal rights and obligations, became greatly resented in the north so that the very word 'feudalism' has come to be debased with connotations of tyranny and exploitation. Allied with a church which, unlike its Celtic predecessor, was organised on a hierarchical basis with firm territorial roots in the form of a parish system, the new nobility spearheaded a wave of penetration into the country and established a chain of strongholds that were particularly numerous in Mar in the northeast.[19] Endowed with substantial estates the feudal authorities could discipline their dependants by organising them into a social structure that would assure their survival, economically and militarily. The king could rest assured in the knowledge that the countryside was being loyally controlled with food surpluses generated for international trade and large numbers of men prepared for military service.

More direct administrative contact was achieved through the royal burghs, privileged communities whose inhabitants were given burgh law by the crown.[20] Some of the leading burghs became the centres of sheriffdoms with clearly-defined hinterlands for the administration of justice. These towns illustrate very well the way in which the medieval town idea involved a combination of economic, ecclesiastical and administrative functions (covering military and judicial matters). The functions were mutually self-supporting and the tax levies were compensated for by the award of monopolies for manufacturing and trade within certain areas. Therefore the theories of Scottish burghs that concentrate on military functions (the garrison theory of G. Neilson) or trade (the commercial theory of A. Ballard) are valid, yet incomplete, for the two approaches reinforce each other and in creating many royal burghs in a short time David I was emulating established European practice.[21] It was in the king's interest to create burghs under a legal system that favoured trade and then divert some of the profits to himself by tolls. Some places would already have a thriving trade. Other burghs were planted perhaps for reasons of control as in Moray. Yet growth would still be determined by success in trade – hence the need for a port and a productive landward region: without these sheriff and castle would stimulate only modest development. A fairly comprehensive chain of such settlements was established throughout eastern Scotland by the time the Wars of Independence first broke out in 1296. But the difficulties of finding economic potential in mountainous areas remote from the main avenues of commerce by land or sea ensured that the distribution would be uneven. While certain burghs enjoyed the greatest prestige, reflected in the large sheriffdoms created round Aberdeen and Perth, there were astonishing variations in the Moray Firth area with the saturation of the coastlands with burghs (Banff, Elgin, Forres, Nairn, Inverness, Cromarty, Tain) contrasting with the total absence of such settlements further west.[22] The boundaries of sheriffdoms reflect this contrast with the vast hinterland of Inverness contrasting with the tiny appendages of Elgin, Forres and Nairn. The rebellious province of Moray was to be pacified by the planting of royal burghs and an interim measure aiming at insulation of the area from the loyal territory of Aberdeen may be the cause of the curiously elongated shape of the intervening sheriffdom of Banff.[23] In view of the anomalies in the distribution of royal burghs and the fact that their monopolies inhibited the development of villages and rural industries it is not surprising that restructuring of the central-place hierarchy has been a prominent element in the modernisation process.[24]

Highland separatism

Resistance to the authority of central government was quite strong. Moray is an example of a 'debateable land' that was taken successfully under control through a military campaign and an effective settlement afterwards.[25] The challenge from Moray was sharpened by Macbeth's claim to the Scottish throne, but although Macbeth was killed in 1057 his descendants were able to sustain a prolonged rearguard action for a further seventy years against the attempts of Malcolm III and his sons to impose the authority of the central monarchy on this recalcitrant province. In 1130 David I defeated Angus of Moray and followed this up by a punitive campaign and an initial 'settlement' of Moray in 1135, but a further campaign by Malcolm IV and a more drastic settlement in 1163 was needed before Moray was brought fully under control. The new order meant the founding of royal burghs and also the introduction of a new aristocracy with the celtic *mormaer* giving way to feudal agents like the Lord of Duffus, based at the motte and bailey castle built on the edge of the Loch of Spynie.[26] Yet many lesser units of the old order survived as thanages, some in the hands of their ancient holders, and a policy of 'selective conservation' is also brought out by the maintenance of certain old dues and obligations alongside the new tenurial conditions. This leads to the conclusion that while reforming monarchs were resolved to destroy local independence and reorganise the structure of government 'they seem to have been conscious of their position as heirs of a Celtic inheritance and disposed to continue such aspects of it as might be to their advantage'.[27] Moray however was an area with considerable economic potential by virtue of its agricultural land and its accessibility by coastwise shipping and overland by the heavily-guarded Mounth passes.[28] It was amenable to plantation through the founding of burghs and the establishment of religious communities, such as the Cistercian Abbey at Kinloss that was founded in 1150 by monks sent north from Melrose. In Galloway too trouble at the turn of the eleventh century was overcome by the familiar strategy that included garrison burghs at such places as Ayr, Dumfries and Lanark, controlling the valley exits. But in the remoter Highlands the centralising impulse faltered and William the Lion's forts along the Great Glen were not complemented by any significant urban or monastic communities. Neither was the solitary Eilean Donan castle whose origins are bound up with an attempt by Alexander II to develop a base on the west coast from which to control the islands.

It is possible that continuation of the feudalising policies of the House of Canmore would eventually have overcome the resistance in the Highlands to stronger central government. Cultural differences, indicated most clearly through language, separated the Highlands and Lowlands yet the task of integration was being pursued with vigour and in 1293 King John planned new sheriffdoms in the Highlands: in Kintyre, Lorn and Skye.[29] But the momentum was lost in the wars of independence that arose out of the attempts of Edward I to reduce to vassal status the successful party in a disputed succession over which the English king had been asked to arbitrate. Edward saw as a precedent the recognition by Malcolm III of William the Conqueror as overlord but this recognition of Norman power and influence did not affect the existence of Scotland as a separate kingdom, nor did the homage that was extended to English kings by certain Scottish barons in respect of lands that they held south of the border. The challenge was readily accepted and the Scottish victory at Bannockburn (1314) is one of the milestones on the route to recognition of the country's independence in 1328.[30] Scotland's resolve had been made crystal clear in a letter to the Pope in 1320. This 'Declaration of Arbroath' may, according to D. Daiches, have been a short-lived rush of national emotion but it was something that could be drawn on for comfort and inspiration.[31] Yet while Scottish national consciousness gained stimulation and the country showed a remarkable recuperative power, relations with England reached a low ebb. Border raiding caused heavy losses, especially since Scotland's most productive farming areas in Lothian and the Merse (Berwickshire) lay exposed.[32] Moreover the crown's obligation to reward loyal supporters tilted the balance of power between the monarchy and the nobility in the latter's favour. The increased landholdings of the baronage meant enhanced economic and political power and a resentment of royal authority nourished in certain cases by cultural differences and traditions of provincial independence. Territories accumulated by John of Islay from Scottish kings in return for military service were further extended by marriage to cover a vast sea empire controlling the Minch crossings and Great Glen approaches. The lordship was made up of a number of semi-independent clans but leadership remained in one family and, with the inspiration of Viking times, the chief was a natural ally of the English despite the fact that much of his power grew in the first place from support against the Anglophil faction in the disputed succession. The so-called Treaty of Ardtornish-Westminster between Edward IV and the Lord of the Isles marks a renewed attempt to give formal political expression to the Highland–Lowland division. But the Scottish King came to terms with the English Yorkists, and many of the territories of the Lord of the Isles were declared forfeit in 1475. After further rebellion the whole title was taken in 1493 and the last lord died in 1503 after living his last ten years as a king's pensioner.[33]

However the growth of centralisation in Tudor England finds an echo north of the border. The two countries moved closer together as the Anglophil faction gained in strength following the disastrous raids on the Borders in 1545. Scotland broke with the old religion and employed English support against the French at Leith in 1560. The prevailing ethos of central government made Highland separatism and lawlessness all the more intolerable. The elimination of the Lord of the Isles indicated a measure of government authority but the vacuum that arose could only be filled by granting commissions to reliable nobles. The danting (or pacification) of the isles was placed in the hands of Argyll and Huntly, leaders of the Campbell and Gordon clans respectively. Yet while these two agents exercised their authority effectively within close range of their own estates they seem to have been powerless to prevent the deepening of local feuds in the islands. The growing difficulties that appear to beset the Hebrides between the visits of Donald Monro in 1548 and Martin Martin in 1695 may arise from a combination of mutually-reinforcing circumstances which led to growing insecurity and placed each island community more consciously on a war footing, ready to strike at marauding neighbours and raid the seaways for plunder. The MacNeil of Barra is regarded as a particularly enterprising sixteenth-century rover in Hebridean waters.

Feudal jurisdictions were strengthened in the 1580s as part of a renewed drive against lawlessness and in 1597 chiefs were required to present their title deeds in a bid to rationalise landholding and provide scope for royal initiatives in land settlement and local industries including fishing. For a few years the planting of lowlanders in parts of the Highlands having a significant economic potential was considered attractive. No doubt events in Ireland formed a precedent. In Lochaber, Argyll appears to have transferred Cameron families from the Great Glen over to Ardnamurchan and Morvern where the MacIan leadership was eliminated. But much more substantial was the plan to settle the Fife Adventurers in Lewis in the period 1598–1609. Their efforts ended ignominiously for no viable bridgehead could be established in the Hebrides, while the local people were naturally disposed to harass the intruders. Eventually the containing role of native leaders was recognised and Lewis, for example, was granted to MacKenzie of Kintail who was considered strong enough to hold the island and prevent lawlessness. Thereafter policy reverted to the traditional one of encouraging local feudal authorities. Successful lowland colonisation (from the counties of Ayr, Renfrew and Wigtown) is reported in Kintyre in the late seventeenth century to settle lands depopulated by plague (and find sanctuary for Presbyterian fugitives evading the religious strife of the 1660–88 period), but this movement stemmed from the initiative of the Duke of Argyll.

However, the chiefs were gradually brought more firmly under government control. Their traditional powers remained unaffected at this time although in return for recognition by government of their authority and title they were obliged to observe various regulations intended to bring their domains into the mainstream of Scottish life. Under the Statutes of Iona (1609) military and naval capacities were to be kept within limits. The wealthier chiefs were to have their eldest sons educated in Lowland schools, wine imports were to cease (though beer and whisky might be produced instead) and the clergy were to assume a greater role in religious and educational matters. This last point is interesting because it marks a trend whereby the established church was used as a very positive instrument for improvement in the broadest sense. Once again therefore the situation seemed favourable for the elimination of Highland separatism but only for prospects for peace to be gravely compromised by religious and successional issues which led to fundamental disagreement and made direct intervention by central government inevitable. Military adventures in the Highlands required a network of reliable bases and a start was made in Lochaber during the enlightened occupation at the time of the Commonwealth. General George Monck was in charge of operations in the Highlands and it was under his direction that the 'Black Garrison' was installed at Inverlochy. It seems that good relations were maintained with local clansmen but the departure of James II precipitated a major crisis: since many Highlanders shared his Catholic faith it was particularly difficult for them to abandon the allegiance that had been sworn to him. Yet explicit support for the Jacobite cause could only be treated with dismay in government circles and this new expression of Highland separatism was viewed with alarm in both Edinburgh and London. The danger of a French landing in the Highlands made a military solution inevitable but in spite of the Glencoe massacre (1692) this did not reach its climax until after the union had been formed. Thus the main study period of this book opens with the Highlands in turmoil and economic advance constrained.

Commercial development

Despite the military aspects of the feudal system it did secure important surpluses through agriculture and fishing that found their way into international trade, while the main ports became significant centres of industry.[34] Dundee was in a good position for trade for it had an extensive hinterland in Strathmore, accessible by easy routes across the Sidlaws, while 'the harbourage within the shelter of Castle Rock was as safe as the medieval mariner could reasonably expect'.[35] The commercial role of Dundee is made plain as early as the thirteenth century by the licence granted in 1402 by Alexander II to the Abbot of Coupar Angus Abbey to export wool and by a reference to the import of wine for Forfar Castle in 1264. The general trading role evidently increased in importance for in 1402 Perth abandoned all claim to a monopoly of trade on the Tay and Dundee provided the main outlet for primary produce from the Highland fringes and for the import of manufactures that were required. By the sixteenth century cloth had become important: the intimate contact with agriculture was lost and at the end of the century Bishop Leslie found it difficult to say whether the town's wealth lay mainly in trade or in industry. Much of the plaiding was derived from locally produced wool and exported to the Baltic, the main sphere of trading operations and the source of hemp and lint which were also consumed by the local textile industry. The soft water of Tod's Burn was made available through a sixteenth-century aqueduct that led through the town from a small reservoir constructed immediately beyond the wall. The seventeenth century sees the persistence of the primary exports: skins and hides, salmon and herring, some of them accumulated by coastwise shipping from an extensive area of the Highlands. But the town was not exclusively dependent on the hinterland. The orientation towards overseas trade increased with the union and the associated decline of the woollen industry, for the linen industry now became dominant and the improved agriculture of the region could not generate the raw material required. With the transition from linen to jute overseas dependence was complete. Of course Dundee's service centre role was maintained, and indeed enhanced by road improvements such as turnpiking, but the town also had its independent existence.

Dundee's experience was reflected to a modest degree in Aberdeen although here the woollen industry appears to have been developed as a domestic trade in the countryside maintained by agents of Aberdeen merchants who distributed raw material and collected the finished goods. The emphasis was on hosiery (the knitting of woollen stockings) and this provides a further point of contrast between Aberdeen and its rival on the Tay.[36] But the most important textile industry was located in Lothian and here, at establishments like the New Mills at Haddington, the production of fine cloth was carefully stimulated until exposed to excessive competition after the union.[37] The importance of the Forth was enhanced by two other considerations. First the existence of coal introduced a new element into the economy. Religious houses were active in coal mining in the early years for the monks of the abbeys of Dunfermline and Newbattle worked drifts back into the hillside. The fuel was used extensively for the production of salt, produced by the evaporation of sea water in large pans (which leave a legacy in such place names as Prestonpans) supplied with coal along the 'salt road' from Prestongrange.[38] The salt found markets abroad and profited from the dislocation of the French salt industry in the late sixteenth century. Deep mines are mentioned at Newhaven in 1609 but the most remarkable account is provided by John Taylor's 'pennyless pilgrimage' of 1618 which took in Sir George Bruce's sea coal mine at Dunfermline 'with its galleries running out for a mile beneath the firth'.[39] The drainage system consisted of an Egyptian wheel: three horses drawing up thirty-six buckets on an endless chain were required to work unceasingly to bale out water from the workings. The coal was used nearby in a salt works that produced about a hundred tons each week for export to England and Germany as well as for coastwise distribution to other parts of Scotland. Bruce's enterprise has left a permanent legacy in the fabric of Culross, the finest surviving small burgh of this period thanks to the attentions recently bestowed by the National Trust. The early-seventeenth-century Culross Palace may be seen as one of the first great mansions to be built by a successful entrepreneur in industry. The second factor lay in the rise of Edinburgh. It was the regular meeting place of the Scottish parliament after 1603 and was graced with a Parliament House during the reign of Charles I. Central law courts were established and in religious matters Edinburgh became an episcopal see in 1633 and was the usual centre for the meetings of the General Assembly. Industries of importance developed including foundry, glass and textile products and progress was made in town planning with the laying out of new squares after 1686 and the conception at least of a new town (though this was not proceeded with until the eighteenth century).

The Forth was Scotland's growth area, or, to put it more elegantly, the fringe of gold on a grey cloth mantle. Sir Walter Scott paints a picture of a flourishing Jacobean metropolis extending from Culross to the East Neuk.[40] In exchange for the staple exports to the Baltic and the Netherlands came timber, hemp and flax.[41] There was also iron from Sweden, for the local iron industry was insignificant (partly because of the protective policy towards woodlands) and a furnace at Letterewe (Ross & Cromarty) in the Highlands that used local timber and bog ore (with some import from Furness) did not survive beyond 1626.[42] Fine manufactures like the bells for the towers of tolbooths and kirks came from the Netherlands. Movement of people was also very significant. Craftsmen came over from the Netherlands while in the reverse direction went considerable numbers of traders and peddlers who settled throughout the Baltic zone: Denmark, Lithuania, Poland and Sweden. Relatively large Scottish communities could be found in Copenhagen, Stockholm, Memel while in both Poland and Prussia practically every town had a stable group of Scottish traders.

Although the emphasis on trade is new, the tradition of Scottish emigration was long established: the sixteenth century had witnessed movement to the Irish plantations while during still earlier times many Scots went abroad to seek education or military service.[43] Finally it should be noted that international trade had a contribution to make in the spread of ideas, and the Protestant Revolution seems to have been stimulated by contact with German merchants and sailors, as well as by the experiences of scholars and soldiers who went abroad. It is to be expected therefore that Protestantism grew and prospered most fully on the east coast from Aberdeen to Edinburgh and that in the Highlands, where no powerful patron emerged, the Reformation was almost unknown until the late sixteenth century.

In contrast to the long-standing trade contacts between east coast ports and the continent of Europe the Atlantic trade was a new element in the seventeenth century. The implications were felt in the far north where New World trade contacts stimulated the growth of Stromness in Orkney. The physical limitations of Kirkwall Bay and the inadequacy of the wharfage there encouraged the development of a separate port. It was early in the seventeenth century that artisans started to take feus or quoys on steeply-sloping land adjacent to a sheltered anchorage. The commercial potential of this new settlement close to the Pentland Firth was recognised throughout Scotland, but the substantial progress made before the union was much resented by Kirkwall whose trading monopoly was being violated. An act of 1693 in effect legalised the new trading centres provided that a proportion of the appropriate royal burgh's tax liabilities was met. However it seems that disagreement over the amount payable to Kirkwall brought litigation, culminating in a Court of Session verdict in 1754 that Stromness was free of any obligation. This appears to have set an important precedent and enabled all similar towns and villages to become totally independent of the royal burghs. However Stromness was not destined to become the Liverpool of Scotland and the industrial growth of west-central Scotland ensured that the bulk of the Atlantic trading would be based on the Clyde.

The Clyde estuary played only a minor role in Scotland's turbulent medieval history, for it was sheltered from English raiding. 'It was only in relation to the Norse power in the Hebrides that the region occupied a frontier role and this phase quickly ended with the defeat of Haakon at Largs in 1263.'[44] There were important routeways, as from Lanark through Glasgow to Dumbarton and from Ayr through the Lochwinnoch or Lugton gaps to Paisley and Renfrew. But until technical and political horizons broadened the physical basis for regional coherence could not be exploited. Glasgow developed as an ecclesiastical centre and until well into the seventeenth century the words 'let Glasgow flourish' were applied steadfastly to endeavour in religious observances.[45] Even when trading opportunities increased there was uncertainty how far the Clyde, as opposed to the Ayrshire coast, could benefit. The availability of the Irish market for Ayrshire coal prompted Sir Robert Cunningham to sink the first real coal pit in Scotland at Stevenston in the 1690s, with a Newcomen engine eventually installed for pumping, and build an associated harbour nearby at Saltcoats. But while the coal trade remained important for Ayrshire the Clyde towns had better hinterlands for commerce in general and it was Glasgow that generated the most successful merchant community.[46] After first cooperating with local rivals (Renfrew and Rutherglen) in unsuccessful attempts to improve the river for shipping, seeking to remove the sands and ford of Dumbuck in the mid sixteenth century, Glasgow gradually acquired the resources to proceed alone. Improvements in the 1630s allowed small boats to reach Glasgow, where the Broomielaw quay opened in 1663, and the importance of the packhorse route from Irvine on the Ayrshire coast was somewhat reduced. However ocean-going ships were obliged to use harbours on the lower river and until Port Glasgow was established in 1668 (after attempts to find accommodation in Dumbarton had been rebuffed in 1658) it was Greenock, a burgh of barony erected in 1635, that syphoned off much of the long-distance trade. Though Glasgow's trade was still modest at the end of the century, suffering from the twin constraints of navigation difficulties on the river and the political barrier to trade with English colonies in the form of the Navigation Acts, it was not a leading centre of commerce and both Leith and Bo'ness generated more customs revenue than Glasgow in 1656.

Trends in agriculture and rural settlement

While a measure of industrial growth is not a matter for dispute the situation in Scottish agriculture is rather less clear. In view of the scathing comments made by propagandists for the new 'improved' agriculture of the eighteenth century there has been a tendency to assume that backward conditions must previously have prevailed: a package of new measures belatedly made revolutionary changes in a countryside where traditional practices had become increasingly archaic. It may be true that the rural areas did not experience any infusion of vigorous capitalistic industrial enterprise until the eighteenth century but that does not rule out any form of innovation to the point where evolution rather than revolution might become the more realistic perspective. Research that drew attention to the important changes in Lothian in the seventeenth century, involving the use of lime to extend the cultivated area and permit a larger rural community to survive, has been overlooked.[47] But recently a major work on seventeenth-century agriculture confirms the impression of change 'if develop-

ments such as the foundation of new market centres, the increased granting
of written leases, the trend of grain prices, the passing of legislation to
encourage agricultural legislation and a host of other indicators are
examined'.[48] Progress was so slow that many contemporary commentators
were hardly aware of it and it required discerning people like Sir Robert
Sibbald, with a relatively broad outlook and long experience, to recognise
that progress was being made and that land was being regarded more as a
source of profit than as a direct basis of political power; such a change of
attitude which implied a willingness to consider new forms of organisation
involving written leases or consolidated holdings was quite crucial for
change over the long term. However, development was most notable in the
south with a widening of the Edinburgh grain market and commencement
of a regular driving trade with England. The large population of the capital
would in any case have stimulated commercial activity relatively early but
through their involvement in law, politics and trade it might be expected
that landowners in this area would not be too hidebound by tradition and
would readily perceive that opportunity existed. Hence while there were
occasional crises, as in the 1640s and 1650s, progress was only temporarily
checked and resumed at the Restoration until the 'ill years' of the
1690s.

The formidable evidence to show the growing importance of liming on
all types of arable land is sufficient to discredit the notion of static
agricultural practice before the eighteenth century and question the reality
of a Scottish agricultural revolution.[49] Yet in addition to the commercial
impulses is the question of inherent stability in the traditional feudal
pattern of rural settlement and landholding. The question is still shrouded
in mystery but some approaches have now been clarified. Continuity is the
keynote of R. A. Gailey's work which suggests that not only do many of
the present farmsteads rest on the sites of irregular nucleated *touns* but that
these touns may in turn have been inhabited since the Iron Age with little
fundamental change in size and morphology.[50] Obviously the continuity
cannot be complete because while some Iron Age settlement sites were
abandoned, where they involved thin soils or sandy land subject to
windblow, many new settlements have been formed by secondary colonisation. And in part of Tayside it has been shown that if the geography of
settlement can be equated with the distribution of Pictish symbol stones
there was a clear shift from sites that were easily defended to places with
the greatest agricultural potential. The most recent Class III stones (post
AD 1000) show an 'intimate' relation to environment when appraised in
the context of Pictish technology for both the uplands and the heavily
gleyed soils of the Carse of Gowrie are avoided.[51] Conceivably such
settlements, with their basic units of agricultural land, known as the
davoch, would become grouped into 'thanages' and 'shires' which repre-

sent an intermediate stage in the development of the county. However some difficulty arises from the fact that place names bearing the prefix Pit-, associated with the Celtic equivalent of Bal-, which have been associated with the davoch, do not accord with the sites of Class III symbol stones, leading to the alternative suggestion (not entirely contradictory with the first) that they emerged as later forest clearing settlements.[52] Regional variations in settlement systems are not thought likely but the general evolution pattern appears to have been rather complicated.[53]

New settlements arose in the late medieval period on account of the colonisation of waste land, indicated by placenames such as Newtown and Woodend, and by the lack of assessment in any form of traditional land measure.[54] But there are difficulties arising partly through a tendency for settlement sites to shift by a trial and error process until they achieved the more efficient spatial relationship with the best agricultural land and partly through township splitting. Basic settlement names appear in pairs distinguished by prefixes such as Easter/Wester, Nether/Over which appear to be associated with the tradition of a sun-wise division of lands. But while the Scandinavian technique of *solskifte* offering a distinction between the sunny (solarem) and shady (umbralem) sides, may have been the mechanism by which a division was made it cannot provide the explanation for a division being necessary in the first place.[55] From documentary study it is clear that some divisions came late, in the seventeenth or eighteenth century, but it is inferred from the complexity of some eighteenth-century estates maps that several stages are involved. The motive may lie in a desire to simplify a landowning structure that has become complex because of partible inheritance and the growing popularity of feuing land leading eventually to highly complex landholding arrangements whereby units of land ownership as well as agricultural holdings were fragmented and intermixed.[56] The situation is confusing (why should there be 'splitting' in Scotland when there is 'balling' in England?) and understanding is made more difficult by the lack of any detailed case studies of rural settlement evolution. But at least it is clear that the geography of rural settlement was dynamic, quite apart from the higher status acquired by some settlements as castletowns, kirktowns and milltowns, or, still more exalted, as estate markets (burghs of barony). As early as the 1470s a village was formed on the estate of Coupar Angus Abbey and it became the Burgh of Barony of Keithick, with its own corn and waulk mill. 'The establishment of the village can be interpreted as an attempt to avoid overcrowding of the farming land whilst yet maintaining in the vicinity a large reservoir of manpower of the kind it was essential to have during harvest'.[57] The differences in privileges between royal burghs and burghs of barony were evidently slight in view of the ease with which one type of burgh could change to another. An act of 1672 gave burghs of barony (and regality) a share of the monopoly of foreign trade hitherto enjoyed by the Royal Burghs.

As for the farming of the agricultural land there is widespread agreement that an infield–outfield system was employed and although these terms were not everywhere used there are as yet no grounds for denial that in all areas of Scotland a distinction was made between a permanently cultivated infield and an outfield where cultivation was spasmodic.[58] It has been shown that many references to 'outfield' indicate land beyond the customary limits of the township and do not therefore refer necessarily to differences in agricultural practice.[59] Yet local variations in land quality do seem to have made it preferable to use a small area (infield) intensively through continuous cultivation and heavy manuring rather than employ a less demanding rotation over a larger area. The logic of this can be seen on the margins of the high ground where a continuous *head dyke* offers an effective separation between hill pasture and arable, with associated meadow.[60] Arguments that see 'infield–outfield' at an early stage in an evolutionary sequences of field systems culminating in English open field patterns overlook the fact that rotation practices on the infield bring it into line with the supposedly more sophisticated 'three field system' of the English Midlands. And the curious anomaly of intensive rotational working of an infield being complemented by a relatively casual shifting system of outfield breaks may be resolved in terms of occasional 'emergency' use of the outfield or as a continuous process reclamation to augment the infield (as has been proposed for the Perthshire estate of Pitkellony) rather than as a regular ritual in the context of stable field boundaries.[61] Where there was a demand to produce more, because of a growth of the community or a demand from the towns, and where lime was available the infield may have extended almost to the limits of the land available. It is also possible that outfield cultivation took place as part of a trial and error process of 'search' for the best infield site. Research has shown that whereas infield normally tends to be on the best-drained land, with close proximity to farm steadings, some infields failed to reflect either of these criteria. A shifting infield, matched by a shifting toun (as mentioned above), may need to be recognised as an important reality.[62]

Where clearly distinct infield and outfield procedures were consistently followed it is likely that they varied from place to place according to the local perception of the potentials of the two types of land in relation to food requirements. It was reported for Lochtayside that outfield land was cultivated half the time: much of it was little inferior to the infield and, with justice done to it, it could have been even more productive.[63] In Islay the distinction between infield and outfield was not striking enough for it to gain any mention in contemporary documents. The 'wintertown ground' is used to refer to all areas of cultivation, permanent and sporadic, that were thrown open to grazing during the winter. Changes are also evident in the balance between individual and community interests with the initial emphasis on regular reallocation of individual holdings equal in both area and quality giving way to permanent holdings for the individuals and some scope for individual enterprise, in which the availability of smaller ploughs was important, exemplified by the appearance of small crofts separate from the community estate. This is implied by Gordon of Straloch's statement of 1662 to the effect that husbandmen had been *formerly* gathered in village settlements. Many a farmer was moving out of the touns to a new site where 'any vein of rich soil attracted him'.[64] The notion of run-rig has undergone a change of meaning. Basically it indicates a ridge and furrow pattern: everywhere there were winding ridges with stone-strewn *baulks* in between, a pattern deriving from the old method of ploughing, the need for drainage and for demarcation of individual rigs. But concepts of fragmentation (for proprietors and/or tenants) and re-allocation of holdings may sometimes be involved.[65] This underpins the dynamism of the infield–outfield system which has for too long been judged harshly for its inefficiency when in fact its only failing was to conflict with the ideal of the consolidated commercial unit that became the norm in the eighteenth century. In writing of the head dyke I. M. L. Robertson claims its position indicates where 'a balance has been struck between fundamental elements of geography: rural man and his physical environment'.[66] The balance is clearly struck in different ways, according to perceptions of the economic situation as mediated by tradition and the available technology.

Conclusion

There is clearly much evidence of progress made in building a unified state with a developed economy. Government had slowly regained initiative after the damaging wars of independence and was taking resolute action in the Highlands to curb lawlessness. 'There was now an institutional cohesion and unity in the country which had been lacking before' and the generally more peaceful conditions had taken castellated houses right out of fashion.[67] A Presbyterian system of church government, thoroughly rooted in popular feeling, allowed Scotsmen to boast that their's was the best reformed church in Christendom. Calvinism has been regarded as an important political development: an extension of feudalism where every-one was free to participate and, subsequently, a means of preserving Scottish national identity against the efforts of Charles I to anglicise the small northern kingdom. Fundamental issues of government were resolved as 'the establishment of presbyterianism closed the struggle over divine right in church and state'.[68] The General Assembly of the church exercised the greatest influence on the nation, but in the context of the ideal of cooperation between civil and ecclesiastical powers, while the acceptance of a more limited monarchy removed much of the strain between king and parliament.

At the same time important economic changes were taking place, for Scotland was turning away from her traditional economy, based on the privileges of the royal burghs and a continental trading system aimed mainly at France and the Netherlands, to a pattern involving greater internal freedom, encouragement for manufacturers through protection and trade with England. Legislation in 1690 to provide compensation for the victims of violence indicates an increased awareness of the value of the livestock trade with England and the consequent necessity for a peaceful trading environment.[69] The commitment to agricultural change is also evident in more general terms in the act of 1661, which made enclosure on a limited scale compulsory for many land holders, while a further act of 1695 reinforced the legal simplicity of enclosure and made it much easier to achieve than was the case in England. Many of the ports had been successful in developing industry out of an initial concern with export of primary staples and import of required manufactures. And the industry in turn stimulated some change in agriculture as the reduced famine risks in the seventeenth century allowed some cultivation of textile crops and as the growing demand for food in the towns induced appropriate improvement in the supply and distribution of grain. The importance of trade was reflected in the authorisation of improvements at some sixteen harbours after 1661, mainly on the east coast, and some official encouragement was extended to shipbuilding, although problems over the quality of timber and lack of skill made capital investment difficult while demand was only modest. While there was a general lack of trading competitiveness fisheries provided an exception and here there is some clear indication of the development of mercantilist politics. Arguably therefore Scotland was moving away from a simple economy with a feudal organisation generating modest surpluses to one where towns and their industries played a key role in modernisation and demanded accommodations from agriculture.

However, such a view must be modified by the difficulty of enforcing legislation. Transport overland was still extremely bad: people and ideas moved very slowly. Whereas the population of the burghs achieved a high level of literacy, and showed through church discipline general respect for the law and administrative hierarchy, the rural areas, especially in the Highlands, were difficult to control, and, while the logic of working through the feudal authorities was logical enough, they could not be expected to act as agents of modernisation until economic, social and political considerations were favourable: improvements would have to repay capital invested, people had to be assured a place in the new order and the need for a military-style organisation had demonstrably to have passed. These factors, which effectively prevented any reforms in the Highlands, called for caution in the Lowlands. A highly mobile population would be difficult to control and might easily undermine the stability of the state if people could not be readily employed in productive industry.[70] The concept of an industrial society was not an attractive one and nothing was done to encourage such a revolutionary change: migration was discouraged by legislation against vagabondage in the 1690s, following previous requirements that the poor be maintained in their home parishes and put to work in 'Houses of Correction'. Industry would be locally based throughout Scotland and the free movement of people to the areas with best prospects would be prevented. However, there was no adequate infrastructure in terms of transport and labour-management skills to justify such a comprehensive regional strategy, there were few compelling raw materials to attract investment, while the burghs were sensitive over their privileges and over the erosion of their 'island economies' by improved communications.

With so many difficulties and inhibitions it may well be doubted whether any recognisable or systematic mercantilist policy existed at all. But was Scotland's performance poor by English or European standards? The general consensus would suggest that it was and that bold initiatives were necessary: hence the great controversy surrounding the union issue. There was a two stage problem of adjustment. Scotland needed to adjust to new economic currents in Europe and overseas while within Scotland the Highland area needed to accommodate more harmoniously with the national ethos as dictated by events in the Lowlands. And while rapid change in Scotland would solve the first problem it would probably complicate the second. For this reason the economic record up to 1707 must reflect a balance of radical and conservative forces. Yet the validity of the perspective presented here must be constrained by the limited evidence available, especially on matters of regional variations. Without any more than the haziest knowledge of population distribution and migration it is impossible to gauge the social problems of economic change and even such fundamental questions as the degree of harmony between Highlands and Lowlands can only be answered crudely and subjectively.[71] It may be that the paucity of information on the socio-economic profile of the different regions of Scotland has led to a rather gross exaggeration of the distinctiveness of 'the Highlands' as an area, with variable limits, which shows the most remarkable deviations from the national norms. If there is one important contribution for historical geographers to make to complement the work done by other scholars it is in the search for greater discrimination in discussion of regional variations to exemplify B. Webster's judgement that Scotland 'was a country of regions rather than of centralised government'.[72] It is encouraging to see that in the agricultural sphere at least there is documentary evidence awaiting study that may allow some progress to be made along this road.[73]

Scotland from 1707 to 1821

3

General review

Scotland made very substantial progress during the seventeenth century and the directions of future growth were becoming clearly established. There is some disagreement on the extent of Scotland's development as compared with that of England, but the achievement of a significant advance is hardly controversial.[1] More clearly in dispute however was the wisdom of securing greater access to the English market through a full political union.[2] Scotland's failure to improve her trading performance was underlined by the crushing failure of the colony on Darien 'that could have been the trading hub of the world'.[3] Yet the complete integration with England that would remove all legal barriers (imposed through the Navigation Acts) to trade with the English colonies was inhibited by the strong grass-roots nationalism deepened by English opposition to Scottish commercial initiatives. T. C. Smout explains that the main lines of Scottish economic progress were laid down in the seventeenth century through cattle, linen and tobacco but 'almost all of them needed the Union if they were to lead to wealth'.[4] This indicates that the events of 1707 were inevitable if Scottish commercial interests were to prosper, but were complemented by a strategic gain to England in eliminating the possibility of a foreign policy in the north that was detrimental to her interests on the continent.[5] And both countries had a further interest in overcoming the problems of government arising from a union of crowns in the context of separate parliaments. But Scottish pride was at stake. The issues were plainly demonstrated in a flurry of legislation concerning the succession to Queen Anne in 1704–5: Scotland asserted her right to independence in the choice of sovereign while England made it clear that failure to agree on the succession would render the Scots aliens and the border would be closed to Scottish linen and livestock, a devastating prospect in view of the precarious economic situation in Scotland just at that time. A settlement was made and gained somewhat grudging acceptance, a measure of the suspicion that persisted in spite of the autonomy that Scotland was granted in her ecclesiastical, educational and legal institutions. A new context was provided for economic development and if at first this failed to inject major stimulation at least there was a peaceful climate, something that could not have been guaranteed otherwise, given the fragility of international relations in Europe at the time.

After the union prosperity came only slowly. War with France disrupted trade, as the Navy refused to provide the convoy services Scotland had a right to expect, and the Jacobite rebellion of 1715 had economic consequences through the confiscation of estates whose owners might otherwise have shown great energy in developing. Foreign speculations diverted capital that might have been better invested at home. Additionally the equivalents (compensation, computed by competent financiers, paid to Scotland for her assumption of a share of the English national debt) were only slowly implemented – despite the patronising attitude by England that Scotland had been 'bought' under the terms of the settlement. Clearly therefore the union had no immediate invigorating effect. Yet Scotland's late-eighteenth-century growth was remarkable and despite the fact that Ireland seemed to hold more promise at the beginning of the century there is no doubt that Scotland's performance was far superior by the end. The value of trade (per capita) for Scotland was fifty per cent above the Irish figure in 1800 whereas in 1700 the Irish level had been higher than Scotland's by the same margin: Ireland's per capita trade advanced from six shillings to seventeen; in Scotland it went from four to twenty six.[6] Arguably therefore the union created opportunities which the Scots had the ability to seize. This was seen most emphatically in Glasgow where the first tobacco ship from Virginia had arrived in 1674. With the support of trade and fishing, and with some expansion of manufacturing, the population of the town increased from an estimated 4,500 in 1560 to 13,000 at the beginning of the eighteenth century. After the union all legal restrictions on Scottish trade with North America were lifted and Glasgow above all was free to reap the benefits of its greater proximity to that continent compared with English ports.[7] There was also the stimulus of personal ties with Virginia, arising from the transportation of some people from Scotland for religious reasons. In 1718, Glasgow sent out the first ship of its own construction (ships from Whitehaven had been chartered previously) and the success of the trade led to the growth of a large prosperous business community.[8] 'The great Glasgow companies with their chains of stores in the colonies practised economies of scale, exploited the London capital market for financial assistance and developed sources of supply all over the European and American continents to feed their outlets.'[9] The tobacco merchants of Glasgow formed a small, tightly-knit group, linked by partnerships, marriage alliances and kinship loyalties, that enjoyed wealth on what was for Scotland an unprecedented scale.[10] There was some diversification through links with the Caribbean as tobacco firms traded there to obtain sugar and rum for their stores in Virginia and Maryland: during the American War of Independence the West Indies became an important centre for clandestine trade with the rebel colonies. These contacts were reinforced through exports from Scotland of herring and coarse linen goods and, late in the century, imports of raw cotton. Thus the tobacco lords presided over highly complex businesses and T. M. Devine concludes that 'their opulence was not based on one activity alone but on the net return from a series of compatible and suitable interlocking investments'.[11]

There were inevitable linkages with other sectors of the Scottish economy, including direct investment by the merchants. Their role in industrial development has probably been exaggerated, although the logic of vertical integration took some of them into cotton manufacture in association with an entrepreneur with skills and contacts yet lacking in capital. The idea that 'the sector concerned with foreign trade could remain an enclave within an industrialising economy is a mistaken view of Scottish economic development'.[12] There is the case of the Glasgow banker Robin Carrick who was involved in trade and industry, including a founding partnership in the Rothesay Cotton Spinning Company. There is also the instance of merchant capital in the malleable iron firm of Smithfield and Dalnottar, with further diversification (in association with the Cramond Iron Company) through the establishment of the Muirkirk Iron Company in order to maintain a cheap supply of bar iron at a time when prices for Russian and Swedish iron was rising. However, most pig iron production in the late eighteenth century arose through investment by English manufacturers and Scottish iron merchants. But there is no doubt that acquisition of landed property was an important aspiration since it was perceived that only through ownership of land on an adequate scale was it possible to embrace fully the life-style of the political and social elite. This in turn led to industry through the working of the coal and ironstone that were found in many estates in West-Central Scotland.[13] In Ayrshire too there was a group of landowners and professional people with proven investment capacity.[14] Coal mining was the more prominent activity, the workings being normally leased to experienced people and not exploited by the landowners themselves.

This chapter conveys the impression of a proto-industrialisation which occurred in a somewhat tentative manner during the seventeenth century in relation to the east coast ports and was then overtaken after 1707 by more powerful impulses which beamed with particularly sharp focus on the one area of the west coast with potential for the complementary growth of trade and manufacture. Moral and material considerations were blended together to create the powerful ideological force of enlightenment which

Table 3.1. *Population data 1755–1801*

Region	A	B	C	D	E
Islands	52.2	68.5	31.2	3.5	7.6[a]
Highlands	212.3	250.0	17.8	20.7	4.8
Grampian	206.6	211.9	2.6	43.0	1.6
Tayside	172.2	214.7	24.7	36.4	0.8[a]
North	643.3	745.1	15.8	103.8	2.2
Borders	82.2	79.9	−2.8	8.9	1.9
Dumfries & Galloway	79.6	106.7	34.1	10.7	2.2
South	161.8	186.6	15.3	19.6	2.1
Outer Regions	805.1	931.8	15.7	123.1	2.2
East-Central	298.8	335.3	12.2	78.4	0.5
West-Central	161.3	341.4	111.7	90.3	0.7
Central Belt	460.1	676.7	47.1	168.7	0.6
Scotland	1,265.2	1,608.4	27.1	291.9	1.3

A Population in 1755 (thousands)
B Population in 1801 (thousands)
C Percentage change 1755–1801
D Number of tradesmen in 1801 (thousands)
E Number of agricultural workers per person employed in trades
[a] Employment data are incomplete for Islands and Tayside
Sources: Census of Scotland and R. O. Forsyth, *The Beauties of Scotland.*
      Edinburgh, A. Constable & J. Brown (1805–8) 5 vols.

envisaged an adjustment throughout Scotland to achieve a common level of material well-being. The rural aspects of the improving movement are also shown to be crucial, although the special studies on agricultural change (Chapter 4) and the creation of planned villages (Chapter 5) means that the general discussion here is biassed towards the related issue of woodlands. But despite considerable effort to improve communications, continued remoteness from markets in parts of the Outer Regions gravely limited the opportunities for agricultural development. And in manufacturing too it is evident that superficial notions of spatial equality in linen manufacture foundered over the 'friction' that continued to be associated with overland travel in the Highlands. Recruitment of additional flax spinners and an exuberant search for suitable water power sites for cotton mills reflected temporary flirtations by Scottish businessmen with the enigmatic potentials of the north after official bodies had seen their promotional efforts frustrated. But while the 'spread effects' of manufacturing did ripple through Scotland their transformatory power was attenuated by distance, due partly to poor accessibility and partly to cultural conflicts – factors that theorists of modernisation are inclined to see as related and mutually reinforcing. The study of the whisky industry (Chapter 6) provides some insights into commercial prospects and government readiness to countenance special assistance in problem regions. Adjustment for the Highlands especially proved more traumatic than eighteenth-century improvers envisaged. The extent of the problem is mapped out by population figures (Table 3.1) which reveal a substantial increase between 1755 and 1801 (above the Scottish average in the Islands) combined with a relatively low level of employment outside agriculture. The period ends with falling (post Napoleonic War) agricultural prices undermining the fragile Highland economy still further while the rise of a steam-power based factory system eliminated the possibility of any further industrial spread and threatened to eclipse the improving ethos of an agricultural revolution combined with rural industry.

The Scottish Enlightenment

The new lairds did much to realise the agricultural potential of their estates and in this way a link is forged between the improvement of agriculture and the expansion of trade. The link was represented in its most tangible form by the traders who became landowners and applied their capital and enterprise to the business of estate management.[15] But it is reflected also in an association of ideas. Perception of potential for development in the countryside was nourished by the confidence that came from their leading role in society and the example of English agriculture that many of them witnessed personally. But a 'freedom from conservative ways', which favoured agricultural development, was combined with a moral earnestness concerning a landowner's obligations to improve society by creating more industry.[16] Moral considerations easily lose credibility when handled crudely and there is no suggestion that such motives were sufficient in themselves to generate investment. But conventional morality effectively prescribed that economic development should harmonise with social development and that in striving for the most efficient division of labour the 'sympathy' that Adam Smith built into his theory of moral sentiments should be shown in full measure.[17]

This combination of virtues finds expression in the Scottish Enlightenment. This is considered to be part of a European movement, an extension of the Renaissance and a form of protest against a traditional theological authoritarianism. But it had a distinct character in Scotland where it was not anti-religious and where much emphasis was placed on the application of empirical knowledge to public affairs. The church played a leading role in society and at the same time proved open to the teachings of modern philosophy and science. Education was accorded a very high value and even before the mid eighteenth century there was seldom a parish in the more developed areas that did not have a parish school and fairly easy access to secondary education. Philosophically the enlightenment occurred during a period when the ruling elite realised that they could understand and control their environment. The experimental method of Isaac Newton was being applied to the study of society where traditional faith and divine right could no longer expect to prevail as unquestioned authorities. Yet approval of material progress was balanced by a certain ambivalence arising from the 'wistfulness' of James Dunbar in seeking to remember the virtues of simpler societies to ensure that 'cultivated society' would be truly superior.[18] The values of the Scottish Enlightenment are well exemplified by Lord Kames (1696–1782) a judge and philosopher with a strong interest in agricultural improvement.[19] He worked on two Boards set up to sponsor development, one in the field of industry generally (Board of Trustees for the Encouragement of Fisheries, Arts and Manufactures in Scotland) and the other with a regional interest in the Highlands (Board of Commissioners for the Annexed Estates). On his own estates he introduced new methods, consolidated farms and offered long leases direct to all his tenants, without the intervention of the tacksman or middleman. He is perhaps best remembered for the drainage of Kincardine Moss on the Blair Drummond estate near Stirling. Trenches or 'goats' were dug parallel to each other and water channelled in from the Teith would float off the peat (previously loosened and thrown into the ditches) into the Forth. Some residual peat was burnt and mixed with the clay subsoil and the Carse of Stirling was then made available for colonisation by displaced families from the Highlands. So, as well as encouraging a progressive agricultural system Kames also appreciated the gravity of the resettlement problem and his example may well have inspired other proprietors to reclaim waste land. This was his way of 'grafting benevolence on self-love', a quotation inscribed on his memorial at the gateway to the estate.

While it is undoubtedly true that the bulk of the work in improvement was done by the tenants and their labourers the importance of the landowners' contribution should not be derided. There could be no sustained investment until prices rose to the point where profits were assured and hence many of the early eighteenth-century enclosures and rotation experiments were restricted to the home farm, or tentatively projected on to outfield land. Yet what is most important is the disposition, indeed the eagerness, to experiment, so that technology was available when the economic climate allowed progress to accelerate. Radical agricultural change is notoriously difficult to accomplish in view of the heavy economic and social costs and it is highly significant for Scotland's entire development that the landowners sponsored agricultural change with great energy while retaining a responsible balance between economic and social considerations. A clear separation of agricultural and non-agricultural employment was desirable for greater efficiency: large commercial farms were not possible as long as the rural population was preoccupied much of the year in carting lime – a situation described by the author of the Old Statistical Account for Grange parish (Moray) and reflected on the ground in West Linton parish (Borders) where the scars of clusters of temporary lime kilns can be seen on the moorland south of Carlops village.[20] Commercial forces stimulated greater specialisation, for in Banff & Buchan 'when shipping and trade became more common upon the coast and exportation of corn commenced at Portsoy then the farmers thought that they could make more profit by the sale of corn than by the lime trade or by subtenants; they therefore enlarged their farms by removing their subtenants'.[21]

Displaced tenants might find employment in rural industry encouraged by the landowners in small towns or in new planned villages. Many new markets had been established during the seventeenth century and proposals for new endowments were a commonplace. In 1708 it was suggested that the Duke of Atholl might establish a new settlement at Logierait (Perth), by the confluence of the Tay and Tummel: the village could become a service centre for the parish and the growth of linen and woollen industries could go ahead in parallel with a reorganisation of farms. Nothing was done in this case but later in the century the subtenants of Grange would have found opportunities in Huntly and Keith, just as their colleagues in Cromdale sought refuge in Grantown, built by the Grants 'to afford a permanent settlement to their ancient dependants without driving them from the country after it had been found beneficial to enlarge the farms as much as possible'.[22] Again the strategy was rooted in self interest because the new village would generate a significant income in rents and it might provide a large enough market to intensify production. It was well known that proximity to the large towns was advantageous on account of 'a constant demand, ready market and a resonable price for every article which the farms produce'.[23] Yet the scheme had a social content too, reflecting the idealism of the time for the elimination of cultural disparities and the creation of an even distribution of industry.

As well as seeking harmony between economic and social interests the improvers looked to an orderly landscape that suited the aesthetic values of the time. The new methods in agriculture meant in most parishes the elimination of the distinction between infield and outfield and also the removal of the baulks, the 'waste spaces between ridges, full of stones and bushes'.[24] Clearance of stones created the resources for building the field boundary dykes, as in Pitsligo parish which 'abounds with stones of all sizes and is therefore extremely well adapted for being laid out in enclosures'. Where stones were lacking earthen banks were raised or hedges planted, alternatives that involved greater difficulty and cost.[25] Fragmented and intermixed holdings were done away with among both tenants and proprietors, as in 1786 when Mr John Menzies of Pitfoddels obtained his half share of the parish of Nigg (Aberdeen) as a consolidated portion instead of the 'alternate ridge'.[26] A geometrical grid was now imposed on the landscape by the land surveyors and the agricultural effort became spatially more continuous as drainage and clearance brought each field to a fairly uniform condition. The new villages for the most part were planned in an extremely regular manner and therefore overcame the highly irregular quality of rural settlement previously displayed by various joint farm townships (recorded so clearly in military surveys), now reduced to single farmsteads.[27]

Woodland conservation

The interest in the landscape extended further, to the woodland. Originally almost the whole country was forested, but climatic change and man's felling of woodland for fuel and agricultural purposes have vastly reduced the forested areas. Burning, as recently as 1654 in the Aberfoyle area to get rid of 'rebels and mossers', is also part of the 'melancholy history of Scottish forests'.[28] By the eighteenth century, timber was becoming scarce in the more densely settled areas and conservation measures had proved inadequate to reverse the process of erosion, though some enclosures were provided to protect woodlands and from this activity came the idea of marking off sections of agricultural land so as to compartmentalise the grazings and arable fields and defend the latter from incursions by livestock. Shortage of timber for use as a fuel and building material was a factor inhibiting development, as at Strachan (Kincardine & Deeside) where the problem was reported as 'a great bar to the progress of improvement'.[29] The constraint was particularly serious in parishes in the outer regions where there was little peat available and where an inland situation greatly increased the cost of distributing coal.

There is considerable mention in contemporary writings of the expansion of plantations. At Monymusk (Gordon) the Grants placed much emphasis on woodlands that would 'in some years not only beautify the country and alter its present bleak and naked aspect but would give advantage to farmers through providing shade and shelter for their cattle in all seasons' as well as 'all needful timber for houses and tools'.[30] The advantages were not immediately appreciated by tenants who reacted to the reduction of the grazing land by destroying dykes and uprooting young trees under cover of darkness, but the programme was eventually accomplished and the visitor to Donside's Paradise Woods will appreciate the scale of the scenic transformation. At the same time Lord Findlater established plantations on Mildary hill at Keith (Moray) where the parish had previously been 'entirely destitute of trees'.[31] Although parishes with little waste land could not reasonably be endowed with great plantations of larch, pine and spruce, small woodlands and shelter belts made a considerable impact on a previously bare landscape. A classification has been suggested that recognises a certain amount of natural growth (frequently alder with birch, oak and ash) on steep slopes in upland situations, the plantations established on low ground in the dales and straths and finally the clumps and windbreaks that adorned most of the houses, especially the great mansions where extensive areas were laid out as parks and gardens.[32] The very elaborate gardens of Castle Kennedy and the terraces of Drumlanrig in Dumfries & Galloway find echoes in Grampian through the grandeur of Gordon Castle (Moray), the tasteful plantations of the Glen of Duntochty (Kincardine & Deeside) and formal gardens of Pitmedden (Gordon).

Investment was motivated partly by prospect of profit and partly by a desire to improve amenity for individual houses and estates. Many proprietors found the economic return was amply rewarding and this stimulated greater interest in the best forestry methods. Land would first have to be drained and fenced and the ground cover might have to be burnt off. Nursery grown trees were commonly used, though seed planting also had its advocates. The advantages of setting plants in clumps for mutual protection was recognised and there was considerable discrimination between species: the Scots pine was quite often used as a quick-growing protective wall for hard wood varieties, while the larch was recognised as a hardy variety that would grow on the most barren muir. Species selection was also guided by aesthetic considerations having in mind contrasting forms and the colours of spring and autumn foliage. In Tayside there were extensive plantations created on the Atholl estates but the Highlands contained extensive stands of natural timber preserved by the relatively feeble penetration of market forces.[33] The situation changed during the eighteenth century however as the coppicing system in the southwest Highlands reached its peak around 1800.[34] Oak tan bark increased in price and gave the drive for a carefully managed system that is well exemplified in the woodlands of the Earldom of Menteith where activity continued until the late nineteenth century. However, the forest economy seems to have suffered from the introduction of sheep since increased pressure was placed on winter grazing land and the area of managed woodland was reduced. Also deterioraton of pastures selectively grazed by sheep led to regular burning, to check the poorer vegetation which would otherwise have become dominant, and this prevented any colonisation of open ground by trees. More specifically, coppicing was adversely affected by grazing and coppices converted rapidly into scrub or non-regenerative woodland.

Exploitation of timber could not normally extend far north on account of the heavy transport costs. On his journey of 1618 John Taylor had noted fine trees on the Mar estate (Grampian) 'so admirable for masts yet worthless since there was no means of bringing them down to the sea'.[35] But the high duties on foreign timber during the Napoleonic Wars increased the range of commercial working within Scotland and the timber of Rothiemurchus (Badenoch & Strathspey) became marketable by rafting down the Spey, with some use of the *curragh* to guide the logs[36] and crude sawmills set up on the forest streams. Activity achieved some notoriety through the management of the York Buildings Company (who purchased Speyside Woods in 1728) but 'these scenes of industrial activity were unfortunately transient' as were the activities witnessed at Rannoch (Perth) where a series of canals and collecting basins were constructed to allow timber to float from Loch Rannoch down the Tummel to the Tay, eventually to reach Dundee.[37] An alternative strategy was to establish timber-using industries and this is illustrated by the eighteenth-century iron furnaces, the most successful being the Goatfield Furnace on Loch Fyne (Argyll & Bute) which survived until 1813 (though a gunpowder factory used the site until 1884) and the Taynuilt Furnace on Loch Etive (Argyll & Bute) which survived until 1866 as a going concern and remains to this day as a monument of industrial archaeology. Both works were situated on the coast and could easily import their timber (for charcoal) from surrounding estates up to a distance of some eighty kilometres. Long term contracts were negotiated and, although there were some difficulties in getting a steady supply, conservation measures were implemented and in the case of the Taynuilt furnace the woodland area available to the company in 1876 was no smaller than it had been in 1750.

Sir John Sinclair's Statistical Account

Knowledge of the effectiveness of the various measures for rural development comes from a series of parish reports published as the Statistical Account of Scotland during the last decade of the eighteenth century. It was a great effort in survey by the questionnaire technique, very much the brainchild of the Caithness improver Sir John Sinclair who believed that detailed knowledge of local conditions throughout Scotland was a precondition of effective legislation to expedite development. The Church of Scotland ministers were identified as the most competent and objective authors of parish surveys and Sinclair addressed them in flattering terms in 1790 as 'an ecclesiastical establishment whose members will yield to no description of men for public zeal'.[38] A total of 166 questions were listed, though answers were not expected in all cases and there was certainly very great variation in the number of issues dealt with and in the thoroughness and accuracy with which information was presented. Heavy pressure was applied through 1791 'so that the state of the whole country should be known if possible at nearly the same period of time'.[39] But progress was rather slower than expected for even at the end of the following year returns for only about half the parishes had been secured. Sinclair then explains in a memoir how he had to 'reiterate the applications from time to time, to present the subject to the deficient clergy in every possible light, sometimes serious and sometimes jocular'.[40] Such persistence was allied with constant support for the project from the General Assembly and promise of financial assistance through a children's fund. Nevertheless pressure had to be kept up for several more years so that only four reports were missing at the end of 1797. The project is certainly a 'memorial to what may be effected by unceasing energy and perseverance'.[41]

The long period over which reports were prepared and the tremendous variations in their quality certainly detract from the value of the survey but considering the novelty of the project and the reservations over confidentiality it is remarkable that so much was achieved. Certainly a very valuable geographical outline emerges from the reports. Reports covered individual parishes allowing local variations to be seen in a way not possible with the studies of whole counties commissioned during the same period by the Board of Agriculture. And although the various parish ministers could not be expected to deal in an authoritative manner on all secular matters, they were reporting from first hand experience and did not hesitate to say how controversial developments affected the community as a whole. V. Morgan has made a thorough examination of this immensely valuable source for historical geography and has found that it is in agreement with other contemporary materials.[42] Considerable reliance is therefore placed on the Statistical Account in the studies which follow this general chapter. A New Statistical Account was produced in the 1840s and this again is a mine of information on each locality. The publication of the reports by whole counties is a great advance on Sinclair's procedure since information on a group of adjacent parishes can be found in a single volume and not scattered through the whole series according to the order in which the reports were received. On the other hand the style is less exciting because the much more settled conditions of the time tend to restrict the number of value judgements made by the authors. Sinclair's inspiration also extended into the twentieth century. In 1946 the Registrar General for Scotland, J. G. Kyd, proposed a Third Statistical Account. The first volumes appeared in the early 1950s but owing to inadequate finance progress has been slow and so far only 24 of the 37 pre-1975 counties and cities have been dealt with.

The ministers supported the process of improvement almost without exception and most criticism is reserved for failure to make adequate progress. But there is considerable misgiving over morality at a time of rapid change, especially in the context of underemployment in agricultural villages and the increased addiction to spirits and exotic drinks. The factual information is in line with the statements of other contemporary authors but it is doubtful whether the latter were quite so sensitive over moral questions. The accounts leave the reader in little doubt that the process of improvement was going on as they were writing. They present evidence of a characteristic diffusion process with backward areas being gradually drawn into the mainstream of economic growth. Thus for example the planned village movement extended the market network into the Highland margins and Arthur Geddes later contrasted the Medieval plantations of the Moray coast with the eighteenth-century development of small towns in the hills.[43] This highlighted the complementary environments of 'laich' and 'brae' with the former displaying the more compelling potential and hence attracting attention at an earlier time.[44] The 'brae' environment reflected not only in the straths as at Grantown but also at the Highland gateways of Stirling and Perth & Kinross (Callander and Comrie) and the insular fishing bases like Lerwick and Stornoway. Transport was an important factor in the delay in the timing of development in the uplands, for, whereas coastal areas were accessible by ships from East-Central ports, inland districts faced the prospect of cartage to the Moray ports or a difficult overland journey south: either way there was little scope for easy intercourse until the military roads and turnpikes of the eighteenth century. Road building at the end of the century attracts a good deal of comment from contributors to the Statistical Account. At Stow in the Borders the Edinburgh–Selkirk turnpike 'produced a total change in the system of farming'.[45] At Blackford (Tayside) a second advantage is mentioned, because 'since a good road was made through Gleneagles and Glendevon, which opens a passage to the south side of the Ochils, a considerable quantity of pit coal is annually imported'.[46] There were local variations too arising from a position in relation to the new roads and specifically the Dundee–Meigle turnpike: 'Such as live near the turnpike and have easy access to it feel its great advantage and readily acknowledge it; while those who live at a distance derive but little benefit from it owing to the wretched state of the bye roads which the commute statute labour will never render tolerable'.[47] On the other hand in his letters the engineer officer Edward Burt mentions objections to the roads by the local people because 'an easy passage is opened into their country for strangers who might upset local people with "their suggestions of liberty"' while 'their fastnesses being laid open, they are deprived of the security they formerly enjoyed'.[48] Eventually the turnpike system was extended through the Highlands, thanks to a special Commission for Highland Roads and Bridges. Commissioners were appointed in 1804 to administer the Road and Bridge Act. They took over the military roads in 1814, though only the roads of economic use were kept in repair. Contrary to some predictions the secondary roads were also improved but the density of the road system remains highly uneven. Improving landowners in the islands, notably Lewis and Shetland, provided local roads although not till the end of the nineteenth century. Even today there are several important missing links in the Highlands which reduce the overall connectivity of the system while even in the Central Belt there are significant variations: the drove road across the Pentlands from West Linton to Kirknewton (Edinburgh) has only been improved for some three kilometres out of West Linton and does not yet cross Cauldstone Slap despite nineteenth-century speculation that it might do so. Such inevitable variations inhibited an even spread of improvement at the local scale.

Even with road improvements however growth potential was restricted by the relatively high cost of carting, a point very relevant in the Scottish case since the great length of the coast in relation to total area makes sea transport accessible to the majority of people and highlights thereby the disadvantage faced by those living deep in the interior. Adam Smith noted how water carriage opened up a relatively extensive market: 'so it is upon the sea coast and along the banks of navigable rivers that industry of every kind naturally begins to subdivide and improve itself; and it is frequently not till a long time after that those improvements extend themselves to the inland parts of the country'.[49] Research on the seventeenth-century grain market shows how the Moray Firth coastlands were drawn into Edinburgh's orbit more easily than parishes within the Central Belt that had to cart produce to the city.[50] In the eighteenth century there is much additional evidence, including lime production and distribution. A large scale of production developed with the use of draw kilns capable of continuous operation and these installations were built where coal and limestone were available, having in mind ease of distribution. The Earl of Elgin erected nine kilns in 1767–8 at Charlestown in Fife, an excellent site on the coast with 'downhill' movement of limestone and fuel to a site from which the finished product could be shipped out. The settlement, which is an extension of Dunfermline's port of Limekilns, dated back to 1756 when accommodation was built for men engaged in the shipment of coal. Lime burning continued to 1937, surviving the adjacent Charlestown Foundry by a few years. There were coastal kilns in Lothian and Grampian (East Mathers) but it was Fife lime that was the main Scottish complement to Sunderland lime in distribution through the Forth and Tay estuaries and, further north, the Beauly and Cromarty Firths, as Robertson indicated in his 'General Views' of the agriculture of the counties of Perth and Inverness.[51] The plight of the inland areas was lessened by the frequent occurrence of limestone in close proximity to peat mosses where fuel to work the kilns could be obtained. In well endowed parishes individual farms would have their own kilns or else the estate would install equipment centrally. But until the railway age solved the problem of inland distribution parishes remote from the coast and lacking in lime found progress difficult.

Similar patterns prevailed over coal supply as A. C. O'Dell has demonstrated.[52] The Central Belt was almost entirely within reach of coal but coastal shipping left interior parts of the Outer Regions beyond the limits of economic distribution.[53] The Forth ports were most active in the trade: Charlestown on the northern side of the Firth, drawing its coal from nearby mines by wagonway (c. 1768), was complemented on the south side by Cockenzie, linked with pits at Tranent by wooden rails laid by the York Buildings Company as early as 1722. Another element was added by the Halbeath Wagon Road that led to Inverkeithing in 1783, not to mention the lines at Alloa and Carron that supplied coal to local industry. Complication arose from the taxation imposed on coal shipments that went beyond Dunbar in the south and the Red Head near Arbroath in the north. First raised in Cromwellian times the tax was reimposed under conditions of war in the 1790s and finally removed by the end of the period. It had the effect of exaggerating the costs of inaccessibility and attracted criticism in parishes where alternative fuels were in very short supply. Understandably therefore the full range of improvements was ruled out until the fuel situation could be reappraised in a more favourable light. But if the tax was levied in the first place to conserve supplies in industrial areas at a time of rapidly rising demand then it is further demonstration of the way that the spirit of enlightenment was being eroded in favour of specialisation and the acceptance of regional disparities as inevitable.

For a time it seemed that there might be some reduction in the accessibility contrasts through water transport. The emphasis lay with small vessels, mostly engaged in short range coastal work.[54] As for movements within Scotland the case of the Orkney island of South Ronaldsay might be taken: there was one sloop belonging to the island and each spring it took the local produce: beef, pork, hides, tallow, yarn, butter and grease to Leith and brought back merchant goods. During the summer she was freighted with kelp consigned to Dundee, Leith or English ports. This seems reasonably typical, for at Brough on the Orkney island of Westray there are still the remains of the modest terminal facilities required by these small craft; more generally, B. Lenman concludes that 'until well into the third quarter of the nineteenth century the bulk of the fish exports of Orkney and Shetland and the grain exports of Orkney were carried in smacks and schooners which also carried the multifarious imports of the islands'.[55] The scope of such exchanges was widened considerably through the building of canals. Powers were obtained for a Forth & Clyde Navigation in 1768; the first section between Carronmouth and Port Hamilton near Glasgow was opened in 1777 and the whole project from Grangemouth to Bowling was ready in 1791. Just one year later the Monkland Branch was able to start feeding in coal from the Airdrie area and in 1822 with the opening of the Union Canal there was a direct link opened through to Edinburgh. In both cities the canals eased the supply of fuel at a critical time and hence the location of the industrial areas shows a close relationship with the wharfs at Port Dundas (Glasgow) and Port Hopetown (Edinburgh) as well as the seaways of the Clyde and Forth.

The idea of an integrated water transport system involving the coastal routes and canal branches was extended by the Caledonian and Crinan Canals but the projected Ardrossan Canal was built from the Clyde only as far as Johnstone in 1812 (the western half of the scheme was overtaken by the railway age) and on the east coast only the canal along the Don Valley from Aberdeen to Port Elphinstone near Inverurie (Gordon) was built (1807); proposals to extend this canal right through the Garioch, to build a canal along the Forth valley above Stirling and link Strathmore with Perth were never acted on. Likewise there was scope for a canal between Sullom Voe and Busta Voe which could connect fishing stations and provide 'a most convenient location for a manufacturing village'.[56] But the idea of cutting a canal inland from Peterhead (Banff & Buchan) and thereby overcoming the lack of access to convenient seaports and markets was implemented by James Fergusson of Pitfour to the extent of six kilometres of canal in St Fergus parish, although the failure to reach either Peterhead or his estates in the nearby parishes of Old Deer and Longside meant that the scheme was of little value.[57] The desired links were eventually provided in the railway age but by that time the technology of manufacturing was vastly different and spread that could have occurred previously with an adequate infrastructure was now constrained by other factors. The government assisted construction of the Caledonian Canal for which it saw an important strategic role, but private investment was only attracted by the prospect of profit.

By the end of the eighteenth century the ports of the east coast were surprisingly unimproved and their capacities were imposing a brake on efficiency in foreign trade. Rapid improvements were to follow, given the tempo of economic development and the introduction of steam power (1821 on the Leith–London passenger service). This led to a transformation in which the only losers were the shipbuilders (represented at nearly every port on the Forth and Tay by 1790) whose sites were repeatedly coveted by the dock builders. But apart from Grangemouth (Falkirk) where investment stimulated by the Forth & Clyde Canal created a rival to Bo'ness it was the Clyde that captured the imagination of the investor. Greenock (Inverclyde) achieved rapid growth: a spacious harbour was built between 1707 and 1710 and the first ship was sent across the Atlantic in 1719. 'So fortunate were its subsequent ventures that by 1740 it has completely cleared off the debt.'[58] Glasgow was determined to minimise the tendency for trade to be syphoned off by ports on the lower river and complaints that Greenock merchants were infringing the monopoly of the royal burghs were followed by more positive action first in building Port Glasgow and subsequently by improving the river. Advice was sought from leading engineers and it was a scheme by John Golborne of Chester to deepen the river to give a minimum depth of 1.8 m at low water that received parliamentary sanction in 1770. Jetties were built to confine the river and the bed was raked to assist the swifter current to scour out loose material. Particular attention was given to Dumbuck Ford where the required clearance was achieved by 1775. Work continued and the depth of the river increased to 4.3 m by 1781 and ships drawing 2.6 m could reach the Broomielaw in Glasgow in 1806. Glasgow became the head port on the Clyde in 1815 and a Custom House was built at the Broomielaw in 1836. As long as the maximum tonnage at Glasgow was between three and four hundred Greenock retained a substantial share of the oceanic trade, in spite of the town's peripheral position and cramped site beneath the Renfrewshire Plateau, and it maintained a notable connection with the sugar industry. But rivalry among the Clyde towns could hardly be excessive: the peculiar topographical conditions, with difficult terrain upstream restricting the scope for further canalisation, gave Glasgow the greatest opportunity as a link between the resources of the interior (water power, coal and iron) and the trading opportunities overseas. And there could be no doubt about Clydeside's dominant position on the west coast of Scotland. The east coast stands in sharp contrast with Edinburgh's sphere of influence curtailed to the north by Dundee, Aberdeen and Inverness.

Industry: linen manufacture

Linen was sufficiently important during the seventeenth century to be viewed by Scots as the salvation of their country and so important was the linen trade that the threat of closure of the English market constituted a major economic pressure making for the union settlement. 'The fortunes of the linen industry and the colonial trades were closely intertwined, with a downturn in the tobacco or sugar trade passed on to the suppliers of linens through delays in payment and reduced orders'.[59] There was considerable investment by colonial merchants in companies manufacturing and finishing linen in West-Central Scotland. More generally linen generated various linkages throughout the economy especially in transport (port facilities and roads) and agriculture (flax cultivation). Though it is hard to assess the total numbers employed in the different branches of the industry direct employment in 1780 must have exceeded a quarter of a million and there is unanimity that linen was Scotland's key industry. After 1707 funds were set aside for certain industries, notably textiles and fishing, and in 1727 a semi-public body was set up to allocate the money through encouragement of development on a wide front. The efforts of this Board of Trustees are of great significance because the efforts to achieve a wide spatial spread by the linen industry provide some insights into the strength of the forces of concentration which eventually triumphed. As a purely domestic industry some local production of flax was necessary. But flax was a risky crop to grow and required greater delicacy in handling, although it did give a larger return than other crops and was suitable for small farms where tenants were anxious to supplement their meagre living from the land before the improving movement made for larger commercial units.[60] Even so areas in the west and north Highlands were physically ill-suited to flax production on any scale although the eastern counties as far north as Caithness and Orkney grew considerable amounts.

An alternative approach for the Highlands was to foster the industry by supplying imported raw materials. After the 1745 rebellion the Board made strenuous efforts to develop the industry through manufacturers organising the distribution of raw materials and collection of finished products through their intakers who were based at strategic points. Promotional interests also come from the British Linen Company, founded in 1746, and the Annexed Estates Commissioners who were responsible for the development of a number of forfeited estates between 1752 and 1784. But labour was not always adaptable and it is claimed that Shetlanders 'could not apply themselves with diligence to the manufacturing process'.[61] In addition, at a time before the turnpike roads had made any impact it was difficult to maintain an efficient network, and instruction of the necessary skills through a chain of spinning schools was also problematical in the more inaccessible places like Lochbroom and Lochcarron (Ross & Cromarty). Even further east in Badenoch & Strathspey it proved impossible to sustain effort because the finished yarn proved too costly despite subsidies from the various authorities until 1784. The Board of Trustees withdrew in 1766 and the British Linen Company ended its spinning relationship with the north in 1773.[62] The demands for more yarn by weavers in the south provided an economic stimulus to recruit more spinners but most of the spread was confined to the lowland parts of the Grampian region where there was some invasion of the area previously geared to the knitting of woollen stockings.[63] Most success was achieved in the coastal areas where communication was maintained by sea and it was with considerable realism that the British Linen Company concentrated their efforts in this most accessible part of the north, in contrast to the misplaced idealism of the other two authorities.

While some parts of the country were unsuited to the industry even in the early days most areas stood to benefit by introducing an industrial component into the earnings of joint farmers. But the improving movement attempted a separation of agricultural and industrial occupations, creating large farms that did not require the support of rural industry while resettling the displaced population in new villages where the linen industry could be pursued with greater singlemindedness. In 1748 the Earl of Findlater introduced linen manufacture to Cullen (Banff & Buchan). Skilled men were brought in from the south and lint mills, weaving sheds and bleachfields were laid out to process the flax imported from Holland. Prosperity spread to the neighbouring parishes of Banff, Fordyce and Keith and the production of linen thread became a local specialism, but the area failed to keep up with the increase in mechanisation and the industry petered out at the turn of the century.

Bleachfields and lintmills were opened as the different stages of production in the industry became more specialised and localised. Lint mills date back to 1730 when James Spalding installed equipment at Monnyton Mills (Edinburgh) and they had a centralising influence as hecklers came to cluster around the mills where flax was brought to be scutched. The number of mills increased in the 1760s with refinements in water powered machinery, but the roughness of the milled product still made for the persistence of hand scutching.[64] Bleachfields were laid out in the 1730s, the same decade that witnessed the first major development of lint mills.[65] The first fields are reported for Ormiston (East Lothian) in 1731, Dunfermline (Fife) in 1733 and Perth (1735). There was expansion of facilities throughout the Central Belt and also throughout the Outer Regions except the west Highlands.[66] The West-Central fields were lost to cotton after c. 1780 and this led to a growth of capacity in the east, extending to new fields as far north as Keith, Laurencekirk and New Pitsligo (Grampian) by the 1790s. The largest fields like Huntingtower and Luncarty near Perth extended to 28 ha and it was on these fields in the core of the linen province that most of the bleaching was concentrated after 1815, especially since the major manufacturers developed links with particular fields, and those in remoter situations, including Ayton, Duns and Melrose in the Borders were closed by the late 1820s. With chlorine the whitening process was accelerated but laying out was still needed. Spinning machinery in the linen industry was introduced at Inverbervie (Grampian) 1787 and at Leven (Fife) the following year, but there was only a low success rate before the 1820s. Brigton was the first mill to spin yarn for linen cloth: a corn mill was converted by William Douglas using the capital of Dundee merchants.

Insistence on a high quality product also led to uneven development; inferior cloth made for disastrous results and, for coarse linen especially, a major problem of the Board of Trustees lay in 'diffusing more efficient

Table 3.2. *Linen production 1730–1820*

Region	1730			1760			1790			1820		
	A	B	C	A	B	C	A	B	C	A	B	C
Angus–Fife–Perth	2.4	64.8	54.7	6.7	57.0	47.2	4.2	82.8	67.3	23.1	87.8	78.3
Lanark–Renfrew	0.6	16.2	20.9	3.1	27.1	32.5	1.9	10.1	19.2	*	0.3	0.7
Other counties	0.7	19.0	24.4	1.9	15.9	20.3	1.2	7.1	13.5	3.1	11.9	21.0

A. Total production (million yards)
B. Proportion of total production (per cent) by quantity
C. Proportion of total production (per cent) by value
* less than 0.1
Source: A. J. Durie (1979) 25

methods of production in a country inured to traditional though inefficient practices'.[67] The legal requirement that linen should be stamped has resulted in the availability of production figures and these reveal that in the later decades of the eighteenth century five counties accounted for approximately ninety per cent of the production by both yardage and value (Table 3.2). The yardage share for all other shires gradually falls from 15.9 per cent in 1770, to 11.9 in 1790, though shares for value of production are slightly higher. Hence there is no evidence of widespread development in the weaving side of the industry. The trends among the major producers show variations, with a growth in Angus, Fife and Perth contrasting with a sharp late-eighteenth-century decline in Lanark and Renfrew. Yet the latter area is clearly much more important in terms of value of production than in yardage with 19.2 per cent of the value in 1790 yet 10.1 per cent of the yardage (comparable figures in 1760 being 32.5 and 27.1). This brings out the emphasis on high quality linen in West-Central Scotland. The polarisation reflects a conscious effort to specialise, but it is based on the fact that skills in West-Central Scotland were of a relatively high order.

Industrial growth in West-Central Scotland

The development process in West-Central Scotland is not fully understood but there was a measure of landlord encouragement in the eighteenth century, as by Lady Blantyre in Erskine parish.[68] Dutch secrets were discovered and their techniques incorporated in the local 'Balgarron thread'. The industry was then taken over by Paisley for 'it was not to be expected that a manufacture of that kind would be confined to so small a district and would be allowed to remain in so few hands for a great length of time'.[69] Nevertheless the Erskine people continued to spin fine yarn for Paisley entrepreneurs imbued with a 'spirit of manufacture' which took them from coarse cloth to 'fabrics of a lighter and more fanciful kind'. But they imitated not only the thread makers of Erskine but the silk, gauze industry of Spitalfields: a 'vast variety of elegant and richly ornamented gauze was issued' on the basis of local labour (within a radius of some thirty kilometres) that was highly skilled and relatively cheap and competitors in London were obliged to relocate in Paisley and enjoy the same advantage.[70] It was the skills in the linen weaving, and in the Paisley silk gauze trade that proved invaluable when opportunity arose in the cotton industry.[71] Momentum also came from the practice of importing French and Flemish yarns, for this trading link created contacts that encouraged interest in the light calico fabics of the continent. Following the striking advance in textile machinery the cotton industry was introduced to West-Central Scotland. The transitionary stage was marked by the practice of many master weavers in Glasgow (Anderston) and Paisley of using cotton for the weft while retaining linen for the warp, since cotton spun on jennies was initially found to be rather too soft for use on its own in weaving. It is significant however that not only did Clydeside have the skill and capital necessary to establish the new industry but that there was a remarkable coincidence of timing between advances in textile machinery and the upheaval of the American War of Independence which disrupted the Glasgow tobacco trade. In Hamilton's words 'when we realise that Glasgow and Paisley already possessed weavers skilled in the production of fine cloths and that just at the time when inventions making possible a great increase both in the quality and the quantity of cotton yarns were being made capital and enterprise in Glasgow were seeking fresh outlets because of the destruction of the commerce of the city by the American War, it is not surprising that the new industry took root and flourished exceedingly'.[72]

The first cotton mill was built at Rothesay (Argyll & Bute) in 1779. It was planted in an area with a reputation for fine linen and was the work of an English engineer seeking to evade Arkwright's patent on the water frame and made use of an ingenious system of canals.[73] The main concentration occurred at the water power sites nearest to Paisley whose manufacturers 'entered the muslin manufacture with their accustomed ardour'.[74] There was a factory at Neilston (Renfrew) in 1780 but there was a greater concentration on the Levern Water at Barrhead and at Johnstone where George Houston founded the first mill on the Black Cart Water in 1782 (after ten years there were five mills there, employing a thousand people). The 1780s saw building move further east into the adjacent shire of Lanark: East Kilbride in 1783 and Woodside (Glasgow) in 1784. But the importance of water power meant that entrepreneurs had to make a wide search for suitable sites and over the following decade people appeared to be infected with an enthusiasm for this new industry everywhere from Annan (Annandale & Eskdale) to Spinningdale (Sutherland). Gatehouse of Fleet (Stewartry) was established as a cotton town and some progress was made on the Don at Aberdeen but the main pressure was on the water power of the Central Belt and the adjacent region of Tayside.[75] Glasgow manufacturers were reaching out into this area, notably to Deanston and Stanley (Perth & Kinross) where large and flexible power sources could be tapped. However the adoption of steam power reduced the value of the remoter sites which were mostly eliminated during periodic depressions.

Progress was neither perpetual nor inevitable: small units were weeded out because only the larger firms could deal satisfactorily with business problems.[76] By 1839, 175 of Scotland's 192 cotton mills were in the two shires of Lanark and Renfrew and there was concentration in the towns at the expense of rural areas which had supported many of the early spinning mills like New Lanark (1786), Catrine (Cumnock & Doon Valley) 1787, and Ballindalloch (Stirling) 1789.[77] Young weavers were migrating to Glasgow and Paisley in the 1790s but many others were working in the rural areas for the urban-based manufacturers. Yet after the first convincing demonstration of power loom weaving at Catrine in 1806 the demise of the handloom weavers rapidly followed, apart from the shawl weavers of Paisley whose fine work made them immune from the power looms until 1834.[78] Thus an industrial potential which first seemed to offer a base for rural industry and a degree of stability in the distribution of population was reappraised, with very damaging social consequences which tarnished the high ideals of eighteenth-century improvement. The finishing section of the industry, requiring copious supplies of clean water, provides some exceptions however, notably in the Vale of Leven (Dumbarton) where the soft water of Loch Lomond was first appreciated by the linen industry. Casual workers from the Highlands flocked to the bleachfields each summer and industry persisted into the nineteenth century, even after the availability of bleaching powder from the St Rollox chemical works in Glasgow (1799) because of the growth of Turkey Red dyeing for extensive new markets found in India. The cotton industry eventually inherited the installations for dyeing and printing and this branch of the industry became sufficiently well established to survive the general decline in the cotton industry after the American Civil War, through closer contacts with Lancashire firms.

Further industrial change was evident in coal mining during the eighteenth century. For much of the period the industry was backward with little use of the Newcomen engine, and associated with serf labour by the tacksmen or lessees who worked the minerals on estates near the coast. The integration with salt production was extremely close in the seventeenth century, so much so that mines away from salt water had great difficulty finding markets, but in the following century the link became more tenuous. There were still six salt pans working at Prestonpans in the

1790s with summer the peak period due to the greater strength of the seawater and the greater speed of evaporation.[79] The same situation is found on the west coast at Stevenston with large scale production complemented by the efforts of some poor people using little pans and kettles, digging coal from near the surface and living in huts on the shore (hence the salt cotes or cottages which gave rise to the placename Saltcoats).[80] But the salt industry was adversely hit by the union and the new fiscal system (and was additionally compromised by producing salt that was unsatisfactory for curing); coal found outlets in lime burning, especially on the Firth of Forth, and was distributed much more widely as a domestic and industrial fuel.[81] Previously the main demand had been in East-Central Scotland and Duckham's estimates give the Forth area an output of 0.35 million tons in 1700 compared with only 0.10 for West-Central Scotland.[82] But the growth of output in the eighteenth century was fastest in the west where coal was found at relatively shallow depths and where pits were consequently cheaper to sink, drain and operate than those in Lothian. Although West-Central Scotland did not overtake the East-Central area until after 1800, at the turn of the century it was producing some 0.80 million tons, forty-two per cent of the Scottish output of 1.90 m.t. whereas a century before the proportion had only been twenty-two per cent. With the building of canals there appears to have been some transfer of coal eastwards to Edinburgh whose local collieries had a notorious reputation for their inability to provide an efficient supply. Deeper pits were delayed by heavy capital demands while local transport was not properly overhauled until the Edinburgh–Dalkeith railway opened in 1831, with links to the Duke of Buccleuch's pits provided in 1838.[83] However, while the greatest enterprise was seen in West-Central Scotland with the Dixon family exploiting collieries in Govan, near Glasgow, and obtaining interests in glassmaking (Dumbarton) and iron production (Calder ironworks was founded at Coatbridge in 1802) the east witnessed the beginning of the modern chemical industry at Prestonpans where a vitriol factory opened in 1749 and through a chain of business connections this led onto the first coke smelting iron furnace lit at Carron in 1760.[84]

The Carron Company has been considered 'one of the great early fruits of the cooperation made possible by the union' since English capital and technology was imported to the extent that the Carron Company became known as the 'English Company'.[85] The locations combined local coal and clayband ore. Charcoal was still needed for good quality bar iron, pending the puddling process of 1783, but local supplies were considered adequate and thence the works were situated away from the Carron estuary. The Carron Company purchased the installations at Cramond in 1759. Furnace, rolling mill and slitting machine had been installed at the Cockie (Edinburgh) Mill on the Almond in the early 1750s.[86] The purchase of equipment and good-will 'not only presented Carron Company with their first operative mills in Scotland but also provided business during the crucial eighteen months of development at the main works at Carron'. The works and its nail trade were sold again, to the Cadells, in 1770, and they supplied rod iron to nail makers in the Falkirk–Kilsyth area (Carron Company having succeeded in planting a colony of English nailmakers as early as 1761). The Cadells also expanded at Cramond by taking over other mill sites: Fairafair for small forgings, Dowie's for spades and nails and Peggie's for spades and hoops (before conversion into Cramond papermill in 1815). There were visionaries who saw Highland charcoal being shipped south in large quantities to supply a chain of coastal furnaces around the Firth of Forth but those iron companies using the Highland fuel chose to locate in that area: Abernethy (Badenoch & Strathspey) and Glengarry (Lochaber) furnaces lasted only a few years, embarrassed by an inland location and by various unfavourable local circumstances, but the furnaces on Loch Etive and Loch Awe (Argyll & Bute) did survive long into the era of coke smelting. However the removal of any obligation to smelt with charcoal in the 1780s established a trend towards inland location of blast furnaces in the Central Belt where ore and coal deposits coincided. By 1802 there were works not only in Glasgow (Clyde Iron Works at Cambuslang dates from 1786) but at Muirkirk (Cumnock & Doon Valley).[87] Wilsontown (Lanark) also featured but most prominent were the Monklands where the Calder, Glenbuck, Omoa and Shotts works were located.[88] The mineral riches of this area had been unlocked by the Monkland Canal but the impetuous pace of coal mining was not fully complemented by iron production until suitable technology was available to smelt the blackband ores. At the turn of the century therefore Glasgow was the leading centre of heavy industry with the one ironworks and a number of foundries that had first been dependent on foreign pig iron; examples include the Smithfield Company with forge, rolling and slitting mills on the Kelvin at Partick (1738) and the Dalnottar Ironworks at Old Kilpatrick (1769).

Industrial prospects for the Outer Regions

The explosion of industry in West-Central Scotland with the sequence of linen, cotton and iron had implications for other parts of the country. Competition for capital and labour on Clydeside had the effect of increasing the potential for the industries that were being superseded in other districts. Thus the invasion of the linen province by cotton meant further opportunity for the east coast producers.[89] Angus was a leading producer in the early nineteenth century with a reputation for 'Osnaburgs' and other brown linens. The industry had first grown in the countryside, for the first Osnaburg yarn was spun at Douglastown near Glamis (Angus). Another early starter was the village of Dairsie (originally named Osnaburgh) which sprang up on the new turnpike route across Fife. The rural industry later contracted and became limited to the Alyth (Angus), Auchtermuchty, Falkland, Freuchie, Dunshelt and Strathmiglo areas of Fife, but this was countered by the growth of a sound factory industry in the main towns through specialisation and early mechanisation. In Arbroath (Angus) for instance the company 'obtained the best machinery that was known in the trade and by devoting great care to the manufacture succeeded in producing a better quality of goods of the kind than was made elsewhere'.[90] Similar growth applied to Brechin, Forfar and Kirriemuir in Angus and the Fife towns of Cupar, Dunfermline, Kirkaldy and Leven. But it was above all in Dundee that the industry expanded through 'the perseverance of the manufacturers in adopting and improving machinery for superseding hand labour, cheapening production and improving the quality of the work'.[91] Dundee had particular opportunities as a leading port for gaining wide experience in marketing and followed the usual practice for the area of gaining maximum benefit from the bounty payable on exports of linen; 'the bounty rates were applied according to the value of the goods per yard and the manufacturers of Forfarshire, including those of Dundee, by setting the price of their coarse product at the lowest limit of the price class for which the highest bounty was paid were able to obtain a bounty as large as that paid to the makers of a finer product'.[92]

There was local specialisation: Osnaburgs at Dundee, Silesias (and sheeting) in Perth, checks and ticks at Kirkaldy, diaper and damask table cloths at Dunfermline. The origins of the specialisation are rather obscure though it is thought that damask weaving was established in Dunfermline around 1720 by James Blake who had observed the techniques in Edinburgh. Specialisation in Dunfermline was encouraged by the development of the London trade in the late eighteenth century. In respect of these industries Turner brings out the close integration of the rural and urban components. The role of the towns in supplying capital and organisation is reflected in the concentration of finishing. The introduction of water powered machinery in the linen industry led to the same search for suitable sites as had been evident for cotton, and Dundee linen manufacturers looked closely at the Ericht valley at Blairgowrie. This points to the prosperity of the Tayside industry, for not until the 1820s (when easy markets for cotton goods were opened up in Latin America) did there seem any chance of linen being superseded. The enterprise of Dundee manufacturers was again demonstrated when jute was first sent there in 1822; experiments were undertaken and spinning began in 1832, the very year in which the export bounty scheme on linen ended. Some minor streams were exploited for bleaching to an extraordinary degree because of their proximity to the important textile towns: the Dighty near Dundee and Leven and Ore for Kirkaldy and Leven. But the Lower Tay and Almond had far more than local significance, lying close to Perth with its 'node of routes where any commercial development dependent for its success on a multiplicity of contacts might well succeed'.[93]

Yet the opportunity was not available throughout the Outer Regions. An integrated linen industry was established only spasmodically and the boom in spinning for weavers in the south was eclipsed by mechanisation. There were other possibilities however. The woollen industry was strangely neglected in the eighteenth century, so great was the obsession for linen and the frustration over attempts to stimulate production of high quality woollens before the union. Wool could be produced locally, where flax was difficult, and although finer grades were eventually secured through import the local wool provided a base for modest advance in the Borders and Grampian, as in some limited parts of the Central Belt. Progress in the woollen industry was dependent on the improvement in the quality and quantity of raw wool supply, over which the Trustees had very little control. Hence it is concluded that 'expenditure on wool would not have yielded a better return than expenditure on linen'.[94] Distilling offered good prospects for the rural areas for there were close linkages with agriculture, as was noted at Kilbagie (Clackmannan) where the Steins, the greatest of the Lowland distiller-capitalists, had a farm that produced the barley and consumed the draff (a fodder particularly valuable during the winter when alternative feed was scarce and expensive). During the Napoleonic Wars many large rural grain mills were built during favourable periods of trade as at Eyemouth (Berwickshire). A large grain mill was also built at the canal terminus of Port Elphinstone (Gordon) but the geography of milling also reflected dispersal according to the availability of water power. At Turriff (Banff & Buchan) a tributary of the Deveron eventually powered two meal mills (as well as two carding mills, a flax mill and machinery for a bleachfield). Wind power was also harnessed in the eighteenth century for corn milling.[95]

Fishing was another important option in the coastal zone. At Bervie (Kincardine & Deeside) the white fishing was divided between an *out sea fishing* in the summer for cod and ling with the boats employed additionally for the carriage of coal and peat and a *near great fishing* in the winter using smaller boats. Fish was sold to Montrose merchants who salted it for export to the Mediterranean. Where other occupations were available it appears that the fishing declined owing to the discouragement of occasional disasters at sea and harassment from the press gangs. But further afield interest was maintained, as in the Moray Firth and Orkney: there was no fishing by trade at Holme in Orkney but 'every individual during the summer and harvest months has a seat or share in a fishing boat and catches fish for his house and family'.[96] In Shetland, the union had the effect of eliminating German traders (through the Navigation Act and the 1712 levy on salt used for curing) and stimulating the lairds to take charge of the island economy, including the fish curing. They had to finance the fishing and also maintain trade links abroad, largely through Scots factors resident in continental ports. The key to the fishing was the *far haaf* (deep sea fishery) which is regarded by some Shetlanders as the mark of a 'heroic age' as the rowing boats with six-man crews (sixerns) set out for the distant grounds. The lairds made some innovations through the use of trading sloops to act as mother ships to the sixerns and thereby cut out the long voyages to and from the coastal stations. But they were most successful in the improvement of the fish drying and curing techniques pioneered by such men as John Bruce Stewart of Symbister, Whalsay. The landholding system in Shetland was related to the fishing and the prime importance of this industry made it appropriate to forgo the option of land reorganisation for commercial farms in favour of a smallholding system that would support the fishermen. The landowner would then make it a condition of tenancy that each tenant of a croft should 'furnish and fit out a fourth share of a fishing boat and prosecute the fishing either in person or by substitution'.[97] Since six people were needed for a boat the four families involved would normally find two boys to join the four men. In the west Highlands and the Hebrides fishing did not emerge as an activity of great importance and it was mainly through the kelp that estate incomes were increased and an increasing population maintained.

Regional problems: with particular reference to the Highlands and Islands

This experience illustrates very well the outlook of the improvers in seeking an economically viable development strategy for their estates yet harmonising it with the maintenance of the population. The various estates in effect show a range of instinctive responses to the challenge of economic and social adjustment. The strategy that worked well in central Scotland and parts of the Outer Regions needed drastic modification in the Highlands where the population could only be supported at low standards of living and with a strong subsistence element in the agriculture. Although there was some 'lag' in the Highlands in applying the ideals of the improving movement the conservatism that this implies should not be exaggerated. It is demography that is the key to the development problem.[98] A slow rate of change reflected the scale of the peasant problem. But by the end of the period rural depopulation was occurring throughout Scotland. Evidence can be drawn from the more elevated rural districts of the Central Belt, reflecting a decline of agricultural effort, as in the Lammermuir Hills (Lothian).[99] Disposition to leave unrewarding upland country is evident in the late eighteenth century and may have been strengthened by a marginal deterioration of climate. For M. L. Parry has shown that farmers will leave marginal areas where the risk of two harvest failures in successive years is greater than once in twenty-five years. Slight deterioration or improvement in climate, by as little as 2°C in mean summer temperatures, can be critical and bring about a shift in the limits of cultivation.[100] The inter-regional transfer of population, involving migrating from the Highlands especially, was evident too. There was a steady flow of Highlanders into Greenock during the eighteenth century though the beginnings of migration to the area are thought to lie two centuries earlier.[101] Some of this movement arose through coercion for there are frequent references in the Statistical Account to the eviction of cottagers which meant removal from the parish where no town or village existed. But even where this did not happen, as at Fodderty (Ross & Cromarty), there was seasonal migration, for the want of labour 'forces those who are industrially inclined to go and find labour in the southern districts of Scotland'. The 'South Country Lads' then returned home and made the locals more aware of luxuries, 'expensive dress and other superfluities'.[102] But the scale of migration was too modest to eliminate serious social problems in the event of a sweeping reorganisation of farms.[103]

The growth of towns is extremely difficult to quantify since no accurate information is available for the period, but if the largest burghal parishes are considered it is possible to indicate that urbanisation was occurring in a highly irregular manner (Tables 3.3 and 3.4). The largest cities were being graced by extensive new suburban developments with considerable architectural distinction. Provost George Drummond saw London's rebuilding as a relevant inspiration for Edinburgh. In 1767, following the Nor' Loch drainage and North Bridge construction he instructed James Craig to prepare a new town plan which would offer better amenity to the city's leading families than the dirty and overcrowded medieval core. Over the next century a series of developments were implemented, extending from the principal axis of George St laid out as an east–west route along a ridge. Strict building controls helped to give the whole 'new town' a remarkable consistency. The initial expectation was that commercial life would remain concentrated in the old city, but decline in demand for services through progressive deterioration of the property in the centre led tradesmen to shift into New Town basements and back lands. The port-city phenomenon emerged with greater clarity, accentuating the theme of urban dominance not only in East-Central Scotland but also in the west where Glasgow's fortunes were rising. At the same time there was a fragmentation of port activity, accentuated by canal building, which provided opportunity for growth at certain other places in the Central Belt especially. The canals offered scope for new town building. Grangemouth

Table 3.3. *Largest burghal parishes 1755 and 1821[a]*

1755		1821	
Edinburgh	64.8	Glasgow	162.0
Glasgow	33,5	Edinburgh	138.2
Aberdeen	15.7	Paisley	47.5
Dundee	12.5	Aberdeen	44.8
Inverness	9.7	Dundee	30.6
Perth	9.0	Greenock	22.1
Dunfermline	8.6	Perth	19.1
Paisley	6.8	Ayr	16.9
Elgin	6.3	Coatbridge/Airdrie	14.4
Alloa	5.8	Kirkaldy	14.2
St Andrews	4.9	Dunfermline	13.7
Campbeltown	4.6	Kilmarnock	12.8
Dumfries	4.5	Inverness	12.3
Kilmarnock	4.4	Falkirk	11.5
Montrose	4.1	Dumfries	11.1
Ayr	4.0	Montrose	10.3
Irvine	4.0	Campbeltown	9.0
Haddington	4.0	Hamilton	7.6
Stirling	4.0	Lanark	7.1
Falkirk	3.9	Stirling	7.1
Greenock	3.9	Irvine	7.0
Hamilton	3.8	Peterhead	6.3
Kirkaldy	3.6	Rothesay	6.1
Kirriemuir	3.4	Brechin	5.9
Linlithgow	3.3	Cupar	5.9

[a] Normally the one parish within which the burgh lies is taken. Additional parishes are taken for Aberdeen (Old Machar), Ayr (Newton, St Quivox), Edinburgh (Collington, Corstorphine, Cramond, Duddington, Liberton, Leith), Glasgow (Cathcart, Eastwood, Gorbals, Govan), Kirkaldy (Abbotshall, Dysart) and Paisley (Paisley Abbey). New Monkland and Old Monkland are taken for Coatbridge/Airdrie.

Source: See Table 3.1

at the eastern end of the Forth & Clyde Canal was successful and its trade grew at the expense of Bo'ness whose custom house was transferred in 1810. But the Earl of Eglinton's ambitious plan for Ardrossan which started in 1805 was undermined by the failure of the canal to get beyond Johnstone and success was deferred until the railway age.

However, adjustment to the opportunities for modernisation in some parts of the Outer Regions failed to achieve a separation of agricultural and industrial employment and did not support the growth of large towns. Whether such adjustment constitutes 'improvement' is a debateable point but it was certainly an umpromising base for further change. The lack of harmony between social and economic criteria in much of the Highlands

Table 3.4. *Distribution of the largest burghal parishes 1755 and 1821*

Region	1755				1821			
	A	B	C	D	A	B	C	D
Highlands & Islands	2	14.3	0.5	0.29	3	27.4	6.9	0.24
Grampian	2	22.0	1.1	0.58	2	51.1	19.8	0.64
Tayside	4	29.1	16.9	0.92	4	65.9	27.2	0.88
North	8	65.4	10.2	0.55	9	144.4	16.4	0.53
Borders Dumfries & Galloway	1	4.5	5.7	0.31	1	11.1	7.8	0.25
South	1	4.5	2.8	0.15	1	11.1	4.7	0.15
Outer regions	9	69.9	8.7	0.47	10	155.5	13.9	0.45
East-Central	9	102.9	34.4	1.87	6	190.6	42.5	1.38
West-Central	7	60.4	37.4	2.04	9	297.4	56.4	1.83
Central Belt	16	163.3	35.5	1.92	15	488.0	50.0	1.62
Scotland	25	233.2	18.4	1.00	25	643.5	30.8	1.00

A Number of burghal parishes (from the 25 largest)
B Total population of the burghal parishes (000s)
C B as a percentage of the total population
D C as a proportion of C for Scotland
Source: See Table 3.1.

meant a breakdown in the monolithic improvement strategy and it raises interesting questions of perception. It is highly significant that government was prepared to recognise that regional problems existed. The desire to eliminate Highland discontent by economic development stimulated several *ad hoc* initiatives which deserve greater recognition as approaches to regional development.[104] But their impact was limited to accelerating the diffusion of some important innovations: there was no prospect of long-term subsidies to allow a more socially-acceptable revision of Highland potentials.

4

Agricultural improvement

Although the improving movement had a comprehensive regional impact, involving the development of industry and the overhaul of transport and settlement systems it was in agriculture where the greatest changes were made. So much so that the notion of an 'agricultural revolution', which is good currency south of the border, has been put forward.[1] There was vigorous action taken to enclose land, to create consolidated holdings and to introduce new rotations, especially during the middle decades of the eighteenth century. Arguably the legislative preconditions had already been satisfied and particular elements of the new agriculture were exemplified in the countryside before 1700. However, a further important act was passed in 1770 relating to entailed estates, authorising longer leases, if tenants agreed to certain improvements, and allowed proprietors to charge to their heirs three quarters of the costs of enclosure and other agricultural improvements. Furthermore the eighteenth century witnessed not simply the application of a number of different ideas to accelerate the growth of agriculture but, rather, comprehensive packages of measures being introduced on each estate. These local development plans involved the landowner taking a lead and concentrating all major decision-making in his hands. Some seventeenth-century proprietors were very much aware of the potential for commercial farming, especially in Lothian, but it has not yet been shown that on any single estate the owner abolished all sub-tenancies and introduced a uniform system of leasing, with associated policies to redeem wadsets, eliminate boundary problems and set up holdings as enclosed and consolidated units. In this respect there was clearly a revolution and, if not every estate was a model of agricultural efficiency, by the end of the eighteenth century at least every estate had been taken in hand by its owner and was being managed as a commercial enterprise. Serious social and economic problems inhibited radical change in some parts of the country until the nineteenth century. But everywhere plans were being implemented and hence the change in attitude which was becoming evident in the seventeenth century accelerated in the eighteenth and resulted in a new concept of landownership. Every revolution has elements of continuity and since there is universal acceptance of radical landscape change over much of the country it is hard to see how the meaning of the term 'revolution' is being significantly abused when applied to Scotland's agriculture at this time.

A distinctive feature of the period was the rise in agricultural prices which created an irresistible stimulus for change by the end of the century. Adam Smith was in no doubt that the rise in cattle prices was the greatest commercial advantage that Scotland received from the Union. The price increase made it worthwhile to cultivate land for fodder crops. 'Had the Scotch cattle been always confined to the market of Scotland, in a country in which the quantity of land which can be applied to no other purpose but the feeding of cattle is so great in proportion to what can be applied to other purpose, it is scarce possible perhaps that their price could ever have risen so high as to render it profitable to cultivate land for the sake of feeding them.'[2] The cultivated area in the upland areas could therefore be increased to embrace all the land physically suitable given the expectation of profit even from the less fertile and less accessible lands. It would no longer be necessary to concentrate on a tiny infield which reflected the maximum area that could be fertilised, bearing in mind the relatively modest cattle herds given the low price levels. The profitability of larger stocks would now stimulate additional cultivation through the demand for fodder and the supply of extra manure. Only ignorance or lack of finance to buy extra stock could possibly prevent the opportunity from being seized. Although Smith's commercial view tends to overlook the subsistence element in farming systems there can be no doubt that the emergence of a lucrative and reliable market constituted a powerful incentive and precondition.

Features of the improving movement

It has been suggested that the bulk of Scotland's better land was enclosed during the forty year period 1750–90, changes being implemented so radically as to remove almost all trace of the old pattern.[3] In accounting for the timing of these changes mention must be made of the new ideas in agriculture, notably the Tullian principles propagated in Scotland by the Society of Improvers founded in 1723. The immediate response was not overwhelming because of a desperate shortage of capital and the low prices that prevailed, in spite of the stimulus of union, until the 1760s.[4] Lord Haddington was active in 1708 sowing clover and rye grass and planting shelter belts at Tynninghame (East Lothian), but he and his colleagues, like Cockburn of Ormiston and Grant of Monymusk, were rich men playing at farming through experiments restricted to the home farm and of little relevance to the ordinary farmer. There was also an important cultural change, especially after 1745, which brought a flowering of intellectual enlightenment and a desire for improvement in the broadest sense. It became not only profitable but fashionable for landowners, many of whom were now merchants bringing capital and ideas to their estates, to make an impact that would 'earn them glory in the same way as their predecessors had earned glory in war and to provide subsistence for a whole dynasty of landlords stretching away into the future'.[5] At a time when the leadership of landowners was undisputed they positively exploited their position by unanimously approving all aspects of economic advance before the end of the eighteenth century, instead of remaining indifferent to economic progress or rejoicing in the poverty of the country as a means of magnifying their own relative affluence. Until town based industrialists and joint stock companies took over the initiative in the early nineteenth century much of the coal mining, canal building and linen manufacture resulted from their efforts. But it was on the land where their influence was most penetrating and the estate unit becomes an essential context for the study of the changing countryside. This is reflected in estate maps which probably constitute the most heavily exploited body of documentary material for historical geography after the census.[6] In several cases interpretation of particular settlements has been assisted by the study of estate maps, for example Ardnamurchan.[7] The magnificent collection available in Register House, Edinburgh, has inspired a formidable research effort which cannot be fully summarised in a short essay.

Reserves of capital and initiative would however have been blunted in their impact had the lairds not enjoyed almost unlimited power to make changes. With possession of land having once depended on ability to hold it, ownership was concentrated in the hands of a few. The balance of power was such that small tenants were unable to accumulate customary rights to arable or rough pasture and hence developments were not retarded by any obligation to negotiate. 'Enclosure' has therefore a relatively simple meaning in Scotland, concerned merely with fencing and dyking, and carries no implication about abolition of customary rights by an elaborate legal process. Legislation was already on the statute book enabling any owner to enclose at will, without the need for recourse to any formal procedure, while the 1695 act on the division of commonties (areas of land common to several owners) allowed for partition by private agreement or through a simple legal process.[8] These acts were the basis to the spread of transformation of individual estates, as was the fact that at the time there were fewer than eight thousand considerable properties in Scotland.[9] However, the ability to innovate does not indicate that change is inevitable: like the availability of relevant technology it holds the promise of action when circumstances are propitious. There had to be a measure of consent from the tenants. Enclosures generated a good deal of suspicion in view of the violent reaction to them by the levellers when the first attempts were made in Galloway in the seventeenth century. At the end of the century there were farmers at Innerwick (East Lothian) who thought enclosures disadvantageous because 'they occupy too much of the high rented corn land and harbour birds'.[10] And at Duthil (Badenoch & Strathspey) 'the people murmur exceedingly at inclosures, their cattle having been accustomed to range promiscuously through the year excepting the summer season'.[11] The prospect of profitability induced by rising prices was a crucial factor. Prices rose from the 1760s as grain imports replaced the previous norm of export surpluses.[12] Yet even so the most astute landowners trod carefully for it was easy to emulate Cockburn of Ormiston and combine technical success with economic failure. Improvement was costly: in areas where little stone was available the difficulty and expense of making enclosures was considerable. Urquhart parish (Moray) was in this situation: thorn hedges could be set but they were 'so long coming to perfection and so difficult to be fenced when they are young that no tenant on a lease of ordinary endurance can attempt them with any prospect of success'.[13] But equally important was the production of a scheme that would assure everyone a place in the new order. For it was a tenet of the improving ethos that everyone should be improved by industry, and redundancies on the land, caused by farm consolidation, had to be balanced by new jobs in manufacturing and services. In this form of paternalism there is a clear strand of continuity with medieval attitudes. There would be economic and social development without excessive migration. The approach was realistic in the Central Belt, with a substantial agricultural potential and scope for industry too but in the north, where there was overpopulation in relation to resources, the way ahead was much more uncertain.

Specialisation

Commercial production became the main objective and more pronounced regional specialisation developed with arable farms in Lothian contrasting with cattle rearing in Grampian and sheep farming in the Highlands. However, these regional interests were not established at once. It is known that sheep moved only slowly into the Highlands: Dumbarton and Perth & Kinross by 1762; Lochaber by 1782 and Sutherland only in 1795. This reflects the misgivings in landlord circles over the social consequences of commercial sheep farming as well as the relatively poor communications and reservations on the part of Border shepherds whose skills were crucial for a successful activity in the North.[14] Even the cattle rearing emphasis in

Grampian was slow to consolidate. Sir Archibald Grant at Monymusk (Gordon) showed the way by clearing boulders off the land (so much so that the enclosed fields became bounded by 'consumption dykes') and by draining the damp patches that had previously broken up the continuity of the arable.[15] Ground was kept free from weeds by fallowing, but this gave way to the more economically attractive method of introducing turnips into the rotation. Turnips could be hoed and weeds eliminated almost as easily as through fallowing while in addition there was a valuable feed crop that offered a solution to the age-old problem of keeping stock through the winter. In turn the maintenance of livestock through the winter offered a ready supply of meat at all times of year and provided copious amounts of manure to boost the harvests of corn, straw and turnips. As J. R. Allan has written so incisively, 'the northern farmer discovered that there is a law of increasing returns: the more the stock, the bigger the midden; the bigger the midden the better the crops; the better the crops the more stock you can keep'.[16]

Yet not all farmers were ready to perceive the advantage of a rotation including one green crop until well into the nineteenth century. Some tenants believed that 'the expense of laying down so much as a fifth of a farm in turnips would be unsupportable' while reducing the cereal area from a half to two fifths would create a 'never-ending scarcity of straw' with less to sell as well.[17] Grant had to use all his powers of persuasion at Monymusk: 'your misfortune is not the want of good soil but your mismanagement of it' was one of the more abrasive remarks in his 'Memorandum to the tenants of Monymusk' in 1756.[18] But tenant reservations were understandable when landowners were liable to change their minds. The initial interest of the improvers lay in cereals and upland country was therefore considered 'ill-calculated' for improvement.[19] Some cereal growing was attempted in enclosures carved out of outfield or waste land to avoid premature disturbance of joint tenants: the Earl of Findlater enclosed land on the uplands of Deskford (Moray) but 'the bleak situation, the bad exposure and the wetness of soil prevented the crops from filling and ripening'.[20] Similarly Thomas Balfour attempted to improve the sheep pasture on Stronsay (Orkney) and convert it into cornland: tolerable crops were grown in good seasons, especially on fields close to the shore that could be dressed with seaweed, but the disappointing results in poorer years forced a reversion to grass.[21] Compared with Lothian only limited parts of the North could expect to prosper as cereal exporters and the logic of concentrating more on cattle was gradually realised. Thus at Monymusk, where Grant first insisted on fallowing in the context of a rotation involving corn and grass, the growth of turnips, clover and rye grass allowed the original orthodoxy to be superseded. In Caithness reliable meal supply through Inverness merchants was a stimulus to improvement there.[22]

It would be interesting to know more about the changing perceptions of landowners towards the potential of their properties. It seems likely that there were considerable doubts over the best cropping pattern and over the size of holdings, with problems of resettlement delaying any rapid transition to large farm units. Even in Lothian it is argued that there was no continuous progress but 'contrast trial and error with advance in one respect and side-tracking retrogression or even reaction in another'.[23] For the uprooting of working settlement pattern might leave an estate short of the seasonal labour that remained so important. 'Seasonal needs required a surplus of people who were self-supporting by their individual small stakes in the soil and stock and who, by providing services in lieu of rents, permitted very cheap running of the Mains farm with almost no cash commitments.'[24] Cash wages became more common in the eighteenth and nineteenth centuries but there were still advantages in having villagers and crofters locally available to be called upon and hence the disturbance of the traditional pattern could not be contemplated without a comprehensive plan. On large estates conditions might vary considerably between districts with big differences in the timing and nature of change. The improvements feature prominently in local histories and through such material the subtle variations can be appreciated.[25] Events on the Gordon estate in the parishes of Inveravon and Kirkmichael (Moray) show how the simple orthodoxy of improvement, that could be applied with comparative ease in Lothian, had to be broken down into a variety of strategies in order to come to terms with the local economic and social realities. It was fortunate that on the eastern fringes of the Highlands the commercial emphasis on cattle raising could be reconciled with small farms and, especially with the scope for taking in new land, the agricultural population was hardly reduced at all. Enclosures would demarcate separate holding as run-rig was abolished but the settlement pattern might still emphasise the toun, perhaps with the holdings radiating outwards and with the farmhouses clustered at the apex. Grampian therefore exhibits considerable flexibility. For example at Alvah (Banff & Buchan) there were only a few farms enclosed yet turnips had been sown in the fields for the previous twenty years while clover and rye grass had become a constant part of the rotation.[26] Figure 4.1 shows the expansion of agricultural settlement in the Glenlivet area of Moray after 1750. The area includes the parishes of Cabrach, Glenbuchat, Inveravon, Kirkmichael and Strathdon. Land with slopes below twenty five per cent is shaded according to altitude and it is evident that there was considerable settlement up to 140 m (c. 450 feet) but seldom above.

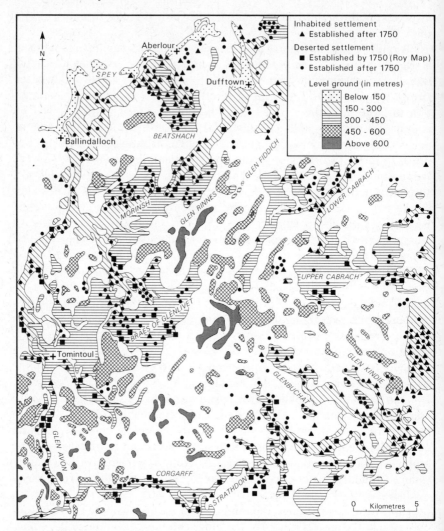

Figure 4.1. Expansion of settlement in Glenlivet (Moray) and adjacent areas after 1750
Source: Roy map and estate documents (Register House)

Field systems

What was the fate of the infield–outfield distinction? It has already been suggested that the practice of using different pieces of ground at different levels of intensity gave rise to many local variations and that it is unlikely for any rigid model to have prevailed. With the availability of lime (and other fertilisers) and the discovery of the value of roots it is probable that the contrasts between infield and outfield were reduced: resources were available to maintain the latter in good heart and both sections would be incorporated together in a geometrical field layout thereby eliminating any landscape distinction. However, differences in the inherent quality of the land would still be expressed through the rotations used on different parts of the farm with the edge of the 'outfield' being finally reached where the soils were so thin, hungry and exposed that even buoyant cattle prices and availability of new grasses and roots would not justify further reclamation. Indeed the flexibility displayed on consolidated farms provides insights that help towards a more credible interpretation on the traditional outfield arrangement. A useful example comes from Funzie in the Shetland island of Fetlar where the interest in the sea (both the local fishing and whaling in distant waters) meant that agriculture had value only for subsistence, with no incentive for rationalisation along commercial lines.[27] The organisation of the agriculture comes out clearly from Sheriff Court Records referring to a consolidation of the landholdings of three proprietors (Funzie exhibiting both proprietary and tenant run-rig). A typical tenant had nine rigs in the infield, amounting to 1.1 ha in addition to his *toon-mal*, an enlarged farmyard of some 0.3 ha. The ground would have been worked communally by delling teams using the traditional Shetland spade. Then came 23 outfield rigs amounting to 1.1 ha with oats alternating with natural grasses and thistles (in contrast to the infield where two conservative crops of oats alternated with fallow). Each tenant had access to the communal meadow as well as the *scattald*, a common hill pasture, which does not seem to have been regulated as well as Hebridean grazings (where a *souming* was often laid down to avoid overstocking). The Funzie case shows that the contrast between infield and outfield cultivation procedures was not as great as is sometimes supposed. References in the Statistical Account to a division in outfield between *folds* which were cultivated and *faughs* which were not indicate a sensitive balance between community requirements and local potentials without the intervention of rigid conventions and excessive conservatism claimed by the improvers.

Funzie is a valuable example because proprietary run-rig rarely persisted into the nineteenth century. In one Orkney parish too great inefficiency arose through the persistence of proprietary run-rig (eleven heritors had an interest) and the lack of proper enclosures which meant that cattle on the hill could easily invade the cropland: 'they must be hunted with dogs to the mountains perhaps after a dozen of them have run through the fields of standing corn'.[28] By contrast the minister at Dollar (Clackmannan) is able to emphasise the advantages in having consolidated units of landownership which included 'cutting off endless quarrels and disputes that were continually taking place between the different proprietors or their tenants about their encroaching or trespassing upon one another'.[29] And the evidence for Berwickshire and Roxburghshire indicates that virtually all cases of proprietary run-rig were dealt with between 1730 and 1770.[30] Consolidation led gradually to the elimination of infield–outfield differences. At Dalserf (Hamilton) 'the old distinction between croft and outfield is fast wearing out and all parts of the farm are now mostly treated in the same manner'.[31] But at Fraserburgh (Banff & Buchan) the contrast remained and 'of consequence an equally regular rotation of cropping ground has not taken place'.[32] The differences were reflected quite sharply in land values at Tullynessle (Gordon) where the best infield land was let at 83p per acre compared with 50p for inferior land and between 2½ and 25p per acre for outfield according to its quality.[33]

Variations in agricultural trends

To assess the general progress of the improvements in agriculture by the end of the eighteenth century the Statistical Account has been used as a basis for content analysis. Although it is not written by experts it has the great merit of describing conditions in every parish of Scotland. Some accounts are so brief and cryptic as to be worthless but in the majority of cases valuable information is given and the variable nature of local conditions is not obscured by the sweeping generalisations that arise in studies of entire counties or the whole of Scotland. From the remarks made by the ministers it is usually possible to gauge whether the improvements were advanced or not. And in the latter case parishes where virtually no beginning had been made may be differentiated from those where some significant pioneering works had been attempted. The picture that emerges in Figure 4.2 shows predictably that the improvements had reached an advanced stage in the Central Belt. However, run-rig still survived in part of Wiston & Roberton (Lanark).[34] In West Kilbride (Cunninghame) lime was only 'just being appreciated' while at Girvan (Kyle & Carrick) lime in the upper part of the parish could not be exploited 'owing to its distance from coal, the want of roads or the unfitness of the neighbouring grounds for agriculture'.[35] At the other extreme, there was little of significance to report on improvement in much of the Highlands and Islands. Yet the other Outer Regions display many local contrasts, though almost everywhere except the remoter parts of the Grampian Uplands a beginning had been made. Typical was Newmachar (Gordon): 'the farms of the heritors are enclosed but the rest of the parish (three farms excepted) is open. The people, however, as they begin to have spots in turnips and sown grasses are led to see the necessity for, and benefit of, inclosures'.[36] Two other parish accounts show the extent of the variation in the transitional stage. In the coastal parish of St Fergus (Banff & Buchan) 'the farmers now appear at church and market dressed up in English superfine cloth and many of their wives and daughters in cloaks and bonnets. The man servant is as

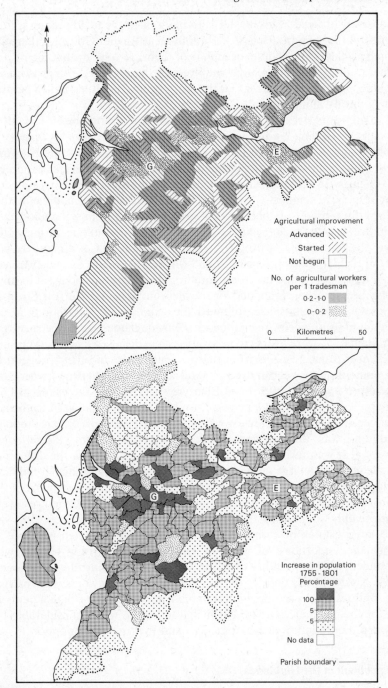

Figure 4.2. Agricultural improvement in the Central Belt c. 1790
Source: Statistical Account and Table 3.1

expensively arrayed as his master and the dress of the maid servant is little inferior to that of her mistress'.[37] But inland at Rayne (Gordon) 'there are so many small crofts and the occupiers of them are so poor that their cattle have not the strength to plough and dress them properly'. The proceeds of stocking knitting paid the rent 'as the crofters have no other way of earning money but by annually rearing a young ox or cow'.[38]

The ministers stress the role of the landlords. At Monquitter in Banff & Buchan the leading landowner Cumine of Auchry pressed his tenants to use lime and 'sow a certain proportion of their land with turnip, flax and grass seeds': 'he frequently walked or rode through his estate, freely conversing with his tenants, rousing them to industry by motives suited to their respective tempers . . . and by the united energy of popular virtues and solid sense he triumphed over every opposition from soil, climate and prejudice, gradually introducing the principles of rational farming and laying the foundation of progressive improvement'.[39] Certainly there was role for the dynamic propagandist and where a particular formula was well suited to economic and environmental realities there was no great harm in strong pressure being applied on recalcitrant tenants. But on Stronsay (Orkney) few tenants had followed the example of Mr Balfour in experimenting with enclosures, done with outside labour, partly because 'the inhabitants . . . were averse to innovations and despised a mode of farming different in some respects from that to which they and their progentiors had immemorially been inured'.[40] And at Erskine (Renfrew) where the agriculture improved after Lord Blantyre succeeded to the estate in 1776 and applied his knowledge gained through practical farming in Lothian it soon became clear that the best way of adapting standard practice to local conditions was through tenants being allowed certain 'discretionary powers'.[41] It was necessary to make adequate allowance for the difference in scale between a large farm in the proprietor's hands and smaller holdings managed by the majority of tenants. At Beith (Cunninghame) many of the improvements had been expedited by small farmers whose methods were 'more readily adopted by the rest than those introduced by persons who have large estates or carry on farming upon a more extensive scale'.[42] Hence the importance of work by the more enterprising tenants who responded to the stimulus of rising food prices during the Napoleonic Wars. No doubt the policies of many improving landowners were premature, with a rapid pace being determined by the need for higher rents to pay for their higher standards of living and there was a considerable lag between the initiation of new practices and their general adoption.[43]

The problem of the Highlands

Figure 4.3 also reveals an element of crisis in the Highlands. Little change

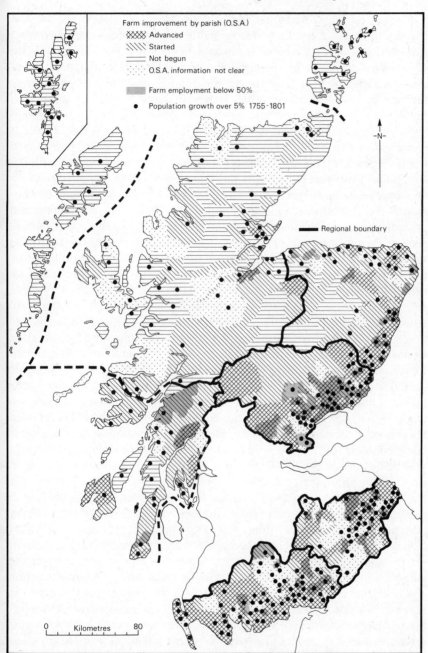

Figure 4.3. Agricultural improvement in the Outer Regions c. 1790
Source: Statistical Account and Table 3.1

had been accomplished by the end of the century, yet the population was increasing and the level of non-agricultural employment was very low. Commercially only a sheep system would be viable yet the serious problem of local resettlement of the subsistence farmers made it impossible to introduce sheep on a large scale. Sir John Sinclair argued that sheep farming could not be profitable 'unless in large flocks and by a well regulated system'. Land would have to be organised into large holdings and their demand for the arable land and sheltered grazings would 'render it compulsory to take from petty agriculture the smaller interspersed tracts'.[44] Sinclair believed that sheep farming might be reconciled with the traditional subsistence system if the joint farms could be converted into cooperative sheep farms. But even in an east coast situation he underestimated the importance of shepherding skills that only outsiders could provide and overestimated the amount of labour that a sheep farm would require. In a west coast situation only a handful of men would be needed to work a sheep farm that might embrace the territory formerly occupied by three or four joint-farm communities. In the event Sinclair never put his theory to the test. Except on farms where the 'great sheep' were a subsidiary enterprise to cattle rearing there was little future for the small tenant farmers who came under growing pressure as the frontier moved north. In 1792 their frustration exploded in a spontaneous demonstration against the invading flocks as the men of Ross decided to take matters into their own hands and drive the Cheviots out. Their gesture was highly symbolic even though it was swiftly contained through intervention by the military, based at Fort George. It pointed to the shortcoming of exclusive land use policies. In fairness to the landowners it must be conceded that they were generally reluctant to introduce sheep unless arrangements could be made for the displaced tenantry, even when revolutionary change was being carried out.[45] There was a considerable income to be derived from cattle, a farming enterprise that was eminently reconcilable with the traditional township organisation, and for many coastal estates the collection of seaweed and its processing into kelp ash for the chemical industry was an effective solution to the increasing population pressure, especially during the Napoleonic Wars when prices were particularly high in view of the cutting off of alternative foreign sources of raw material.[46] But the collapse of both cattle and kelp prices in the 1820s demanded drastic action and emigration, which had run counter to the improving ethos of the eighteenth century, was now regarded officially as inevitable.[47] Nevertheless, in the revolutionary adjustment that was now made, with an ample measure of cruelty and insensitivity, there was still an effort made on many estates to hold a balance and allocate to small tenants particular areas with scope for land improvement and ancillary employment. Unfortunately the literature often fails to hold a balance and there are important works that stress the problems of the landlords and, alternatively, the injustices suffered by those evicted.[48]

Some indication of the problem is provided by the survey made of Barrisdale estate in Lochaber for the Annexed Estates Commissioners. All the corn land on Barrisdale was on the hillside: the gravelly soil was delved with the spade, manured with sea wrack or ferns and cropped with black oats. Cropping was discouraged by 'the tediousness and expense of delving, the frequent and heavy falls of rain in the spring, summer and autumn, the danger and uncertainty of reaping, and the steepness of the hills'.[49] One particular farm, Skiary, was considered to have 'a most horrid appearance from the steepness of the hill and the numberless impending rocks . . . which bring on great losses to the tenants by the death of their cattle occasioned by falls from the rocks when in search of their food'. The farms also suffered much from the encroachments of the herring fishers who cured their fish on the verges of the grasslands. Fish caught in Loch Hourn were an important part of the economy and featured prominently in the diet: 'the herring are boiled with potatoes and their butter cheese and milk maintain them the remaining part of the year'.[50] There was little potential for improvement apart from raising some inclosures for hay crops and no way that substantial rent increases could be met. In any case 'to lay a high additional rent upon them at once would certainly dispirit them and tempt them either to grow desperate in the country or, like their neighbours, to emigrate to America which I apprehend is quite opposite to the intention of the honourable Board'.[51] Speaking of Lochaber in the early eighteenth century, Edward Burt claimed he had never heard of any limestone, chalk or marl being available 'and if some of their rocks might serve for limestone, in that case the kilns, carriage and fuel would render it so expensive it would be the same thing to them as if there were none'.[52]

Similar groping for an acceptable formula is evident on the Argyll estates where the seventeenth-century stratagem of infiltrating the ancestral lands of the MacLeans of Duart (in Mull, Morvern and Tiree) with Campbell tacksmen was followed by a policy of direct leases to tenants from the Duke, in the hope that elimination of the middlemen would allow a substantial increase in rent to pay for expensive development plans at Inveraray. The intention was partly political, to reduce the influence of certain Cameron tacksmen who did not always further the Argyll interests.[53] But the new system introduced by Duncan Forbes in 1737 did not have the expected outcome. Tenants could not 'improve' without significant encouragement from the landlord and instead their position deteriorated with the elimination of the protection and financial assistance previously given by the tacksmen (some of whom retained their place in society as leading tenants). The increased rents could not be paid and there was much opposition to the offering of leases to the highest bidder. The proprietor would not reinstate the tacksmen but rents were moderated and a system of private offers for leases introduced a strong element of continuity. Even sub-letting was revived to avoid emigration.

Conclusion

It seems that the record of achievement is highly uneven and the heroic methods of the Lowland improvers in the mid eighteenth century appear distinctly tarnished when applied to the Highland situation half a century later. Overpopulation in the Highlands, allied with the problems arising from its position and resources, makes it inappropriate to expect a single improvement model to be diffused throughout Scotland in such a way that a relatively slow rate of change or the appearance of local anomalies can simply be attributed to conservatism.[54] But where change could be accomplished so as to improve the situation of every family affected there could be considerable advance and those who failed to conform to the local norm would hardly win sympathy against eviction. There could be a more determined advance towards individualism as it became less necessary to retain the security of communalism in agrarian organisation. The continuance of the pendulum swing, which had already gained some momentum in the seventeenth century through reduced emphasis on reallocation of infield holdings, was assured through total elimination of run-rig. If there had been major differences in cultivation methods between infield and outfield, for instance in manuring and fallowing, this was perhaps partly due to the weaker communal restraints in the outfield, where people might consequently be reluctant to take a responsible attitude. With the consolidation of holdings there could be a more judicious mixing of techniques to assure regeneration and infield–outfield distinctions would be blunted. Thus at Garvald (East Lothian) 'the greatest improvement in agriculture is that of sowing the land with grass seeds and turning it into pasture for a few years. This species of improvement is found to be the best restorative where manure cannot be procured.'[55]

Yet in any event there would be considerable turmoil in the township. Which of the joint tenants (if indeed any of them) would become tenant of the consolidated holding? Which of his former partners would be prepared to accept the inferior role of farm labourer in the new system? What alternative employment would be immediately available for those who had no place in the new order? Not surprisingly therefore the improvers began in the less sensitive areas, the outfield and common land. The disruption of the joint-farm community could only come when some acceptable basis for social differentiation was available, and when certain families would accept demotion to small-holdings on the edge of the moorland, to undertake land reclamation on a scale that would not have been contemplated under the old communal system of basic subsistence with minimum effort. As the minister at Dalmeny (Edinburgh) pointed out, large farms did not necessarily mean a smaller population because many married workers might be employed. But it would mean fewer farmer families and a different balance between the classes in the countryside.[56] Where there was no way that the desired agricultural efficiency could be made socially acceptable then change was postponed. It is interesting to note that while the Earl of Breadalbane commissioned a thorough survey of his estates beside Loch Tay (Perth & Kinross) in 1769 he was unable to implement any radical changes because the introduction of new technology by outside farmers would create insoluble resettlement problems.[57] Equally in Arran (Cunninghame), a large island in the Firth of Clyde, it has been shown that a rising population posed great problems for advocates of agrarian change: the proposed reorganisation by Burrel in 1772 could not be implemented and progress was only possible in 1814/15 when consolidated holding in the interior of the island was matched by the laying out of many small lots near the coast.[58] In 1830, as the island's population passed its peak, some enlargement took place, while in Breadalbane too the nineteenth century allowed a solution. Values in the nineteenth century were rather different: a more highly specialised economy combined with the greater self-confidence of the landlord class applied an abrasive edge to the rather benign quality of 'sympathy' advocated by Adam Smith. Yet even so there were many interesting survivals of traditional farms like the farm at Auchindrain (Argyll & Bute) which persisted as a joint tenancy into the twentieth century with an irregular nucleated settlement layout that has most appropriately been preserved as a croft museum.[59]

5

The planned village movement

The planned villages became an essential element in the improving movement, distinctly complementary to the reorganisation and expansion of farming. The creation of new settlements was not an entirely new phenomenon. When the feudal system was first imposed some of the royal burghs, such as Elgin (Moray) and Nairn, were stimulated by plantation and did not develop spontaneously. The origins of Newton Stewart (Merrick) lie in the founding of a burgh of barony by Walter Stewart in 1677, while further seventeenth-century precedents are evident in the support given by the Earl of Argyll and Earl of Seaforth to Campbeltown (Argyll & Bute) and Stornoway (Western Isles) respectively. New villages were also being created at this time, notably Houston (Renfrew) where the old settlement was resited to 'ensure more distance between mansion and village', a motive that was subsequently to transform both Cullen (1820) and Fochabers (1778).[1] However, the eighteenth century shows a very significant surge of interest in developing new market centres especially in areas remote from existing centres. Of course estates were no longer closed economic entities: even in the seventeenth century the Earl of Seafield, with estates on the Moray coast, found the Edinburgh grain market extremely lucrative and an agent was maintained to look after his interests when ships arrived. But, nevertheless, a local market provided some security when national markets became difficult and also stimulated more intensive activity than would otherwise have been justified. Even with the designation of various burghs of barony the very uneven urban system arising through the royal burghs was only partially modified and hence it was reasonable to try and exploit the improved climate for growth to rectify the outstanding deficiencies.

Certainly the importance of local markets is one of the more persistent themes to emerge in discussions of agricultural development in the Statistical Account. Because of the demand for food in Glasgow, dairying and market gardening developed in nearby parishes. That local demand 'gave life and vigour to the exertions of the farmer' was evident not only in Cambuslang but at Dunlop.[2] The local cheese was being brought almost to equal perfection with some of the better sorts of English cheese and could find acceptability in distant markets, but the Glasgow trade was an important incentive to increase production.[3] The whey was fed to swine which again attracted attention because of the ready outlets nearby. Fruit growing in the Clyde valley was gaining in prominence: Archibald Hamilton had laid out forests and orchards in Dalziel but the same emphasis was noted much further away at Carluke.[4] Even in Fife the potential of the Glasgow market was felt: for the farmers of Anstruther the Forth–Clyde Canal had given them access to the city 'which takes off vast quantities of wheat barley and beans'.[5] But Edinburgh was also available to the producers in East-Central Scotland: for example, milk, butter, eggs and poultry were supplied to Edinburgh from Kirknewton and Uphall. The towns were also important to farmers in nearby parishes because manure was available and could be taken back to the farm as a return load.

Integration was furthered, moreover, by the tendency for wealthy urban dwellers to acquire land in the country. This was noticed in New Monkland where there were a vast number of gentlemen's properties 'many of them finished in the greatest taste'. It was argued that 'when a merchant has been successful he purchases a piece of land, builds an elegant villa and improves his property at the dearest rate'. And it was supposed at Muirkirk (Cumnock & Doon Valley) 'that new implements and new modes will be introduced' on account of much land being acquired by 'men of fortune who have money to spare in making experiments'.[6] And it was not just the cities that had a beneficial local effect on agriculture. The farmers in Kilmacolm (Inverclyde) have 'a ready market for every article at Port Glasgow and Greenock, and a high price', while it was also reported that at Old Cumnock, where export of food to Ireland had been ruled out by the high cost of transport overland to the harbour at Ayr 25 km distant, the distance from markets was 'happily removed by the works of Muirkirk and Catrine'.[7] And the same trend was evident at Lanark: 'some years ago a considerable quantity of oat meal was yearly carried from this parish to the Glasgow market; but now since the introduction of cotton manufacturers it is all consumed at home; and frequently Irish meal is sent up from Glasgow to supply the demand at the cotton mills'.[8] Hence it became an important objective of improving landowners to stimulate local demand and to induce the reciprocal relationship that had developed spontaneously in some parts of the country.

The village would do more than simply stimulate agriculture through local demand. Employment in manufactures and services would help overcome the problem of redundancies arising from the reorganisation of farms. Furthermore a church and school in the village would introduce a dynamic cultural element and enable the new settlement to become a means of propagating the ethos of the improving movement. By no means insignificant either was the scope for the reclamation of marginal land. It would not be sensible to take good agricultural land for a village except in special circumstances. Better to site the village on improvable muirland where those who occupied the various plots on the feuing plan could reclaim a strip of land as a garden and allotment. There was a danger that such sites could be bleak and inaccessible but since the turnpike roads were frequently bypassing the old kirktouns a number of sites would be found where all the relevant criteria could be adequately respected.

Aspects of planning: the case of New Lanark

Villages were typically created through a planning project undertaken by the landowner. The basic resolve to establish a new settlement was backed up by a physical plan, allocating sites according to a prescribed pattern, sometimes with architectural specifications as well as conformity to a given street system. Choice of site would inevitably be concerned with the basic planning decision: this might involve an extension to an existing settlement or else could relate to a greenfield site. Further elements of planning might emerge through the development of industry and the provision of various community facilities, as well as promotion of the scheme by publicity in neighbouring parishes. It cannot be assumed that every 'planned village' carries all these attributes and apart from the basic act (and the inevitable elements of site selection and feuing plan) each settlement must be studied on its merits. It is therefore very difficult to draw up a complete list of these settlements unless arbitrary criteria are clearly laid down. Certain projects like Garmond (Banff & Buchan) might be planned but only very partially executed. Modest extensions to existing kirktouns, as at Monymusk (Gordon), could escape attention because there was no major transformation. While small quarry or mining settlements like Wanlockhead (Nithsdale) might evade recognition because of their slow development or lack of a regular layout. Some efforts have been made to draw up a comprehensive list but not all of Scotland has yet been covered.[9] Another area of uncertainty lies in the evolution of the planned village idea. As with the royal burghs of the medieval period the source of the inspiration has not been properly traced and it may be that, basically, the restructuring of settlement was seen as an inevitable part of the modernisation process. But like so much of the improvement inspired by the Scottish Enlightenment a good idea was given additional credibility through prevailing fashions, perhaps to the point of encouraging disregard of the financial risks involved.

New Lanark is one of the more spectacular examples. The mellow sandstone buildings of this model village are situated in the Clyde gorge just two kilometres from the centre of the ancient burgh of Lanark. It was founded in 1784 as the result of a visit paid to Glasgow by Richard Arkwright, the pioneer of mechanical cotton spinning. He was shown the Falls of Clyde by David Dale, a Glasgow linen merchant and banker. There was ample power to drive Arkwright's new spinning machine, the water frame, and Dale therefore decided to finance the building of cotton mills. The site was completely undeveloped and in addition to securing the water power by building a tunnel from the top of the falls an entire village was built and a road from Lanark put in. It seems that the original mill was destroyed by fire in 1786 and the oldest industrial building standing today is the second mill opened in 1788. The replacement for the first factory opened in 1789 (originally with five storeys but later reduced to three) and is rather unconventional in being built over the lade with the water wheel placed in the centre of the building. New Lanark was the largest cotton mill in Scotland in 1799 but it continued to grow and two additional mills were erected alongside: the third mill (built in 1826) still stands but the last one was lost by fire in 1883.

Housing was provided in tenements, the first block being the New Buildings of 1789. Built by David Dale they form an attractive centre piece in a plain classical style, complete with a bell which would ring from an ornate bell cote to summon workers to the factory opposite. Religious meetings took place in the New Buildings until a church was built in 1898. Further tenements were added between 1790 and 1795. Although density was high the housing was excellent for its time and through the standard of accommodation and the importance attached to education he established a philanthropic tradition that was maintained by Robert Owen.[10] Owen sought to marry Dale's daughter and as an indication of his ability to provide for his bride he formed a partnership to buy the mills and village. The new management took over in 1800. Owen added a Counting House to the end of Caithness Row, enlarged the New Buildings and installed gate houses (probably to control traffic) but his main contributions came through the Institute of 1816 and School a year later. Such endowments reflected his preoccupation with enlightened management which involved him in schemes for community building in other places after the Napoleonic Wars. New Lanark remained at work and the textile industry continued till 1968. The mills are presently occupied by Metal Extractions and a New Lanark Conservation and Civic Trust has been formed to maintain the fabric of the village. Restoration has already passed from Caithness Row to the New Buildings and the survival of this remarkable village, 'planned' in the widest sense, is assured.

New Lanark thus became an important element in the industrial geography of the Central Belt (Figure 5.1). It was complemented by other

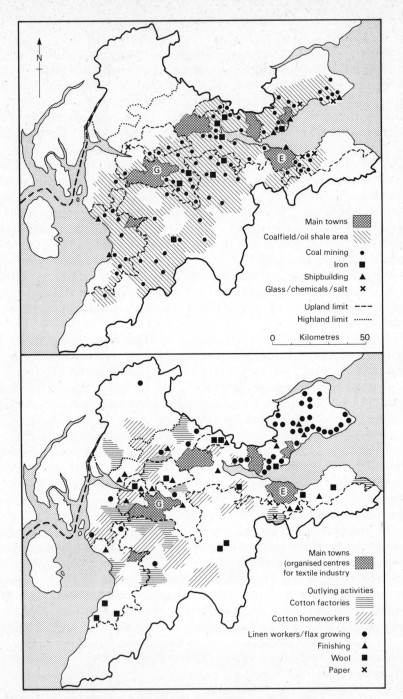

Figure 5.1. Industrial development in the Central Belt c. 1790
Note: Upland parishes are those with more than half their land over 150 m (c. 500 ft) Highland parishes also have a predominance of land over 150 m but include some land over 600 m (c. 2,000 ft)

Source: Statistical Account

villages using local water power like Catrine (Cumnock & Doon Valley). And the Outer Regions were affected as well because places like Gatehouse of Fleet (Stewartry) and Stanley (Perth & Kinross) also attracted attention as the cotton industry entrepreneurs sought suitable sites for their capital investment.[11]

Highland experience

Scope for the development of the cotton industry on the basis of water power should not however be regarded as a key to the planned village movement as a whole. Interest started before this late-eighteenth-century industrial boom and a measure of responsibility may be laid at the feet of the Commissioners for the Annexed Forfeited Estates. The Disarming Act of 1746 was followed by an effort to civilise the Highlanders through an experiment in regional development and nationalisation. The idea was to convert a number of the estates that had been forfeited by owners implicated in the Jacobite Rebellion into a permanent crown holding that would act as a model to private owners. The Annexing Act (implemented in 1755) was primarily political, seeking to promote amongst the Highlanders the protestant religion, good government, industry and manufactures as well as principles of duty and loyalty to his Majesty. Some thirteen estates were involved, distributed loosely over an area stretching from Kippen (Stirling) in the south to Loch Broom (Ross & Cromarty) in the north and from Glenelg (Skye & Lochalsh) in the west to Crathie & Braemar (Kincardine & Deeside) in the east. Thus a very large part of the Highlands could be influenced by the innovations on these model properties.[12] Farming was of course fundamental but when elaborate surveys were carried out it was perceived that new villages were an essential component of any agricultural plan. Surveying the Lochiel estate for the Commissioners in 1771–2 William Morrison found 'no branch of commerce' in the area, 'linen manufacture being in a manner unknown' and the woollen industry carried on no further than to supply local people.[13] Earlier schemes to develop the Highlands had rested on the creation of new burghs and sheriffdoms and the Commissioners would have been aware of contemporary developments at Fort William (Lochaber) and Fort Augustus (Inverness). In seeking to combine strategic and economic interests they were following a well-tested formula, but past failings would suggest that compelling economic potential and a tractable disposition on the part of the indigenous population would be crucial. In 1757 it was suggested that new settlements could be built at Beauly (Inverness), Callander (Stirling), Kinloch Rannoch (Perth & Kinross) and New Tarbet (Ross & Cromarty): the first two places already existed in modest form (work at Callander had been started by the attainted Earl of Perth) whereas the others were to be entirely new developments. All the four candidates were on the eastern fringes of the Highlands but Ullapool (Ross & Cromarty) was eventually preferred to New Tarbet and that meant some development on the west coast. Furthermore, the initiatives were broadened considerably by the plan to settle disbanded members of the army and navy: there was an obligation to provide for the servicemen, who might set an example of industriousness, though equally their attitude might disappoint and their intrusion might be resented by the local people. Several settlements were started on the Perth and Struan estates, the longest lasting colony being Strelitz (named in honour of George III's wife Charlotte of Mecklenburg-Strelitz). But the soldiers seem to have caused a great deal of trouble and attempts to settle them as fishermen at Ullapool and on the west coast estate of Barrisdale at Inverie (Lochaber) were no more successful.

It is easy to find evidence of failure in Highland development schemes. There is little doubt that the Commission's objectives were too grandiose and their capital resources inadequate. When the Board concluded its activities in 1784 (the estates being restored to the families that had previously owned them) the land was not in a significantly better condition than on other properties. Yet development could not reasonably proceed beyond what the potential allowed and with so much to be done in building up a road system (including numerous bridges) and training skilled labour even the theoretical possibilities were modest. Scarce resources might have been used more effectively had they been concentrated on a more limited number of schemes. Yet, as in subsequent Highland development strategies, political considerations demanded as wide a spread as possible. It has been suggested that the injection of industry through fishing and linen was a Lowland obsession which should have been treated with greater caution. But the process of Highland adjustment could only be accelerated by what appeared at the time as the most promising economic developments. It is perhaps the fate of any backward area to share in a profitable activity only briefly before the forces that encourage a wide geographical spread are eclipsed by new circumstances favouring consolidation. Though the industrial scene soon did favour consolidation in the Central Belt the settlement policy was not discredited, for, as even private landowners saw, the cultural argument for a more centralised provision of services was clear. In the year after the Board wound up its activities J. Anderson published his 'Account of the present state of the Hebrides and western coasts of Scotland' and attempted 'to explain the circumstances that have hitherto repressed the industry of the natives'.[14] Tradesmen might live in 'detached hamlets' but such settlements were 'a poor base for commerce' since they lacked adequate facilities for marketing and the exchange of information.

The importance of smallholdings

In their experiments on the Annexed Forfeited Estates the Commissioners had supposed that a beginning could be made by establishing a community of smallholders who might then feel that they had a secure base from which to develop an interest in trades. This was an extension of the concept of a purely agricultural settlement where small tenants could be resettled following the consolidation of the joint farms. Improving landowners were in a dilemma in several senses. Although dedicated to a more efficient farming pattern they recognised an obligation to all their tenants and this meant making some provision for those displaced. At the same time it was desirable that a substantial labouring population should be retained so that the heavy seasonal labour demands on the farms could be met and various development projects on the estate implemented without having to bring in the work force. The parish reports in the Statistical Account pay much attention to this issue. At Alvah (Banff & Buchan) there had been much depopulation because of the 'eagerness of some improvers to take all their land under their own management by which means mechanics and even day labourers are deprived of their crofts; and as there are no villages within the parish betake themselves to other places where they can find accommodation'.[15] At Cawdor (Nairn) it was 'found convenient to have cottagers in the neighbourhood'; employed as day labourers they were extremely useful particularly in the more busy seasons of the year, while the winter months could be spent in weaving, tailoring, shoemaking or carpentry.[16] At Kettle (Fife) 'many farms have cottages, whence they obtain assistance in hay time and harvest'.[17]

Yet smallholders who worked their allotments or pendicles could become so committed to their holding, which they would have to work thoroughly in order to pay rent and gain subsistence that there would be little opportunity to take other work. At Sorn (Cumnock & Doon Valley) such holdings were considered disadvantageous for the tenants were 'neither entirely farmers nor entirely labourers and generally in a worse condition than either'.[18] The problem was elaborated by an outline of the circumstances of Orkney cottagers: 'he is allowed to keep a few sheep of which some have half a dozen, some a dozen and some more. From these he has a little wool which his wife in winter makes into stockings and coarse clothes for the family . . . He sometimes can spare a few hours for the fishing which is often of great use to his family . . . He cuts divots on the common and also peats in the isle of Eday; and the cottagers assist each other in bringing them home. So that their fuel, bad and little as it is, costs them a great deal of labour, though not much money; but it prevents them from being otherwise employed during the time.'[19] Serious conflict could arise as cottagers sought to overcome the limits of their holdings. In Ross

& Cromarty the mailers could not raise enough feed for their cattle and therefore wished to have the whole country a common after the harvest. Smallholder–tradesmen were described as great depradators: 'in declared hostility to all inclosures and improvements of any higher nature than their own and unmerciful destroyers of all grounds around them'.[20]

There would inevitably be some migration where better prospects existed nearby and at Inchinnan (Renfrew) a population decline was noted as cottagers were attracted to Paisley by a flourishing manufacturing industry.[21] A smallholding in the congenial surroundings of a village might prove more attractive, but only if there was adequate employment. The comments made about Callander (Stirling) might well be taken as a valid generalisation. 'Thriving villages', the minister wrote, 'afford a ready market for whatever the farmer has to sell; and in return provide him with artificers and labourers.' Also 'it is to these nurseries of human species . . . we are to look forward now for men to recruit to our army and navy in the hour of danger, while our hardy peasantry are decreasing daily'. Yet increasing the population of villages is wise only 'providing the people are rendered industrious; otherwise it is the greatest curse that can befall a place'.[22] The same reasonable argument was expressed for Kirkpatrick Durham where a village 'though as yet in its infancy has given a liveliness and animation to the place, formerly unknown in that part of the country'. But 'as villages will always become nurseries of dissipation and profligacy when the inhabitants are idle plans have to be formed to give them honest and creditable employment'.[23] His colleagues at Borgue (Stewartry) could certainly have agreed because in that area it seemed that villages provided haven only for 'the most worthless and wretched part of society': 'thither the dregs of the community from all quarters are poured in. Every incentive to vice is presented and no proper police is established to give a check to the growing evil.'[24] The idea of an agricultural community was therefore unviable. Certainly smallholdings were attractive in association with other, regular employment. This could not be provided in agriculture since farmers would normally prefer work to be done by labourers living on the farm with their families or staying for the term as hired servants. The clear separation of agricultural and non-agricultural employment became gradually more evident. It meant that farm labour costs were subject to market trends and wages rose sharply at the end of the eighteenth century with Alford (Gordon) parish for instance being much affected 'by the great demand and high price of labour in southern parts of Scotland, together with that occasioned by the number of extensive manufactories recently erected in Aberdeen'.[25] But this was the inevitable consequence of the transition from feudalism to capitalism.

Small scale manufacturing in the Outer Regions

The concepts of the planned village was therefore subject to revision as it became clear that an essential part of the plan to develop a successful community was the encouragement of industry. An excellent example is afforded by Monquitter (Banff & Buchan) where Joseph Cumine of Auchry began to enclose land and consolidate holdings after he succeeded to the estate in 1739. But 'observing that his tenants were frequently at a loss for a market he determined to establish a permanent one on his own estate. For this purpose he planned a regular village, contiguous to the church, upon a moorish part of a farm. He prevailed upon a few to take feus; he assisted the industrious with money; obtained premiums for the manufacturer; decided every difference by his arbitration; and animated all to the utmost exertion by his countenance and counsel.'[26] The village was a success and the landlord was able to draw £150 per annum in rents from land which had yielded only £11 before the improvements began. Naturally the scheme was widely imitated throughout the Grampian region, not least on the Gordon estates where Huntly (Gordon) and Fochabers (Moray) were rebuilt.[27]

Entirely new village communities were created at Rhynie (Gordon) and Tomintoul (Moray), the latter dating back to 1776 when the Duke of Gordon decided to encourage the scattered population of Kirkmichael to consolidate as far as possible in a central community. The first applications for new feus were made in that year and the village gradually developed.[28] A public house was to be built for travellers along the military road of 1754 (Coupar Angus–Fort George), realigned to fit in with the main street, and it was expected that the kirk and parochial school would become relocated in the village. Land was allotted according to a regular plan, partly arable and partly improvable muir. But the key to village economy lay in the cultivation of lint and the spinning of linen yarn which had been introduced to the district about 1760. A lint mill was to be built and Tomintoul was seen as the proper place for a bleachfield and spinning school. But the industrial developments did not materialise and the village developed only slowly as a service centre, though one gaining some patronage from the landlord since the Duke of Gordon lodged in one of the Tomintoul inns during the shooting season. The message from the region was clear. Industrial potential was limited (Figure 5.2) because there were few skills and raw materials to hand while transport costs in the Outer Regions imposed additional burdens.

But villages were still viable as market centres provided they were carefully sited and provided they were located in districts where no burghs already existed and where rival villages did not emerge. Contemporaneous with the efforts made in Grampian was the development of Inveraray by the

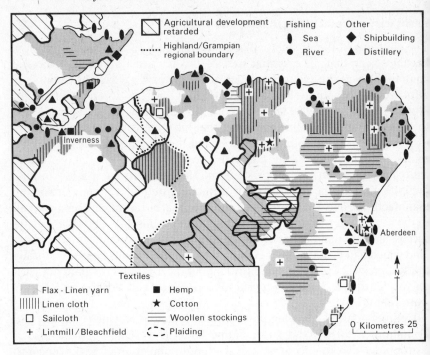

Figure 5.2. Industry and commerce in the Grampian and Highland regions c. 1790
Source: Statistical Account

Duke of Argyll. The new town was started in the late 1740s and an elaborate town plan was drawn up around 1750. A spinning school was opened in 1751 and attempts were made to settle weavers in 1753. Again, however, the industry failed to take a firm hold, the difficulty in raising adequate amounts of flax locally being a serious problem that required imports and consequently higher costs. So the town would have appeared rather forlorn: in 1770 'the gap between its visionary plan and the small part so far realised remained depressingly wide'.[29] Nevertheless the village proved to be a viable service centre and is seen as a model for late-eighteenth-century developments elsewhere. Families connected with the Argylls applied the planned village idea in other parts of Scotland: like Newcastleton (Roxburgh) built by the Duke of Buccleuch for handloom weavers in 1793 and the port of Ardrossan (Cunninghame) started by the Earl of Eglinton in 1805. The Annexed Estates Commissioners would certainly have been aware of the Inveraray project and perhaps for this reason their policies encountered the same failings, though they were miscalculations compounded by political pressures to resettle ex-servicemen. The Highlands were not however exempt from further initiatives, for there remained the strong urge to increase rents taking advantage of whatever potential could be identified. The sheep were advancing northwards and landowners in the remoter parts of the region (some of them having recently had their estates restored to them) were now seeing the constraint that a large population of subsistence farmers imposed.

Prospects for the fisheries

An element of idealism was contributed by the independence of the American colonies, suggesting more emphasis on colonisation at home, followed by the Napoleonic Wars which made emigration appear all the more unacceptable. The fisheries offered some opportunity in the west Highlands in the 1780s. The herring shoals seemed to favour the west coast but it was difficult for the fishing to be increased without better organisation: financial assistance to enable local people to buy boats and improved marketing. The bounty laws (designed to stimulate British fishermen) were altered so as to remove the rendezvous system (whereby all the boats that wished to qualify had to meet off Bressay (Shetland) for the summer fishing and at Campbeltown (Argyll & Bute) for the autumn season) and supplement a boat bounty with a 'barrel bounty'. John Knox was impressed by the logic of fishery development for it offered the prospect of worthwhile employment to people who experienced the destitution of 1782 while the installations would prove useful as part of a basic transport system. The growth of fishing would also serve as a nursery for sailors to be recruited into the navy in the case of emergency.[30] With stimulation to exploit the fishing grounds more flexibly and to increase catches Knox proposed a chain of forty fishing villages along the Highland coast from Dornoch (Sutherland) round to Arran in the Firth of Clyde. Each village would have between thirty and forty houses (with gardens), plus a school, church, various craftsmen: a large enough community to provide a market for farmers in the vicinity. Anderson endorsed the plan, although a smaller number of larger settlements was preferred: this was a sensible modification because, despite the parallel proposal that a road be built right along the west coast, it would not be possible to create real urban settlements if a large number of sites was selected. Most landowners were already dabbling in the fisheries and a survey of the west coast fishings by Lord Lovat in 1785 mentions proposed developments by the Duke of Argyll in Oban and the Ross of Mull (Argyll & Bute), MacLeod of MacLeod at Dunvegan (Skye & Lochalsh), as well as two schemes further north at Isle Martin and Tanera (Ross & Cromarty) both involving English interests.

The British Fisheries Society made a careful study of various sites on the mainland and in the Hebrides in 1787 and decided on Tobermory and Ullapool as suitable bases for the southern and northern parts of the Minch respectively.[31] These places also provided sheltered harbours and land suitable for the creation of smallholdings. Stornoway in the Outer Hebrides was a strong contender by virtue of its custom house but it was thought that the costs of development there would be unacceptably high. To encourage local people provision was made for smallholdings at Ullapool and there was considerable encouragement of agriculture to make the community self-sufficient while the spinning of yarn for net making caught on in the 1790s. A cod fishing base at Isle Ristol (Ross & Cromarty) did not succeed but small scale herring fishing, with local curing, did get under way and the Society's aims were achieved in a small way. By contrast Tobermory became primarily a trading centre while at Lochbay in Skye, where the Society attempted development in the late 1790s, the smallholders proved too much of a distraction and the village became a crofting community. Even Ullapool's fishing dwindled in the early nineteenth century and the Custom House was removed in 1812 after several years of poor trade. The movements of the herring shoals were most unpredictable and while the local people could catch fish for themselves when supplies were available such spasmodic activity was no basis for commercial success. Herring were reasonably plentiful after 1832 but deep sea fishing was now involved and the Ullapool base was less well situated for this than Stornoway, while large boats and nets were required.

Overall therefore the Society did not enjoy great success on the west coast and although there was some private village development on the Society model at Dornie, Jeantown, Kyleakin and Plockton (Skye & Lochalsh) its prestige fell. Much greater success attended the efforts made at Pulteneytown, Wick (Caithness), in the first decade of the nineteenth century. Telford recommended that the harbour be improved and the work was well advanced in 1808. Smallholdings were not included in the scheme and the local fishermen found full-time fishing a much more congenial occupation than the natives of the west coast. Pulteneytown forms part of an amazing development of fisheries which involved the sweep of the Moray Firth. The physical potential for industrial growth in the east through ample sites and easy lines of communication with the overpopulated west had little economic foundation in terms of textiles once the cotton mill project on the Dornoch Firth failed.[32] But through fishing there was a basis for change which was given a grim expression through the Sutherland clearances.[33] If the west coast failed to realise the dreams of Anderson and Knox then the Moray Firth easily made up for the disappointment and showed how, given suitable resources and encouragement, fishing could provide the underpinning for a programme of planned villages.

Conclusion

The improving movement led to the destruction of many small villages, or touns, where agriculture had been combined with various trades and services. The experience at Aberlady (East Lothian) where the formation of large farms was found 'unfriendly to population' leading to the destruction and decay of villages was the rule rather than the exception.[34] But commercial agriculture required the services and manufactures that towns provided and since these functions seemed capable of diffusion into each locality in the eighteenth century it is not surprising that many of the larger landowners appreciated the opportunity to make the local market the centre piece of their development plans. The standard of planning was generally much higher than it had been in the seventeenth century and few criticisms were raised on the grounds of unhealthy living conditions. Of course there were cautionary words from those who questioned the material benefits of improvement, including the various luxuries of the time, and who emphasised the danger of immorality as the villages became larger. Some reservation can be detected over the element of compulsion in the transfer from the farms to the villages: 'it is one thing to build a village to which people may resort if they choose it, and another to drive them from the country into villages where they must starve unless they change at once their manners, their habits and their occupations'.[35] By 1800 building a model village was an established and popular method by which a landowner could undertake capital investment. That it was a good idea is brought out by the long period over which the villages were built: taking the 107 villages that are listed and accurately dated by T. C. Smout, nine were built before 1760 and seven came from 1820 onwards, leaving 31 for the period 1760–79, 35 for 1780–99 and 25 for 1800–19.[36]

But the greatest controversy was not over the villages themselves but their functions. Settlements inspired directly by industrial potential, like New Lanark, were straightforward but where industrial growth was to be contrived in order to expedite improvement on the land there were procedural difficulties and no certainty of success. The economic planning was infinitely more complex than the physical component and with difficulties encountered, especially in the Outer Regions, of finding skilled managers to look after local industries it is not surprising to find that smallholdings were sometimes given unreasonable emphasis. Yet it would be wrong to regard the whole movement as a failure. It was quite logical that improvement of agriculture, involving among other things the separation of agricultural and non-agricultural employment, should lead to a restructuring of the old kirktouns either by remodelling the older settlement as at Manymusk, or by creating an entirely new settlement in a more convenient location as at Tomintoul. Except for a small number of conspicuous failures, usually where unsatisfactory sites or locations were selected, all the villages retain a servicing role and are appreciated by local authorities for housing developments much more than the cores of parishes which never experienced a consolidation of local services. During the period over which villages were founded the industrial climate changed significantly with the peak of enthusiasm for linen coming between 1745 and 1770 and the cotton boom restricted to the decades after 1780. Industrial functions have changed rapidly but in no settlement, whatever the size, has industry remained stable. Several villages are important historical monuments. New Lanark is the most impressive case but it is complemented by Eaglesham (Eastwood), a seventeenth century kirktoun remodelled in 1769 to become a centre of handloom weaving. Modern estates have been added but the old cottages have been renovated.

The villages have adapted to the changing climate and this has meant tremendous variations in experience. Dufftown (Moray) started off with a textile industry but is now surrounded with whisky distilleries, although its original form is still well preserved. By contrast the industrial development of Alloa (Clackmannan) transformed the village into a large town that went far beyond what the Earl of Mar had anticipated. Industrial change was certainly a factor in the decline of village building: the factory scale of operation and the link with coal invalidated earlier notions about an even spread of industry.[37] But of course by the 1830s many of the gaps in the central place system had been filled and it was no longer so necessary to plan villages as a part of an area development exercise. The fact that barely twenty of the villages included in the previous calculations were in the Central Belt, where there was a relatively close network of burghs, reinforces the relevance of the service or marketing approach. Equally it is unnecessary to seek grounds for failure in the declining influence of the landowners in economic development in the nineteenth century nor in the gradual rejection of the paternalism that was such a feature of eighteenth-century improvement: the style of management is a separate consideration from the function of the settlements. But one weakness that does emerge from the association of villages with improving landowners is the failure to take a broader spatial view and plan the settlement pattern as a whole. J. Anderson was aware of the danger of small villages being isolated if they were too far from the large towns. It appears that the 'general progression is first to establish large towns and then to allow villages to spring up of themselves around them; and not to attempt, as many have thought was natural, first to make villages in the hope that these would gradually rise to be great towns'.[38] Some villages were somewhat premature in aspiring to urban functions before they had become adequately connected, but regional planners are still groping for the most effective strategy today; the landowners of the eighteenth century can hardly be condemned for setting out on the same road.

6

The whisky industry

The whisky industry is probably not the greatest of Scotland's eighteenth-century industries but is exhibits a growth pattern and a geography that reflect the complex nature of adjustment to new values and opportunities and also the problem of creating an efficient system of government regulation that did not discriminate unreasonably against certain regional interests.[1] There was considerable controversy over moral issues in the late eighteenth century, and the concern shown by the Church of Scotland for whisky distilling in its Statistical Account in the 1790s (in contrast to a generation later) shows how difficult it was to accept it as part of the improvement ethos. The early history of the industry is obscure, a situation that carries the advantage of allowing romantic speculation to stimulate demand for the product but frustrates any scholarly investigation. It may be true that knowledge of distillation accompanied the celts to Ireland and that through the subsequent movement of Scots to Dalriada interest developed in North Britain: 'the Highland fastnesses provided a sanctuary for the people and an eminently suitable laboratory for the perfection of that malt spirit which commonly served both for victual and drink'.[2] The first documentary reference dates back only to 1494 with an entry in the Exchequer Rolls referring to eight bolls of malt for a certain friar 'wherewith to make aquavitae'. It might therefore be supposed that monastic communities were most addiduous in practising the art of distillation. Such an idea could accommodate the hypothesis of diffusion from Ireland, through Christian missionaries, and also harmonise with the present day geography through association with areas of monastic settlement. But there is no clear evidence for the Irish link while the correlation has little significance in view of the many different sites used for the establishment of religious houses.

From the north the industry allegedly 'crept down to the Lowlands after the Battle of Culloden' but this rather sensational notion of a major eighteenth-century relocation has no solid foundation in fact.[3] Tenants in parts of Argyll & Bute and Perth & Kinross were paying their rents in acquavitae in the seventeenth century but recent research suggests that until the end of the eighteenth century distilling in the Highlands was not particularly widespread and that much of the whisky then drunk in that region came from the south.[4] The common drink was ale, while Highland gentlemen generally preferred claret (free of duty until 1780), not to mention rum and brandy that could be smuggled to the west coast and distributed across the country. The earliest production figures available certainly show the bulk of the effort in the Central Belt. This does not rule out widespread activity in the Highlands at some previous time, but there is no evidence of such a preoccupation and if distilling was a traditional activity it is curious that in 1769 Pennant should find the Duke of Argyll making great efforts to discourage it: he obliges 'all his tenants to enter into articles to forfeit five pounds and the still in case they are detected . . . but the trade is so profitable that many persist in it to the great neglect of manufactures'.[5] Equally the minister of Mortlach parish (Moray) would hardly refer to the popularity of both whisky and tea as a 'miserable change'.[6]

Basic characteristics

It seems generally agreed that distilling in the Highlands expanded because it was an easy way of converting grain of indifferent quality into a readily saleable product. The greatest production might therefore be expected in areas producing large quantities of grain, or in places well-situated to collect supplies from a surrounding catchment area. It is not therefore surprising to hear of production on the Ferintosh estate in Urquhart parish (Ross & Cromarty). The case is well known because in 1690 the owner, Duncan Forbes of Culloden, was awarded an exemption from excise duties on spirits distilled because 'by opposing the disaffected, and supporting the loyal subjects in his neighbourhood at much expense, he was materially instrumental in quashing a rebellion which at that time threatened the north of Scotland'.[7] Although Forbes was required to make a fixed annual payment in lieu of excise duty this was small in relation to the value of his production which was significant enough for 'Ferintosh' to become virtually synonymous with 'whisky', a distinction which later passed to Glenlivet. The tenants benefited from the concession as 'the acknowledged superiority of the spirits produced from their small stills occasioned a demand for them from all quarters and a constant circulation of cash in the place, which brought the people in general an ease of circumstances and a fullness of the necessities of life beyond what commonly falls to the class of farmers'.[8] The Ferintosh privilege was withdrawn (with compensation) in 1786 but after a short period of adjustment it appears that the industry resumed on a viable basis with capacity outstripping the barley supply of local farms and therefore requiring 'a very considerable annual importation'.[9]

A similar picture is painted for the nearby parish of Urray where nine stills (in contrast to 29 in Urquhart) consumed all the barley grown in the parish. As many as a dozen tenants might be involved in each of these businesses which were in effect farmers' cooperatives enabling each man to manufacture his own growth of barley. Grain is speedily converted into money, with which to pay the rent, since 'Highlanders from Lochaber, the extensive west coast of Ross-shire and the Isle of Skye buy the spirits at between ten shillings and fourteen shillings per Scotch gallon.'[10] This suggests a pattern of activity whereby distillers in the eastern Highlands supplied customers in the west. The practice probably dates back to the beginning of the eighteenth century when export to the Lowlands was relatively unimportant. Certainly there was too high a local consumption of whisky for local ministers to withhold censure: the cheapness of the spirits gave rise to a 'pernicious tendency' in the form of 'an inlet to intemperance and a bane to the industry and morals of the people'.[11] Yet distilling was one of the few ways in which the Highland economy could be commercialised in a socially acceptable way. Much skill and ingenuity was involved in production and considerable labour involved in growing and transporting the raw material and in guiding the pony trains to the Lowlands where the whisky could be exchanged for manufactures: textiles and metal goods. In his pioneer study of Scottish economic history H. Hamilton stresses the value of the direct and indirect employment.[12]

In the Central Belt distilling was concentrated in relatively large units, frequently exceeding 20,000 gallons annual production in 1798–9. The largest unit in the Outer Regions produced no more than 10,000 gallons and in the Highlands the vast majority were producing less than 1,000 gallons. The top ten distilleries in Scotland were all in the Central Belt with outputs ranging from 23,900 to 101,200 gallons. Altogether for 525,200 gallons which meant that 11.1 per cent of the distilleries accounted for 60.4 per cent of the total production. The Lowland units in general offered contrasts with Highland counterparts in other ways. They were owned by distillery companies and not by farming interests and although the functional links with agriculture were obviously close through purchases of grain and distribution of waste products this did not extend to ownership. Market areas were rather different with the Lowland distiller having much better access to the urban areas of central Scotland and England while quality, though variable in both regions, was on the whole lower in the south.

Government policy

The fundamental contrast between the Highland and Lowland sections of the industry created difficulties for government seeking simultaneously to gain revenue while curbing excessive consumption. In the context of a united Britain (including Ireland after 1801) it was desirable to equalise levels of duty between Scotch whisky and English gin. Yet any significant increase would be resented in Scotland: there had been no attempt to restrict whisky distillation until 1579 (and then only to conserve grain) and no duty imposed until 1643 when a regime of moderate levies was started.[13] It might also undermine the fragile economy of the Highlands where, additionally, any taxation system would be hard to enforce. So complex was the problem that free trade in spirits within the United Kingdom was not achieved until 1858 when a uniform regime of excise duties and distillery regulations applied in England and Wales, Ireland and Scotland. After the Union of 1707 Westminster imposed the English malt tax in Scotland at half the normal rate (1725), but this compromise was resented both in Scotland, where it represented an increase over the duty levels laid down in 1693 by the Scots Parliament, and in England where it seemed to allow Scottish distillers unfair access to the southern market.

A new system took effect in 1786, at a time when action against the smuggling of foreign spirits was creating greater interest in whisky. The system was ingenious for its efforts to give special recognition to the Highland industry through a moderate imposition of twenty shillings per gallon of still capacity (Figure 6.1). This was in recognition of the more problematical business environment, with harvests precarious and capital resources low, and it also acknowledged the ease with which illicit production could take place. Yet the understanding of the Highland situation was clearly deficient in the subsequent insistence on a minimum still content of thirty gallons and the restriction of each parish to two stills. A consolidation of the industry was premature and a widespread illicit industry was the inevitable outcome. A further problem lay in the necessity of demarcating a Highland distillery area where the special 'concessions' would apply and in effectively closing this 'frontier' to trade in either malt or whisky. Although to a large extent the Highland distillers used local grain and traded the whisky within the Highlands exclusion from the southern markets was unfortunate and again it meant widespread defiance of the law. Lowland distillers had to accept much higher minimum still capacities and higher levels on tax (thirty shillings per gallon of capacity). Further levies were made through a malt tax although the assessment of its importance is complicated by the drawback, or remission, that was partially allowed to whisky distillers in recognition of the other duties to which they were liable. But since the Lowland distilleries were large

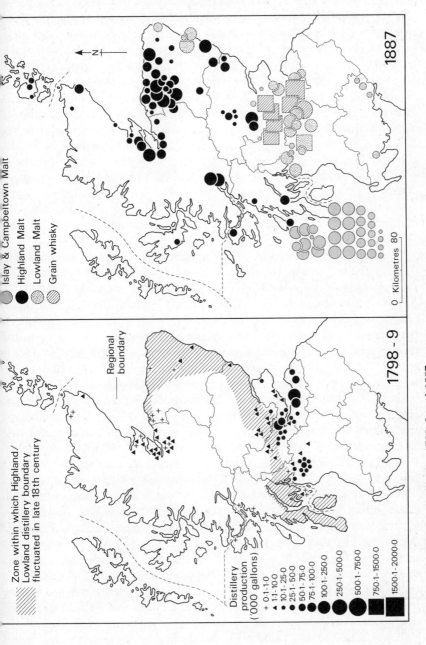

Legend (top left):

Zone within which Highland/
Lowland distillery boundary
fluctuated in late 18th century

Islay & Campbeltown Malt

Highland Malt

Lowland Malt

Grain whisky

Regional
boundary

Distillery
production
('000 gallons)

+ 0.1-1.0
▲ 1.1-10.0
▲ 10.1-25.0
• 25.1-50.0
● 50.1-75.0
● 75.1-100.0
● 100.1-250.0
● 250.1-500.0
● 500.1-750.0
■ 750.1-1500.0
■ 1500.1-2000.0

1887

1798 - 9

0   Kilometres   80

Figure 6.1. Whisky distilleries 1798–9 and 1887

Source: A. Barnard, *Whisky distilleries of the UK*, London, Harper's Gazette (1887) and Note 1

101

businesses in accessible situations there was no way the taxes could be avoided. Whisky from Kilbagie and Kennetpans in Clackmannan parish was shipped to London but 'great distillers could not smuggle . . . being constantly subjected to the surveys of the excise'.[14] As exporters they were subject to even more stringent criteria with minimum still capacities of two hundred gallons of wash (fifty for low wines) and a duty levied in London on each gallon shipped in. The shipping of Scotch whisky was the only situation where tax was levied on the actual product and the particularly strict controls placed on exporters followed from the difficulties of administering pre-1784 taxation systems which had all been based on the quantities of wash and spirits actually generated. The new approach, concentrating on still content, encouraged distillers to make the fullest use of their equipment. While the amount of wash to be derived from a given quantity of malt was prescribed there was no legal sanction against modification of equipment and production methods to increase the speed of distillation and hence the number of distillations that could be completed each day.

The details of the legislation are complex and frequent modifications increase the confusion. The rates levied on still content were progressively stepped up to £6.50 in the Highlands and £54.00 in the Lowlands in 1797. The Highland boundary line was moved in 1792 back from the northeastern lowlands. In 1797 an intermediate area was formed, with duty levels between the Highland and Lowland rates, as an attempt to isolate the market towns along the Highland line (Kintyre was also in this 'middle zone'). Then in 1814 the whole system was scrapped in favour of duties to be levied on wash and spirits at an equal rate throughout Scotland and various requirements over distilling methods and still capacities. The English system was first applied: tax was levied on the wash (reckoning that 18 gallons of spirits would be derived from 100 gallons of wash) with minimum stills of 2,000 gallons in the Lowlands and 500 in the Highlands. But in 1815 a special Scottish formula was introduced allowing a minimum still size of 40 gallons and levying duty on the whisky, with maximum strength seven over proof (compared with twenty which was common with illicit spirit). The results were unsatisfactory: the Lowland distiller was frustrated while the Highland operator went outside the law. The illicit distiller was in a good situation because although he might have to accept certain inconveniences in order to escape detection and offer various considerations to guard against informing (practices that might extend to bribery of the excise officers) the margin of saving from avoidance of duty was sufficient to yield an acceptable profit. Moreover because the illicit operations also evaded both the controls on distilling methods and the technical innovations to achieve faster distillation the product was generally of higher quality than the legal product and marketing opportunities in the Lowlands increased. Since the income earned by the illicit sector was crucial to the maintenance of rent payments it was difficult for proprietors to take any resolute action. All the more so because the viability of a legal distillery would have been doubtful even assuming that capital and management skills were available.

The excise were understandably reduced to despair in their search for a 'conceivable ultimatum'. However, it appears that between 1816 and 1821 some reduction in the rates of duty and a greater tolerance towards the smaller stills made a small licensed distillery a viable proposition and the number of such units increased even in the Highlands. A number of proprietors like Fraser of Brackla, Munro of Teaninich and the Duke of Sutherland at Brora persevered in their attempts to find a legitimate outlet for their grain. The distilleries they opened are still functioning today. But in order to make substantial inroads into the illicit sector it was necessary to reduce duty levels still further so that the saving of duty would become too small to keep the stills in business when such penalties as the payment of 'hush money' and the impossibility of marketing the spent grains were taken into account. This point had been recognised by the landed interest in 1786 when a challenge was issued to the new distillery regulations. Smaller stills would allow large farms to install the equipment: 'agriculture and distillery will be united to their mutual advantage whereby the waste lands will be cultivated and the population of Great Britain increased to an astonishing degree'. High duties constituted 'an alluring bait to the smuggler of foreign spirits' which ought not to be tolerated.[15] The Duke of Gordon was a key figure at this time by virtue of his stature in Scottish landowning circles and of the locations of his estates on the eastern flanks of the Grampians. Proposals made in the House of Lords were acted on through the act of 1823 and this legislation, coming right at the end of the period, opened the way to a rapid increase in the number of licensed distilleries. The duty was reduced to 12p on each gallon of proof spirit (and a £10 licence fee on each still – minimum capacity 40 gallons) from 47p in 1816. Landowners who had previously felt obliged to neglect their responsibility to enforce unpopular and unreasonable excise laws now supported the government for the licensed distillery was now economically attractive and it also carried the potential as a focal point for the modernisation of the estate.

Adjustment on northern estates

For obvious reasons it is impossible to measure the full extent of illicit activity at the turn of the eighteenth century. However, the average annual number of illegal stills seized and condemned in Scotland over the period 1780–97 was 2,758 of which sixty two per cent were in the Highlands. If

Table 6.1. *Distillery capacities 1798–1833*

| Region | Number of distilleries (A) and total capacity (million gallons) (B) in: | | | |
| | 1798–9 | | 1833 | |
	A.	B.	A.	B.
Highlands & Islands	34	0.03	67	0.80
Grampian	8	*	51	0.45
(Moray)	4	*	27	0.30
Tayside	8	0.01	45	0.50
North	50	0.05	162	1.75
Borders	—	—	—	—
Dumfries & Galloway	—	—	4	0.10
South	—	—	4	0.10
Outer Regions	50	0.05	166	1.85
East-Central	26	0.65	63	4.30
West-Central	14	0.17	40	1.95
Central Belt	40	0.82	103	6.25
Scotland	90	0.87	216	8.10

Source: Note 1.

T. M. Devine is correct in suggesting that there were twenty stills that went undetected for every one uncovered then the quantity of illicit whisky must have been very substantial.[16] That it was at least equal to the output of licensed distilleries is suggested by a virtual doubling of whisky on which duty was paid from 2.23 million gallons in 1823 to 4.35 in 1824 with the introduction of the new excise system (Table 6.1). It should be remembered that there would still have been a significant illegal activity remaining in 1824 while the figure for licensed production in 1823 represents some improvement over 1816 after extremely high levels of illegal activity during the Napoleonic Wars. At the same time there was a growth of demand for whisky in preference to claret and brandy, alternative beverages that were cut off by war (additionally so since heightened naval activity discouraged smuggling) and eclipsed with the return to peace by heavy duties and a patriotic opposition to French spirits: 'the smuggling of foreign spirits is now in a great measure suppressed and whisky is substituted in their place'.[17] Distilleries that had previously been licensed were driven outside the law by the increases in licence fees during the 1790s and the substantial industry in Kintyre was entirely illegal between 1797 and 1817, when the Longrow Distillery in Campbeltown opened. There were two licensed distilleries on Tiree in 1790 but both had stopped by 1794: as already mentioned the industry encountered much discouragement from the Duke of Argyll who was anxious to receive his rents in grain at a time of high cereal prices and therefore resented the diversion of local grain surpluses to the distilleries. The effectiveness of the landlord's strictures cannot have been overwhelming in this instance, but his attitude was certainly a factor that helped determine the scale of illicit operations.

For an estate that was not substantially reorganised illegal distillation enabled the smallholder to pay a high rent and poor land thus acquired considerable value. Furthermore a large population could be supported and the consequent avoidance of radical adjustment by the community was probably appreciated, though it is arguable that the perpetuation of the medieval concept of a large rent roll meant only that change was delayed with traumatic effects inevitable in the long term. However, the landowner who was anxious to develop his estates would find that the illegal distillers were usually uncooperative tenants whose activities would be particularly unacceptable to lairds who had invested in licensed distilleries. Noting that 'whisky follows the Highlander from the cradle to the grave, and often accelerates his progress from the one to the other' one writer expressed the view that illicit distillers were the tenants 'least able to fulfil their engagements'.[18] The organisation and status of the whisky industry in the Highlands therefore harmonises with the broader issue of 'improvement'. The Sutherland clearances involving eviction of small tenants from the inland straths and resettlement in coastal crofting–fishing townships find an echo in the particular case of the whisky industry with the disturbance of illicit distillers in the Creich, Lairg and Rogart areas and the establishment of a licensed distillery at Brora. In the same way the minister of Birse (Kincardine & Deeside) noted how 'a considerable number of families formerly supported by illicit distillation have been obliged to remove to town and other parishes'.[19]

The geography of illicit distilling remains rather enigmatic. Devine states that 'illicit distillation flourished most strongly in deprived areas fringing regions of grain surplus'.[20] Such a view is supported by evidence from Strathconon (Ross & Cromarty) and Glenlivet (Moray). People with only small farms and no capital could maintain themselves by distillation and smuggling, so much so that the industry may be seen as the eastern equivalent to kelping in the west Highlands and Islands. It was certainly similar in the sense that the smallholder was only a modest beneficiary, apart from the insurance against eviction that his industry generated. For the distiller would have to buy in a lot of the grain required and this would often mean seeking credit from the supplier. On the other side the distiller was pushed by the landlord for rent and by various local people who felt that their sympathy and cooperation should be recognised in a tangible way. So it is not unreasonable to claim that the illegal distiller was driven outside the law simply to gain a modest living and that the activity could only survive given the coherence of Highland communities with a certain fellow feeling against the law. Otherwise it would have virtually been impossible for the industry to flourish. It was not simply a case of concealing a small still but rather of taking a whole industrial system underground: grain supply might require sailing from the south into the Moray Firth or carting from the Grampian lowlands into the mountain glens while the transport of the whisky was a particularly hazardous occupation. Much of Kintyre's grain came from Islay where distilling was discouraged by Campbell of Shawfield. And Kintyre incidentally provides a rare exception to Devine's generalisation about illicit distillation being a near monopoly of deprived rural areas. But there may well have been others if almost forty per cent of the stills that were seized by the excise between 1780 and 1797 were in the Lowlands. Equipment had to be procured and this involved some difficulty as has been noted in the case of Robert Armour, a maker of illicit stills in Campbeltown who concealed his activities as a coppersmith under the cover of a plumbing business in the town: the expansion of licensed distilleries eventually seems to have deflected his activity back to legality.[21]

Conclusion

The whisky industry's development is thus a barometer of the times. It reflects government concern to control an industry whose product could be abused while simultaneously deriving revenue and maintaining the delicate equilibrium of the overpopulated areas of Britain. Early legislation was well-intentioned but inevitably suspect because of a lack of understanding of the Highland situation. It was also inevitable that the option of going illegal would become more popular at the height of the Napoleonic Wars with rising cereal prices, rising licence fees (and a 500 gallon minimum still content in 1814) and rising malt tax. With considerable community and landlord backing illegal production could flourish. Any real superiority the illicit product enjoyed over the legal counterpart (arising from the pressure on the legal distiller to increase the wash from a given quantity of cereal, to use a proportion of raw cereal rather than malt and to accelerate the distillation process) was increased by the mystique associated with smuggling and with the life styles of those who occupied the 'whisky bothies'. 'The smuggled spirit was generally preferred to that of the legal distiller on account of its bouquet and pleasing flavour.'[22] The cachet derived from this association certainly assisted in penetrating the Central Belt market. Even if the claims of the Lowland distillers that Highland spirits were dominating the market were exaggerated, they undoubtedly deprived Lowlanders of trade. With a return to peacetime, government was ready to take resolute action. Reduction in duty to encourage legal activity was followed by drastic action against the illicit sector as the extent of lawbreaking was evealed in investigations carried out in 1821–2. The Illegal Distillation (Scotland) Act of 1822 meant much stronger court penalties and led to more use being made of the army and navy to suppress the illegal trade. But a crucial factor also was the ability of virtually all landowners in Scotland to reconcile their own interests with upholding the law provided there was a realistic level of duty. The 1823 act therefore involves a harmonising of regional and national interests that was not attainable in 1785. The change is an indicator of greater government understanding but also one of considerable adjustment in the Highlands to the national pattern of development.

In some places there is a clear transition to legal operation. In Glenlivet (Moray) George Smith took out a licence for his bothy business at Upper Drumin and gradually increased his production, most of which was shipped through the Moray ports of Burghead and Garmouth. The demand for barley was satisfied mainly from nearby farms that Smith leased and improved. After a fire at Drumin he relocated his distillery at Minmore which was more convenient for both the farms that supplied his barley and for the road to the coast. It is at Minmore where the much-enlarged Glenlivet distillery stands today. This example bears out Devine's argument that with the suitable reform of the revenue regulations the Highland area 'produced the capital resources and the entrepreneurship essential to the development of a successful industry'.[23] This example also illustrates the tendency for changes to take place in the siting of distilleries. Previously they had been in remote spots to minimise risk of detection but now that there was nothing to fear from the gaze of the excise officer locational efficiency was dictated by more conventional criteria. The consolidation process was very clear in Campbeltown where there were twenty five distilleries by 1850 and in Dufftown which acquired its own seven stills during the railway age. The development of the legal industry, combined with more effective control, meant that the illegal operators were virtually eliminated on the Highland fringes by the 1830s. Persistent smugglers remained at work and their enterprise is legendary, but the scale of their activity became comparatively trivial as the legal product became superior in quality.[24] Illicit spirit was now liable to have bad effects, 'producing the general boisterous demonstrations' before imbibers declined 'into a maudlin state of insensitivity with the appearance of being under the influence of some drugged poison'.[25] There was no longer any widespread distribution of illicit stills for the improvement of communications eroded the advantages of isolation which had previously been a great comfort. Armed groups trudged south over the Ladder Hills from Glenlivet but their ardour was blunted by sharp encounters with the excise men in Strathdon, with military assistance from the fort at Corgarff.

In remoter parts of the Highlands illegal activity lasted longer because control was less effective while the growth of legal distilleries in the far northwest was restrained. This situation reflected the lack of locally-produced cereals once the reorganisation of estates on a basis of commercial sheep farming had been completed and a perception of relatively high costs compared with east coast situations. More generally it reflects a tendency for legalised distilling to move more fully into line locationally with areas where there were cereals produced and also cattle to consume the spent grains.[26] For the distillery integrated well with certain types of agriculture and this was a significant factor in its economics, so much so that many distilleries continued to be vertically integrated with farming. The distillers of Muthill (Perth & Kinross) were 'advantageous in the consumption of the grain, the feeding of cattle and the manuring of the ground, as also in employing many workmen'.[27] But against this were several problems, apart from the inevitable difficulty of maintaining skilled management on all fronts in a highly diversified business. The whisky trade became extremely competitive, especially with the introduction by the large Lowland distillers of the patent still which introduced greater efficiency by making distillation a continuous as opposed to a batch process.[28] Differences in price were acceptable in the market if the more expensive whiskies had a suitably attractive character and bouquet. All malt whiskies are unique and this arises from the water supply (with its distinctive mixture of 'secondary constituents'), maturation climate and both the shape and dimensions of the stills.[29] Variations in taste and discrimination and hence in demand accordingly influenced the fortunes of distilleries, a trend accentuated by the growth of large blending firms. Bladnoch (Merrick), for instance, is the sole survivor of a group of ten units scattered across Dumfries and Galloway by 1850.[30] So the geography of legalised distillation did not only fail to reflect closely the geography of illicit distillation it replaced but slowly evolved to the present pattern where the popularity of medium malts of Speyside and the heavier peaty malts of Islay has induced a remarkable degree of concentration.[31]

Scotland from 1821 to 1914

7

General review

The period 1821–1914 witnesses the rise of the regional city to the point where it plays a dominant role in the economic and cultural life of the country. Eighteenth-century growth had been accompanied by the multiplication of local marketing centres, but these places were seen as accessories to rural-based 'improvement'. The expectation that they could attract manufacturing reflected the improvement ethos, encouraged it would seem by landowners seeking to capitalise on their assets, and also by the desire to maintain continuity in local communities: there was some popular misgiving over urban life in large towns, arising perhaps from perceived 'culture shock' in transferring from a rural to an urban environment. The situation was now drastically modified by the continuing revolution in technology. The use of coal-fired boilers to produce steam introduced a new scale of industrial production that required greater discrimination over location (particularly in relation to labour supply and coal distribution costs) and placed manufacturing both financially and managerially beyond the capacities of lairds brought up on the 'general practitioner' ethos of eighteenth-century estate management. And as steam was also raised in locomotive boilers the constraints of inaccessibility that had defied the canal builders and turnpike road administrators were eventually eliminated. Scotland became a functionally unified country focussing on a group of great cities. Changes in settlement patterns can now be more readily illustrated thanks to the accumulation of census data. It may be helpful to introduce maps of population distribution in Scotland (Figure 7.1) and, in more detail, the Central Belt (Figure 7.2) at this stage. Statistical tables will help to clarify regional contrasts in settlement patterns. They are based on census information for 1871 and 1891 which list the population of individual towns and villages as well as parishes and counties. Settlements may be classified into size groups (Table 7.1) and trends examined (Table 7.2). Parishes may be classified according to the nucleated settlements within them (Table 7.3).

111

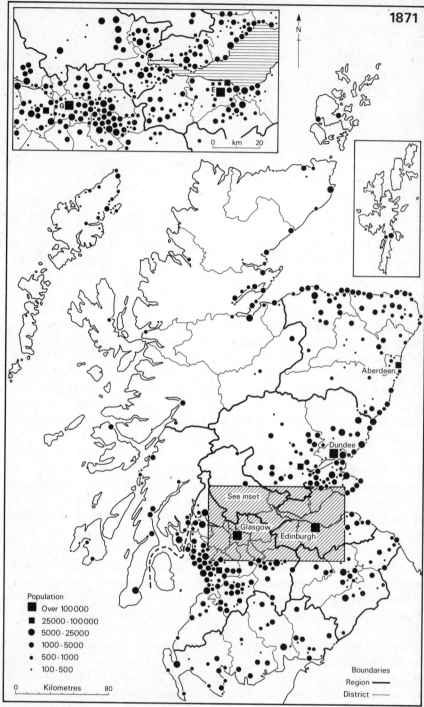

1871

Population
■ Over 100000
■ 25000-100000
● 5000-25000
● 1000-5000
• 500-1000
· 100-500

Boundaries
Region ——
District ——

Figure 7.1. Distribution of population 1871
Source: Census of Scotland

Table 7.1. *Distribution of settlements 1871 by settlement size groups*

Region	Settlement size groups: Below 300		300–499		500–999		1000–4999		Over 4999		Total	
	A.	B.	A.	B.	A.	B.	A.	B.	A.	B.	A.	B.
Islands	80.3	—	5.0	13	4.6	8	12.4	5	—	—	102.3	26
Highlands	201.2	—	8.3	21	17.1	23	30.3	16	37.1	4	294.0	64
Grampian	191.2	—	8.5	21	20.7	30	48.9	24	111.7	4	381.1	79
Tayside	104.9	—	4.6	12	9.7	13	34.7	16	204.3	7	358.2	48
North	577.7	—	26.4	67	52.1	74	126.2	61	353.2	15	1,135.6	217
Borders	59.4	—	3.7	10	7.3	10	27.0	11	21.7	2	119.1	33
Dumfries & Galloway	89.6	—	5.1	13	9.9	14	29.5	14	21.4	2	155.5	43
South	149.1	—	8.8	23	17.2	24	56.5	25	43.1	4	274.6	76
Outer Regions	726.7	—	35.2	90	69.3	98	182.8	86	397.3	19	1,410.2	293
East-Central	188.8	—	16.3	40	22.5	33	117.0	50	343.7	12	688.4	135
West-Central	149.1	—	30.8	79	62.1	88	213.1	98	806.3	21	1,261.4	286
Central Belt	337.9	—	47.2	119	84.6	121	330.2	148	1,149.9	33	1,949.8	421
Scotland	1,064.6	—	82.3	209	153.9	219	512.9	234	1,546.2	52	3,360.0	714

A. Total population (thousands)
B. Number of settlements
Source: Census of Scotland

Table 7.2. *Population trends 1871–91 by settlement type*

Region	Settlement type: Town		Village		Dispersed		Total	
	A.	B.	A.	B.	A.	B.	A.	B.
Highlands & Islands	78.5	30.4	59.5	8.4	250.8	−11.7	388.8	−2.6
Grampian	198.4	33.9	53.3	13.5	173.0	−8.6	424.6	10.5
Tayside	280.0	21.5	30.6	−9.5	99.7	−7.9	410.3	10.1
North	556.8	26.9	143.4	5.7	523.5	−10.0	1,223.7	5.9
Borders	62.6	44.3	13.7	−14.0	52.0	−9.6	128.3	9.8
Dumfries & Galloway	47.3	12.4	20.8	−12.5	82.2	−8.3	150.3	−3.4
South	109.9	28.6	34.4	−13.1	134.2	−8.8	278.5	2.3
Outer Regions	666.7	27.2	177.8	1.5	657.6	−9.8	1,502.2	5.2
East-Central	602.8	34.2	125.2	24.8	137.8	−1.8	865.8	25.5
West-Central	1,361.7	39.2	162.9	46.1	133.1	−12.6	1,657.6	33.5
Central Belt	1,964.5	37.6	288.0	36.0	270.9	−7.4	2,523.4	30.6
Scotland	2,631.3	34.8	465.8	20.4	928.5	−9.1	4,025.6	19.8

A. Total population (thousands)
B. Percentage change 1871–91
Source: Census of Scotland (county figures)

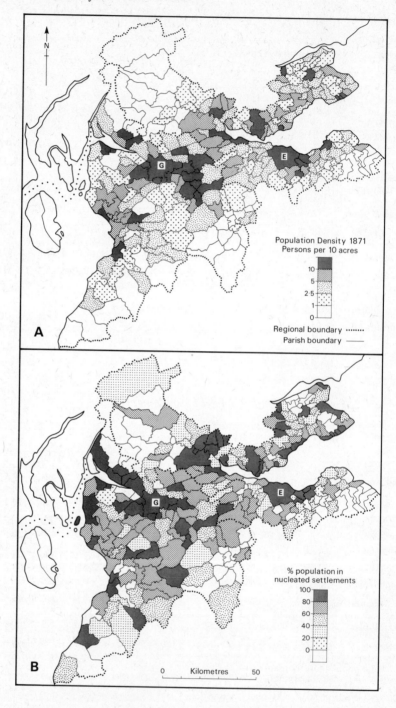

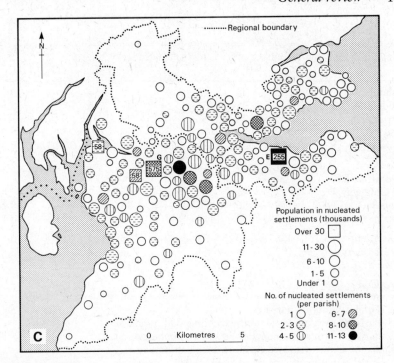

Figure 7.2. Population in the Central Belt 1871 by parishes
A. Density
B. Nucleated settlements (percentage shares)
C. Nucleated settlements (total population)
Source: Census of Scotland

The traditional primary activities were complemented by an ample development of manufacturing. Scotland had resources for industry in roughly comparable fashion with other parts of Britain and, with her independent port system, could win a fair share of trade with the empire. Of course the same improvements in transport that integrated Scotland as a single entity simultaneously integrated Scotland with other parts of the UK and created the possibility that Scotland's industries, even with the utmost efficiency in location and management, might not be competitive with those elsewhere. But the breakdown of 'regional' economic systems has been seen most dramatically since the First World War and the new scale of production, geared to national distribution, has found Scotland's peripheral location compounded by loss of major raw material advantages. But arguably at the end of the period in 1914 these problems were small in relation to the accumulated success of the Scottish economy that had found

Table 7.3. *Classification of parishes 1871*

Region	Number of parishes in each category:[a]							
	A.	B.	C.	D.	E.	F.	G.	H.
Islands	42	34	5	3	3	—	—	19.0
Highlands	124	75	31	5	17	1	—	39.5
Grampian	139	78	32	4	28	1	—	43.9
Tayside	108	70	16	3	18	3	1	35.2
North	413	257	84	15	66	5	1	37.8
Borders	81	55	14	—	10	2	—	32.1
Dumfries &								
Galloway	78	41	21	—	15	1	—	47.4
South	159	96	35	—	25	3	—	39.6
Outer Regions	572	353	119	15	91	8	1	38.3
East-Central	136	40	35	9	56	4	1	70.6
West-Central	107	28	14	8	56	8	1	73.8
Central Belt	243	68	49	17	112	12	2	72.0
Scotland	815	421	168	32	203	20	3	48.3

A. Total number of parishes
B. Parishes with no settlement exceeding 300 population
C. Parishes with settlements of 300–999 population
D. As for C but with two or more such settlements
E. Parishes with settlements of 1,000–9,999 population
F. Ditto 10,000–99,000
G. Ditto exceeding 100,000
H. C–G as a percentage of the total number of parishes
[a] Present parish boundaries are used and some grouping is allowed where large towns embrace several parishes.
Source: Census of Scotland

ample possibilities for growth, gradually losing the colonial character it had assumed prior to 1707 thanks to resources and infrastructure (in which the union was fundamental) that inspired sustained innovation. Arguably the nineteenth century introduced a balance of constraints and opportunities that allowed Scotland to reach her peak performance in the national and global contexts.[1]

Regional specialisation

Although Scotland's economy was well-balanced overall the various constituent regions were extremely specialised. This is seen most clearly in agriculture, but manufacturing also reveals important variations although they are more difficult to recognise. West-Central Scotland may be regarded as the centre of innovation where a succession of profitable

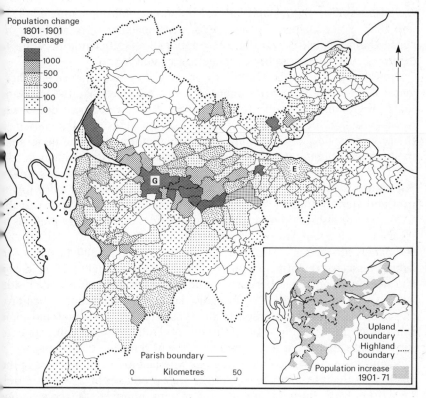

Figure 7.3. Population growth 1801–1901 and 1901–71
Source: Census of Scotland

industries were introduced: linen, cotton, iron and engineering. Despite a rapid growth of population (Figure 7.3) competition for capital and skilled labour meant that each new industry displaced the existing specialisms. Trades that were being superseded dwindled to comparative insignificance, but if suitable conditions existed there could be compensation for the loss through development in other regions. The displacement of textiles from West-Central Scotland was balanced by expansion in East-Central Scotland and in the Outer Regions of Borders and Tayside. Dumfries & Galloway and Grampian gained only modest textile industries while the Highlands found virtually no compensation for the disappointing failure to induce spread in the industry in the eighteenth century. Once again the census permits some quantitative assessment of spatial contrasts in specialisation. Extremely elaborate employment tables covering individual counties can be simplified down to a relatively small number of headings and the standard regional systems adopted for this book. Appendix A

includes absolute figures and indexes based on total population for 185
and 1881. Some changes in the employment headings were made by th
census between these years but descriptions are sufficiently accurate t
achieve broad comparability over the aggregated figures.

Industrial growth in the Outer Regions was not fully sustained and ther
was little inclination by government to revive initiatives like the Highlan
linen programme of the eighteenth century. But development did exten
to other sectors besides textiles. Some existing industrialists maintaine
their locations despite the technical changes that threatened to undermin
them. An excellent example is ship-building which was prominent in eas
coast ports before the age of steam powered vessels using iron and steam
Alexander Stephen's business followed the logic of location close to th
iron and steel producers by transferring from Burghead (Moray) to th
Clyde by a series of relocations that parallel the 'step by step' migrations o
so many individual families during the nineteenth century. But othe
companies survived in east coast locations: not only the builders of woode
fishing vessels at the principal ports of the Moray Firth but builders in iro
and steel functioned in Aberdeen, Dundee and Grangemouth while Leith
with six graving docks by 1868, specialised in repairs. It became difficult fo
east coast yards to expand their facilities as ships became larger and som
firms that did re-equip like Gourlays of Dundee were vulnerable t
subsequent slumps that left them incapable of servicing their debts.[2]

Again, distillers in the Outer Regions who had taken out licences in th
1820s and sought to compete with larger scale producers in the Central Bel
were frequently unsuccessful as government removed the concession
previously granted in the Highlands and gradually brought in a standar
regime of excise duties throughout the UK. The smaller distillers were als
threatened by the patent still (allowing continuous production of whisky
which the large producers were able to install. Fortunately batch produc
tion by the traditional pot still was found most suitable for malt whisk
while the special physical resources of parts of the Outer Regions, throug
water with 'secondary constituents' and climatic conditions conducive t
optimum maturation, gave some of the small remote distilleries an assure
place in the industry. Blending of grain and malt whiskies generated muc
opposition from malt whisky distillers resentful of the adulteration of thei
product, but the fashion has guaranteed a future for malt whisky and th
boom in trade in the late nineteenth century was reflected not only i
the building of blending and bottling plants in the Central Belt but in th
multiplication of malt distilleries on Speyside where the 'Highland Malt
whisky was eagerly sought by the blenders. Other forms of spread can b
seen in special cases where the Outer Regions seemed to have the bes
resources given the specific location requirements. For metallurgy th
Central Belt had overwhelming advantages in the nineteenth century, bu

when aluminium first entered commercial production it made use of electric furnaces that required power considerably cheaper than the output of conventional thermal generators. Hydro-electric plants were built to exploit catchments of appropriate scale and these were found in the Highlands. Moreover since transmission of electricity to the Central Belt was not considered feasible when the Foyers (Inverness) and Kinlochleven (Lochaber) schemes were being implemented the aluminium smelters set down roots in locations that were incredibly exotic for that period.

Despite the exceptions, which run to quite a long list when supplemented by extractive industries (such as lime burning or the quarrying of granite and slate) or processing branches (like brewing, leather-working, milling and woodworking), the industrial core of the region was clearly the Central Belt with the West-Central area the most dynamic and prosperous.[3] Imbalance in opportunity was reflected dramatically in migration, especially from the Highlands after failure of industrial projects. The Duke of Argyll had introduced industries to his estates and followed a pragmatic policy over land: in Tiree he reversed a doctrinaire plan to create large farms and resettle surplus tenants ('supernumeraries') in fishing villages and substituted a crofting pattern that meant consolidated holdings but with a low average size. It was a genuine attempt to modernise the Highlands without the need for emigration: indeed E. Cregeen sees it as the historical function of the house of Argyll to draw the Highlands into the mainstream of contemporary life.[4] But the industries failed and the schemes were also undermined by a deep mistrust of Campbell 'imperialism' in the northern outposts of their domains, a sentiment which had previously contributed to the force of the 1745 rebellion. But problems could also be seen throughout the well-populated north in a search for employment that would be as labour-intensive as possible, commensurate with profitability. Had there been more opportunity for industry in Grampian it is inconceivable that there would have been the same commitment to crofting and fishing: both activities offered a return to those who invested capital or provided land and gave a meagre living to the workers in return for facing heavy work and considerable danger. But in the Highlands the situation was more difficult since fishing was less well developed as an indigenous industry (local grounds came to be worked most successfully by 'stranger' boats) while crofting was generally less attractive to landowners for it meant forgoing the rents that a sheep farmer might pay in return for the heavy potential responsibilities of assisting a numerous tenantry overwhelmed by famine. Not surprisingly there were times of desperate confrontation when small tenants grimly held on to what they had in the face of eviction threats.

It is hardly remarkable that the first government initiatives over regional protection should involve cases of rural distress. The crofting legislation of

1886 and follow-up through the Congested Districts Board came afte
famine relief in 1850 and earlier support of educational and religiou
programmes. In 1823 government money was provided for buildin₤
additional churches and in the years 1824–40 thirty-two churches were buil
and more than forty manses. Thomas Telford carried out this work, whicl
formed a part of a powerful effort by the established Church of Scotland t₤
improve its organisation: presbyteries, covering groups of parishes, ha₤
been formed during the 1720s but some of the more populous an₤
extensive civil parishes were divided for ecclesiastical purposes in 1834
support was later made available for schools to be set up in these *quoa₤*
sacra parishes while the Church of Scotland's General Assembly main
tained many small (sometimes ambulatory) schools in remote areas.
'Schools in remote districts are signal blessings, the teacher in numerou
instances becoming a sort of pastor or missionary to the inhabitants' an₤
there is a clear allusion to regional aid in the assertion that 'many othe
circumstances in the lot of the Highlanders strengthen their claims for ₤
general extension to them of the blessings of education by their mor₤
favoured countrymen throughout the kingdom'.[6] The plight of the High
lands, unable to shake off its colonial image, is brought out clearly i₤
travellers' accounts. The Borders region 'is divided into corn and pastur₤
lands, well inclosed, interspersed with neat villages'.[7] But the Highland
seemed dreary, as 'the people live in as wretched a state as can b₤
conceived: a little hut built with sticks and covered with sods, with a smal
hole in the wall to supply the place of a window in their habitation'.
However, in retrospect it is evident that all the Outer Regions suffere₤
from a serious weakness that has only become critical in the twentietl
century. The growth of towns was mainly a function of their industria
importance and outside the Central Belt only the regional cities gained an
real prominence in the Scottish urban pattern. At the lower levels it is ver
noticeable how the minor industrial centres acquired larger population
and better services than those geared primarily to supplying an agricultura
hinterland.[9] Thus in Grampian the largest towns after Aberdeen were th₤
fishing towns of Buckie, Fraserburgh and Peterhead.[10] In the twentietl
century, cities have become all powerful in triggering new developmen₤
and those sub-regions that did not inherit large towns have found divers₤
fication very difficult.

Some industrial trends

The remainder of this chapter is geared to a review of the nineteenth-centur
geography. In the industrial sphere the coalfields were fundamental. I₤
1910 the Central Belt yielded 41.3 million tons, just over two-thirds of ₤
coming from West-Central Scotland: this region had contributed only fort

per cent of the output of 1.9 m.t. in 1800. J. A. Hassan has referred to entrepreneurial failure to meet Edinburgh's coal demands at the beginning of the nineteenth century: yet it seems that Lothian collieries were then wetter and deeper than those in the west, while the iron ores, including some blackband, were again less compelling than those of Monkland.[11] Although the first coke furnace was built at Carron in 1760 the most rapid expansion of iron production took place in the Coatbridge area in the 1830s and 1840s, a theme examined in Chapter 9. East-Central Scotland comes back into the picture only modestly as additional blackband ores are sought. The chemical industry had moved to a new stage when the salt industry of the Forth was diversified by John Roebuck's sulphuric acid works at Prestonpans in 1749: indeed it was through Roebuck and another English industrialist, Samuel Garbett, entering into partnership with William Cadell, a Cockenzie coal owner, that Carron furnaces were built. But the permanent establishment of the chemical industry is mainly due to Charles Tennant who obtained a patent for bleaching powder in 1789 and set up in Renfrewshire before founding the St Rollox works in Glasgow in 1800.[12]

However, East-Central Scotland did regain some prominence when the Glaswegian James 'Paraffin' Young developed an academic interest in oil and found a promising raw material in the 'Torbanite coal' of Bathgate (West Lothian). Successful experiments resulted in the first commercial oil works in the world at Bathgate in 1851 and Young made his fortune selling paraffin oil, lubricants, wax, naphtha candles and fertiliser. As the Torbanite gave out the abundant shales (with a slightly lower oil content) were used as an alternative and it was on this raw material that the industry boomed after Young's patent expired in 1864.[13] It was very profitable, offering cheaper products than those gained from animal and vegetable sources, and was able to stand up to competition from mineral oil. Some three million tons of shale were mined at the beginning of the twentieth century. There was a sharp decrease in the number of units. There were 26 in 1890 but only seven survived in 1921: Addiewell, Broxburn, Dalmeny, Oakbank, Philipstown, Pumpherston, and Tarbrax. The last shale refinery closed in 1962 and the Grangemouth mineral oil refinery and petrochemical complex maintains a connection with the industry through its location. However, by 1914 shale oil was hardly able to rival coal as a fuel and raw material and Young's success does not fundamentally alter the impression of an industrial revolution mainly centred on the Central Belt. Ready access to coal remained a significant advantage up to the First World War. Gas provided an alternative fuel for industry but costs of production in local gas plants varied substantially according to the scale of output and the distance over which coal had to be transported. The economics of gas engine operation varied in sympathy and the more sparsely populated parts of the Outer Regions were clearly disadvantaged.[14]

Textiles demand close consideration. After the strong tendencies towards spread discussed in the previous chapter the advent of steam power now made concentration the order of the day. It has been pointed out that Dundee's port facilities and its entrepreneurial skill had made it an obvious focus for industrial activity, but its limited available water power had given places such as Blairgowrie, Brechin and Forfar (Angus) some advantage despite the transport costs to and from Dundee. Several Dundee capitalists erected mills at the turn of the eighteenth century and 'in every case the need for water power had driven firms whose business activities were centered on Dundee to look outside the town for sites for their production departments'.[15] However, steam power made location in Dundee much more feasible and indeed the advantage of being close to the harbour, for raw materials and markets, and to the engineering industry that was stimulated by the local demand for machinery 'made it essential even for those firms based outside the city to establish mills within it'.[16] Concentration stimulated a range of special services that increased the efficiency of such a geography. It also meant that ideas could circulate and innovations could more easily evolve to maintain the industry's competitiveness. In Dundee there is the remarkable transition from linen to jute beginning in 1832 as part of an attempt to develop new cheap bagging materials (to meet competition from the cotton industry). It was found that jute fibres could be softened with whale oil and used as an acceptable bagging fabric that was widely sought by the 1840s. It led to a decisive shift in the 1850s when interruption of flax supplies during the Crimean War increased interest in alternative fibres, and the jute industry was fully mechanised during that decade.[17] The scale of demand for jute became sufficient to attract jute clippers directly to the Tay and the trade was a valuable stimulant to the port at a time when the coasting trade was in decline. The need for whale oil to soften fibres helped to maintain the whaling industry in the city and this in turn had implications for the port and for local shipbuilding.

Dundee's jute industry also involved linkage with the textile town of Kirkaldy (Fife). The trends are similar with a tradition in linen spinning and weaving that was somewhat embarrassed when water powered spinning became possible: there was no stream of adequate size within the town and Kirkaldy manufacturers eventually took over cotton mills at such places as Kennoway and Kinghorn. Later mills powered by steam were built in the town and power weaving was exclusively urban in location. Indeed the first successful power loom factory was built at Bute Wynd, Kirkaldy, in 1821, though low hand weaving rates inhibited rapid development until the 1860s (Bute Wynd mill was in the meantime converted to spinning). Then power weaving factories clustered into the old hand weaving suburb of Linktown, followed by spread in search of labour to higher sites in the northeast (Pathhead, Sinclairtown and Gallatown)

expedited by a piped water supply from the Lothrie. The association with
Dundee arises out of the diversification of the coarse linen industry to
loorcloth, first produced by Michael Nairn in 1847. Nairns went into
inoleum in 1876 and obtained their jute backing from Dundee by rail.[18]
Other large towns expanded their linen industries, notably Dunfermline
with its damask weaving linked with the Perth bleachfields, but the
Strathmore towns did not experience great dynamism. Aberdeen's mixed
extile industry only survived thanks to quality and specialisation,[19] but the
city demonstrates the link between linen and paper production.[20] Although
the mill building in the industry in the mid-nineteenth century (1825–61)
was related to imported rags (later esparto grass and wood pulp) the local
inkage with textiles was originally crucial. Cotton is similar to linen, with
ts heavy concentration in Glasgow before the industry was weakened by
competition (in local capital and labour markets) from heavy industry
which prevented modernisation at a time when the Lancashire industry had
few inhibitions.[21] The woollen industry is different however because while
t emerged in concentrated form on the frontiers of cotton and linen
provinces in the Borders and Clackmannan the growing market for the
high quality 'homespun' woollens prompted further spread into areas
where domestic traditions had survived: Harris Tweed and Shetland
hosiery were most successful and have survived to the present.[22]

Specialisation in agriculture

Trends in agriculture are easier to recognise at the end of the period than at
the beginning because reliable statistics become available from the 1870s
and important advances have been made recently in mapping this
information.[23] In much of the country, including the Central Belt, large
farms were the rule and agriculture rested almost entirely on a commercial
basis. Correspondingly the industry employed relatively few people and
non-agricultural occupations were prominent. However, in parts of the
Outer Regions the high level of population in relation to employment
opportunities outside agriculture is reflected in smallholdings: the number
of people per agricultural holding is particularly small in the Grampian and
Highland regions where distinctive crofting systems emerged. The formation of large farms was not greatly impeded since many of the small units
were situated on reclaimed land and in Grampian especially there were
close functional links in terms of both labour and livestock. However, the
emphasis on smallholdings was essentially a response to overpopulation
and acceptance of meagre living standards; improvements in rural education and clearer perceptions of opportunities elsewhere (including the
colonies) accelerated the decline in numbers in most areas during the
depression years. The large farms were becoming more sophisticated and

this is indicated by greater use of machinery which, in its turn, required increased accommodation on the farm. Fixed farm equipment like the threshing machine required considerable adaptation since it was central to the activity of most farms: the Scottish system of threshing was geared to production of feed and bedding for animals on a weekly basis and travelling mills, an important nineteenth-century innovation in England, gained only limited acceptance north of the border. Power for the mills was provided wherever possible by water and so the construction of dams and leats added a new dimension to farm layouts, especially in the Grampian uplands where it was already quite common for farms to have their own lime kilns.[24] Horse power was an obvious alternative and in parts of Orkney the landscape still bears the stamp of this option, frequently selected by the leading tenants, and of the less-reliable wind power that many of the smallholders employed.[25] Some of the largest farms in the Central Belt were able to afford steam power, first noted in Lothian in 1803, though its use remained experimental until the late nineteenth century.

However, the most remarkable feature of Scottish agriculture is the clear pattern of regional specialisation, with, for instance, East-Central Scotland's emphasis on cropping and that of the Highlands on sheep, to give examples at either end of the intensive–extensive spectrum.[26] The physical underpinnings of the system of 'agricultural regions' that highlight the dairying of Dumfries & Galloway and the cattle rearing of Grampian have been adequately explored and there is much in the contemporary agricultural literature to show how the selected enterprises were improved. On the Gordon property in Grampian livestock breeding among the Duke's tenants was encouraged during the prosperous middle decades of the nineteenth century by the example of the home farm and through premiums for cattle, horses and sheep 'to be competed for by those who occupied his farms; the show to be held alternately in the Fochabers, Huntly and Glenlivet districts and the annual dinner to follow it'.[27] Annual public sales of young stock were established at Gordon Castle (Fochabers) 'which gave every farmer in the country, whether he was a tenant or not, opportunities of obtaining blood, both in cattle and sheep, drawn from the most celebrated stocks in Scotland and England'.[28] Landowners with their home farms and built-in mechanisms for the diffusion of innovations were not the sole agents of change however. Association of agriculture and distilling is illustrated by the case of Walter Scott of Glendronach whose Shorthorns fully matched the success of his whisky. There was also something approaching a tradition in cattle breeding growing out of the droving trade, fundamental to the livestock industry of the region before the opening of the railways and the provision of regular steamer services.[29] The most celebrated case concerns the McCombie family who settled at Tillyfour in the Vale of Alford in 1830 and did much to establish the polled

Aberdeen Angus breed. William McCombie eventually combined his father's cattle dealing business in lean animals (for fattening in the north was hardly feasible as long as overland droving was the usual means of export) with fattening on a small scale: he began prize-taking at the Vale of Alford Society's shows about 1832 and 'had extended and perfected his cattle feeding to such an extent by 1840 that in that year he began to send picked animals to the Smithfield and Birmingham Christmas shows'.[30]

McCombie had a formula prepared which could be greatly extended once better transport from the north was available. This kind of backward linkage into breeding by dealers was quite rare and when the trade in dead meat started to grow the Aberdeen butchers who controlled the business maximised their profits by buying up 'turnips, straw and byres – sometimes all that the farm gives' and then putting in stores purchased in the rearing areas. Payments to farmers remained moderate because 'when they have difficulty in buying the quantity they require for market, they fall back on their own stocks'.[31] Nevertheless efficient organisation contributed to the progress of Grampian agriculture and the success was to be seen not only in Aberdeen mansions and slaughter houses but also in the new crofts broken in on the high ground, on the Beatshach below Ben Rinnes or close by in the Braes of Glenlivet, to meet the rising demand for stores. There was still a peasant population ready to labour on marginal land: 'from the increase in population, the limited extent of this country and the natural desire of man to occupy land there is scarcely any difficulty in obtaining tenants who will agree to any conditions of letting and camp on the most barren hillsides'.[32] And buoyant prices even provided incentive for proprietors and leading tenants to reclaim 'stoney wastes, thin moorland and heath clad hills', trenching out the stones and applying artificial manures that the railway could now distribute. We have an impression of widespread commitment to a going concern in Grampian agriculture, but it would be interesting to know more about the circumstances in which this and other regional enterprises emerged.

To a considerable extent Strathclyde displayed a microcosm of Scotland's varied agriculture (Figure 7.4, Table 7.4). Argyll & Bute provide the Highland dimension while the Clyde Valley achieved remarkable intensity through the expansion of market gardening.[33] Physical conditions were permissive, for the valley trench gave warmth and shelter – witness the orchards of the monks of Lesmahagow (Lanark). However, it was Glasgow's market, and manure supply, that triggered the nineteenth-century growth. Within about ten kilometres of the city potato growing was well established, this being the area over which carting of manure was feasible. In the late nineteenth century, rhubarb growing in the Hogganfield Loch area was prominent too. Land reclamation was demonstrated impressively by the forty hectares of Fulwood Moss in Renfrewshire. Further away up

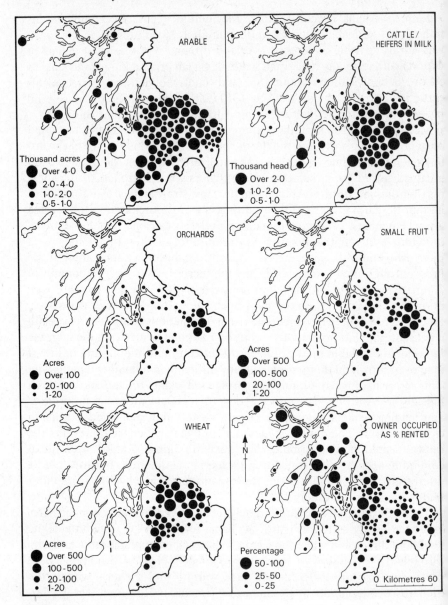

Figure 7.4. Agriculture in Strathclyde 1911
Source: Agricultural returns

Table 7.4. *Aspects of agriculture in Strathclyde 1911*

District zone	A.	B.	C.	D.	E.	F.	G.
Lowlands	115.0	84.5	30.5	361.7	70.2	10.3	459.2
Ayrshire	56.9	42.6	14.3	335.3	27.8	6.9	496.6
Dunbartonshire	15.5	11.7	3.8	320.6	60.9	1.7	403.3
Lanarkshire/Renfrewshire	42.6	30.1	12.5	415.7	121.4	16.8	428.8
Uplands & Highlands	232.6	186.3	46.3	248.3	5.9	22.3	365.3
Argyll & Bute	63.2	48.3	14.8	307.4	0.5	2.5	418.7
Ayrshire	67.1	56.1	11.1	197.0	6.2	3.3	370.4
Dunbartonshire	4.3	3.3	1.0	299.3	62.6	19.4	501.5
Lanarkshire/Renfrewshire	97.9	78.5	19.4	246.7	6.9	48.5	323.5
Strathclyde	347.6	270.8	76.8	283.7	31.5	17.6	394.5

A. Area of crops and grass (thousand ha)
B. Area of grass (thousand ha)
C. Area of crops (thousand ha)
D. Area of crops per 000 ha of grass
E. Area of wheat per thousand ha of crops
F. Area of soft fruit and orchards per thousand ha of crops
G. Cows and heifers in milk per thousand ha of grass
Source: Agricultural returns
Boundaries of Upland and Highland areas are shown on Figure 5.1

the Clyde Valley the orchards of Carluke, Dalserf, Dalziel and Hamilton parishes were being enlarged early in the nineteenth century, although the industrial growth tended to displace activity southwards. Soft fruit, notably strawberries, were noted in Lesmahagow around 1830 but the practice of planting gooseberries, currants and raspberries as undercrops in orchards received a fillip through the opening of a jam factory at Carluke. The main interest lay in strawberries, though other soft fruits, and orchard fruits (apples, pears and especially plums), gained ground. Another feature of Clyde Valley agriculture was the appearance of glass-houses for tomatoes and flowers: by the First World War the Lanark–Carluke belt was clearly established with spread subsequently occurring over the surrounding areas as far as Abington, Carnwath and Renfrew. The various elements still exist: especially plums, strawberries and tomatoes but the industry has become much more competitive, through overseas suppliers, and derelict greenhouses are a commonplace. Strawberry growing was seriously hit by disease in the 1920s and new varieties had to be established. Finally it should be pointed out that there is an important dairying industry in Strathclyde which was prominent even in the eighteenth century: farm-based cheese making at Dunlop provided a model widely copied elsewhere including the parishes of Avondale (Lanark) and Glassford (East Kil-bride). The demand for fresh milk tended to reduce the importance of milk products manufacture, gradually transferred from farm to creamery as at Kilmaurs (Kilmarnock & Loudoun) and at Dolphinton and Thankerton (Lanark). The stage has now been reached where Strathclyde dairy farmers concentrate almost exclusively on the fresh market (hence the closure of many local creameries) while milk products manufacture is concentrated further south in Dumfries & Galloway: creameries were established here through the enlargement of the urban milkshed (the Annandale Dairy Co. at Lockerbie was founded in 1899 and the Edinburgh & Dumfries Dairy Co. in 1919) but the larger scale of marketing through the Scottish Milk Marketing Board has led gradually to greater specialisation.

Forestry and fishing

Considerable areas of agricultural land were being lost through urban development. There were also significant transfers in the upland zone where forestry was a significant land user. Even in the Central Belt where there was plenty of alternative fuel, woodlands were established for amenity purposes and the generally greater profitability of agriculture did not prevent some plantations of Scots pine (which often failed on the higher ground around Leadhills). In the Outer Regions where substantial forests remained, several owners were able to run their own sawmills and place timber on the market to compete with imported supplies: about eighty mills were mentioned in the New Statistical Account (1840s), mainly distributed along the east coast. There is a particularly well documented case of Abernethy (Badenoch & Strathspey) where heavy felling took place in the early nineteenth century: extraction was concentrated along the Nethy and numerous dams were built in the forest to provide water for timber floating.[34] But there was a movement in favour of conservation towards the middle of the century and a nursery for pine seedlings was set up at Dell near Nethy Bridge in 1854. Private landowners cumulatively made substantial efforts but 'they were uncoordinated and were rarely if ever carried out on the basis of the principle of sustension' while small plantations for shelter or ornament were seldom large enough to be economic.[35] Cessation of the use of home-grown tan bark by 1914 eliminated a valuable inducement to sound management of woodland while the end of charcoal smelting in 1866 broke a profitable link with the iron industry that was poorly compensated by the steelmen's demand (through the cementation process) for bundles of birch twigs which brought exploitation to the Great Glen by 1911. Nevertheless there were substantial areas of woodland revealed in pre-war agricultural returns and the undeniable case for state intervention should not imply that private enterprise was totally ineffective. Foreign competition was severe however and, furthermore, estate owners saw prospects of a better return through sport.

At Abernethy the change can be dated to 1869 when the 'Upper Forest' was enclosed as deer forest. The increasing popularity of a traditional recreational activity was just one expression of the late Victorian indulgence in leisure, but one which rested on the solid reality of better communications and the rather less permanent dictates of fashion, nourished for some decades by a romantic view of remote rugged country and by Queen Victoria's example of Deeside vacations. Until Scott adopted the area as the subject of a romantic story the West Highlands was a land of mystery to the London summer tourist.[36] The faltering profitability of sheep farming made conversion of many grazings to exclusive deer forest an irresistible policy.[37] Very high rentals stimulated investment in lodges, gardens, approach roads and forest paths and also made deer forests (along with grouse moors, shootings and fishings) the dominant element in the rateable value of many Highland parishes (Figure 7.5, Table 7.5). The smallholder might be troubled by marauding animals but on the whole he benefited from the employment and patronage extended during a hectic season. 'Old people in Raasay [Skye & Lochalsh] still remember this period when the house reached the height of its luxury and the four-fold chime of the clock-tower above the eighteenth-century stables rang each quarter across the island.'[38]

Fishing was another activity that had particular significance for the Outer Regions. Their monopoly was not complete, for the inshore fishermen of Fife and the trawlermen of Granton provided important exceptions but in general it seems reasonable to argue that enterprise in the Central Belt was largely absorbed by more profitable activity. On the larger scale it is interesting to see how the interest in whaling, which affected Dunbar, Dundee, Kirkaldy, Leith and Peterhead in 1788 was entirely centred in Dundee in 1872 when it was also Britain's leading whaling port: a factor in this was the linkage with jute, which was treated with a mixture of water and whale oil, and with shipbuilding through the firm of Alexander Stephen which designed and operated whaling ships and diversified into seal fishing in Newfoundland.[39] The industry collapsed due to falling prices in the 1890s. A tradition had developed whereby whaling ships called to pick up crew members in Shetland and it was here that Christian Salvesen & Co. set up a base for Arctic whaling using the latest Norwegian technology. The Shetland operations continued until 1929 and sites at Collafirth (Northmavine), Olnafirth and Ronas Voe were used. 'Pollution from the stations at Ronas Voe was at the time held responsible for the failure of the important West Side herring fishery in 1905 when a near-riot atmosphere prevailed.' But it was lack of whales rather than local opposition that brought the final close-down.[40] Salvesens had turned to the

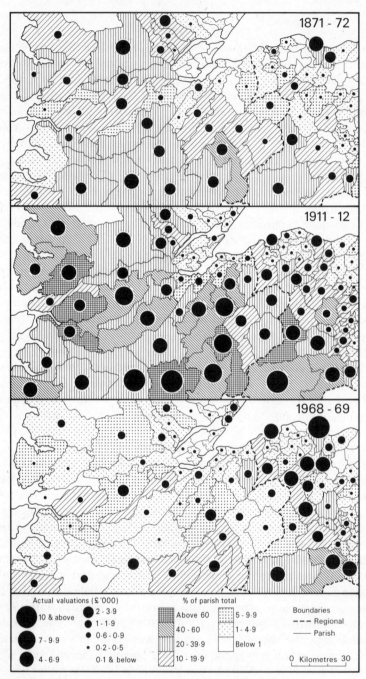

Figure 7.5. Sporting valuations in part of north Scotland 1871–1969
Source: Valuation Rolls

Table 7.5. *Sporting valuations in part of north Scotland 1871–1969[a]*

Area	1871–2			1911–12			1968–9			
	A.	B.	C.	A.	B.	C.	A.	B.	C.	D.
Highland Section	55.2	412.7	13.4	145.5	525.9	27.7	43.7	1,334.7	3.3	51
Moray Firth Coast	11.4	178.7	6.4	23.2	203.5	11.4	11.3	417.9	2.7	25
East Highlands	29.4	148.5	19.8	78.4	207.0	37.9	21.1	410.3	5.1	16
West Highlands	14.4	85.5	16.8	43.9	115.4	38.0	11.3	506.5	2.2	10
Grampian Section	24.8	308.5	8.0	68.5	380.4	18.0	85.1	949.4	9.0	44
Moray Firth Coast	8.6	121.2	7.1	12.2	138.0	8.8	30.6	491.9	6.2	16
Uplands	16.2	187.3	8.6	56.3	242.4	23.2	54.5	457.5	11.9	28
Study area	80.0	721.2	11.1	214.0	906.3	23.6	128.8	2,284.1	5.6	95

A. Total valuation of deer forests, shootings and fishings (in £000s)
B. Total valuation (in £000s)
C. A as a percentage of B
D. Number of parishes in each area
[a] For study area limits see Figure 7.5
Source: Valuation Rolls of relevant counties

Antarctic and although they had a link with Leith most of their employees were Norwegians and Shetlanders. Deep sea trawling again sees the major nineteenth-century interest in an Outer Regions' port, namely Aberdeen. Following the example of fishermen at South Shields an Aberdeen syndicate purchased a paddle tug in 1882 and experimented with trawling in Aberdeen Bay where there was then no three mile limit in force. Trawling became more efficient with the introduction of the otter trawl in 1894 and growth was rapid right through the First World War. In 1912 when Aberdeen was Scotland's leading fishing port (third in Britain) there were 230 trawlers at work landing high quality white fish that could be processed locally (filleting and fish meal production being just two of a host of ancillary industries) and railed south directly from the harbour.

But fishing was not restricted to the large operators. It found its opposite extreme in the craig fishings, a traditional activity based not on boats but on 'craig seats' where individuals could work rods, lines or the circular *poke* net.[41] Between the two extremes lay the 'inshore' white fisheries which at the beginning of the period used open boats that did not require harbours. J. R. Coull has shown how a considerable industry had grown up along the Grampian coast by 1800: seven settlements are mentioned before 1500, but additional centres participated subsequently: 11 more by 1600, 17 more by 1700 and another 15 by 1800. 'The numbers of fisherfolk had increased to be a reservoir of skilled manpower, despite the hardships and periodic disasters of life, and had achieved by the standards of the time a fair measure of prosperity.'[42] Only five new fishing settlements are

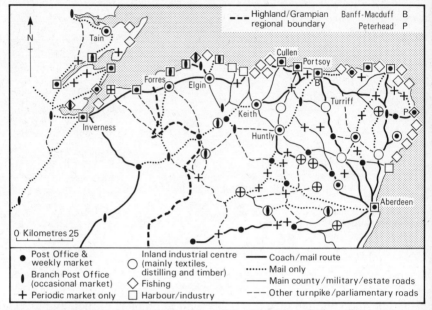

Figure 7.6. Transport and commerce in the Grampian and Highland regions c. 1840
Source: New Statistical Account

mentioned after 1800 but this conceals a massive expansion that involved a considerable measure of concentration (Figure 7.6). Herring fishing swept round the Moray Firth and a process of selection began which saw larger decked boats (steam drifters eventually) based in harbours at the edges of the Firth, with best access to the grounds and integration with herring curing and boat building/repairing. It was, however, just possible for the fishermen to remain independent of the processors with skippers, and frequently crew members too, having shares in the boat.[43] Boats from Wick, Fraserburgh and Peterhead eventually followed the herring shoals from Shetland to East Anglia during a long 'season' that saw a corresponding migration of curers and their workers.

In the West Highlands and Hebrides there was very little scope for emulation. The white fishing could not expand because the commitment to the croft meant that 'capital and energy were drained away from a fishing which remained subdued and ineffective': provision of a new harbour at Ness in Lewis was a failure, partly for technical reasons but mainly because crofters would not transfer from their townships when the fishing was intermittent for much of the year.[44] Herring fishing attracted the more enterprising Hebrideans, but relatively poor access to capital restricted them to second hand sailing boats which meant they could not compete effectively with their east coast rivals. Shetland's story is rather different with a haf fishing that was well organised by proprietors in the outlying parts of the islands who based the organisation of their estates on a fishing tenure. This style of white fishing, involving delicate handling of open boats, persisted well into the second half of the nineteenth century (though with some specialisation: saithe at Dunrossness and haddock at Burra). But by 1830 a merchant community had arisen in Shetland: investment in the cod fishing involved longer voyages (ultimately to Faroe, Rockall and Iceland), and required larger boats which in turn sought bases in the central part of Shetland where the ridge and valley topography gave rise to long, narrow and comparatively sheltered voes. The central areas were also the places where some commercial farming had been established and where small estates provided a base from which proprietors could launch more singlemindedly into trade than their colleagues situated on the island peripheries (Figure 7.7). Before the regular steamer services fish could be exported fresh to Granton or Grimsby in well smacks. Herring fishing complemented both the cod and the haaf, so both interests invested and the fishing bases were initially dispersed throughout Shetland. However, the steam drifters made a dispersal of curing facilities unnecessary and as the whole herring fishery became accessible from a single port (in the context of a night's fishing) the steamer terminal of Lerwick came to dominate. The drive contributed by the merchants was lost by the ending of the truck system yet individual initiative among innovative fishing communities in Burra and Whalsay has maintained a Shetland interest in both herring and white fish.[45]

Improvements in water transport

The trends in industry and agriculture already noted would hardly have been possible without great improvements in transport, so conditional is growth and specialisation on the efficient transfer of persons and materials. The study of transport in the previous period ended with the emphasis resting with water transport: the coastal shipping routes and the canals built across the Central Belt. With the completion of the Union Canal in 1822 there was not only contact between the Clyde at Bowling and the Forth at Grangemouth but also a through route from Port Dundas in Glasgow to Port Hopetoun in Edinburgh, by way of the fine Almond, Avon and Slateford aqueducts which remain as stately monuments to the canal age. The integrated system of canals and seaways did not necessarily constrain locational choice and certain mineral-based industrial enterprises like the iron works of Dalmellington (Cumnock & Doon Valley), Shotts (Monklands) and Wilsontown (Lanark), as well as the lead mining and refining at Leadhills (Lanark) and Wanlockhead (Nithsdale), persevered

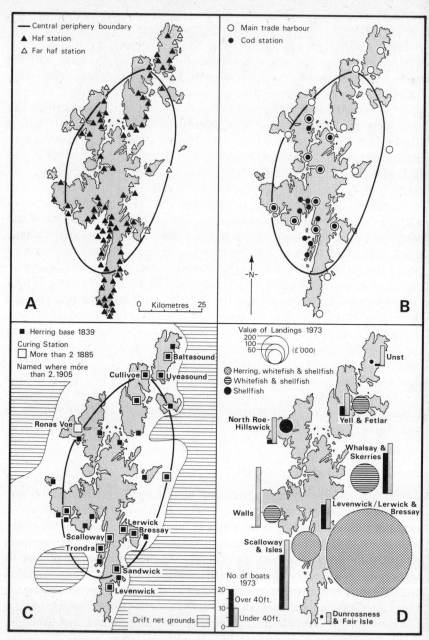

Figure 7.7. Shetland fishing industry since the late eighteenth century
A. Haf fishery, late eighteenth century
B. Cod fishery, early nineteenth century
C. Herring fishery, late nineteenth century
D. Boats and landings 1973

Source: Scottish Sea Fishery Statistical Tables and note 45

with road transport before the railways arrived. The Shotts Company made considerable use of the roads, for the works were situated on the Edinburgh–Glasgow route, while the Edinburgh–Ayr turnpike (opened in 1828) passed within one kilometre of the works. The Company had its own stables and employed carters and wagoners until railways were eventually found more efficient and a branch was built from the Coltness Railway in 1846.

However, the coastal emphasis was a rational one in the early nineteenth century and visionaries saw potential in extensive coastal sites where industry inspired by local raw materials and/or markets might profitably develop. There was increasing support for such a view as the complex web of sailing ship movements became complemented by steamer services. Until 1818 steamers had been built only for service on the smooth waters of rivers and canals but with the advent of *Rob Roy*, built by Denny's of Dumbarton and engined by Napier's of Glasgow, a steamer service connected the Clyde with Belfast during the summer season.[46] Within five years, regular services were operating to Liverpool and Dublin, while the east coast came into the picture with the formation of the Dundee, Perth & London Shipping Company in 1826. Sheltered coastal routes had already been graced by Bell's *Comet* but the 1830s saw great improvements in the services to the Highlands with the entry of Messrs J. Martin and J. & G. Burns into the trade: making full use of the Crinan and Caledonian Canals steamboats penetrated as far as Fort William, Inverness, Cromarty and Invergordon. Bell's successors were joined in 1824 by J. McLeod and A. McEachern and by the end of the decade the competition had brought a broadening of the operations to take in the Outer Hebrides. However, the West Highland trade proved too limited to justify competition and from the beginning sailings were coordinated to provide the best overall service. It was logical that this would lead to amalgamation and in 1851 Messrs Burns emerged with Thomson & McConnell, who had taken over (in 1838) the fleets that David Napier had previously acquired from the Bell and McLeod/McEachern interests in 1832.

On the east coast a local steamer service began in 1815 with crossings of the Forth from Granton, Leith and Newhaven to such Fife ports as Aberdour, Burntisland, Kinghorn and Kirkaldy. Then a steam yacht was introduced between Aberdeen and Leith in 1821 and four years later a rival service started, with each company providing three services per week (using alternate weekdays). Takeover of both vessels by the Aberdeen Leith & Clyde Company in 1826 was followed by some reduction in service to adjust to demand but the vessels were employed in a widening in the scope of the services: 'for a few years a pattern of expansion was steadily pursued as the steamers pushed even farther north, first in summer, then in winter, at first fortnightly, later weekly'.[47] A regular weekly summer run to

Inverness began in 1829 and a fortnightly voyage to Wick started in the summer of 1833 (occasionally to Kirkwall). With the support of a government mail contract in 1838 regular summer services were extended to Lerwick. Regular winter services by steamers came only slowly: Inverness in 1848–9, Wick in 1857–8 and Lerwick in 1858–9: the early steamers were not too successful in stormy northern seas and sailing ships retained a key role into the 1850s, while the inadequacy of the lighthouse system was a serious constraint on any shipping operations. It is hardly a coincidence that the regular winter Shetland steamer service followed immediately after the opening of Bressay lighthouse, at the approach to Lerwick, in 1858. Mainland east coast services were badly affected by railway competition but the deviations arising from Beauly, Cromarty and Dornoch Firths helped to maintain steamer links between Burghead and Littleferry (north of Dornoch) until the First World War. This bears out the general claim that coastal shipping remained competitive apart from perishables and cattle.[48]

Railway development

At this point however it is necessary to pause and consider the developments that were taking place on land. Railways in Scotland may be traced back to the Tranent Wagonway of 1722: a project completed by the York Buildings Company on a forfeited estate with the aim of transporting Tranent (East Lothian) coal to the port of Cockenzie and the salt industry of Prestonpans.[49] Trucks rolled downhill from the colliery by gravity and the empties were hauled back by horse power. Tranent provided a model that was widely copied around the Firth of Forth during the late eighteenth century. The technology was gradually diffused more widely.[50] On Tayside the idea of a Strathmore Canal was translated into railway terms and the Dundee & Newtyle Railway emerged in 1831. It was built very much on canal principles with almost level sections, where horses could be used, linked by inclines (Law Hill, Balbeuchly and Hatton) where the assistance of stationary steam engines would be required. As steam locomotives reached higher levels of efficiency the railway was rebuilt along a new alignment via Lochee (1860–1) and the inclines eliminated.[51] But it was in Strathclyde where the railway first proved to be of crucial importance. The Kilmarnock & Troon Railway of 1812 merely linked collieries with navigable water on the Tranent model, and the early railways in the Monklands, like the Monkland & Kirkintilloch (1826) and Ballochney Railway (1828), were essentially tributary to the canal (Figure 7.8). But the vision of *Scotsman* editor Charles Maclaren in 1824 anticipated railways as transport networks in their own right and not as mere canal feeders. It was in 1831 with the Glasgow & Garnkirk Railway that Scotland first acquired

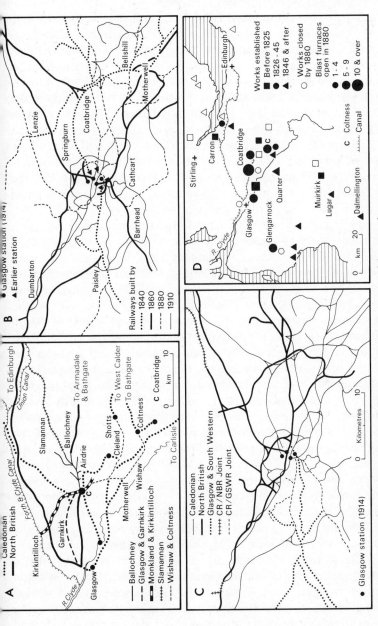

Figure 7.8. West-Central Scotland: development of railways and ironworks

A. Principal developments to 1850
B. Stages in the growth of the Glasgow network
C. The Glasgow networks by companies
D. Location of ironworks

Source: R. Miller & J. Tivy (eds.) (1958) and note 50

a railway that was directly competitive with the water-based system (in this case the Monkland Canal). Dundee had an early rail link with Arbroath, and an extension to Forfar, provided in 1836.[52]

The future pattern was not immediately clear at first and as late as 1840 when the Slamannan Railway crossed the plateau to reach the Union Canal at Causewayend (Falkirk) there were serious hopes entertained of an inter-city canal–rail link, a regional expression of the Glasgow–London service in which the Ardrossan–Liverpool steamer service of 1840 (Ardrossan to Fleetwood in 1843) played a part. However, all-rail crossing of the Central Belt was provided by the Edinburgh & Glasgow Railway in 1842. More ambitiously, by taking over the Glasgow & Garnkirk as well as the Coltness Railway of 1833, the Caledonian Railway acquired a launching pad from which it could build southwards over the Clyde–Annan watershed at Beattock (314 m) to make an end-on junction in 1847 with the Lancaster & Carlisle Company (later London & North Western) which had struggled to Carlisle through the Cumbrian Hills at Shap Fell (290 m).[53] It was supposed that one railway to England would suffice and the selection of the Nithsdale route had been a controversial decision. Yet the mania years widened horizons dramatically and by 1850 there were two other routes open to the south: the North British followed the east coast to Berwick while the Glasgow & South Western reached southwards into Nithsdale from Kilmarnock and joined the Caledonian line right on the border at Gretna. Indeed a fourth route was opened when the North British extended their Hawick branch of 1849 through Whitrope Tunnel to Newcastleton, Longtown and Carlisle. This decision meant Langholm was bypassed: 'the most serious commercial set back in its history'.[54] The same company advanced over the border from lonely Riccarton Junction (Roxburgh) to the Plashetts coalfield and on by Reedsmouth and Scots Gap to Morpeth: with the cooperation of the Blythe & Tyne Railway this meant an alternative Edinburgh–Newcastle service, independent of the North Eastern Railway which partnered the North British on the coastal route.

The rivalry between the three companies displayed on the railways towards the Border is an essential context for consideration of the network in the Central Belt in general and the Glasgow area in particular. The Caledonian improved their access into Glasgow by extending from the original terminus of the Glasgow & Garnkirk at St Rollox through heaps of chemical waste to reach Buchanan Street in 1849, the same year that a direct route from the south along the Clyde valley reached Bridge Street in the Gorbals. From here the Caledonian and GSWR were already serving Paisley and Kilmarnock. The Edinburgh & Glasgow Railway spawned a branch from Cowlairs on the northern edge of the city to Balloch and Helensburgh (Dumbarton) in 1858, before this system was absorbed by the

North British in 1865. Competition sharpened thereafter. The Caledonian could offer a rival Edinburgh service through Carstairs but a shorter route between the two cities by extending their Edinburgh–Bathgate line into Coatbridge and Glasgow (1871) and from this line assaults were launched on Bothwell and Hamilton from Shettleston (1878) and Coatbridge (1879). The Caledonian meanwhile had reached Coatbridge by a new line from Rutherglen (1865) but now the north–south route through Coatbridge was improved by the new line into Bellshill (1880) following an earlier bypass of Motherwell. In the west the Caledonian encountered competition from the GSWR building through Kilmacolm to Greenock (1869) and forging a connection across the heart of Glasgow to the NBR at Springburn in 1875. Their new terminus of St Enoch north of the river could now be opened (1876) and the Caledonian were forced to follow suit by crossing the Clyde from Bridge St to Central Station in 1879 (though Bridge Street remained in use for suburban traffic until Central Station was widened in 1905).

The urban railway increased again in complexity after 1880 due to the twin stimuli of suburban development and the expansion of Clyde shipping. Wealthy Glaswegians could live out on the East Kilbride branch where construction through Busby had first been stimulated by the bleachworks and quarries. Some positive encouragement might come from railway promotion: the Edinburgh & Glasgow promoted Lenzie by offering free season tickets to people who built houses on this lineside site: the 'villa ticket' was valid for five years, with an extra year for every £100 spent on the house over £1,000. Industrial growth in Scotstoun and Clydebank was accelerated by the excellent rail services provided: the huge Singer Works opened within a year of the railway's arrival in 1882 and morning rush-hour trains converged on the factory from Balloch, Bridgeton Cross and Springburn. Given the very high demand for transport services the competition was hardly excessive: it ensured a good quality of service by train or steamer at reasonable fares. It was the electrification of horse tram routes beginning in 1898 that caused the greatest difficulty for railway companies. The consequences were not immediately understood because when the Govan–Springburn service of the GSWR closed in 1902 there was a simultaneous opening of a new service to Paisley and Barrhead which was itself forced out of existence seventeen years later.

The rivalry in Glasgow that reached a climax in Caledonian/GSWR assaults on Barrhead at the beginning of the twentieth century found an echo in Cunninghame in the Caledonian advance to Glengarnock/Kilbirnie in 1889 and Ardrossan (Montgomerie Pier) in 1890. But the case for duplication was quickly dissipated as the railway pushed outwards from the great urban centres. Certainly problems of land acquisition could be an important factor in route selection as the case of the Gifford & Garvald line demonstrates.[55] Equally the major companies might quietly sponsor local promoters so as to minimise controversy in sensitive areas such as Peebles (Tweeddale).[56] But abrasive competition is generally absent and if the touching of the Highland and Great North of Scotland networks on the Lower Spey, where distilleries and fisheries were thriving, stimulated some duplication through rival routes to Buckie, the contact of the G.N.O.S. and Caledonian at Aberdeen became harmonious enough to permit an ambitious joint station project in 1867.[57] This reorganisation of urban railways is repeated on a grander scale by the changes in Fife. The first railways, from Burntisland to Ladybank and Cupar in 1847 and the extensions from Cupar to Ferryport (later Tayport) and from Ladybank to Perth the following year, were connected by ferry crossings over the firths and eventually replaced by bridges in 1887 for the Tay (the first bridge, built in 1877, collapsed in 1879) and in 1890 for the Forth.[58] Penetration of the Highlands was particularly slow, in view of heavy construction costs and limited traffic (Figure 7.9). However, the Irish precedent for government support of railways was not followed up immediately by assistance to problem regions in Britain: no doubt there was a fear that private enterprise might be discouraged even where adequate resources were available and 'special cases' might be difficult to identify.[59] Construction went ahead sluggishly, though some landowners accelerated the process, such as the Duke of Sutherland who built the Golspie–Helmsdale section of the Highland Railway at his own expense.[60] Only in the 1890s was there some special aid: the Light Railways Act of 1896 made rural branch lines cheaper to build while financial concessions allowed the extension of the Inverness–Strome Ferry line to Kyle of Lochalsh and the completion of the West Highland Railway from Fort William to Mallaig.[61] However, branch line building was cut off by the growth of bus services and hence the north of Scotland, where the rail system was never completed, shows some of the earliest cases of integration of rail and road services, notably on the G.N.O.S. system where the company operated a number of motor vehicles introduced between 1904 and 1912, with services from Aberdeen to Cluny, Midmar and Newburgh and from Ballater, Fraserburgh and Huntly to Braemar, New Aberdour and Aberchirder respectively. There was also integration of rail and steamer services and here the Highland experience is interesting if unremarkable.[62] Several local operators were already working in conjunction with the major Glasgow-based operations when the railways arrived but the railheads became relatively more important for passenger traffic and although the Glasgow–Stornoway service still carried passengers up to the First World War (and freight services only died away in the 1970s) the most important services were now based on Oban, Mallaig and Kyle. The railway strengthened the link between Caithness and Orkney by simplifying the land journey north to the port of Scrabster near Thurso (Caithness) but the Aberdeen base for both Orkney and Shetland services was retained.

Impact of the railways

The influence of the railways is a major topic which merits more research.[63] In one sense the railway increased opportunity by cheapening transport over land relative to movement by sea to the point where inland locations acquired great potential. It is hard to see how the shift of the iron industry into the interior could have been sustained without the railway (or further canal building). Yet in another sense the railway reduced opportunity by enabling such an increase in scale in urban and industrial development that centres profiting from an 'early start' were able to acquire economies of scale that made competition more difficult. Specialisation was the opportunity that arose from the destruction of protection that had previously gone to local producers through high transport costs. At the UK level it was fortunate for Scotland that the hot blast was able to increase the efficiency of the iron industry and allow the railway to improve market outlets for a product that would otherwise have succumbed to English and Welsh competition.[64] Within Scotland producers in the Outer Regions were more vulnerable. Destruction of local industries in Grampian might be balanced by the scope for land reclamation to produce more store cattle for fattening farms that had intensified in the face of railway services, and by the growth of tourism on the coast, some of it promoted directly by the railways as in the case of the G.N.O.S. hotel at Cruden Bay (1899), complete with electric tramway service from the terminus of the Boddam branch.[65] But the new opportunities were found mainly in the cities and in the regions of the Central Belt, so migration within and between regions accelerated.

One interesting study of railway influence concerns the ports, where it might be supposed that the railway would consolidate the importance of larger places.[66] This is basically true: on the west coast the fortunes of Glasgow and Greenock remained in the ascendant (as the subsequent case study shows), though while Greenock began dock construction in the eighteenth century Glasgow persisted with riverside quays exclusively until the late nineteenth century. On the east coast there was dock elaboration (the fourth stage of development in J. Bird's 'Anyport' model) at Newhaven in the 1820s and at Granton by the Duke of Buccleuch in the 1830s and 1840s. At Dundee there was contemporaneous development with King William IV Dock in 1825 and Earl Grey Dock in 1834.[67] Thereafter the record is less convincing. Glasgow shows amazing growth towards the end of the century while Greenock's Great Harbour project was a partial failure. At Leith, Victoria Dock (1851), Albert Dock (1869) and Imperial Dock (1904) went ahead smoothly and accommodated a large and complex trade but in Dundee the Victoria and Camperdown schemes ran into difficulties and were completed only in 1865 and 1875 respectively thanks to the stimulus of massive increases in jute imports. Larger ships

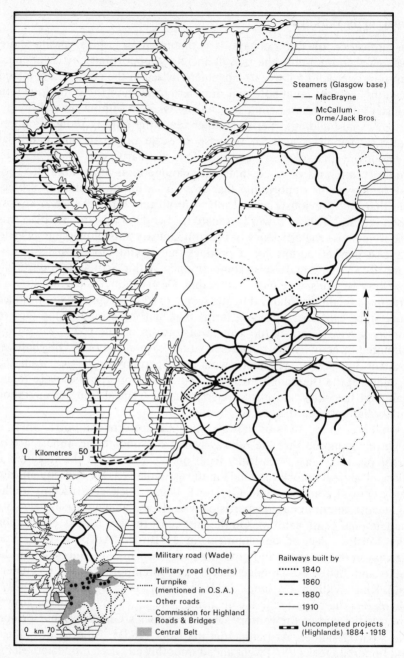

Figure 7.9. Railway and steamer networks c. 1910
Source: Miscellaneous railway/steamer route maps and timetables

were provided for at King George V Dock where the first phase was completed in 1915. The impact of the railway on the smaller ports was not universally adverse and Lenman concludes that it would be wrong to see the impact of the railways on the smaller ports of the Tay and Forth as other than 'a complex and protracted phenomenon'.[68] Arbroath settled for imports of jute through Dundee but Perth's tidal dock (1835) provided for a range of bulk imports and some export of seed potatoes (some potato merchants actually entered the shipping business) and Montrose acquired a wet dock in 1839 which supported a successful timber trade later in the century. Fife coal exports created potential for one important port and this was Methil: Alloa, Dysart, Inverkeithing and Leven failed to compete but Burntisland with much support from the North British Railway did prove a serious rival. The north shore of the Firth was also the site of a naval repair base, at Rosyth where work began in 1903. Defence from naval attack was then the major consideration and this was assured by the fortification of Inchkeith and Kinghorn Ness, with further installations on either side of the Forth between Dunbar and Dalmeny and again between Crail and Burntisland. On the south side of the estuary Grangemouth profited from the interest of the Caledonian Railway: Carron Dock (1882) and Grange Dock (1906) were used for the export of coal and the import of iron (overshadowing Bo'ness where a wet dock was built in 1881) and some oil import, storage and distribution after 1900.

Development of ports on the islands may well have accelerated as a result of the railway since the ferry links with the mainland became extensions of the railway system and regular, reliable schedules were demanded. It has already been shown how the poor facilities at Kirkwall led to the establishment of a separate trading town at Stromness. However, Kirkwall's harbour improved in the nineteenth century. The Peerie Sea, a sheltered lagoon at the very head of Kirkwall Bay and separated off by a spit known as 'The Ayre' through which a narrow entrance ('The Oyce') was available for vessels, gave access to the business quarter of the town and allowed boats to be drawn up on the beach in safety. But the depth of water was inadequate for large vessels and a big improvement was effected in 1811 when the first substantial pier was built into Kirkwall Bay. This was replaced by an iron pier in 1866, with additional accommodation added later in the century for the steamers from Aberdeen and Leith. Meanwhile the old wooden drawbridge across the Oyce was replaced by fixed structures and the removal of shipping from the shores of the lagoon paved the way for land reclamation on the margins of the Peerie Sea. Stromness also acquired deep water piers to simplify landing in the sheltered anchorage: the South Pier of 1879, used by steamers from the Caithness railhead, was followed by the Lighthouse Pier in 1902. Harbour improvements in Shetland were concentrated on Lerwick. By virtue of the large

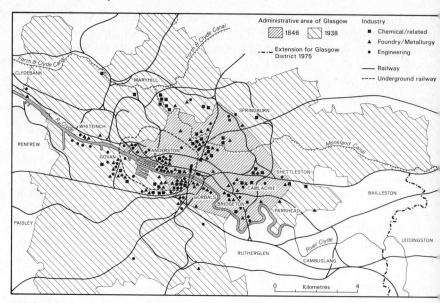

Figure 7.10. Nineteenth-century Glasgow industry correlated with the railway system

Source: J. R. Hume, *Industrial archaeology of Glasgow*, Glasgow, Blackie (1974). Note: the industrial pattern is a cumulative one and does not relate to any single point in time

expanse of deep, sheltered water in Bressay Sound, with an easy approach and no problem of silting from major river estuaries, Lerwick has been the main port for Shetland ever since the Dutch came to fish in the northern waters. Scalloway became an important fishing centre and attracted calls from steamers on the 'west side' routes but it has not seriously challenged Lerwick in modern times. The Lerwick shoreline has altered beyond recognition over the last hundred years. Several piers were constructed during the nineteenth century but development reached a new scale of magnitude with reclamation of Morrison's Beach and the construction of a retaining wall, leading to a renaming as Victoria Wharf in 1866. Further harbour works in 1883–6 supplemented this wharf with Hay's Pier and Albert Wharf, while the Fish Market and associated Alexandra Wharf of 1907–8 allowed Lerwick to reap full benefit from the herring boom.[69]

In causal terms the role of the railway is difficult to judge with accuracy without sophisticated exercises in counterfactual enquiry. But there was a very strong functional association between the railway system and various forms of economic activity. Large industries would tend to occupy lineside sites, often with private sidings, and the links are clearly demonstrated in Glasgow by Figure 7.10. However, the connections are most clearly shown in mining (and in public works projects like reservoir building) since the geography of minerals cannot be expected to harmonise with the basic railway network.[70] In consequence large scale production may well be conditional on special railway links being provided. The case of lead mining in the Lowther Hills may be cited as one example. Ore was found around Leadhills and Wanlockhead in the late seventeenth century and after the union these mines were the most consistently successful projects in an eighteenth-century upsurge of mineral enterprise that saw many discoveries reported and attempts at exploitation at such places as Glenesk (Angus), Islay (Argyll & Bute), Minigaff (Merrick), Strontian (Lochaber) and Tyndrum (Perth & Kinross). Lead mining in fact furnishes one of the first examples of large scale English investment in the Scottish economy and perhaps the only example of widespread immigration of English labour into a native industry.[71] Leadhills and Wanlockhead never produced less than four fifths of Scottish lead output despite the transport problems, carting by road to Leith via Biggar. Transport was also difficult for coal that had to be brought in from Sanquhar (Nithsdale) to allow steam pumping: the cost of this operation meant that steam power was installed in 1789 and was given up with the fall in metal process after the Napoleonic Wars. Instead water power was used exclusively, with the Mennockhass Tunnel (1764) and the Straitsteps Beam Engine (a water bucket pumping engine probably of late nineteenth century date) still visible along with many of the leats. Improved prices in the 1860s encouraged more investment and the transport of the refined lead, eased by the building of the Glasgow–Carlisle railway, was further expedited by the branch that struggled up the valley from Elvanfoot in 1902. At 440 m Wanlockhead was the highest point reached by standard gauge railways. Figure 7.11 shows the Wanlockhead installations tied to the terminus of the branch by a narrow gauge line and inclined plane. It was unfortunate that the loaded wagons had to be hauled up the gradient to Wanlockhead station, but the displacement of smelting further down the valley as far as Meadowfoot did make it easier to harness water power and also kept fumes away from the village. The railway was maintained only for a few years (the remaining passenger service was discontinued in 1939) because the mines closed with the slump in lead prices after the First World War and an attempted reopening by a new company in 1948 was not successful.

Other examples of railway branches in mining areas include the small Machrihanish coalfield near Campbeltown (Argyll & Bute) where a canal link with the port was later replaced by a light railway,[72] and Dalmellington (Cumnock & Doon Valley) whose local blackband ironstone attracted the Houldsworths of Coltness in 1845.[73] Their Waterside furnaces were opened in 1848 on the assumption that a railway would soon arrive as a branch pushed along the Doon Valley from the Ayr–Portpatrick trunk route. In fact the railway did not appear until 1856 and, incredibly, in the

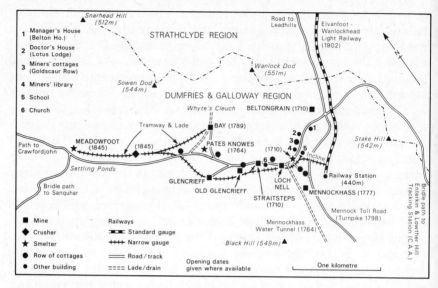

Figure 7.11. Lead mining at Wanlockhead: aspects of development from 1700
Source: Wanlockhead Museum and fieldwork

meantime all plant came in by road and both limestone and pig iron had to be moved in this way. But eventually Dalmellington spawned a complete system of local railways (shifting in sympathy with the growth of mining at Benwhat and other plateau settlements overlooking Waterside) but this is now a memory since the coalmining has run down in the post-war period (the furnaces were blown out in 1921).

Urban development

A number of small towns went into decline, such as Portpatrick (Merrick), which lost its function as a ferry port.[74] But on the whole the period brought a massive increase in population to the towns and the available census data expedite quantification of the new urban geography (Figure 7.12). Even at the beginning of the period there are signs of the urban explosion: Edinburgh's New Town was being rounded off by William Playfair, master of the Edinburgh terrace, who showed considerable flair with the Calton scheme of 1819 and the Royal Circus a year later.[75] Aberdeen implemented a bold and costly programme of street planning that provided new roads, such as Union Street with gentle gradients maintained over undulating terrain thanks to the Denburn Viaduct and the levelling of St Catharine's Hill, and river crossings such as Telford's Bridge of Don (1830).[76] Yet at the same time William Baxter built the first steam powered mill in Dundee at Lower Dens in 1822 and started a period of

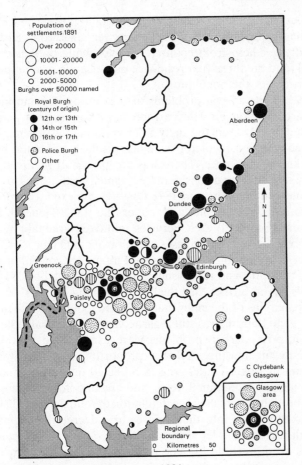

Figure 7.12. Large nucleated settlements 1891
Source: Census of Scotland
Note: The following settlements have been omitted: Campbeltown, Kirkwall, Stornoway, Thurso and Wick

vigorous industrial expansion.[77] And it was this industrialisation that swamped eighteenth-century idealism and created cities within cities so well exemplified by the east and west ends of Glasgow with their stark contrasts in culture, status and amenity.[78] Demographic studies reveal a slowing down in population growth after 1831 with increased mortality and a new wave of emigration (countered to some extent by Irish immigration).[79] Death rates were particularly high in the towns – perhaps twice the rural level – and not until the 1840s were there attempts to find solutions to the appalling urban health problems. There was the irritant of poverty on a scale that authorities could not comprehend. 'In small communities the scale had been manageable and poverty more obvious to the rich: in large towns much of the poverty remained concealed.'[80] People could hardly get help from country relatives while poor law allowances were small (and the three year residence qualification disqualified the most mobile sections of the population).

Nevertheless the special problems of this period of rapid industrialisation and urbanisation provided a foundation for modern planning. The state became involved increasingly in urban affairs as the market proved itself inadequate as a regulator of major conflicts generated by powerful economic and social forces. There was acceptance of the need for overall control of large cities and considerable boundary extensions are evident in the late nineteenth century: in 1891 Glasgow annexed a number of 'villa burghs' that had been tolerated under the 1862 General Police and Improvement (Scotland) Act. Services improved gradually although the diffusion process was in some cases long drawn out (Figure 7.13) and there was greater coordination of services with municipal control of water, gas, electricity, transport and telephones generally achieved by 1914. But land use controls got no further than the Town Planning Act of 1909, relating to land on the margins of the cities that would be required for their inevitable expansion. And housing was still regarded as being basically the domain of private enterprise. Urban problems were exacerbated by reluctance to spend heavily on housing. A lower proportion of wages was spent on housing than in English cities: this is reflected in the prominence of the tenement, involving minimal rent, and making for efficiency in local transport through very high usage in relation to route length. 'The people of Glasgow were packed into their houses to a degree unimaginable in the larger English cities. Under such conditions, family morale collapsed and the results were terrible.'[81] Yet these monumental shortcomings are perhaps the inevitable consequence of the large city phenomenon that proved the key to nineteenth-century innovation to such an extent that it gradually blunted its efficiency and left an appalling backlog of social problems.[82]

However, a considerable number of improvement schemes were implemented to deal with some of the worst housing problems. Indeed the improvement scheme stands as an important signpost in the history of planning since it established the basic principle that collective will is superior to individual rights in the urban sphere. Parliament would sanction the acquisition, demolition and redevelopment of a designated area, the aim being to improve the standard of housing and, by the creation of new street alignments, to allow traffic to flow more efficiently. A reform campaign in the Scottish burghs led by the provost of Leith led to legislation in 1862 expressing the notion of slum clearance. Although it proved ineffective above the level of the individual property it was a

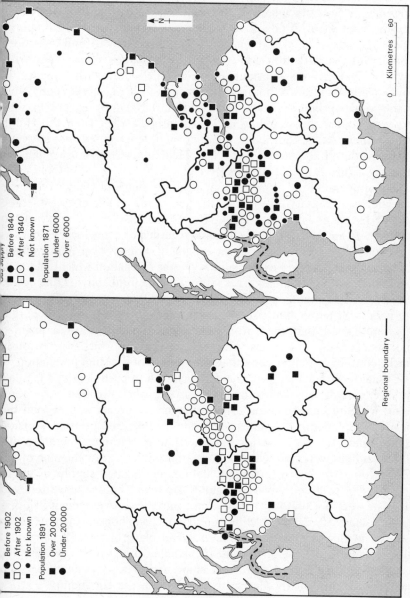

Figure 7.13. Diffusion of electricity and gas supplies

Source: I. H. Adams (1978)

Note: The years 1840 and 1902 represent the mid-points in the two diffusion periods

149

suitable instrument for small projects and it helped to map out the powers and responsibilities of medical officers. The principle of wholesale demolition was introduced in the Artisans and Labourers' Dwelling Act of 1875, although this was anticipated by the local act of 1866 that provided for an Improvement Trust in Glasgow. Similar schemes followed in Edinburgh (1867), Dundee (1871), Greenock (1877), Leith (1880) and Aberdeen (1884). Not that attention was confined to the largest cities. The textile town of Hawick was substantially remodelled during the nineteenth century: a new entrance through Buccleuch St in 1815, subsequently lined by the principal churches of the town, and a new North Bridge (1832) came four years after the widening of Drumlanrig Bridge. Then the Burgh Improvement Act of 1861 led to the removal of tenemented alleyways and the laying out of new streets, especially High St on which a town hall was built in Scottish Baronial style in 1884–6.

The momentum for redevelopment came fundamentally from 'the beachheads of sanitary reform' and the fear of the middle classes over the risks of disease and epidemic arising from the slums.[83] But it is difficult to deny that an improved street system was regarded by some local officials as a most valuable accessory. And the mixing of motives over improvement schemes is compounded by the subtlety in the legislation which tended to place emphasis on insanitary areas rather than their inhabitants; the device was accepted as a public health measure rather than a means of providing the poor with better houses. Discussing the 1867 scheme in Edinburgh, P. J. Smith states that 'the Corporation's actions could always be justified under the criterion of responsibility to the ratepayers, which was obviously perceived to be a greater good than the welfare of the slum population'.[84] The usual tendency therefore was for clearance to push deprived families into accommodation in surrounding areas that were already at saturation point, while the new housing usually commanded rents well beyond the means of the poorest families. The late-nineteenth-century depression reduced incentive to build for the lowest wage earners. Therefore displaced families were 'left with no alternative but to redraw the map of the slums, competing fiercely for the tighter and tighter supply of cheap housing which filtered down to them'.[85] However, bourgeois attitudes to the poor were not uniformly indifferent. Further redevelopment in Edinburgh in the 1890s did include the building of cheap housing including such facilities as drying greens, wash-houses and playgrounds. This provides some evidence at least of a trend of planning practice in a progressive direction although there were still some articulate opponents of slum clearance because of the destructive impact on the community. Patrick Geddes was perhaps the most effective spokesman although further comment on his view will be left over until Chapter 11.

Yet while Scotland became predominantly an urban nation it is evident

Table 7.6. *Largest towns and cities 1891 and 1971 (000s)*

1891		1971	
Glasgow	658.2	Glasgow	897.5
Edinburgh	332.4	Edinburgh	453.6
Dundee	153.3	Dundee	182.2
Aberdeen	124.9	Aberdeen	182.1
Paisley	66.4	Paisley	95.4
Greenock	63.1	Motherwell & Wishaw	73.7
Motherwell & Wishaw	34.0	Greenock	69.5
Coatbridge	29.9	East Kilbride	64.1
Perth	29.9	Coatbridge	52.1
Kilmarnock	28.4	Kirkaldy	50.4
Kirkaldy	27.2	Dunfermline	49.9
Hamilton	24.9	Kilmarnock	48.8
Ayr	24.8	Clydebank	48.3
Arbroath	22.8	Ayr	47.9
Dunfermline	22.2	Hamilton	46.3
Inverness	19.2	Perth	43.0
Hawick	19.2	Irvine	42.5
Airdrie	19.1	Airdrie	37.7
Falkirk	17.3	Falkirk	37.6
Stirling	16.8	Inverness	34.8
Port Glasgow	14.6	Cumbernauld	31.6
Montrose	13.0	Stirling	29.8
Dumfries	12.9	Dumfries	29.4
Peterhead	12.2	Dumbarton	25.6
Forfar	12.1	Bearsden	25.6

Source: Census of Scotland

that the process of town development was very uneven (Tables 7.6 and 7.7). The Central Belt embraced a much larger number of the twenty-five largest towns in 1891 than was the case in 1821. Consideration of smaller nucleations also reveals great disparities between the regions, with the Highlands clearly the most poorly urbanised in terms of both towns and villages.[86] It was therefore inevitable that rural–urban migration would be overshadowed by inter-regional transfers and the shift of demographic strength from the Outer Regions to the Central Belt took place more rapidly than it did before or after this period.[87] All the Outer Regions show net migration losses although the dynamism of the leading towns allowed a modest overall growth.[88] The Highland population, however, shows a significant decline while natural increase also fell away from the high level reached in the late eighteenth century. But the adjustment in the Highlands was hardly painless. Certainly there was a steady flow of migrants into the Central Belt: 'the pull of Greenock on the Highlands reached out

Table 7.7. *Distribution of the largest towns and cities 1891 and 1971*

Region	1891				1971			
	A.	B.	C.	D.	A.	B.	C.	D.
Highlands & Islands	1	19.2	5.0	0.11	1	34.8	11.3	0.22
Grampian	2	137.1	32.5	0.72	1	182.1	41.5	0.80
Tayside	5	231.1	58.5	1.32	2	225.2	56.6	1.09
North	8	387.4	32.2	0.72	4	442.1	38.7	0.75
Borders	1	19.2	14.8	0.34	—	—	—	—
Dumfries & Galloway	1	12.9	8.6	0.19	1	29.4	20.5	0.39
South	2	32.1	11.4	0.26	1	29.4	12.2	0.24
Outer Regions	10	419.5	28.3	0.64	5	471.5	34.1	0.66
East Central	5	415.9	48.0	1.08	5	621.3	46.5	0.90
West Central	10	963.4	57.5	1.29	15	1,606.6	64.0	1.24
Central Belt	15	1,373.3	54.2	1.21	20	2,227.9	57.9	1.12
Scotland	25	1,792.8	44.5	1.00	25	2,699.4	51.6	1.00

A. Number of towns and cities (largest 25 in Scotland)
B. Total population of largest towns and cities
C. B as a percentage of the total population
D. C as a percentage of C for Scotland
Source: Table 7.6

in a wave-like motion, affecting first districts close at hand and later the more distant places within an ever widening radius in successive periods through the eighteenth and nineteenth centuries'.[89] And contacts with the colonies forged through previous migrants gradually made movement overseas a more 'natural' answer to limited opportunity at home. Yet voluntary migration was insufficient to avoid a Malthusian crisis after 1815.[90] Peaceful conditions in Europe meant that enlistment into Highland regiments could no longer keep young adult males from matrimony and parenthood while falling agricultural and raw material prices reduced access to imported food previously assured by the exports of cattle and kelp. Landowners now positively encouraged migration as their small tenants became dangerously dependent on the potato. Blight in the mid-1830s and mid-1840s did not create destitution on the Irish scale, for the areas seriously affected were relatively small; this was helped by earlier migration partially enforced through clearance, and where it did occur relief was quite effective.[91] Emigration increased as landlords granted considerable assistance, and help also came from government through the Emigration Act after Sir John McNeill's report to the new Poor Law Board of Supervision in 1851.[92] These issues are examined further in the study of the crofting system.

8

Glasgow and the Clyde

The rise of West-Central Scotland must surely rank as the classic story of Scotland's economic history. The focus of activity is the Clyde, an extensive and sheltered maritime inlet well connected with the system of 'western seaways' which have been shown to be so crucial to an understanding of trade and migration in prehistoric and later times.[1] Apart from its use for trade and commerce there were valuable natural resources in herring and salmon, and although medieval commerce was concentrated by law in the burghs fishing was open to all the coastal settlements. However, these advantages counted for little before the development of the Atlantic routes, conditioned by the colonisation of America and the removal of legal barriers to trade with English colonies by Scottish merchants in 1707, and before the technology of the industrial revolution had revealed tremendous possibilities which local entrepreneurs were ready to exploit. This transformation of regional potentials led not just to the dominance of the Clyde valley in Scottish economic affairs but to the emergence of Glasgow as the key city in this dynamic complex of industry and trade. 'That the ecclesiastical burgh of Bishop Jocelin should attain such distinction would certainly have appeared incredible to the inhabitants of the older king's burghs of Rutherglen and Renfrew, and equally so to those of Dumbarton, the ancient and strategically situated capital of Strathclyde'.[2] Yet by the end of the sixteenth century Glasgow had achieved greater taxable importance than her rivals in the west and was the second city in Scotland by 1670.

Glasgow and her rivals for the Clyde trade

Downstream settlements had more direct access to open sea but their hinterlands were restricted. Glasgow on the other hand lay at the lowest bridging point, yet where the river was shallow and extremely difficult to navigate: at Dumbuck, Erskine, Renfrew and Glasgow Bridge the river

153

was easily forded at low water. In contrast to the lower Clyde, where glaciers had eroded deeply into solid rock, the section above Port Glasgow was excavated by water cutting through clays, sands and gravels. This did, however, mean that the river could be deepened artificially and recorded efforts date back to the mid sixteenth century when Dumbarton, Glasgow and Renfrew cooperated at Dumbuck. This work extended into the next century accompanied, however, by indications of greater rivalry between the main competitors. Renfrew lost its port during the century when a serious flood diverted the river away from the town to the northern side of King's Inch and hardly features in the subsequent history of Clyde commerce, but Glasgow had formidable rivals in Dumbarton, and in Greenock (erected a burgh of barony in 1635). Neither town would make land available to Glasgow so that the Broomielaw (where a quay was built in 1663) would be complemented by downriver facilities. So Glasgow had to acquire the Newark site in Kilmacolm parish (1668) where an outport was built. All Glasgow merchants were obliged to use this facility, to the exclusion of all other downriver harbours.[3] This regulation was reimposed in 1691 after some relaxation when use of Greenock warehouses had been tolerated, but it could not be effectively maintained and a feature of the remarkable growth of commerce in the eighteenth century, in which the tobacco trade was the cornerstone, is the greater importance of Greenock than Port Glasgow. Greenock had 291 arrivals and departures between 1742 and 1744 while Port Glasgow had 231: Glasgow merchants were using Greenock and often had shares in Greenock ships. 'One can only presume that there just was not room at Port Glasgow, either in the harbour or warehouses, for all the traffic.'[4]

Greenock and Port Glasgow between them took the lion's share of Clyde shipping activity. Glasgow itself could receive only the smallest vessels while Dumbarton was being rapidly eclipsed.[5] The old capital of Strathclyde was endowed with a volcanic plug, an excellent base from which to control invasion forces heading up the Clyde valley by either land or sea, but its importance in conditions of peace was becoming less obvious. Dumbarton appears to have rejected any option of port development in 1658, fearing the evil effects of the 'influx of mariners'. In the eighteenth century there is no mention of a flourishing port and industry was not expanding 'owing to letters of deaconry preventing strangers from working at their trades without costly entries'.[6] Furthermore the shallow water of the Clyde discouraged ocean going ships of the eighteenth century and the bridging of the Leven reduced Dumbarton's importance as a staging post for road travellers. The depth of water meanwhile was greater on the Renfrewshire side and Greenock's harbours lay at the deepest water nearest to Glasgow. 'The deep-water roadstead lay close to the raised beach at the point where the clotted river enters the deep sheltered firth' and this 'Tail o' the Bank' was much trusted by mariners.[7] It was entirely logical that a burgh of barony should grow out of the fishertowns of Cartsdyke and Greenock and become an entrepot where large vessels anchored in the roads and transferred cargo to lighters which proceeded up river to Glasgow. The construction of a harbour at Newark led Greenock to follow suit in 1710, enabling her to enlarge the fishing industry and increase trade with America. A graving bank was included in the scheme, to facilitate ship repair, and this was followed up with a dry dock in 1783.

Glasgow now responded with further surveys of the river. John Smeaton sounded the river in 1755 and proposed a dam and lock at Marlinford in order to achieve deep water at Glasgow, adequate for coasting vessels: accommodation for ocean-going ships was not seriously contemplated at the time. However, grave setbacks were encountered and damage from spring floods in 1762 precipitated formal abandonment of the scheme by the end of the year. John Golborne took a different approach, building jetties, or wing-dams into the river (downstream from the mouth of the Kelvin) to increase the scour and yield 1.5 metres or five feet of water at high tide by 1772: the progress was consolidated by building the Lang Dyke through Dumbuck Shoal the following year. Successful completion of this work was followed by the important canal schemes in Central Scotland. Yet this work merely increased the efficiency of the inland navigation system without any significant difference to the movements of ocean shipping. Greenock continued to capitalise on her natural advantages: an East India Harbour was ready in 1809 and the following year saw Greenock with 40,000 tons of registered shipping compared with Port Glasgow's 13,100 and Glasgow's mere 2,600. Greenock crowed its success with a new dry dock (1818) and a fine Custom House that still dominates the waterfront. At this time there was a fairly clear division of effort between Greenock with a virtual monopoly of ocean-going ships, and a base from which many Glasgow firms now chose to operate their vessels, and Glasgow which was accessible to small coasting vessels (including those handling the Irish and European trade). When the canals were built they provided a better route into Glasgow than the Clyde, and vessels from European ports could be seen regularly at Port Dundas. It was the canal rather than improvements on the upper Clyde that first led to Glasgow's recognition as an independent port (for the collection of customs dues) in 1780. The Clyde waterway seemed in distinct danger of being overshadowed not only by Greenock's dominance on the river but by a further canal scheme from Glasgow through Paisley and Johnstone to a new deepwater harbour at Ardrossan proposed by the Earl of Eglinton in 1803. However, the canal building was completed only between the Clyde (at Port Eglinton) and Johnstone, reached in 1810.

The port of Glasgow: river deepening and dock construction

By the 1830s consolidation of Golborne's work had made Broomielaw more accessible and ships of up to 250 tons could use the shipping lane offering a minimum depth of almost 2.5 m at low tide. Glasgow became a port of registration in 1808 and a head port in 1815, but the very modest Custom House built at the Broomielaw in 1837 emphasised Greenock's superiority, underlined by the rapid growth of the passenger traffic to America during an era of sustained emigration. What transformed the situation in Glasgow's favour was the development of steam power, which eliminated the hazard of unfavourable winds on the upper river: 'the discoveries of steam gave assurance that a shallow stream would no longer be a barrier'.[8] As the old laborious method of lightering goods up the river to Glasgow 'by rowing and poling and horse towage was superseded by towing lines of lighters by small vessels propelled by steam engines' (the first steam tug was built in 1819), it was feasible for Glasgow to have serious pretensions as a port for ocean shipping.[9] Parliamentary assent was forthcoming in 1840 for a project to secure a minimum depth of six metres but this was not achieved until 1886 because of the need to evolve techniques of underwater blasting to cope with the problem of Elderslie rock encountered in 1854. By 1907, however, the rock had been reduced to some eight metres below low water, the minimum depth now achieved between Glasgow and Greenock thanks to the blasting techniques and the powers of the steam powered bucket dredger. Small vessels could leave Glasgow at any state of the tide while ships drawing nine metres could reach Greenock on one tide. Glasgow now convincingly overtook Greenock. Greenock had had an overwhelming lead over Glasgow as regards tonnage of shipping handled in 1830: 122,500 tons against 19,500. In 1840 Greenock's 168,000 tons still compared favourably with 122,700 at Glasgow but comparable figures for 1850 were 148,900 and 296,900.[10]

This mammoth development called for a huge increase in berth facilities in Glasgow. Back in the canal era plans had been discussed for docks in the vicinity of the Broomielaw but for many years an alternative solution to the demand for more quayage was found in extending the riverside wharfs: for the tidal range was not so great that locking was needed and many riverside sites were still available for development. This strategy was linked with the introduction of steam powered dredgers to deepen the river for ocean going ships. There was controversy for some years as to whether the river should be narrowed or widened: it was eventually shown that the ebbing tidal flow had the greatest deepening effect and hence that the tidal volume should be maximised. In 1834 the traditional policy of dykes and training walls was abandoned in favour of widening as well as deepening. Quayage on the north side of the river was extended upstream (Custom House Quay, 1852–7) after the resiting of the weir, but the main development came downstream with Anderston Quay (1814) followed by Hydepark (1840), Lancefield (1844) and Finnieston (1848). Accommodation was also provided on the south side opposite Broomielaw at Clyde Place (1837) and this work extended downstream to Windmillcroft (1839), Springfield (1848), General Terminus, with railway access (1849) and Mavisbank (1858). Quayage might have extended further downstream to Govan and the mouth of the Kelvin, but need for docks was eventually conceded as the riverside facilities extended further and further from the heart of Glasgow and increasing competition for land arose with the shipbuilders. Kingston Dock (1867) involved a remodelling of the Windmillcroft Quay but the later docks at Stobcross (Queen's Dock) and Cessnock (Prince's) were excavated at the downstream ends of the riverside quays.[11] There was then a break in continuity for it was at Clydebank that a special mineral dock (Rothesay Dock) opened in 1907 although much of the riverside between Queen's and Rothesay Docks was developed for quays handling cattle (Yorkhill), grain (Meadowside) and timber (Merklands). In the search for further accommodation attention shifted to the south side of the river between Govan and Renfrew Ferry. The burgh of Renfrew was anxious to see developments within its boundaries but the Clyde Trustees preferred to exploit an extensive site at Shieldhall where a timber wharf opened in 1884. An elaborate scheme for five basins with nine metres minimum depth was drawn up in 1913 but confidence was sapped by the unpromising economic conditions after the First World War and only one dock (King George V opened in 1931) was ever built.[12] There was some displacement of shipbuilders as, for example, the Kelvinhaugh yard was eliminated in the development of Yorkhill Quay. Several firms relocated downstream: Alexander Stephen began the process with a move to Linthouse in 1870.

Meanwhile Greenock remained in the running and the Victoria Harbour, for trading and for the fitting out of steamships, was successful. But the grandiose scheme for a great new harbour in the grounds of Garvel House, on the eastern edge of the town adjacent to Port Glasgow, was quite unable to divert ships which now had the choice of proceeding upstream to Glasgow. Greenock maintained an important stake in the sugar and timber trades, and the growth of railway services made Greenock a convenient base for steamer services to the Argyll side of the river: hence the Glasgow & South Western Railway development at Princes Pier (1867) and the Caledonian Railway's project at Gourock in 1889 (relocating from Custom House Quay). But Greenock had lost its primacy and although a secure future has now been found in the context of a unified port authority for the Clyde (1966) through a modern container terminal (1969) the underused Great Harbour still stands as a monument to frustrated Victorian ambition when Greenock sought to maintain its distinguished role as the Liverpool of Scotland.[13]

The growth of the shipbuilding industry

It is necessary to emphasise the role of the Clyde in Glasgow's growth even further by considering the rise of shipbuilding, the growth industry that brought nineteenth-century prosperity to its climax. Activity was very limited indeed until after the union and the founding of Scotts of Greenock in 1711. The construction of wooden sailing ships increased to meet part of the local demand and the association between ocean trading on the one hand and shipbuilding and repairing on the other is particularly clear in the various harbour development plans for Greenock. Yet until well into the nineteenth century the Clyde launched less than five per cent of Britain's total tonnage of shipping and consequently 'there is little evidence to support the proposition that the later dominance of the Clyde in shipbuilding rested on traditional skills and long-standing importance in ship construction'.[14] Rather the origins lie in the development of new techniques of construction and propulsion. Scotland was in the forefront of experiments by engineers inspired by the invention of the steam engine. William Symington is remembered for his experiment with a paddle-driven steam-boat on Dalswinton Loch (Nithsdale) in 1788 and the steam barge that sailed in the Forth & Clyde Canal in 1802. But even more significant was Henry Bell's success in 1812 in assembling three components (a hull from John Wood's Port Glasgow yard, a boiler from David Napier's Camlachie Foundry in Glasgow and an engine from the engineering works of John Robertson in Dempster Street, Glasgow) to produce a successful sea-going vessel, the *Comet*, which operated in Clyde and West Highland waters. A link was forged between riverside boatbuilders and engineers located in the East End of Glasgow where they had sprung up initially to serve the cotton industry. Such simple assembly work could easily be taken on elsewhere, but the Clyde maintained a formidable lead through a succession of innovations. David Napier started at the Camlachie Foundry as an ironfounder and boiler maker, but produced a marine engine in 1816 and then relocated his works on the Clyde at Lancefield (1821) where engineering and shipbuilding could be combined for the first time. Boiler efficiency was improved, the screw propellor developed (in place of the paddle), while the compound marine steam engine made greater use of energy by successive feeding of steam into two cylinders. Incredibly David Napier also played a leading role in the use of iron hulls with his *Aglaia* which sailed on Loch Eck (Argyll & Bute) in 1827. Despite reservations by the Navy and by Lloyds, increasing numbers of iron ships were launched in the 1830s and by the middle of the century about forty per cent of the tonnage launched on the Clyde was iron. The proportion was almost seventy per cent in Glasgow, while at yards in Dumbarton, Greenock and Port Glasgow it was less than a quarter. Glasgow launched sixty per cent of the iron ships completed by the four towns together but only thirty-four per cent of iron and wood ships combined.

It is attractive to relate the growth of iron ships on the Clyde to the supply of cheap iron. This certainly had some influence over the location decisions of would-be builders of iron ships. Alexander Stephen began building wooden ships at Burghead (Moray) in 1750 but the firm was successively relocated to Aberdeen (Footdee), Arbroath, Dundee and the Clyde at Kelvinhaugh in 1850.[15] The same process can be seen again in 1906 when Yarrows moved from the Thames to take advantage of the lower labour and material costs on the Clyde. Yet iron supplies satisfied only a precondition and without the successful innovations in engineering it would have counted for nothing. As it was the iron–steam technology became widely known among a compact group of builders on the Clyde, especially in Glasgow, and capacity was well able to meet the rapidly increasing demand for ships of this type over the period 1850–70. Clyde tonnage rose from 0.20 to 0.34 million tons per annum during the 1860s, with the Clyde's share of British launching rocketing from thirty to seventy per cent. There was expertise in other branches of course and this is well exemplified in the 1860s by the success of Greenock builders (especially Robert Steele & Co.) in tea clippers: composite sailing ships involving the use of iron frames and wood planks, like the *Taeping* of 1863.[16] But innovation was most marked in the use of metal, with steel now attracting attention. There was suspicion of steel plates made by the Bessemer process but the invention of the open-hearth furnace, with the refinements of Thomas & Gilchrist, was decisive and William Denny of Dumbarton staked his reputation on the launching of the *Rotomahana*, the first ocean-going steamer using mild steel, in 1879. Acceptance of steel in boiler making paved the way for higher steam pressures and further elaboration of engine design (much of it pioneered by Denny's). This in turn made for the greater efficiency that ousted sailing ships from the ocean routes during the following decade.

As steel ships came to dominate there were new linkages in the industry, involving shipbuilding and steel making. Some separate boiler firms came into existence, notably Babcock & Wilcox who set up at Renfrew in 1897 to make water tube boilers. Denny's at Dumbarton extended first into engine making (in partnership with other builders) through the Dennystown Forge in Dumbarton and then into steel through the installation of an open hearth furnace. In the other direction came Beardmore's of Parkhead Forge where malleable iron production was followed by steel making. The company acquired Robert Napier's shipyard at Govan in 1900. This linkage process was often associated with relocation of yards further downriver in order to find more spacious sites and, at the same time, free land nearer Glasgow for the construction of docks. As already noted

Stephen's moved from Kelvinhaugh to Linthouse in 1871: the new site was more spacious and carried a lower rateable value although the infrastructure was initially poor, requiring workers to walk more than a kilometre from the tramway terminus and plates to be carted from Govan station. Beardmore's transferred to Dalmuir in 1906. English steel makers were also gaining a footing in Clyde shipyards: J. & G. Thomson were established as engineers and shipbuilders at Finnieston by 1851 but relocated in Clydebank in 1872. This new yard was then taken over by John Brown of Sheffield in 1899, giving that company an assured outlet for heavy forgings. Cammel Laird & Co. of Birkenhead became major shareholders in Fairfield Shipbuilding at Govan. There was some breakdown of regional independence and this trend was underscored by the application of external technology such as the steam turbine first used on the Clyde by Denny's in 1901 and, with geared machinery, at Fairfields in 1912. As with ocean shipping, therefore, Glasgow, along with Govan and Clydebank, came to acquire a dominant role in shipbuilding. But larger ships have impaired the efficiency even of those yards that were relocated at the turn of the century. The trend is now in favour of the downstream yards like Lithgows at Port Glasgow which has been able to take over part of Greenock's Great Harbour and so overcome the problem of a short frontage on a narrow river.

Diversification of Glasgow's ecclesiastical function

The events on the Clyde form the basis of Glasgow's transformation.[17] St Ninian is reputed to have consecrated a cemetery on the cathedral site and 'one might well view Bishop Jocelyn's civic charter from William the Lion (1175–8) as being merely another monument to the importance and sacred associations of the site between the Molendinar and Glasgow burns'.[18] There is no doubt about Glasgow's association with a great ecclesiastical foundation and 'the concentration of academic and clerical institutions' was powerful stimulus to growth, reflected in an urban axis from the cathedral running southwards along the High Street to the north bank of the Clyde. Medieval trades (fulling, tanning, skinning and fishing) were present here and modest secular building induced a second major axis parallel to the river consisting of Gallowgate and Trongate where much of the late medieval marketing is reported. There appears to have been no serious friction between town and church: ecclesiastical administration was not oppressive and the burgesses benefited from the wealth and influence of the bishops. There was a considerable fund of enterprise and initiative which found an outlet in the opportunities of the seventeenth century and more especially the eighteenth century when the population rose from approximately 13,000 to 84,000. Glasgow's growth might have faltered with the decline in the influence of the church after the reformation and the vigorous local response to the widening of commercial horizons might not have happened. However, the merchant community grew rapidly between 1560 and 1707 and this might be linked with the feuing of church lands 'to the effect that the tenants, being thereby become heritable possessors of their several possessions, might be encouraged by virtue and policy to improve that country'.[19] Landed wealth formed a likely base for further enterprise and many of the owners of small estates became part of the mercantile elite. The process of development for this great individual and corporate enterprise requires further clarification but basically it seems that 'the inheritors of civic power and episcopal land were also the founders of a new mercantile tradition' and this provides the link between medieval and modern Glasgow.[20] It meant that opportunities would be seized with vigour and, because there was such a close association between merchants, burgesses and landowners, that the physical expansion of the town would not be hindered. Even the lands skirting the city were in the ownership of a small number of civic leaders and, in the first decades of the eighteenth century, industrial villages arose close to the river at Anderston to the west and Calton to the east. Later in the century as the Forth & Clyde Canal reached Port Dundas to the north the Cowcaddens lands became another industrial location for dyeing and chemicals, malting and brewing.

The eighteenth-century expansion of the city was most evident along Trongate. The western gate (West Port) was removed in 1751 and the road extended across the now-culverted Glasgow Burn as Argyll Street (later Argyle Street), to proclaim its social pretensions. New streets were then laid off this axis at right angles beginning with Virginia Street in 1753 and continuing with Buchanan Street in 1778, Hutcheson Street in 1791 and Glassford Street in 1796. The westward shift of the city was then consolidated by the fact that Jamaica Street (1761) led south to a new crossing of the Clyde. The westward movement accelerated into the nineteenth century and a sequential pattern of occupance may be observed with buildings raised initially as residences for gentlemen but gradually converted for use by various professional services, commercial, financial and legal.[21] The central business district came to polarise on the Buchanan Street/Argyle Street intersection and new housing erected still further west came to form the high status residential zone of the city in the nineteenth century. There can have been little perception of this Victorian destiny because desirable residences were also built in the east, notably on Charlotte Street which was taken off the Gallowgate in 1779 and led down to the Green on the banks of the Clyde. Further open land was taken for Menteith Row and St Andrew's Square, both of which attracted wealthy residents. But within a generation the high status character of this neighbourhood had been lost and plans for further East End squares were abandoned. Attractive accommodation was also provided on the south side of the river on the Hutcheson estate, close to the village of Gorbals and between the two Clyde bridges. The merchants and other professionals were successfully enticed over the water (and until the turn of the century at Laurieston and Tradeston too) but again there was subdivision and the 'once fashionable town houses degenerated into warrens of one and two-roomed homes for casual labourers'.[22]

It is not clear just how these alternative suburban developments came to acquire a bad name in the early nineteenth century but the cotton industry was graduating to a factory scale of operation and taking firm root in the East End, while south of the river the Govan ironworks began a tradition of heavy industry which would tend to repel high status residents through the pollution and the development of working class neighbourhoods. The houses at Blytheswood by contrast lay on rising ground, punctuated by drumlins aloof from the twin industrial axes of the Clyde and the Forth & Clyde Canal.[23] The differentiation within the city remained strong throughout the nineteenth century. In the East End the cotton factories stimulated engineering and this industry became increasingly complex as new opportunities arose.[24] Locations also became more diverse but the attraction of the Lanarkshire ironworks supplying metal was reflected in a consolidation of the East End with the industry in Parkhead and Springburn, extending further out from Bridgeton and St Rollox respectively, while the shipyards eased downriver to Clydebank and paved the way for further relocation, such as Singer's sewing machine factory, opened in 1882. By the beginning of the twentieth century the car industry was developing. There were workshops in Bridgeton but again the ambitious companies moved to secure more spacious premises and the Argyll Company combined their Bridgeton premises with a new factory opened in the Vale of Leven (Dumbarton) in 1906. None of these trends affected the West End which was free to expand further outwards along the axis of Great Western Road.

Expansion in the suburbs and renewal in the core

The process of expansion is one that merits close attention. Despite the Scottish practice of tenement building, vast areas of land were needed and questions dealing with land acquisition, land use planning and provision of infrastructure can be followed through the Victorian period of cyclical fluctuation in housing demand. Glasgow's West End has been used to illustrate the arrangement of residential and 'institutional' land uses which is thought to correlate with building cycles. At times of high demand, in the early 1870s and again through the turn of the nineteenth century, speculative builders will be able to offer high prices to secure plots immediately adjacent to the edge of the city. Institutional developers, wishing to secure land for parks, hospitals, schools and barracks, will settle for less accessible sites with lower prices. During depression, when speculative building will practically cease, institutions will have virtually no competition in the area where they previously secured land; land that has now become more accessible since the boom in speculative building pushed the city limit further out.[25] Consolidation in this new fringe belt will now create a zone with a distinct institutional character. The pattern will then be repeated over the next boom–slump succession and give rise to urban spread through a sequence of fringe belt developments of alternating character. There is much empirical evidence to support this approach.

But of course the model does not take account of the attitudes and aspirations of landowners, assuming that they automatically sell to the highest bidder: a landowner might wish to become involved in suburban development and aim for a mix of residential and institutional land uses in defiance of economic forces. It also overlooks the tendency for institutional demands to vary through time and it is notable that during the predominantly boom period of 1840–58 the ability of institutions to take up proximal sites was greater than 'expected', due to the strength of social considerations which led Glasgow Corporation to compromise the economic argument for housing development. In 1851 some influential citizens submitted a proposal to acquire land for Kelvingrove Park and thereby enable West End residents to have the same facilities as those in the east, who had benefited from the laying out of the New Green as a recreation ground about 1810. South of the river land was acquired for Queen's Park in 1857 and additions made in 1894 when the adjoining Camphill lands were obtained.[26] Finally any analysis of suburban development in the late nineteenth century must take into account the lack of unified administrative control: Anderston, Calton and Gorbals were included in the city only in 1846, followed in 1891 by the previously separate burghs of Crosshill, Govanhill, Hillhead, Maryhill, Pollokshields East and Pollokshields West, in 1905 by Kinning Park and in 1912 by Govan, Partick and Pollokshaws. Separation from Glasgow meant lower rates for middle class owner occupiers but it reduced the resources that could be mobilised for major projects like the Loch Katrine water supply scheme of 1859 and the sewage purification works that were eventually opened in 1894 at Dalmarnock (subsequently at Dalmuir and Shieldhall too).

Suburban development must be seen in the context of transport provision. Main lines into the city were forged by the Glasgow & Edinburgh Railway of 1842. In addition the Caledonian Railway took over the Glasgow & Garnkirk Railway of 1831 and extended it to a terminus at Buchanan Street in 1849, the same year that a new line was brought up the

Clyde Valley to a terminus at Bridge Street south of the river (superseded by Central Station on the north side in 1879).[27] The Glasgow & South Western forged a connection across the heart of Glasgow with the North British (which had absorbed the Glasgow & Edinburgh) at Springburn in 1875 and then allowed the company to open a new terminus north of the river at St Enoch the following year. This provided a base for the development of suburban railways, anticipated by the Caledonian's Busby Railway to East Kilbride (1868), by the North British building south from their Helensburgh Railway of 1858 to Stobcross (1873) and northwards to Milngavie (1863) and the Kelvin Valley settlements as far as Kilsyth (1879). The greatest development came after 1880. The growth of the western suburbs and the phenomenal growth of Clydebank led the North British to expand their earlier penetration into Stobcross by extending to Clydebank (1882) and then provided a more direct approach from the heart of Glasgow (Queen Street Low Level Station) to serve not only Clydebank and Dalmuir but also Coatbridge, and Bridgeton in the East End. The Caledonian built a duplicate line, passing beneath their Central Station (1896), extending westwards to Dumbarton, and eastwards to Dalmarnock (for Rutherglen) and Carmyle (for Coatbridge). At the same time there was a loop right round the north of the city to reach Possil and Springburn from either Rutherglen or Stobcross. Meanwhile south of the Clyde the Caledonian's thrust into Ayrshire via Cathcart and Neilston provided a base for suburban services by the Cathcart Circle from Central Station (1894) and by the loop from Patterton through Barrhead to Paisley. The Glasgow & South Western was the Caledonian's competitor here with a new line to Paisley (1885) from which Barrhead was reached: a circular route could be followed to Barrhead via Paisley and Pollokshaws (1902). These suburban routes were quickly undermined by the trams, which were particularly effective against railway services from grimy underground stations: the Barrhead service which two railway companies had launched through a costly 'battle of the braes' was killed by the end of the First World War. Yet suburban transport was a highly competitive field and provides an essential context for the late Victorian growth of Glasgow.[28] It also obliges a widening of the perspective to embrace the whole conurbation since the journey to work was now relatively easy. Indeed the commuter trains and connecting steamers were extending Glasgow's West End across the water to Argyll and Bute.[29] This was hardly remarkable considering that back in the 1850s the Edinburgh & Glasgow had tried to seduce affluent families out of the city by offering five years free travel to anyone building a house of £500 value within a mile of Campsie Junction (Lenzie).

During the nineteenth century the central core of Glasgow had changed from being a self-contained town to become first the heart of a great city in which industry had migrated to suburbs like Parkhead and Springburn and then through further 'metropolitanisation' to become the centre of a vast city region efficiently integrated by railway services. This is expressed in extensive remodelling of the centre to accommodate railway stations and warehouses as well as a great increase in retail and professional services. This led to some further invasion of West End residential areas but it also involved slum clearance in the East End where there were considerable social problems. By the 1870s there was considerable differentiation between working class areas. The centre contained the largest groupings of poorer families, who found employment on the quays, in warehouses and with small manufacturing concerns. Part of the central area had the character of an Irish ghetto for there had been heavy immigration in the 1845–65 period into former high status areas where town houses were subdivided, the classic case of the 'invasion' of a neighbourhood and 'succession' to a new cultural pattern.[30] Under these conditions the clearance of slum property for commercial development increased the distress by forcing people into surrounding properties that were already saturated. The time was ripe for municipal intervention in housing and an act of 1866 provided for an Improvement Trust in Glasgow to acquire land in the centre and redevelop with new, wide streets and the culverting of the Molendinar and Camlachie Burns. However, once again initial clearance meant displacement into congested properties round about, while depression slowed the pace of new building until 1888 when the Improvement Trustees were prepared to start building of their own account.[31] Another Improvement Act in 1897 led to extensive evictions, yet there was little awareness of the plight of low income families who could not afford economic rents. Corporation houses (1,500 of them by 1900 in four storey tenements) were let to selected tenants and only in 1902 did Glasgow apply for an act to enable municipal housing to be built for the poorest people. In view of the controversy over municipal control of housing and services it is hardly remarkable that a socially acceptable solution proved elusive. Yet although the abrasive ethos of Haussmanism had only been slightly modified there was a clear precedent for public sector influence in housing in the inner city where rapid growth for more than a century had left social problems of a scale and complexity previously unknown.

Conclusion

By 1921 Glasgow had attained a population of 1.03 million which made it the second city of the United Kingdom. The achievement struck many contemporaries as amazing, including H. J. Mackinder (one of the city's MPs) who wrote a short piece on the future of Glasgow in 1921. 'In each successive phase of civilisation Glasgow has flourished up to the possibilities of the time' and 'being a great going concern Glasgow has changed her geographical environment, has brought the seas to her doors and made tributary distant ores and granaries'. Yet the potentials that had triggered past enterprises were approaching exhaustion and the great city that had taken root 'in a far corner of the damp and chilly north in a little sterile land beside an unnavigable mountain torrent' might be hard pressed to maintain its momentum.[32] It would be unreasonable to suppose that there was anything accidental in Glasgow's development for the potentials were real in their times and any regional economic system requires its capital. Scotland as a whole was inspired by Glasgow's enterprise and patterns of interdependence became more complex as Glasgow-based rail and steamer services integrated the highly specialised sub-regional economies and provided an effective vehicle for migration. Yet the 'cumulative and self reinforcing growth' that produced the greatest of Britain's provincial cities and provides the best model of a spontaneous 'growth pole' through linkages in heavy industry led Professor Checkland to employ the analogy of the Upas tree, a growth in Java reputed to be so voracious as to consume all rivals within a range of some thirty kilometres.[33] Certainly an exaggeration in view of the establishment of some light industry in the Glasgow region yet an indicator of the force and quality of Glasgow enterprise and morale. Questions surrounding its generation in the seventeenth and eighteenth centuries, its maintenance in the nineteenth century and eclipse in the twentieth amount to a puzzling enigma which historical geography is bound to acknowledge.

9

The iron and steel industry

The early history of iron making in Scotland is obscure but it seems that despite a lack of self-sufficiency in the early modern period, reflected in trade with England and overseas countries going back to the fifteenth century, there were a large number of bloomeries, perhaps as many as 2,000. Some were situated in an exposed position to benefit from strong winds while others achieved greater efficiency through harnessing water power. Bog ore was acceptable, with an open porous structure amenable to smelting with charcoal from forests and peat mosses. These resources gave some prominence to the Highlands as a potential exporter to other parts of the country and there is a hint of such a dimension in the decision of George Hay (entrepreneur of the Wemyss glass works in Fife) to build a furnace at Letterewe (Ross & Cromarty) in 1607. It is known that the iron was of good quality, taking advantage of the expertise of some English workers employed in smelting and casting and from the use of some haematite ore from Furness, and also that Hay's influence at court exempted the works from the prohibition on the use of timber for smelting in 1609. But the ultimate fate of the venture is unknown and the most reasonable assumption is that it closed on the expiry of the nineteen year lease. Further efforts were made in the Highlands in the eighteenth century with the York Buildings Company leading the way with their project for Glenkinglass near Loch Etive (Argyll & Bute) in 1725. The company purchased a number of Highland properties, including some estates forfeited in 1715, and attempted to reach a new scale of exploitation in minerals and timber resources. Although their activities were distinctly impermanent and lacked sound management (Glenkinglass closed in 1731) the concept of a charcoal iron industry in the Highlands, drawing ore from the south and exporting iron to refineries there, was supported by other firms and the Lorn Furnace at Bonawe, near Taynuilt on Loch Etive, operated from 1753 to 1866. As J. Butt explains, the site is now looked after by the Ministry of Public Buildings and Works.[1] It is complete and

eminently worthy of preservation with a fine mason-built furnace (without
lining but with chimney complete), a filling house, three sheds (one for ore
and two for charcoal), and ruins of a casting house.

Coke-smelting in Central Scotland

A new pattern was created by the technology of coke smelting, embodied
in the Carron furnace that was lit in 1760 and stands at such a prominent
milestone in Scottish economic history that the country's industrial revolution might arguably begin with it.[2] Some timber was required initially but
the high cost of fetching wood from Loch Ness encouraged an exclusive
reliance on pit coal, supported by the presence of workers from Coalbrook-
dale who were familiar with the process.[3] There was some difficulty over
the blast: a water wheel was needed, and a steam engine to pump water
back into the reservoir. In the following decades past the turn of the
century a series of other furnace developments created a dispersed location
pattern which extended across the Central Belt from Balgonie (Markinch)
in Fife to Muirkirk (Cumnock & Doon Valley).[4] The other units were
Devon, Carron, Wilsontown, Calder, Clyde and Glenbuck (Figure 7.8D).[5]
The industry was not very competitive but despite relatively high production costs the poor transport system provided a degree of protection
against iron from other regions. Clayband ore was used but, with an iron
content of fifty per cent at best, calcining was needed before smelting, and
then the lack of good coking coal increased the quantity of fuel needed: in
1797 the production of one ton of iron at Muirkirk required a charge of
fifteen tons of coal, ironstone and limestone. This was about double the
quantity used in Wales where ironmasters had the additional advantage of
larger furnaces.[6]

   The basis for change arose with the development of coal mining and iron
working in the Monklands. An iron works was built at Calder (Monklands)
in 1795 and in the course of construction David Mushet discovered the
blackband ore. Abundant resources were revealed in the area. It was
laminated with coal (between two and eight per cent) and could be calcined
without the addition of more fuel to produce a concentrate for the furnaces
with an iron content of seventy per cent. High temperature was necessary
to smelt the ore however, but this could not be achieved using the local
coal with the conventional cold blast, considered essential for a high
quality iron. J. B. Neilson's hot blast technique was eventually proved
satisfactory and experiments at Glasgow gasworks were tested at Clyde
and Calder ironworks. At the latter the formula of an air temperature of
over 300 degrees (centigrade) and raw *splint* coal was found most econo-
mical, with a greatly reduced coal consumption (only one third the
previous level) and the cost of coking eliminated.[7] Productivity increased

dramatically and with improved transport, first by sea and later by rail, Scottish iron was able to penetrate the English market. The efficiency of the industry was remarkable with both ore and coal available in shallow pits and the Monkland Canal available to connect either with Glasgow (Port Dundas) or with Clyde/Forth shipping. The earliest railways first eliminated canal detours (Monkland & Kirkintilloch) and then provided alternatives (Glasgow & Garnkirk). The furnaces were improved in the course of solving technical problems relating to the use of the new raw materials. The only shortcoming was a lack of integration between the pig iron production and the finishing sections for the new opportunities stimulated a crop of new blast furnace companies and many of them never entered the malleable iron trade.

The greatest success in the industry was achieved by the Bairds, a farming family that went into the coal trade and then extended into iron as the trade recovered from depression in the late 1820s. Alexander Baird took nineteen year leases in Old Monkland parish at Woodhead in 1785 and High Cross in 1804 (supplemented by Kirkwood in 1811). Farms managed under the 'old fashioned style of cultivation namely in broad crooked rigs' were levelled and divided into fields of between three and six hectares: 'so thoroughly was this done by the use of both plough and spade that no vestige of the old ridges could be seen'.[8] His wife managed the dairy, regularly carrying butter on her back to Glasgow before road improvements made carting possible, while the sons shared their father's business sense and capacity for hard work. The Bairds were also small time coal miners and it was the aptitude of Alexander's eldest son for colliery management that led to the original lease for Woodside coal being replaced by larger undertakings at Rochsolloch, Merryston (New Mains) and Gartsherrie. Inclusion of Gartgill with the latter in 1827 meant a total of six pits in a small area close to the Monkland Canal, the Monkland and Kirkintilloch Railway and the turnpike road. The profits from coal mining provided the means of entry into the iron industry which was now attracting larger orders. The decision was taken by Bairds in 1828 when a lease of the Cairnhill limestone was obtained and work began on blast furnace construction on land obtained at Gartsherrie. The first furnace was lit in 1830.

Locational efficiency was compounded by sound management and investment policy, increasing the capacity in the early 1830s ready for the upswing in demand in 1836 which provided profits for further development to 100,000 tons capacity in 1843. Sixteen furnaces were arranged in two parallel rows on either side of the branch canal, with railways behind: raw materials could be discharged directly into the furnaces from railway wagons while pig could be loaded straight into *scows* for distribution by canal. It was the largest iron works in the world after Dowlais in South

Wales. The firm was particularly discriminating over raw materials with calcined ore subject to inspection so that impure material could be taken out by hand: this led to a high proportion of top grade iron which commanded substantial premiums. Recovery plant was installed and Gartsherrie practice became so widespread as to virtually eliminate open-topped furnace working in Scotland. Other companies came into existence in north Lanarkshire: Chapelhall had opened in 1826 but the following decade saw units appear at Dundyvan (1833), Calderbank (1835), Coltness and Summerlee (1837), Carnbroe and Castlehill (1838), and Govan (1839). Development spread to Ayrshire with Blair near Dalry, and Cessnock near Galston (both opening in 1839).

Spread from the Monklands

The following decade saw further spread from the Monklands because the one new works in that area (Langloan of 1841) was complemented elsewhere in West-Central Scotland by Glengarnock (near Kilbirnie) in 1842, Nithsdale (New Cumnock) in 1845, Eglinton (near Kilwinning), Lugar (near Cumnock) and Portland (Hurlford, near Kilmarnock) all in 1846, and Dalmellington in 1847. In the east there was Kinneil near Bo'ness (1845), Oakley (1846) and Lochgelly and Lumphinnans, both c.1850. By this time some of the early works had been closed: Glenbuck, Markinch and Wilsontown, but the distribution of iron production was nevertheless extensive, with further locations to follow at Ardeer near Stevenston (1851), Causewayend near Linlithgow (1855), Wishaw (1858), Bridgeness near Bo'ness (1863) and Quarter near Hamilton in 1865. Yet growth from the late 1850s was very slight overall and closures became the order of the day even in the industry's heartland: Omoa and Dundyvan (1868), Castlehill (1884), Quarter (1887), Calderbank (1888) and Chapelhall shortly after. By this time all the works in East-Central Scotland had failed except Carron (beginning with Devon in 1857) and both Cessnock and Nithsdale in Ayrshire had also closed. Carron was in a poor state at this time, being managed in a very conservative style, and it required extensive modernisation in order to survive. How are these fluctuating fortunes to be accounted for?

Various companies with their own scales of production and capital/ management resources were active on the 'chess board' of the Central Belt where the fixed value of various squares in terms of raw material endowment was being constantly reappraised in the light of changing accessibility (associated with railway developments) and market trends. Individual business histories are not generally available to a sufficient degree to allow each enterprise to be examined. But there is evidence for Coltness where Henry Houldsworth, active in the cotton trade, 'avoided the dismal balance sheets of other mill owners by gradually reducing his commitments in cotton spinning and entering the iron trade'.[9] Securing of minerals was a major preoccupation and during the firm's existence the search extended to Caithness and the Isle of Man as well as overseas. Also, the management at Shotts was finding it very hard in the late 1840s to secure high quality minerals at favourable prices close to the works. And the main reason for the takeover of Wilsontown by William Dixon of Govan was to secure valuable minerals.[10] The Baird fortunes are particularly well documented.[11] The securing of adequate supplies of iron ore was always a high priority. By the 1840s it was clear that the industry had reached its maximum scale in the Monklands.[12] Even maintaining production would be a challenge as the local blackband reserves were worked out. The Airdrie field in Monklands faced rising costs as available seams became thinner and poorer in quality. Slamannan proved to be of limited value and it was pits in the Denny–Kilsyth area of Falkirk that supported Gartsherrie through the 1860s and 1870s. Before this, however, Bairds had decided that in order to increase output new works would be needed and this provoked a burst of interest in Ayrshire in the 1840s.[13] Independent companies found themselves taken over by the Monkland concerns: this happened at Glengarnock and Ardeer which Merry & Cuninghame (of Carnbroe) acquired in 1842 and 1854 respectively, and at Dalmellington which was taken over by the Coltness Company, but the Bairds provide the best example. After searching for minerals near Glengarnock the firm was approached by the Earl of Eglinton and eight furnaces were built on his estate near Kilwinning (Cuninghame) between 1846 and 1859. The Gartsherrie experience was repeated, thanks to ample capital and capable management, so the works acquired predominance in Ayrshire (whose resources were attractive given the building of the railways in the 1840s and exhaustion of the best reserves in the Monklands) and acquired a series of small independent companies that had failed to prosper: Blair (1852), Muirkirk and Lugar (1856), and Portland (1864). Interestingly Lugar had been promoted by the Clyde and Dundyvan companies but their venture was not profitable.

This meant that the giants of the iron industry around 1860 (when Scotland had about 160 furnaces) were Merry & Cuninghame with 25 furnaces divided between three locations and Bairds with 42 furnaces at six locations, of which Gartsherrie was the largest (although now with only one third of the company's total capacity of 300,000 tons). Their empire was vast and rested on the labour of some 9,000 people in the collieries, ironstone pits and furnaces. It was immensely profitable and allowed the family to acquire large estates. Expansion was not apparently an end in itself but a means to survival because until transport improved sufficiently to make the import of ore feasible the company reasoned that the best strategy lay in control of the largest possible blackband reserves. This took their operations into Ayrshire where distance was too great for efficient transfer of ore to Gartsherrie and hence furnaces had to be acquired. Some of the furnaces taken over had good ore supplies, as at Lugar which was fully rebuilt in 1864, but lacked the capital and skills which only the largest companies could provide, including their marketing arrangements and expertise in efficient furnace layout. Not all outside interests flourished in Ayrshire however. The prospect of the railway extension to Cumnock prompted English interests from Durham to found the Nithsdale Iron Company. Production started with the help of key workers brought from Consett and Shotley Bridge but costs were unacceptably high because the Dalmellington Company had leased the local minerals in a bid to forestall a rival concern. Reservations have also been expressed over adequacy of capital and commercial competence. A new company, New Cumnock Iron Company, representing backward integration by a foundry firm into iron making, was no more successful and the works was broken up in 1855. Nor did interventions in the east bring instant success: the Wilsons of Dundyvan were behind the Kinneil furnace in 1845 but it did not establish itself as a viable plant.

The problem of dwindling local ore supply

There was, therefore, an initial period of rapid and extremely profitable growth in the Monklands in the 1830s, as Scottish iron production rose to c.400,000 tons in 1844 compared with 40,000 in 1830. The tenfold increase in fourteen years compares with the half century needed to achieve the same increase from the output of 4,000 tons that was reached in 1780. And after 1844 there was again gradual progress, over the next two decades, which saw Ayrshire's resources more fully appreciated.[14] But the 1860s introduced new problems over ore supply at a time when North East England was providing very strong competition and only in the high demand years of the early 1870s did prosperity return, with peak production of 1.2 million tons. The large Scottish firms could adapt, although they were no longer major innovators, having been overtaken by their competitors in furnace size, blast temperature and utilisation of waste gases. As more ore was imported – haematite from Cumbria, but more importantly from Spain in the 1880s – plant rationalisation was needed.[15] The blackband ore and splint coal were too fragile to permit a high column of materials but failure to enlarge capacity is difficult to account for. Equally puzzling is the disregard for the contribution that chemists and other scientists could make to the prosperity of the industry. Gartsherrie was modernised and a by-product plant installed in the 1890s. Eglinton, which had been enlarged in 1862 through an alteration to the course of the

Garnock river, was also modernised, since it was conveniently placed for imports and for supplies of Paisley clayband ores that were exploited in the 1880s. Blair was sacrificed in 1871 in favour of concentration on Eglinton, and Portland was eliminated by contraction of the Cumnock ironstone field in the 1890s, though Lugar and Muirkirk had sufficient blackband to enable them to survive in the meantime. Coal was not a major problem for new leases could be acquired as necessary within acceptable distances of each works: expansion of mining took place in the Blantyre/Bothwell and Cumnock/Old Cumnock areas, sometimes on properties from which ironstone had previously been extracted.[16] Yet the decreasing dependence on domestic ore (down from 86.5 per cent of requirements in 1882 to 34.6 in 1900 and 18.5 in 1912) undermined the logic of scattered inland plant and after the closures of the 1920s Bairds were restricted once more to Gartsherrie and Glengarnock was the only works left in Ayrshire. Calder, Carnbroe, Coltness and Langloan were also closed by the end of the depression. Fate, however, decided that rationalisation in the face of increasing import-dependence would focus attention on the best-situated of the *inland* works. Few of the iron works built in the nineteenth century flourished in a coastal location that would have shown benefits under new iron ore supply conditions. Bridgeness and Kinneil in Lothian (like Garscube in Glasgow) failed to establish themselves while neither Ardeer nor Govan attracted investment at critical times sufficient to become the centre pieces of rationalisation programmes.[17] If the Scottish iron industry was fortunate in its mid-nineteenth-century development its subsequent restructuring has been fraught with difficulty because of a failure to accommodate realistically to prevailing trends.

Secondary trades: rolling and malleable iron production

Study of the secondary trades may appropriately begin with the Cramond works in Edinburgh which showed a formidable capacity for survival, refining domestic and imported iron for the production of nails and implements. It also has a history as a steel producer, being the first installation to make steel commercially in Scotland. The works eventually covered a series of four mills on the banks of the Almond, downstream of Cramond Bridge. The water power sites were first developed for milling corn and fulling cloth but the premises were taken over by the iron industry in the eighteenth century, beginning with Cockle Mill at the seaward end. Rolling and slitting was reported here around 1750, processing imported bar iron to supply rods to the nailers in both Fife and the Stirling area (Bannockburn and St Ninians). With almost five metres of water at high tide, coasting vessels could enter the small harbour beside the mill and lie up at low tide. Cockle Mill was taken over by the Carron Company and was vital to this organisation in its early years with 'every drop of water properly employed'.[18] The mill passed on to the Cadells in 1770 and it was under their management that the business expanded by taking in the upstream mills: Fairafar in 1770, Peggy's Mill in 1781 and Dowie's Mill in 1782. The range of goods produced at Cramond then increased to include hoops, spades and shovels. However, there was neither capital nor space to expand in the nineteenth century. By the middle decades the water-powered works were definitely old fashioned: water flowing with uneven force jolted machinery and broke gear wheels. But a horse railway was built as far as Fairafar by 1839 and a steam engine was operational in 1855. However, the Cadell connection ended in 1860 and all ironworking had definitely ceased by 1873. Plant was sold during the following decade. Cramond's closure marks the end of the first generation of factories which had been established in the eighteenth century and broken the grip previously exerted over the secondary trades by domestic craftsmen.

In the nineteenth century most of the works were in West-Central Scotland, reflecting demand, and inevitably when rising bar iron prices stimulated production in Scotland the secondary trades in the Glasgow area exerted an influence: Clyde shows the link most clearly but the Carron location was chosen with an eye on the Glasgow market, via the Forth–Clyde Canal. Other early furnaces were well located in relation to raw material (Glenbuck, Muirkirk, Omoa and Wilsontown) but marketing was a problem before the railway age. This tended to encourage the building of finishing works at the furnace sites. Wilsontown was rolling rods and bars by 1790 and became the first maker of plate iron in 1802. Muirkirk produced malleable iron in the 1790s though the works was planned as a supplier of bar iron to the malleable works at Cramond and Smithfield & Dalnottar.[19] Thus although the development of iron making was expressed in terms of backward linkage from the secondary trades, the raw material locations used by the furnaces eventually modified the geography of the finishing sector. The move into the interior was not conditioned solely by the attractive force of the iron works however: around 1800 the old steel and file works were transferred from the Molendinar Burn in the heart of Glasgow to the old forge at Calderbank and in 1826 there was backward linkage into iron making with the opening of a blast furnace nearby at Chapelhall. The process is one of relocation from a congested site in a city centre to another location that offered space, with adequate coal supply and transport services.

The link between pig iron and malleable iron production was somewhat tenuous. With excellent export opportunities for pig iron during the boom there was no great stimulus for vertical integration in firms that set themselves up initially as pig iron producers. Moreover the Welsh were more highly skilled in this branch of the trade and could work up Scottish pig and deliver it back to Glasgow at prices competitive with the local forges. There were several notable failures by ironmasters attempting to enter the malleable trade in the 1840s and R. H. Campbell suggests that 'these early failures had a much more lasting adverse effect on the Scottish economy than has generally been credited to them'.[20] The Bairds puddled iron only at their Muirkirk works, where the pig iron had a reputation for softness and malleability, though they had another stake in the trade (by marriage) through Coats Malleable Iron Works. However, the growth of engineering and shipbuilding provided a much greater demand for malleable iron and new firms sprang up to exploit the opportunities after 1850. There was little integration with the pig iron producers and the closest links were probably between the malleable iron producers and the engineers. Thus the Neilson family established the Mossend malleable iron plant and also acquired extensive interests in heavy engineering. Hence it might be anticipated that chosen locations would be less dispersed, yet without any massive concentration in the heart of Glasgow. In fact an intermediate situation obtained, with works on the eastern side of Glasgow (Blochairn, Parkhead, St Rollox), around Coatbridge (where several tool making firms were expanding), and, increasingly after 1870, in Motherwell and Wishaw. The Coatbridge–Glasgow axis is logical given the geography of pig iron production while Motherwell's belated prominence follows from its nodal position on the Caledonian Railway well placed to draw pig from north Lanarkshire and to deliver malleable iron to Glasgow shipyards.

Spread from Coatbridge may also have been encouraged by difficulty in finding suitable land and labour. The phenomenal growth of the Coatbridge iron industry, with some sixty furnaces at mid-century, required a great influx of people, many of them from outside Scotland. Curiously, however, the increasing use of Cleveland iron, which was brought in by sea to Grangemouth, did not stimulate any shift of malleable iron capacity to the coast although sites on the Clyde (Kilwinning and Saltcoats) and the Forth (Dunfermline) were considered. This inflexibility was to prove highly significant because 'the forges localised in the interior were to become the main stock on which steelmaking was grafted'.[21] Yet the logic of a tidewater location was not nearly as compelling a century ago as it is today and relatively small firms saw little merit in moving out of the area that provided their markets and their skills. Under the circumstances the emphasis on Motherwell presented a radical shift. At a time when Scottish firms were going in for bridge building and hence required extensive sites entrepreneurs raised their sights. David Colville opened a works at Clifton (Coatbridge) in 1861 but left his partner in 1870 and set up a new works at Dalzell near Motherwell in 1871–2.[22] There was no pig iron production in this locality apart from the Wishaw furnaces which represent backward linkage by the Glasgow Iron Company to supply their two malleable works (one of only four cases, with Calderbank, Govan, and Muirkirk, where this integration existed in 1872). A response to the flow of Cleveland iron can be seen in the casting section of the secondary trades with a clustering of foundries in the Falkirk area, on the Forth–Clyde Canal, and in the Maryhill district of Glasgow which was also in direct touch with Grange-mouth by canal. Links with the engineering industry were again close and this can be seen in the history of the Wilkinson Foundry established in Johnstone (Renfrew) in the 1820s. The foundry work developed into boiler making and the production of steam engines for factories and collieries, not to mention wood-working machinery in which an international reputation was eventually acquired.

Steel making and the prospects for integration

As described above, steel was first made commercially in Scotland at Cramond in the eighteenth century. Good quality Swedish and Russian bar iron was heated for some twelve days in a charcoal furnace and, to improve quality where necessary, the resulting blister steel was broken up, bound with faggots and alternately heated and hammered. These methods were still used in the 1790s, although it seems that Huntsman's crucible process was slowly accepted. Six firms were making crucible steel in the 1880s, about 1,500 tons per annum. Efforts were made to introduce the Bessemer converter in the 1850s: Dixon cleared away some of his puddling furnaces at Govan to make way for the new equipment but the phosphorous content of Scottish pig made it unsuitable and interest lapsed (apart from Atlas Works where collaboration with Bessemer was successful) as no firm came forward to produce pig from imported non-phosphoric ore.[23] However, in 1871 the initiative was taken to open Scotland's first open hearth steel-works. The Steel Company of Scotland was not based on pig iron interests but reflected a union of the engineering and chemical industries. Spanish ore could have been imported and processed at an integrated works on the Clyde coast (e.g. Ardrossan) but Scotland had large quantities of non-phosphoric iron residues, a waste deposit accumulated by the Tharsis Sulphur and Copper Company who refined iron pyrites, also obtained from Spain.[24] Charles Tennant of St Rollox, Henry Dubs of Glasgow Locomotive Works and Arrols, another engineering company, joined with Tharsis to establish a company that would use the residues in a direct conversion process involving Siemens–Martin rotary furnaces. The loca-tion on the Caledonian Railway at Hallside, Glasgow, was convenient for the interests represented. A location on the Ayrshire coast was seriously considered, bearing in mind the need for a large level site free of mineral working and with a good water supply and rail communication, but Hallside combined the necessary attributes with proximity to Tharsis.

Excellent puddled iron was made from a mixture of 'purple' and other ores by direct reduction but the costs were prohibitive and the method was abandoned. Instead steel manufacture depended on the use of haematite, pig iron and scrap. Further difficulty arose because the opening of the works coincided with depression in the rail trade. Production was geared increasingly to shipbuilding and a plate mill was laid down in 1876. Additional premises were opened at Blochairn in 1880. The company was purchased by the Clyde Shipbuilding Group in 1920 and passed to Colvilles in 1934.

Growth of Scottish steel companies was understandably slow until the open hearth system demonstrated its profitability in Scotland. Locally produced pig was unsuitable while marketing was complicated: Scottish malleable producers were not deeply involved in the rail trade while the shipbuilders' interest in steel was restrained until 1879 (when Hallside plate was used in the *Rotomahana*). However, Hallside's eventual success with ship plate brought other producers into the industry, notably Beardmore's at Parkhead (Glasgow) and the Glasgow Iron and Steel Company at Wishaw (Motherwell) in 1879. Mossend and Dalzell followed in 1880–1 and finally in 1884 two other malleable producers at Clydesdale and Milnwood installed open hearth plant. Some entirely new firms appeared in the open hearth steel industry: Clydebridge (opposite Clyde ironworks) in 1888, Flemington at Motherwell (Lanarkshire Steel) in 1890 and Calderbank in 1891. But no iron producer installed steel making plant except Glengarnock and Wishaw (and the latter originated as a malleable company). Curiously both these locations included Bessemer converters, though only on a temporary basis: they were added at Wishaw to supplement the open hearth furnaces of 1879, whereas at Glengarnock they represented the first investment in steel (1884) backed up with open hearths in 1887 because of the ban on the use of Bessemer steel in shipbuilding that was imposed by Lloyds in that year. Coatbridge, the boom town in the pig iron era, had no steel furnace at all until the small Northburn plant of the Scottish Iron and Steel Company opened during the First World War. Association with the Gartsherrie furnaces subsequently yielded an integrated unit, but with cold metal working.

The Scottish steel industry was tied up overwhelmingly with the production of acid steel for the shipyards, and this made Scotland a leading open hearth steel district. With the Gilchrist–Thomas process of 1878 the local pig could have been used for basic steel but was not in demand at home, while overseas the continental basic Bessemer boom made Scotland's competitive position extremely feeble. In 1913 the Scottish steel industry produced only 0.24 million tons of basic steel compared with 1.12 million tons of acid steel. So the industry depended heavily on non-phosphoric ore that was not available in Scotland. The need to import meant an additional cost that was partly offset by the use of scrap, which in turn indicated a preference for the open hearth furnace. But the most serious weakness was the lack of integration with iron production through hot metal working. There were possibilities at Clyde/Clydebridge (which faced each other across the river, although the companies were separate), Coltness (with steel making plant installed around 1900), Glengarnock and Wishaw. Yet there was no realisation until 1937. It should be added however that Glengarnock's melting shop used hot metal in 1919–20 but the practice was discontinued by the availability of low priced war scrap and not reintroduced.

Hindsight of course is a luxury that should not permit over-indulgence. It would have been feasible for Scottish iron and steel interests to follow the example of the Dowlais Iron Company and build an integrated works on the coast: ore would have been received more cheaply with the rail haul eliminated, and this saving would have been greater than the additional charge for coal. Furthermore, since the bulk of Scotland's pig was then being converted, hot metal working would have secured worthwhile economies. Yet against this was the fatal dichotomy of iron and steel business interests. The former struggled with obsolete plant and changed only slowly to acid haematite pig. The latter overcame high costs in the supply of haematite ore (some of it from England) by increasing dependence on scrap: Shotts was the first ironworks to make haematite pig regularly for the new steel industry in 1872 but Bairds followed suit in 1877 (Eglinton 1881), producing according to market demand. It could hardly be foreseen that increasing scrap costs would make this option less attractive after the war and that relatively rapid increases in the costs of furnace fuels would make hot metal working not simply attractive but a precondition of survival. Fuel problems inhibited decisive action at the turn of the century because splint coal, to which the furnaces and recovery plants were geared, was running out, while there was no assurance that the coking coal available in Central Scotland would give satisfactory results. It was only after the First World War that some ironworks successfully changed to exclusive use of coke and thereafter the new technology was diffused through the industry to remove the chief constraint that had hitherto inhibited building of large capacity blast furnaces. Finally there was the attraction of greater investment in coal mining. It seems that at the critical time ironmasters 'having weighed up the relative merits and potential profitability of moving forward into steel or intensifying their backward linkages with coal, chose the latter path'.[25] A greater commitment to steel making would have diverted funds from more profitable investment in coal mining and led to difficulty in competing with steel makers who melted pig purchased at the lowest possible market price. So there were good reasons why the heavy burden of the past resting on the Scottish iron and steel industry should only be properly recognised in the inter-war period.

10

Crofting in north Scotland

Crofting is closely associated with the Highlands in the popular mind and there are certainly some districts in the region where smallholdings are still a prominent element in the landscape. This should not obscure the reality of large farm dominance overall, as the nineteenth century generally witnessed a persistent diffusion of commercial farming. But in the Highlands the failure of the planned village movement to provide an effective solution to the problem of overpopulation led to the persistence of traditional agrarian structures until after the Napoleonic Wars, with only limited intrusions by sheep farmers. The compromise was a dynamic one, much affected by the generally upward trend in the profitability of sheep farming and the generally downward trend in the ability of small tenants to support themselves. Yet the economic factor, seeking the highest return from each piece of land, had to be balanced against small tenant perception of opportunity elsewhere, landlord interest in land reclamation by subsistence farmers, and the general estate interest in having a local labour supply available. Reliable information was sparse in remoter parts of the Highlands and Islands and this made the cohesive fabric of the local community all the stronger. Any adjustment would be painful with population growing fast in relation to commercial opportunities. Some security was provided by the retention of the gaelic aristocracy as landlords on the southern model (in contrast to the expulsion of native landowners in Ireland). But the elimination of tacksmen (middlemen in the traditional landholding system who had provided considerable support for dependants) and the appearance of new landlords, when traditional owners were rendered insolvent by the depression of the 1820s, created a new situation in which the small tenants were culturally isolated.

The nineteenth-century reminiscences of one gaelic speaking landowner, Osgood Mackenzie, provide valuable insights into the relevance of the cultural factor in Highland discontent.[1] Resentment of radical change was inevitable in dealing with a conservative peasantry but would arguably be all the stronger when there was no cultural contact between the parties. In Sutherland it is claimed that 'sullen apathy mixed with a malicious joy when failure occurred was an impenetrable barrier to development'.[2] Hence the reorganisation of land holdings in the Highlands generated a passionate idealism for the old order that is not evident in other parts of Scotland where society as a whole embraced a common culture. In essence the Highland solution was conventional, for the crofting townships in which many small tenants were accommodated corresponded to the villages elsewhere. But communal facilities were virtually non-existent, industry was limited to crafts and fishing and the agricultural holdings combined an arable strip with a share of a common grazing.[3] Some traditional practices like the use of summer shielings were eliminated by the reduction in the land available to small tenants: the system was preserved in the Hebrides but on the mainland most shielings were incorporated into sheep farms and while some sites were perpetuated through the building of shepherds' cottages the majority became simply a part of an extensive grazing over which sheep ranged instinctively according to weather conditions.[4] The Highland landscape was reorganised as thoroughly as elsewhere: some relict features persist, like the old field dykes in Morvern that lay beyond the limits of the enclosed arable and the clachan form at Achnaha where the traditional cluster in the depression within the eucrite dyke of Ardnamurchan is amenable to a constellation of holdings radiating out from a central point. But generally the landscape was remade as linear settlements with houses planted in individual crofts and aligned on the township road, replacing the run-rig layout. However, the pastoral system of farming in the Highlands, with very large sheep farms that embrace the territories of several former open field communities, provides opportunities for research on old settlements that are not available in the Lowlands where consolidated farmsteads appear to have been built on the joint farm sites. Old dyke systems can be traced at Drimnin in Morvern (Lochaber) (Figure 10.1) while extensive research has been done elsewhere by H. Fairhurst.[5]

The crofter may be regarded as the local equivalent of the settler in a planned village but his position was less secure through having no long lease (and certainly no feu) and little opportunity to set himself up in business. The crofters were always vulnerable because they could not make themselves indispensable to the landowners and large tenants. Their labour was required but not usually on a large scale or on a permanent basis. Educated opinion was inclined to be patronising, acknowledging, as did J. MacCulloch, 'the difficulty of moving men', which is 'plainly connected with ignorance; with a low degree of mental cultivation' yielding strong local attachment 'which knows not that there is as good a world beyond its own immediate home'.[6] It was envisaged therefore that crofting

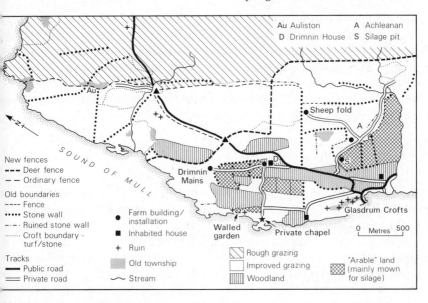

Au	Auliston
D	Drimnin House
A	Achleanan
S	Silage pit

New fences
– – Deer fence
– – Ordinary fence

Old boundaries
---- Fence
•••• Stone wall
–·–· Ruined stone wall
•••••• Croft boundary -
turf/stone

Tracks
▬▬ Public road
══ Private road

● Farm building/
installation
■ Inhabited house
＋ Ruin
▨ Old township
∼ Stream

Walled
garden

Private chapel

⬚ Rough grazing
□ Improved grazing
▥ Woodland

Sheep fold

Glasdrum Crofts

0   Metres   500

"Arable" land
(mainly mown
for silage)

Drimnin
Mains

SOUND OF MULL

Figure 10.1. Drimnin estate (Lochaber) 1978
Source: Fieldwork survey in 1978

would be a temporary phenomenon for 'no other circumstances than a crowded population and low value of labour can preserve the cultivation of such lands; and whenever . . . capital and labour shall seek for more legitimate and profitable employment in the breaking up of large tracts the occupation of the crofts as such must be abandoned'.[7] So unlike the planned villages which played a new part in the marketing system, crofting townships were not the first stage of a general improvement but the last improvement of an ancient system which could not be made perfect. They were an accommodation to people who could not participate in any viable commercial farming system but who might subsist with only minimal constraints on the efficiency of sheep farming. Of course no issue is clear cut and while MacCulloch's opponents were unrealistic in demanding capital investment to support small scale agriculture there was a possibility that fishing could become so profitable to landowners as to justify the allocation of a substantial area of land to smallholdings, as in Shetland.[8] But otherwise 'emigration is in every way preferable to this system of retaining the peasantry after they have lost their lands and confining them within bounds too narrow to afford them subsistence'.[9] Against a background of landlord ambivalence which shifted between tolerance, not altogether lacking in sympathy, and a hard-faced determination to evict in the interest of greater efficiency and reduced poor law liabilities, it is remarkable that the Highlanders have clung to their modest inheritance and stamped their culture on it to the point where it passes for the genuine article: the traditional celtic community. They have succeeded without the help of their natural leaders, for a new 'elite' was bred in the harsh climate of the mid nineteenth century, and gained the ear of government so effectively that ever since 1886 the crofting system has been a pillar of the regional development policy for the Highlands.[10]

The clearances in context

The story of the clearances has been told many times and the issues have been thoroughly debated. Even allowing for the values of the times it is difficult to deny that the implementation of the clearance programme was often outrageously brutal and insensitive. It is also hard to avoid the impression that clearance became fashionable as landowners sought High land estates without the embarrassment of a numerous tenantry that migh induce financial strain at times of scarcity and pollute what would otherwise be an exclusive private playground. Arguably the pendulum need not have swung so far. Yet there are imponderables. Too little is known of the adaptability of small tenants faced with limited schemes of reorganisation. M. I. Adam has argued that 'if the average Highland landowner seemed dubious of the advantages of the new methods and strangely unimpressed by the propaganda of the scientific agriculturalists of his day how much more was this the case with the tenants who possessed the same conservative temperament as the owner, quite unmodified by any contact with the non-Highland mind'.[11] Tacksmen were allegedly outraged that landlords should put up their holdings to the highest bidder and become land speculators. Yet J. S. Keltie was surely exaggerating when he claimed that 'for centuries previous to 1745 and indeed for long after agriculture appears to have remained at a standstill'.[12] How far may an innovating society in the Lowlands be contrasted with a fundamentally conserving society in the Highlands? It cannot be assumed that the Highlands were uniformly settled with small tenant communities on every farm. Evidence for Argyll farms in Morvern (Lochaber) in 1779 suggest that there were two categories of holding: small tenants' farms and tacksmen's farms, with the latter further divisible into farms with a modes population (more than ten persons per square mile) and others with a lighter settlement.[13] Only in the case of small tenants' farms would dramatic clearance be involved. Similarly in parts of Ardnamurchan and Sunart (Lochaber), especially in the Strontian valley, large commercia units for tacksmen were established.

At what time did these commercial units become established and what happened to the small tenants who were displaced? The implication would be that there was considerable reorganisation before the nineteenth-century clearances but that there was little conflict because local resettlement was allowed: thus in 1788 when MacLean of Drimnin's lease expired the Duke of Argyll decided to allocate the west coast of Morvern, from Auliston to Portabhata, to small tenants. The general effect of reorganisation was a displacement of small tenants from the glens to the lochsides, leaving interior grazings free for sheep farming while enabling small tenants to colonise raised beaches that provided an opportunity for subsistence farming while offering a base for kelping and fishing. The model may well have been introduced by the Annexed Estates Commissioners, for sheep appeared in Lochaber on the forfeited Lochiel estate in the 1760s. Some of the Camerons became skilled shepherds and may well have followed the progress of sheep into other parts of the Highlands. Reorganisation took place in 1777 (and subsequently, at twenty one year intervals in 1798 and 1819). Small tenants were removed from Loch Arkaigside and Glendessary, a policy which may have been partly aimed at the flushing out of cattle rievers and army deserters from remote parts of the property. Resettlement took place on crofts lotted out at Banavie and Corpach, accessible to both Loch Linnhe and the Caledonian Canal, then under construction. Radical schemes were also carried out in Sutherland, where the planned village solution was seriously implemented.[14] But there was a great deal of friction over development plans and 'within a few years the relationship between the planners and the people became permanently soured'.[15]

At the turn of the century the landowners were strongly opposed to emigration and resented the departures of prominent tacksmen and their dependants. Through the Highland Society government was pressed to legislate in 1803 for better conditions on the Atlantic passenger ships, a humanitarian measure but one contrived in order to increase fares and put emigration beyond the reach of the majority of tenants. But circumstances changed. The end of the Napoleonic Wars removed any stigma that might previously have made emigration appear unpatriotic and simultaneously depressed prices to the point where the Highland economy was threatened with collapse as a large population was thrown back on limited land resources. Emigration now appeared inevitable and those who had advocated the 1803 controls now pleaded successfully for their repeal in 1827. Tenants with resources of money and initiative had been leaving while the poorer people were left behind. But there was no immediate desire to take advantage and the Highlands remained overpopulated, excessively dependent on the potato crop. Tolerant of lime deficiency and responsive to manuring with seaweed the potato provided about four fifths of the food for small tenants in the early nineteenth century. It meant that more people could gain subsistence from a given area of land, yet it left them highly vulnerable to crop failure and gave each community only a small surplus with which to pay rents. A new compromise had to be drawn between farming and crofting interests and it meant an extension of the Lochiel model throughout the areas where the kelp industry had previously forestalled the need for drastic change. Thus the factor of Ardnamurchan reported in 1834 that the only remedy for the problem of overpopulation was the purging from the rent roll of all those tenants in arrears, accompanied by their emigration or their resettlement on less valuable holdings. Clearance of the Ben Hiant townships in the 1830s was thus contemporaneous with the lotting of holdings elsewhere in the 'West End' of the estate, while clearance from the Swordles was associated with the creation of holdings at Kilmory and in the new townships with good potential for sheep farming.[16] Morvern presented fewer opportunities for resettlement on marginal land but there was nevertheless a will to compromise until the famine of 1846. Achabeg, Knock and Kinlochaline were retained for small tenants on the Lochaline estate while the Bunavullin and Rhemore crofting settlements contrasted with the farms of Barr and Mungasdale organised on the Glenmorvern estate. At Drimnin, sheep farming was introduced to Achleanan and Drimnin though Patrick Sellar introduced more drastic measures when he acquired the estate of Acharn in 1838.[17]

The famine of 1846 brought a government response through a Central Board of Management which gave out meal in return for labour on public works such as the 'famine' roads. But the withdrawal of the Board in 1850 coupled with a statement in favour of emigration by the Board of Supervision (responsible for the poor) put landowners in a mood for further clearance. There were removals from Drimnin and Lochaline estates in Morvern and notorious clearances were implemented elsewhere, notably Knoydart. Over the years the reorganisation of land had restricted small tenants to very minor portions of the Highland estates. Their inability to survive in the economic climate of the time (with no consistent government policy of regional protection) provoked a final solution, with its grim realities of emigration under coercion and the burning of villages. Yet the process of Highland depopulation has been coloured too deeply by the occasional excesses and it is easy to overlook both the voluntary migration that took place and the large crofting population that remained. Local variations are enormous and historical narratives that follow the record of nineteenth-century crises can easily mislead with a picture of unremitting gloom.[18] The contrasts between Ardnamurchan and Morvern (Figure 10.2) (repeated further north in North Morar and Knoydart) could hardly be greater and it is to these variations, and the reasons for them, that historical geographers might devote more attention.[19] The physical bases for resettlement, as perceived by landowners and their agents, is

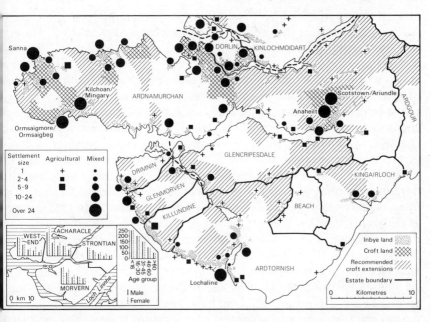

Figure 10.2. Landholdings and settlement in Ardnamurchan and Morvern (Lochaber) in the late nineteenth century. Inset: population in 1871

Sources: Ordnance Survey maps and fieldwork. Estate boundaries and croft extensions from: Royal Commission on the Highlands and Islands, *Report*, London, HMSO (1895) C 7681. Population data from Census of Scotland 1871

apparently crucial. But how far did the precarious financial situation of Highland properties demand radical change? And how far did prevailing fashion for Highland playgrounds, coupled with the opportunities for emigration, bring about a reappraisal of eighteenth-century values of 'sympathy'?

Government protection: the 1886 act

By a remarkable transformation the crofting system attracted extensive political activity and in 1886 privileges of security of tenure, 'fair' rents and compensation for improvements were won. Shortly after, the most over-populated districts were given relief through the provision of new holdings and the enlargement of some existing holdings and common grazings. The result of the land settlement policies extending through to the First World War and beyond was to restore to smallholders virtually all the lands from which they had previously been evicted in the Outer Hebrides. Other Congested Districts' benefited from the same policy while the act of 1919 applied to the whole of Scotland. This success may be related to action taken by the crofters themselves and this aspect is stressed by J. Hunter who has carefully examined the religious contribution to the emergence of the modern crofting community. The Free Church was in many ways a creation of the small tenants and there is close connection with the events of 1886 'for the Disruption and revivals which preceded it were largely instrumental in welding a disparate collection of small tenants into a community capable of acting collectively and possessing a distinctive character and outlook'.[20] H. J. Hanham, however, provides a complementary perspective through Scotland's readiness for a period of political and social reform. One consequence of this new climate was the development of a radical land movement in the Highlands. Crofters had occasionally been driven to defend their interests by force: in 1853 crofters at Coigach (Ross & Cromarty) clung desperately to what they held and their grim defiance of eviction attempts prompted some scrutiny of landlord policies.[21] Violence had not previously won concessions but the mid-Victorian social conscience was troubled by the plight of Highland smallholders, especially in view of the Irish precedent. The crofters' protest became more articulate and escalated dramatically in 1883. But success must be seen in the context of a series of reforms that occurred 'largely because there was within Scottish Liberalism a sufficient body of radically-minded men to turn vaguely-held aspirations into political programmes and to provide the leadership necessary to make out of isolated grievances a political movement'.[22]

It is also important to recognise that the case for regional protection reflected a consensus in British politics at the time, so that despite frequent changes of government there is a marked continuity of effort through to the First World War. Visitors to the Highlands were appalled by the plight of the crofters and wrote emotionally about hunger and despair, instancing 'the greatness of the misery in the Ross of Mull from which the people have flown as if from a plague . . . nowhere does death seem so great a blessing as we thought it must be here'.[23] Although the support to crofting was basically a political gesture it was economically rational in recognising that non-agricultural employment was too spasmodic and unstable to justify the same functional specialisation that was feasible in other parts of the country. One progressive landowner giving evidence to the Napier Commission pointed out that *permanent* industry was necessary if people were to be labourers and since this was not available it was desirable that people should have sufficient land to raise crops and rear cattle and sheep.[24] There is a strong social and cultural underpinning to the crofting community but this is conditioned by the economic realities which instil a reluctance to sever ties with the land, as Lord Leverhulme found when he tried to introduce a more efficient division of labour in Lewis after the First World

War. His programme was politically inept in not working with the system to create ancillary employment which, if permanently rooted, would gradually erode the smallholding ethos of Hebridean society. But sadly for the Highlands the crofting label has tended to beguile planners into regarding agricultural development as a worthy objective, overlooking the fact that agricultural efficiency cannot be reconciled with maintenance of the crofting population. The Congested Districts Board sought regional development in the context of a crofting system but their resources were very limited. The Highland and Islands Development Board are following the same course today and it is their pursuance of a broad harmonising with a crofting system with its powerful vested interests that makes their efforts particularly remarkable.

In view of the hardships suffered by the crofting population in the late nineteenth century it is curious that more interest was not taken in the fishing. It seems sadly ironic that a hard-pressed peasantry should leave a valuable resource open for exploitation by 'stranger boats' whose crews sailed from relatively prosperous areas. The situation is all the more anomalous in view of the coastal location of many crofting townships and the association between crofting and fishing in the minds of those proprietors who initiated the programme of resettlement. M. Gray has advanced a number of reasons for the failure of the indigenous Highland fishing industry to develop: 'the remoteness of the area from the main markets, the nature of the land system which kept the people trapped in a fatal mixture of occupations, lack of capital to allow even the beginnings of improvement, a tyrannical social system which removed from the ordinary man both the incentive and the means to improve, the lack of a merchant class, and the hidden traps in some of the evidently easy forms of fishing in the treacherous conditions of the area'.[25] But the late nineteenth century witnessed a determined government effort to stimulate the industry on the grounds of welfare for depressed areas and not simply national strategic and economic interests. At a time when the herring industry had good prospects, government assistance was involved in extending railways to the Highland coast at Kyle of Lochalsh (1897) and Mallaig (1901) so that a combination of rail and steamer services would place many outlying communities in close touch with markets in the south. There was also help for the construction of harbours and low interest loans (1886–91) helped fishermen to acquire larger boats. For 'fishing has become more and more a distinct trade, pursued not merely by local persons but by regular fishermen who follow the fish round the coasts'.[26]

A clear regional focus was provided in the 1890s by the Congested Districts Board. Yet adaptation to the new scale of fishing and the streamlined marketing system required a degree of adjustment that many loch fishermen could not accept. Yields from white fishing (by lines) were only occasionally high enough to polarise activity, as with the Badachro cod fishery at Gairloch (Ross & Cromarty), even before trawlers invaded the inshore banks, while herring fishing with government loans involved financial risks (for they were fully commercial transactions) that few smallholders had the resources to contemplate seriously. Use of obsolete, second-hand equipment would reduce risks yet perpetuate the inferiority of the local fishermen. Further difficulty arose through the necessity to centralise the fishing at places with satisfactory harbours and processing/marketing arrangements. But it is unnecessary to emphasise the need for fishermen to leave remote townships which had previously been satisfactory bases for small scale fishing, for seasonal migration to work was well established and many people found jobs as crew members on east coast boats (though a viable white fishing industry could have been maintained with greater willingness to range widely). It is also unnecessary to emphasise that fishermen used to operating in sheltered firths 'were less skilful sailors and less ready therefore, to follow the fish round the stormy coasts of Scotland'.[27] 'Shortage of capital was the most serious frustration' especially in herring fishing.[28] Economic forces meant an inevitable thinning of the ranks of owner fishermen and the Highlanders suffered disproportionately in this process. In 1914 when steam drifters were very active in the Minch only one was owned by a west coast crew.

Small farms in Grampian

Nineteenth-century crofting was not restricted to the Highlands. Small farms were to be found all over Scotland but the northern section of the Outer Regions was most distinctive when small farms are related to large units and demographic criteria are considered (Table 10.1). There are obvious reasons why small farms should exist: allotments may be granted to farm workers and people engaged in rural industry such as quarrying may desire a small farm to run as a spare-time occupation. Even though the smallest units were generally left outside the official agricultural statistics these explanations would account for many of the smallholdings included in the table. But the numbers of small farms in the Grampian region clearly require special discussion (Figure 10.3). It seems that the desire of landowners to consolidate farms and maximise efficiency was strengthened by the new poor law liabilities of the 1840s that made it appear necessary to remove families that might become a burden to the parish. Yet there was a large area of marginal land in the uplands that could be reclaimed by crofter tenants willing to accept the challenge. Advance to higher levels was frustrated by higher risks of failure but during the early nineteenth century climate appears to have been relatively favourable.[29] Even before the end of the eighteenth century it was not uncommon to find that 'by a

Table 10.1. Agricultural holdings 1871–1969

Region	1871[a]				1911				1939				1969			
	A.	B.	C.	D.	A.	B.	C.	D.	A.	B.	C.	D.	A.	B.	C.	D.
Islands	11.5	96.0	39.7	112.1	12.5	94.9	28.4	124.0	12.6	95.0	39.5	157.4	10.6	91.7	40.6	164.7
Highlands	16.4	85.6	44.3	57.2	17.8	86.6	40.6	68.8	16.9	85.9	33.8	75.4	12.2	81.3	29.0	52.7
Grampian	20.1	69.5	20.8	51.4	18.1	61.6	14.3	38.9	16.1	55.6	10.8	35.7	10.5	42.7	6.9	23.4
Tayside	8.3	61.5	30.5	22.3	7.1	51.8	19.3	17.3	6.4	48.4	14.7	16.1	4.3	38.8	11.8	10.4
North	56.3	78.4	32.9	48.8	55.5	75.8	26.6	44.9	52.0	74.1	25.7	45.0	37.6	68.6	24.1	32.5
Borders	2.7	51.5	24.4	23.2	2.7	48.0	13.9	23.2	2.7	46.2	14.2	25.1	2.3	42.7	7.8	23.4
Dumfries & Galloway	5.5	49.1	16.1	35.1	5.7	47.8	16.6	39.7	5.6	46.6	13.8	39.5	4.0	34.6	9.4	27.6
South	8.2	49.9	18.9	30.0	8.4	47.9	15.7	32.3	8.3	46.5	13.9	33.3	6.2	37.5	8.8	25.9
Outer Regions	64.4	74.8	31.1	45.2	63.9	72.2	25.2	42.7	60.3	70.3	24.1	42.9	43.9	64.2	22.0	31.3
Central Belt	16.4	49.7	n.a.	8.5	13.3	39.7	16.4	4.1	15.4	57.0	19.4	4.3	9.3	46.0	12.0	2.4
Scotland	80.8	69.7	n.a.	24.0	77.1	66.6	23.6	16.2	75.7	67.6	23.1	15.1	53.2	61.1	20.3	10.2

A. Number of holdings (thousands)
B. Percentage below 20 ha (50 acres)
C. Percentage below 2 ha (5 acres)
D. Number of holdings per thousand population
[a] Figures for Central Belt and Scotland are estimates

Source: Agricultural Returns and Census of Scotland (county base – Nairn with Grampian)

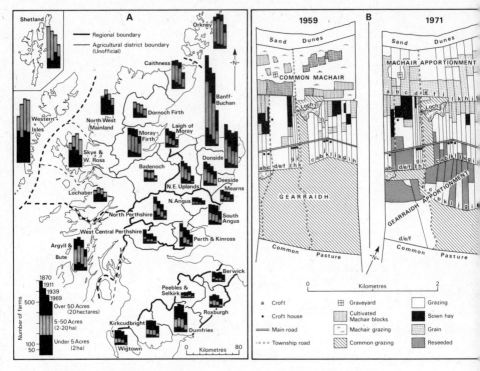

Figure 10.3. Smallholdings in the Outer Regions 1870–1971
A. Changes in the number of holdings 1870–1969
B. Change in the crofting township of Sollas (Western Isles)

Source: Agricultural returns and J.B. Caird, Changes in the Highlands of Scotland, *Geoforum,* **12** 5–36 (1972).

union of farms that lately took place many of the small tenants were obliged to retire to the waste grounds, a limited portion of which is assigned to them by the proprietors'.[30] This solution offered many small farmers an assured place in the community and it gave the landowner a means of improving his estate at minimal cost. Furthermore the large tenant farms were able to draw their labourers from the crofts and also enjoyed a local supply of store cattle, for fattening became a leading enterprise after the middle of the century.

This rationale was effective at the time of the improvements because where villages were not feasible a solution to the resettlement problem could be found in planting families on the edge of the waste land. Whereas previously land reclamation had been a communal activity, extending the infield into the outfield, there was a social division between a class of leading tenant farmers, who inherited the infield land and worked this ground to yield a large surplus to enter into commerce, and smallholders who accepted a less profitable role in rural society rather than migrate to an uncertain future in the towns. The differentiation of the agricultural population was clear by the middle of the nineteenth century and it persisted until the depression. J. R. Allan captures the spirit of the age magnificently when he writes how 'the momentum of improvement carried people to fantastic things. When all the likely land had been taken up young men were driven by a sort of land hunger beyond the reasonable limits of cultivation. For a long time men with no capital except their own strength had squatted on some rough moor, had cleared a few fields and built a house and steading'.[31] The seeds of decay were sown by falling cattle prices and lack of further potential for reclamation (given the prevailing price levels). Further amalgamation left the crofters with no scope for survival in the north, while the education act limited the tenant's control over his family's labour. Of course many small farms remained in 1914 where tenants accepted lower consumption levels but according to I. Carter the crofting system had lost its integrity.[32] The relations between large and small farms are clearly described in a recent study that shows Kincardine the only major area of Grampian where there was no physical basis for crofting (and little social pressure on account of the greater acceptability of migration in this most southerly part of the region). The bothy system (with labourers looking after themselves in a separate building) prevailed here and the men lived more independently than under the chaumer system of the crofting areas with 'kindly' relations (including farmhouse meals) and a stifling protocol.

In two respects, however, Carter's thesis is suspect. First he blames the failure of the Grampian crofters to enjoy the privileges of the 1886 act on their political error of joining the large tenants in a Scottish Farmers Alliance which could not be an effective instrument for projecting specifically crofter grievances, especially when the leadership of the organisation at both national and branch level was in the hands of large farmers. This situation reduces the strength of the argument about the class consciousness of the crofters, but more importantly overlooks the desire by government to use the smallholding as the basis of a regional protection policy only in those areas where a truly special case could be pleaded. There was some debate over the most desirable boundary for the crofting area that was to benefit from the privileges of the 1886 act, but there is insufficient evidence to suggest that with more political muscle the Grampian crofters would have shaken government from their resolve to restrict the act to counties visited by the Napier Commission. Although the eastern boundary of the 'Crofting Counties' did not reflect any clear contrast in rural wellbeing the initial requirement that certain criteria should be satisfied on a parish basis before the privileges would apply shows the government anxiety to avoid standing on a slippery slope where the limits could not be defended. Secondly, it is misleading to attribute the prominence of crofting in the Grampian region to an immaturity of capitalism. Certainly the crofting system represents a departure from the 'normal' arrangements of large farms worked by a labouring proletariat, but essentially because of the physical resources of the region and the perception of them by the various interests involved in rural development. Likewise the decline of crofting does not result from some conscious ideological effort to bring capitalism to maturity but from a new socio-economic climate in which the smallholding has lost much of its viability. The danger of Carter's Marxist framework is that the evolution of class relations is given credibility as a discrete force in the development process aside from the concrete socio-economic conditions that form the essential context. Crofting in the Grampian region flourished in the last century when there was a very large rural population and no alternative form of employment. It lost its viability with falling prices, coupled with a better education system and more efficient information flows which facilitated a transfer to the towns and also overseas where opportunities were now perceived to be manifestly superior to the croft with its falling living standards as the order of the day.

Scotland since 1914

11

General review

In the period since the First World War the importance of the cities has been reinforced through a rapid expansion of their tertiary functions combined with retention of an important stake in manufacturing, albeit with much diversification. The accessibility of cities has improved through a rapid growth in road transport offering a far more developed system than the railway network, which has been drastically reduced in consequence. This has meant the avoidance of a 'dual economy' type of development in which city growth is associated with increasing urban isolation and diminishing influence or contagion throughout the region. But it has, equally, not induced urban growth evenly throughout Scotland: disorderly urban sprawl would not be possible anyway given the relatively stringent planning controls that have evolved during the period but even in the context of government and local authority control of urban layouts it is evident that the growth areas are restricted, especially in the Outer Regions where the urban network remains poorly developed. Thriving industries require the full range of urban amenities such as may usually be found in the regional centres of Scotland, but spread away from these cities is difficult. For an industry can only flourish in the context of favourable environmental circumstances.[1] The spread of industry to the Outer Regions is socially necessary, in view of the reduction in employment in primary sectors which are no longer so labour intensive, but the recent improvements in terms of power and transport are not balanced by a satisfactory urban pattern.[2] Planning can encourage large units of settlement endowed with improved services but such projects are costly and encounter opposition from those who believe that development can be accomplished within a traditional framework.

In the Central Belt the infrastructure is generally more conducive to continuing development but the advantages have been reduced by serious deficiencies in the inherited fabric, especially in Glasgow, and by the decline of basic industries. There can hardly be any stable economic development policy in a rapidly changing world yet it is remarkable how the proud record of nineteenth-century industrial leadership has been followed up by frustration at the failure to find successful replacements in the present century. This is reflected politically not only in strong support (beyond the average for Britain as a whole) for the Labour Party and its philosophy of regional protection, but in the growth of support in the early 1970s for the Scottish National Party which stood for devolution and possibly complete independence.[3] The lack of any clear majority in favour of a Scottish parliament in the referendum of 1979 shows that Scots are not convinced that devolution is an effective remedy for economic problems. Although it would offer the possibility of greater originality in industrial development incentives with the oil revenues as a source of wealth there has been little progress in the suggestion of a development package significantly different from the one that has evolved through the British connection.[4] It is also significant that the SNP made little progress in gaining parliamentary seats in West-Central Scotland and most of its eleven seats in 1974 covered rural constituencies. Redevelopment has become an important task and the severity of the problem has meant that regional planning in Scotland has become quite sophisticated. Unfortunately even in the Central Belt the crucial importance of the city has been overlooked. A dogmatic policy of decentralisation has been implemented, linked with the notion of 750,000 as the desirable size for Glasgow. Overspill, both planned and voluntary, has brought the population towards this reduced level but migration has been selective in terms of both age and socio-economic status so that the city has been denuded of vitality in the interests of new towns whose future depends ultimately on the dynamism of the largest centres.[5] Edinburgh has succeeded in establishing a good relationship with Livingston new town but the failure to implement a positive decentralisation of Glasgow (in which the lack of regional administration until 1975 has been a factor) has crippled Scotland's first city and limited the region's prosperity. Overshadowing these difficulties is the peripheral position of Scotland in Britain so that the decline of export-orientated industries based on local raw materials has not been followed by light industry on a sufficient scale: the latter finds more profitable locations further south.[6]

Crisis in Scottish industry

Lack of confidence on the competitive position of Scottish industry was evident before the First World War as profits from the jute and iron industries were used for the export of capital rather than for reinvestment in Scottish industry. But it needed the 1930s depression to reveal major weaknesses in the economy. External assistance was provided through the

Special Areas (Development and Improvement) Act of 1934 and part of West-Central Scotland became one of four special areas in Britain. The designated area did not include Glasgow itself, where unemployment rates were not as high as in the blackspots of Clydebank and Wishaw, and regeneration was hindered by excluding the focal point of the community. But the scope was limited anyway by the fact that there was no provision for direct assistance to industry or for major public works projects. Much more important was the public sponsorship of industrial estates which was provided for in 1936: the following year the first such estate in Scotland was established at Hillington (Glasgow) and the Scottish Industrial Estates Corporation had three others open on the edge of the city by 1939.[7] Progress has continued through to the present and the Scottish Development Authority which took over responsibility from the SIEC in 1975 has properties throughout Scotland, including a growing number of advance factories which represent one of the post-war refinements in Scottish regional development policy (Table 11.1).[8] Another form of elaboration has been the physical expansion of the assisted areas. Under the Distribution of Industry Act of 1945 'development areas' were set up, roughly comparable with the special areas, although Dundee was included at the outset and a Highland development area round Inverness was added in 1949: although the incentives were not thought suitable for rural areas there was recognition of a special need in the Highlands and the Inverness area offered greatest potential.[9] It was significant that Scotland should see the first use of development area policies to stimulate a growth centre in a rural region (Figure 11.1). Further extensions were made up to 1971 by which time the whole of Scotland was being assisted in some way by government incentives. Edinburgh had only 'intermediate' status but growth areas recognised in a white paper in 1963 were boosted by recognition as development areas, while two of them (Glenrothes and Livingston) along with Glasgow and some coal mining areas were designated special development areas (allowing more generous factory rent concessions and settling-in benefits for migrant firms).[10] So the Scottish Office has become an effective force in regional planning with development area policy being used to harmonise with regional development objectives: the full weight of government incentives is thrown behind the redevelopment of the Central Belt. Policy evolved quickly through the 1960s after rising unemployment suggested the need for a thorough rebuilding of the industrial structure of the region. The Toothill Report outlined a consensus that induced changes in the Scottish Office.[11] The Scottish Development Department was formed in 1962 to embrace both economic and physical planning, and led to the production of a regional strategy in 1963.[12] Soon after, this perspective was broadened through the 'Scottish Plan'.[13] This held out the prospect of a second-stage programme

Table 11.1. Advance factory floorspace 1960–79[a]

Region	1960–7			1968–75			1976–9			1960–79[b]		
	A.	B.	C.	A.	B.	C.	A.	B.	C.	A.	B.	C.
Highlands & Islands	2	1.2	4.2	8	5.2	17.1	6	2.9	9.4	16	9.3	30.6
Grampian	6	8.0	18.2	7	4.7	10.7	9	4.5	10.3	22	17.2	39.3
Tayside	2	5.0	12.6	8	11.9	29.9	10	16.3	40.9	20	33.2	83.4
North	10	14.2	12.5	23	21.8	19.1	25	23.7	20.8	58	59.7	52.3
Borders	1	0.9	9.1	10	7.2	73.9	14	10.9	111.2	25	19.1	194.6
Dumfries & Galloway	4	5.9	40.7	7	8.4	58.7	12	9.9	69.0	23	24.2	169.2
South	5	6.8	27.6	17	15.6	64.6	26	20.8	85.8	48	43.3	178.9
Outer Regions	15	21.0	15.1	40	37.4	27.0	51	44.5	32.2	106	103.0	74.5
East-Central	14	36.2	28.4	5	9.2	6.9	18	17.4	13.1	37	62.8	47.0
(Fife)	10	23.9	74.5	2	3.7	11.3	11	10.0	30.6	23	37.7	115.3
West-Central	39	92.2	36.6	48	105.9	42.2	39	80.8	32.2	126	279.0	111.1
(Glasgow)	17	17.9	17.0	16	40.3	44.9	10	26.1	29.1	43	84.3	94.0
Central Belt	53	128.4	33.9	53	115.1	29.9	57	98.3	25.6	163	341.8	88.9
Scotland	68	149.4	28.8	93	152.5	29.2	108	142.8	27.3	269	444.8	85.1

A. Number of factories
B. Combined floorspace (thousand square metres)
C. Square metres of floorspace per thousand of the population
[a]Excludes all factories built with a specific tenant in mind at the outset
[b]Some discrepancies occur in the additions (horizontally) because of rounding and because of differences in base population figures used

Source: Scottish Development Agency and Highlands & Islands Development Board

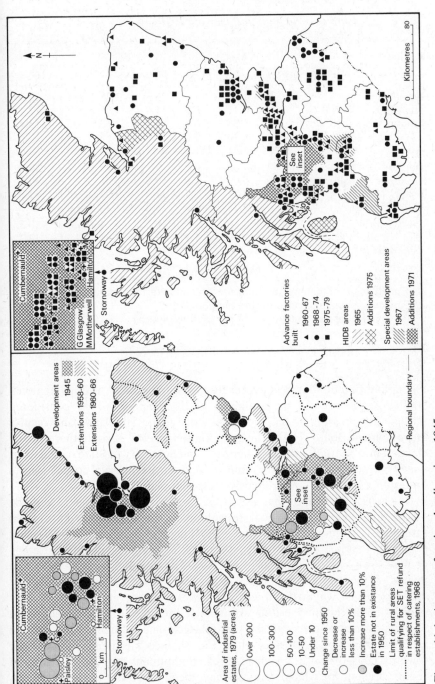

Figure 11.1. Aspects of regional policy since 1945

* *Source:* Scottish Development Department

Table 11.2. *Employment in manufacturing 1950–74*

Region[a]	1950–4			1955–9		
	A.	B.	C.	A.	B.	C.
Islands	1.15	1.6	26.5	1.25	5.7	24.7
Highlands	4.11	−0.3	14.8	4.05	−2.1	13.1
Grampian	32.55	0.8	13.7	33.83	−0.1	13.4
Tayside	50.70	1.2	12.3	54.85	−0.8	12.6
North	88.51	1.0	13.1	93.98	−0.5	13.1
Borders	14.38	0.8	9.1	14.93	*	10.4
Dumfries & Galloway	6.34	6.9	19.7	8.55	−2.2	14.7
South	20.73	2.7	12.3	23.47	−0.8	11.9
Outer Regions	109.23	1.3	13.0	117.45	−0.6	12.8
East-Central	134.10	1.0	11.2	140.74	−0.4	10.5
West-Central	415.59	1.1	13.3	438.65	−0.6	12.2
Central Belt	549.69	1.1	12.7	579.39	−0.5	11.8
Scotland	658.92	1.1	12.8	696.84	−0.6	11.9

A. Employment in manufacturing at the beginning of the period
B. Percentage annual change during the period
C. Percentage annual turnover (new jobs and job losses)
* less than 0.1
Source: Scottish Economic Bulletin No. 17 (1979) 14–32
[a]Official regions (with Argyll & Bute allocated to West-Central)

to exploit potential in the Outer Regions (identified through regional studies).[14] Meanwhile the situation in the Highlands was considered particularly pressing and a special authority (the Highlands and Islands Development Board (HIDB)) was appointed in 1965. It could therefore be claimed that Scotland, through her MPs and Secretary of State, could exert heavy political pressure at Westminster and attract financial concessions to underpin a uniquely comprehensive regional plan.[15]

But a new geography has not been evolved easily (Table 11.2). The nature and value of regional (development area) policies have been scrutinised, yet more fundamental is the danger of building a 'branch plant economy' that is subject to external control. The regional planning strategy of new town growth areas has been assessed over the location, size and layout of the various designated areas, but this overlooks the risks of excessive rundown in the towns and cities that are expected to export population. Although the 1963 white paper envisaged further development of new towns it also recognised that Glasgow needed help over road and rail modernisation and since then the balance has been shifted back towards Glasgow with a high level of commitment now to its industrial redevelopment for which resources have been taken out of the new town programme. But it will not be easy to find a new industrial role for

Table 11.2 (*cont.*)

1960–4			1965–9			1970–4		
A.	B.	C.	A.	B.	C.	A.	B.	C.
1.62	1.7	18.9	1.75	1.7	23.1	1.90	−0.5	23.4
3.61	6.9	21.1	4.85	2.6	22.6	5.47	18.9	33.2
33.68	1.0	13.2	35.39	2.2	16.2	39.22	−1.4	13.3
52.61	0.7	13.0	54.57	*	13.5	54.71	−2.6	13.0
91.52	1.1	13.5	96.57	1.0	15.1	101.30	−0.9	14.4
14.89	0.5	11.7	15.23	−0.3	12.2	115.04	−4.5	14.7
7.62	2.0	13.7	8.38	5.1	16.0	110.53	0.1	11.6
22.51	1.0	12.4	23.62	1.7	13.6	25.58	−2.6	13.4
114.03	1.1	13.3	120.19	1.1	14.8	126.88	−1.3	14.2
137.69	1.0	12.8	144.27	1.2	15.0	152.60	−0.7	13.4
425.92	−0.5	14.4	414.87	−0.5	14.4	404.42	−2.4	13.5
563.62	−0.2	14.0	559.14	*	14.6	557.02	−1.9	13.5
677.65	*	13.8	679.32	0.3	14.6	683.90	−1.8	13.6

Glasgow when the scale of shipping and of maritime industrial complexes has grown beyond the capacity of the upper Clyde. Ideally there should be promotion of industries that can thrive in inner-city locations in preference to diversion of enterprises that may survive more easily outside.[16] Proposals to enlarge the Scottish iron and steel industry by building a new complex at Hunterston (Cunninghame) on the Firth of Clyde gave rise to an 'Oceanspan' concept with the Scottish Council (Development and Industry) envisaging a series of manufacturing industries in the Central Belt between the Firth of Clyde, with its capacity for handling large ships conveying raw materials, and the Firth of Forth from which smaller consignments of processed goods could be sent on to Europe. But although expansion of port facilities in Europe would be costly because of need to obtain by dredging the deep water close inshore that was available naturally in the Clyde it was inconceivable (on the grounds of both politics and economics) that European governments would allow the Clyde to develop such an exalted role.[17] Moreover, no companies have yet decided to establish manufacturing capacity on the Oceanspan principle. But the potential of sites adjacent to deep water for maritime industrial development areas is real enough: it is reflected in concrete developments in the aluminium industry of Invergordon (Ross and Cromarty) and also in a number of large fabricating yards associated with the North Sea oil industry. Most of the latter are located in the north of Scotland. The upper Clyde is involved through the use of the former John Brown shipyard at Clydebank but most of the potential lies downriver where greater depths of

water are available for production platform building as at Ardyne Point
(Argyll and Bute).

Industrial decline has been very pronounced in heavy engineering
(especially locomotives and shipbuilding). It is hardly surprising that
construction of steam locomotives has fallen off with the introduction of
diesel and electric traction across the world and it must be equally
unremarkable that with other countries building modern shipyards the
limited capacities of the many units in Scottish industry should prove a
great weakness. The Glasgow area has been severely affected on both
counts with the collapse of locomotive works at Springburn and the
elimination of most of the Upper Clyde shipyards between Govan and
Clydebank: the miracle is rather that several units have survived. Yet the
distinctive forms of entrepreneurship and labour outlook which performed
the incredible feat of developing a shipbuilding complex of world fame in
the upper reaches of an artificially enlarged river have conspired in the
twentieth century to attract an equally incredible amount of government
assistance. Some of it has been geared to shipbuilding in Britain as a whole
but much of it has been tied specifically to the Upper Clyde, beginning with
state participation in the rescue of Fairfields and the formation of Upper
Clyde Shipbuilders. Thus the economically logical process of a shift
downriver to deeper water has been resisted for social reasons, although
the Lithgow yard at Port Glasgow has a much greater capacity, including a
graving dock for ship repairs. The full impact of changing scale can be seen
by comparing new construction at the Lithgow yard with the replica of
'*Comet*' built in 1962 and laid up in an adjacent park in Port Glasgow as a
memorial to Henry Bell and the Port Glasgow craftsmen: it forms an
evocative link with the past, complemented in a Greenock shopping centre
by Naomi Hunt's sculpture, unveiled in 1975, featuring 'Men of the Clyde'.
What is much harder to explain is the failure of Scottish industry to
diversify away from the basic industries of the nineteenth century to
achieve an indigenous growth of new industries comparable with other
regions of the UK. Both automobile and aircraft building seemed well
established in West-Central Scotland before the First World War and the
motor vehicle industry seemed particularly well placed for a major
expansion: William Beardmore & Co. produced private cars, taxis, buses
and commercial vehicles at works in Coatbridge and Paisley, as well as
their main premises in Parkhead (Glasgow). The Argyll Motor Company
expanded from Bridgeton in Glasgow to the Vale of Leven while the
Albion Motor Company were established at Yoker (Glasgow).

Yet in 1930 only Albion was still in production, with the emphasis on
commercial vehicles, and they continued as an independent producer until
absorbed by the Leyland Group in 1951. Equally in the aviation sector only
one firm stayed alive through the 1930s and the outcome was the Weir

helicopter of 1938. The failure of Beardmore's is most surprising since they withdrew from both motor vehicles and aircraft. They were concerned over the consequences of reduced government purchases and dispensed with those sections of their business that were not immediately profitable. Thus a policy of retrenchment brought a fall-back on basic industries when the new branches had reached a critical stage, requiring a large scale of development that would attract a range of component suppliers. The area was left with the new industries too small to stimulate firms in the engineering and metal trades to adjust their output. With the background of solid success in the staple industries, reinforced by the naval orders of the First World War which boosted the less strategically sensitive west coast locations, it was perhaps inevitable that diversification would be discouraged under conditions of depression. And so 'the upas tree of heavy engineering killed anything that sought to grow beneath its branches'.[18] Through government encouragement, motor vehicle industries returned to Scotland in 1961 (Bathgate, West Lothian) through the British Motor Corporation, now British Leyland, and in 1963 (Linwood, near Paisley) by Rootes, subsequently taken over by Crysler and again by Talbot. But although the latter development included an adjacent factory by Pressed Steel the small size of the Scottish industry has prevented the growth of component manufacture. And the closure of the Linwood plant in 1981 has further undermined the credibility of this once-promising initiative.

However, there is evidence to suggest that Scotland has achieved considerable success in diversification, considering the extent of its dependence on 'basic' industries, its peripheral location in the UK and the reluctance of organised labour to accept relatively low wages as a stimulant to outside companies. Powerful groupings have emerged in engineering (Bruce Peebles and Weir to mention two examples), and firms that have acquired international prestige can maintain their position with technical assistance from the National Engineering Laboratory at East Kilbride and from universities in Edinburgh and Glasgow which have developed close links with industry through various initiatives. Electronics proved to be a powerful growth industry, especially during the 1960s, and its origins can be traced back to the wartime activity of the Ferranti company producing gyroscopic gunsights. The company was strongly supported with defence contracts and after the war Sir John Toothill (as he became) was able to take advantage of the firm's healthy condition and a substantial element of autonomy for Ferranti's Scottish plant to diversify into electronics. With powerful emphasis on research and development Toothill created an environment that was favourable for the immigration of American electronics subsidiaries. He had close ties with the Scottish Council (Development and Industry) and was associated with an unofficial report which had considerable influence on government thinking when the white paper of

1963 was issued. Numerous major companies are now represented and in the area of computing alone the following may be cited: Burroughs at Cumbernauld, IBM at Greenock, NCR at Dundee and Univac at Livingston.[19] Labour has been found eminently adaptable and the assistance of the universities is again an asset, but this does not adequately compensate for the danger inherent in external control and a perpetuation of the branch economy. However, ownership by foreign companies does not occur solely in respect of new industries.

Trends in metallurgy, chemicals and distilling

Relocation can be seen dramatically in metallurgy. In the iron and steel sector the difficult circumstances surrounding the industry after the First World War – non-integrated works in traditional locations and exhaustion of local ores, with replacement by imports – suggested the building of new integrated plant in a tidewater location.[20] Several firms considered a joint scheme for the Houston (Renfrew) area of the lower Clyde (and other locations) but the initiative was undermined by the decision of one firm to relocate outside Scotland (Stewarts and Lloyds developed at Corby) and the other companies lacked the resources to contemplate any radical change. Meanwhile, use of increasing quantities of scrap provided some alternative to hot metal working which was continued only at Clyde–Clydebridge by the Second World War. New integrated plant was built after the war under the first period of nationalisation but the selection of a tidewater location was resisted on social grounds in favour of Motherwell where a site was developed at Ravenscraig adjacent to the existing Dalzell plant.[21] Gradually the older works closed down, continuing a trend established in the nineteenth century and maintained through the inter-war period. The result was an almost total annihilation of the former industry. Gartsherrie closed in 1967 and the site is now used as an inland port and freightliner terminal. Clyde–Clydebridge closed in 1978 and the site forms the Cambuslang Recovery Area which is being cleared for use by new industry in association with the Glasgow Eastern Area Renewal (GEAR) scheme. Closure of the steel furnaces at Dalzell brings to an end open hearth working in Scotland and means that the Basic Oxygen (BO) steelmaking vessels at Ravenscraig will be the 'kitchen' making steel for small specialised processing works like Dalzell, which is the main producer of heavy plates.

However, Ravenscraig itself had considerable finishing capacity, for the decision to divide the much-publicised strip mill investment between Scotland and Wales meant that the commissioning of the iron and steel works at Ravenscraig in 1957 was followed by a hot strip mill in 1964. The new investment of that period was, however, divided within Scotland and led to the redevelopment in 1959–61 of a rolling mill site at Gartcosh near Coatbridge (a site first used during the late nineteenth century by Smith & McLean but acquired by Colvilles in the inter-war period) for a cold reduction mill. The completion of rationalisation led to proposals for new capacity at Hunterston to handle imported iron ore that would be diverted from Glasgow's General Terminus Quay which was becoming too small to handle modern ore carriers. But once again the idea of a fundamental relocation was resisted and ore received at the new terminal (capable of handling ore carriers of 350,000 tons) will be transferred to Ravenscraig where a sinter plant, remodelled blast furnaces and expansion of BO steelmaking capacity from 1.5 to 3.2 million tons will make up for the capacities lost by closure. However, Hunterston is being equipped with direct reduction plant for the pelletisation of iron ore for the electric furnaces at Ravenscraig. Ultimately electric furnaces might be built at Hunterston for the 'Midrex' direct reduction process has been perfected in step with the concept of the electric furnace mini steel plant. It yields a metallised material of great purity which can be introduced into electric furnaces by continuous charging which improves the economics of steel-making. But for the present the new complex is essentially a service base for Ravenscraig and the decision not to operate the direct reduction plant on account of rising gas prices now makes the prospect of eventual steel production at Hunterston still more remote.

By contrast the aluminium reduction industry first expanded on the basis of hydro-electricity, with a three phase development at Fort William using power generated from water derived from Loch Treig (1929), Loch Laggan (1933) and the upper Spey (1943), but has since enlarged output through a grid supply to smelt imported alumina at a coastal site (Invergordon).[22] However, it is interesting to reflect on the first smelters in the Highlands as coastally located. Although bound closely to power stations based on water catchments· that extended deep into the interior they were nevertheless accessible by sea, even in the case of Foyers which was situated on the Caledonian Canal.[23] Since neither Foyers nor Kinlochleven enjoyed a direct rail service and since alumina came initially from Ireland (bauxite from the Antrim Plateau was processed at Larne) it was most efficient to base the transport primarily on water. Ships could reach the Greenock carbon factory and also entered the Mersey to discharge ingots (forwarded overland to the rolling plants in the English Midlands) and load up with locally-produced chemicals. The system was broken down progressively after the First World War as the Fort William plant was accessible to rail transport and a new factory at Burntisland, Fife (1917) supplied alumina by this means: Kinlochleven continued to receive alumina from Larne (now processing French bauxite) but the closure of this factory after the Second World War led to a switch of supply to Burntisland using rail transport to

Ballachulish, with transfer to road vehicles for the short journey on to the smelter, and to Fort William after the closure of the Ballachulish branch in 1966. Today Invergordon needs relatively generous harbour facilities since alumina is imported from the Caribbean and large ocean-going vessels must be accommodated; the handling of alumina is increased by the fact that Invergordon is a distribution point for Fort William and Kinlochleven factories (Burntisland is retained as a chemical plant). Nevertheless, although little used today both the older plants retain harbour installations which help to identify them as representatives of the first generation of coastally-located heavy industrial plants in Scotland.

Another plant whose coastal location has become less significant over the years is the oil refinery at Grangemouth.[24] Although the site continues to be highly satisfactory in terms of supply of developable land, enabling a substantial growth of downstream activities to be accommodated along-side, the limited capacity of the Upper Forth has meant that crude supplies have been switched to the Clyde estuary and crude oil has been piped across the Central Belt from the Finnart terminal on Loch Long since its opening in 1951. A second raw material supply has been provided by the development of the Forties Field in the North Sea by British Petroleum, who own the Grangemouth refinery. The pipeline runs overland from Cruden Bay (Banff and Buchan) and an extension to Dalmeny lower down the Forth with facilities for export of the crude that the refinery cannot handle points still more clearly to the importance of the deeper coastal waters. It is rather remarkable that the North Sea oil developments have not yet stimulated any new tidewater processing units but the present over-capacity in the world's oil refining industry has inhibited any new project. The plan for the Sullom Voe terminal in Shetland includes a refinery but the only serious possibility discussed in the late 1970s concerned Nigg on the Cromarty Firth where an oil-based petrochemical complex has been mooted.[25] However, the attractiveness of the Rotterdam spot market for small North Sea companies without refineries of their own has undermined the scheme. There remains a possibility of petrochemistry based on natural gas liquids derived from North Sea gases piped to the Buchan coast. But the first supplies to become available have been piped to Mossmorran (Fife) for conversion to ethylene (and possible downstream activities). Further deliveries may also be taken south, although at the time of writing there remains a possibility of gas being piped from Buchan to Cromarty Firth to allow the Nigg project to go ahead on the basis of this alternative raw material. However, for the present the traditional location pattern is continuing and, fortuitously, being strengthened by the Tayside textile industry making heavy use of polypropylene for fabrics and packaging material.[26]

The growth of the food and drink sector is underlined most emphatically by the continued buoyancy of the whisky trade, now characterised by a significant level of foreign ownership. Foreign-based blenders have extended backwards into distilling, following the lead of the Scottish blenders. The Canadian firm of Hiram Walker acquired their first Highland Malt Distillery in 1930 and now own five others, along with a complex at Dumbarton which includes Lowland Malt and grain whisky production. Control of blending and bottling plant completes the vertical integration and matches the structure of the American firm, Schenley Industries (who acquired Long John International in 1956), and British companies such as the family firm of Grants and the massive holdings of Distillers (with their subsidiary Scottish Malt Distillers). It is impossible to establish a completely self-sufficient whisky business since a very large number of different malts are combined in any blend and some buying and selling is inevitable. However, what is probably more significant for the future of Scotch is the ability to maintain its position in foreign markets (which account for more than four fifths of all sales) which is determined by taste and the ability of foreign companies to produce spirits of similar character. For the present this seems unlikely and the industry continues to lay down stocks well in excess in current demand on the assumption that this will be justified by the market when the maturation period ends (legal minimum of three years). Distilleries are being enlarged and new ones built. The Highland malts of Speyside continue to play a key role and most of the new developments have been in this area with the current emphasis on road transport making feasible some dispersal up tributary valleys like Glen Rinnes and Glenlivet (Moray) which were not favoured in the boom of the 1890s. Centralised malting has reduced the labour requirement at the distillery sites but some additional processing at the downstream end has come about through the production of animal feed from the draff and effluent: such dark grains plants are built on their own sites or adjacent to distilleries to serve a group of distilleries which form a geographical cluster or one united by company affiliation.

Agriculture and crofting

In the Outer Regions the primary industries are still of very great importance in the employment structure. In 1971 agriculture, forestry and fishing provided 13.4 per cent of all employment in Dumfries and Galloway, 9.2 per cent in Grampian and 9.0 in the Highlands (shares for manufacturing being 24.9, 28.6 and 14.3 respectively). Broadly speaking, traditional enterprise patterns brought out by C. P. Snodgrass in her farm classification of the Outer Regions are perpetuated as Figure 11.2 makes clear.[27] But there has been a considerable amount of geographical research, particularly on sheep, which provides valuable insights into the

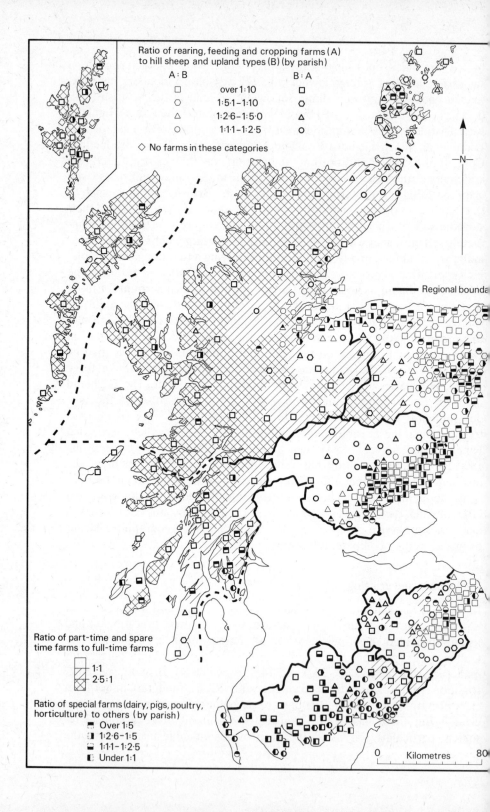

Ratio of rearing, feeding and cropping farms (A)
to hill sheep and upland types (B) (by parish)

	A : B	B : A
□	over 1:10	◻
○	1:5·1–1:10	○
△	1:2·6–1:5·0	△
◐	1:1·1–1:2·5	◑

◇ No farms in these categories

──── Regional bounda[ry]

N

Ratio of part-time and spare
time farms to full-time farms

1:1
2·5:1

Ratio of special farms (dairy, pigs, poultry,
horticulture) to others (by parish)
Over 1:5
1:2·6–1:5
1:1·1–1:2·5
Under 1:1

0   Kilometres   80

workings of the various farm systems.[28] And the enterprise patterns are quite dynamic as recent trends indicate.[29] But the most dramatic changes are perhaps in farm structure and the level of agricultural employment.[30] Amalgamation has brought about a rapid decrease in the number of holdings while mechanisation and some shift in emphasis from cropping to grass has led to labour shedding on an unprecedented scale.[31] The area of crops and grass has been reduced over the last century and this indicates a withdrawal from marginal land where cultivation was only justified in the context of relatively high prices and low rewards for labour. On the eastern side of the main Highlands watershed, slopes are relatively gentle and there is no clear boundary between potentially improvable land and irredeemable moorland: it has been noted that 'there is a marked tendency towards the head of each strath for arable land to fade out into permanent pasture enclosures and these in their turn, at a slightly greater height, into reverted rough pasture with abandoned holdings and ruined farmsteads'.[32] However, the extent of the deterioration is partly a function of accessibility: while the principal lines of communication are marked by the development of tourism and other ancillary industries which have helped to retain a high level of agricultural activity, the side valleys and 'annexes' have been left to dwindle with emigration and withdrawals of local services reacting in the downward spiral which brings excessive farm amalgamation and transfer of land to forestry. There have been calls for greater emphasis on the reclamation of 'debatable land' including substantial areas in the Central Belt.[33] It is clear that, in the context of grass growing, areas of good soil at high altitudes would not be so vulnerable to low yields as they were under cropping regimes at the time of their abandonment.[34] During the Second World War a better use of land was encouraged by the Marginal Agricultural Production Scheme (which allowed for government provision of up to half the cost of approval schemes of development) while the subsidy schemes for hill cattle and sheep increased productivity of hill grazings and released low ground for cropping (Figure 11.3). Help has continued in slightly varying forms since the war and presently harmonises with EEC policies. While this assistance has not prevented a net decrease in the area of crops and grass since 1870 it is hard to deny that without help the retreat from the marginal land would have been greater. Professional advice has been helpful in spreading the results of research such as that carried out by the Hill Farm Research Organisation: surface treatment with lime and phosphate can be a relatively cheap way of increasing grass for grazing or silage and inexpensive forms of drainage on soils of low permeability have been found.[35] Progress is inevitably piecemeal since

---

Figure 11.2. Farm classification for the Outer Regions 1969
Source: Department of Agriculture & Fisheries for Scotland

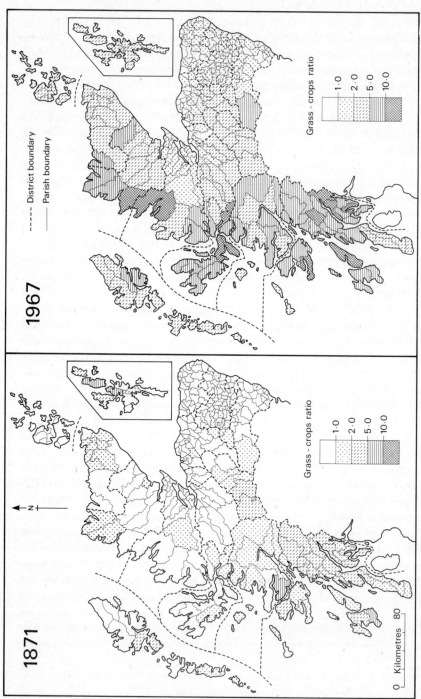

Figure 11.3. Arable land in the Grampian and Highland regions 1871 and 1967

potential sites vary in accessibility and farmers vary in their attitude to intensification. Yet in areas where there is a strong social argument for maintaining a strong farming community particular efforts have been made to provide incentives not only for reclamation but for breeding, fattening and marketing as well.[36]

As already noted a very striking anomaly in the farm size table (Table 10.1) is the importance of smallholdings or crofts in the Highlands and Islands.[37] It is significant that these holdings continue to enjoy a distinct legal status (first granted in 1886) which provides effective security of tenure, though there can be no certainty that holdings will continue to attract tenants and the legal safeguards against arbitrary eviction and excessive rent increases can only be a precondition for a stable community.[38] The critical factor is the acceptability of a small farm where it is very difficult to gain an adequate income without the support of ancillary employment.[39] It seems clear from surveys which have been made in recent years that crofts are highly valued where other work is available. This is hardly surprising since the crofter is strongly encouraged to maintain a high level of agricultural activity and tourism can yield a useful income, but the issues are not all simply economic: in the islands especially, where virtually the whole community is croft-based, the smallholding is fundamental to society as well as economy. It is therefore eminently logical that any strategy for regional development should build up from the croft and accept its stabilising role in maintaining communities in areas where non-agricultural employment has not always been readily available. However, 'the crofting constraint on migration is not a simple check on outward movement; it is rather the balancing of outward movement at one period in time by inward movement at another': for many people entering crofts are approaching middle age and are valuable members of the community because of the experience they have of the wider world.[40] In other words the croft is an important stimulus to return migration as people who left home in their youth return to inherit the family smallholding. This can create difficulty because 'some of those who return late in life are obsessed by their recollections of the township as it was in their youth and are resolutely opposed to change'.[41] In practice it is very difficult to combine the social function of the croft system with maximum agricultural efficiency. The social life may be strengthened by a strong communal element in agriculture (such as the use of common grazing) and a large number of tenancies, including new holdings created by sub-division. Yet agricultural efficiency is best served by larger holdings and the removal of community restraints on the decision-making of the individual (Figure 10.3B). The dilemma is evident in official surveys conducted over the last hundred years and in the policies of the Crofters Commission which have sought to encourage the individual crofter without damaging the community.[42] A balance must be struck because while excessive emphasis on agricultural progress (through amalgamation) would destroy the community, neglect of agriculture would so depress incomes as to induce a steady decline in activity that would be equally debilitating in terms of the crofting population. So agricultural development can present a mirage, offering the prospect of higher incomes yet not to the point where agriculture can provide full-time employment.[43]

Crofters exerted strong political pressure after the First World War for a further increase in the amount of land available to smallholders and farms were acquired for land settlement, both in the Highlands and elsewhere (though the privileges of croft status were not available for the latter).[44] But such action could only be a political gesture since there was insufficient non-croft land in the main areas of demand to provide worthwhile holdings for all applicants. In Lewis the extension of crofting was opposed in the early 1920s by Lord Leverhulme who aimed at progress through provision of non-agricultural employment on a scale that would render crofts irrelevant. His argument was theoretically sound yet the failure to maintain investment vindicated the crofters' instinct to make full use of government sympathy to gain a more secure base in the land. Associated with land settlement on farm land is the call for reclamation of rough grazings to increase carrying capacity: there was great scope on the peat lands of Lewis if economic methods of reclamation could be found. In Leverhulme's time the ecologist, Patrick Geddes, argued that the significance of the land was being overlooked: the proposal that a survey should be made by a botanist, Dr M. E. Hardy, whom Geddes knew personally, was accepted and the work was eventually published as part of a major study of Lewis and Harris by Arthur Geddes (son of the planner Patrick Geddes) who had assisted Hardy in his work.[45] Reclamation of peat, it was argued, should be linked with division of farms and an expansion of fishing: on slopes with good drainage, where peat was already thinned by cutting, dressing with sand might make for a big improvement. Pilot schemes were started at Arnish and Tong and the former scheme recommenced after Leverhulme's withdrawal (1923) with funds provided by T. B. Macaulay. By 1938 it was shown that while reclamation to provide arable land was too expensive, lasting improvement could be made on moorland grazings with favourable slope at reasonable cost, thereby permitting a higher level of stocking. Since the Second World War much progress has been made by communal activity in dumping shell sand from the beaches on the common grazings. The addition of phosphate and seeding with clover and rye grass has completed the transformation and the lower slopes of the moor have regained their former greenness.[46]

However, the Lewis experience demonstrates that land reclamation cannot be a panacea: local possibilities must be explored in the light of available technology, likely returns and availability of subsidies.[47] Dams across marine embayments appear too expensive: A. G. Ogilvie's plea for reclamation on the Beauly and Cromarty firths has not been heeded while a small scheme for Vallay Strand in Uist (Western Isles), in connection with a bulb growing enterprise encouraged by the HIDB, was shown to be not feasible. Further difficulties arise in persuading crofters, and farmers, to cooperate in projects that are viable: schemes for comprehensive development to make full use of land resources (including the benefits of integration with forestry) in the interests of crofters, and other sections of the community, have foundered over lack of support.[48] It is interesting to note that in the Highlands, where the land is still regarded as a major element in economic and social development, there are continual pressures to modify the usual conventions of landholding.[49] The nineteenth century witnessed a conflict over the landowners' rights to evict smallholders and now the HIDB is seeking a procedure that will allow an element of compulsion to ensure the proper use of land. The notion of a special case in the Highlands, with its roots in the eighteenth century schemes for industrial development to be stimulated by improved communications and removal of burdensome duties on coal and salt, thus continues to express itself in novel forms.[50] It is perhaps paradoxical that with the continuing growth of manufacturing and services the fortunes of the crofter and other occupiers of rural land should come under closer scrutiny. But arguably this is not anomalous – it is an indication of the maturity of regional development policies in using expertise to seek out potential wherever it may lie.[51]

Land use in the twentieth century must continue to make allowance for forestry (discussed in a later study), tourism and recreation. The deer forests, grouse moors, salmon rivers and trout streams still attract wealthy sportsmen but much more important is provision for a generally more affluent and mobile population that seeks access to open space in the immediate vicinity of urban areas, and further afield in places that are considered attractive enough to justify the cost and effort of making a longer journey.[52] But country areas are not the only beneficiaries of tourism: the cities which generate demand for recreation facilities in rural areas are simultaneously among the most attractive tourist centres. Thus Edinburgh and Glasgow have not only the most tourist accommodation in the Central Belt but are also the leading resorts in Scotland as a whole. Even this industry, which is influenced by attractive scenery such as the Grampians and historic sites such as Iona (Argyll and Bute), is heavily conditioned by the organising power of the cities with their relative ease of access, choice of accommodation, range of entertainment and intrinsic charm through historic monuments and associations. Spread of tourism to remoter areas has become an important element in regional development but it encounters a dilemma: the more adventurous or discriminating visitor will explore in depth beyond the major tourist routes but such enterprise, even with the encouragement of information services, improvements in accommodation and transport, will hardly allow tourism to become more than a modest ancillary. On the other hand, the promotion of a large tourist complex like Aviemore Centre (Badenoch and Strathspey) and related developments in the Cairngorms threatens to undermine the scenic resources on which its success depends.[53] And justified fears about the adverse ecological consequences of heavy tourist pressure on sensitive environments have helped to strengthen interest in the protection of scenic areas – and indeed preservation of certain remote districts from all forms of 'development'.[54]

At the beginning of the period the main concern tended to be over access to remote areas and this meant better public transport, including new roads (like the Glen Feshie road to link the Dee and Spey, which was advocated unsuccessfully by the Cairngorm Club in 1925) but also more secure rights of access to private land, exemplified by the long campaign waged by Aberdonian James Bryce up to his death in 1922 for free access to mountains and moorlands. But the growth of tourism in many remote rural areas has given rise to a conflict between conservation and development.[55] There are many cases of enlightened development, such as the careful management of Glencoe (Lochaber) by the National Trust for Scotland (formed in 1931). And although a national park system has not materialised (partly because it might inhibit a wider dispersal of tourism and simultaneously constrain, within the designated areas, the development of roads and hydro-electric power stations on which the future of the indigenous communities depends) a Countryside Commission for Scotland has been appointed (1967) to deal with landscape conservation and recreation provision throughout the region.[56] Nevertheless, wilderness concepts have been employed widely in the last decade, with international stimulus through European Conservation Year (1970) and the ecological work of F. Fraser Darling, expressed through his Reith lectures on 'Wilderness and Plenty'. The question of tourist development remains highly sensitive and hardly any developer in the remoter rural areas will find himself immune from controversy. Certainly a project like the Glen Feshie road would be unthinkable in the present climate. The notion that certain areas (not necessarily those with most attractive scenery) should not be developed in any way is not inherently unreasonable, although idealism should not blind itself to the fact that wilderness in Scotland is rarely natural, being generally a product of depopulation, and that explicit designation of such areas, even if it were possible to secure wide approval for an appropriate management system, would attract interest and undermine the basic objective.

Fishing

Despite recent contraction the fishing industry continues to flourish, especially in the northern Outer Regions of Scotland (Table 11.3). Deep sea trawling has been hit very hard by recent extensions to territorial waters and the decline at Aberdeen and Granton (Edinburgh) has been severe. However, the inshore sector has been able to derive some benefit from similar protective measures in the UK although the situation remains confused due to failure, at the time of writing, to reach agreement over an acceptable EEC fisheries policy and because of extreme shortages of herring which have called for the most drastic conservation measures. Herring fishing was already contracting after the First World War because of the loss of foreign markets for cured fish, while reorientation towards the home market was complicated by the depression.[57] The Herring Industry Board (HIB) was formed in 1935 to regulate this branch of fishing and provide grants and loans for the building and conversion of boats: subsidies and guaranteed prices helped to maintain interest although many fishermen preferred to change to the more profitable white fishing. However, in the context of supply of fresh herring to the home market a seasonally fluctuating output leads to problems of surpluses and although profitable outlets may be found in canning, curing and 'klondyking', sale to fish meal factories at relatively low prices was unavoidable (Table 11.4). Through much of the post-war period the HIB has been concerned with the optimum distribution of fish meal factories but progress has been upset first by competition from Peruvian fish meal and, more recently, after adjustment through introduction of industrial fishing techniques (mid-water trawl and purse seine systems), through a catastrophic fall in the catch, which is now regulated by conservation measures.

The modern white fishery was made possible by the introduction of the seine net, a Danish invention first tried at Lossiemouth in 1921.[58] It was suitable for bottom fish but because the tackle was not dragged along the sea bed the boat did not have to be as powerful as the steam trawler: indeed small motor boats proved eminently satisfactory. Although regarded as 'inshore' boats the seine netters may fish up to 40 km from the coast and because of opposition (on the grounds that spawning grounds were being spoiled) from line fishermen working close to the shore seiners were generally obliged to fish beyond a three mile limit. Thus the seine net led to an increase in the scale of local white fishing and induced a similar concentration on the principal harbours (such as Lossiemouth and Peterhead) as was already applying to herring fishing. Small villages may however still retain a strong stake in the fishing even though their harbour can no longer accommodate the fleet: the Gardenstown men continue a tradition of resourcefulness and persistence although their boats are now

Table 11.3. *Fisheries 1938–78*

Region	1938			1963				1978						
	A.	B.	C.	A.	B.	C.	C1.	A.	A1.	A2.	B.	C.	C1.	C2.
Islands	1,448	3,434	48.1	1,046	1,875	18.2	1.4	738	143	6	1,593	66.1	3.3	45.7
Orkney	373	514	2.7	297	439	0.4	0.4	201	21	.	366	1.1	1.0	*
Shetland	295	638	32.2	314	736	12.6	0.4	211	59	4	660	46.4	0.6	43.6
Western Isles	780	2,282	13.3	435	700	5.2	0.6	326	63	2	567	18.6	1.6	2.0
Highlands	1,324	2,753	22.0	494	1,381	65.5	2.7	661	157	.	1,622	145.9	11.3	18.6
Grampian	1,551	8,428	143.5	933	5,349	163.3	2.5	753	493	77	4,317	168.7	4.6	142.8
Tayside	84	283	3.0	67	236	4.0	0.4	69	25	.	191	3.7	0.3	3.4
North	4,407	14,898	216.5	2,540	8,841	251.0	6.9	2,221	818	83	7,723	384.5	19.4	210.4
Borders	72	366	3.1	52	195	3.6	0.5	61	26	.	277	7.4	1.0	6.5
Dumfries & Galloway	140	149	0.5	32	60	1.3	0.3	39	10	2	103	3.1	2.7	0.4
South	212	515	3.6	84	255	4.9	0.8	100	36	2	380	10.5	3.6	6.9
Outer Regions	4,619	15,413	220.1	2,624	9,096	255.9	7.8	2,321	854	85	8,103	395.0	23.0	217.3
Central Belt	566	2,512	54.6	357	1,431	50.5	2.5	295	161	6	1,188	33.6	3.7	16.4
Scotland	5,185	17,925	274.7	2,981	10,527	306.4	10.3	2,616	1,015	91	9,291	428.6	26.8	233.7

A. Total number of fishing boats
A1. Boats between 12.2 m (40 ft) and 24.3 m (80 ft) in length
A2. Boats over 24.3 m (80 ft) in length
B. Total number of fishermen
C. Total landings (thousand metric tons)
C1. Landings of shell fish
C2. Landings of demersel fish (the difference between C and C1/C2 combined is made up of herring and other pelagic fish)

Source: Scottish Sea Fisheries Statistical Tables

Table 11.4. *Herring fishing 1948–78*

Period	Landings (thousand mt)	Offtakes (percentage distribution)						
		A.	B.	C.	D.	E.	F.	G.
1948–53	621.9	28.8	0.2	6.2	113.0	20.0	1.9	31.7
1954–8	520.8	21.9	0.5	7.6	10.2	13.3	12.4	34.0
1959–63	428.4	33.7	3.8	8.8	7.9	19.6	14.8	11.5
1964–8	438.6	51.0	4.1	6.5	3.1	6.1	13.1	16.0
1969–73	658.2	48.0	1.7	5.5	1.7	22.4	5.5	15.2
1974–8	353.1	77.6	0.6	0.5	1.0	13.6	2.2	4.4
1948–78	3,021.2	41.4	1.7	6.0	6.5	16.5	5.7	20.2

A. Fresh (includes quick-freezing and kippering)
B. Marinating
C. Canning
D. Curing
E. Klondyking
F. Pet Food
G. Oil & Meal
Sources: Department of Agriculture and Fisheries for Scotland Annual Reports on Scottish Fisheries and Scottish Sea Fisheries Statistical Tables.

based in Fraserburgh (and may work out of more distant ports according to seasonal trends).[59] The traditional small line fishing is much reduced but crofter–fishermen in the Highlands continue to employ this method while, on a larger scale, the women at Gourdon (Kincardine and Deeside) still bait the lines that enable the local fleet to catch prime flat fish. But whereas Scotland's 437 seine netters accounted for 39.0 per cent of white fish landings in 1973, 423 boats using lines or other non-trawl methods scored only 2.3 per cent: many of the latter were small boats fishing only intermittently. There has been a spectacular growth of shell fishing to meet a strong foreign demand and this has helped to disperse the fishing industry, especially in the Highlands where special incentives have been offered. Whereas significant landings of demersal or pelagic fish were restricted to 51 ports in 1973 (41 of them in the Outer Regions) shell fish landings were made additionally at 110 ports (98 in the Outer Regions). However, the future for sea fishing is not good although a new branch of industrial fishing based at Breasclete (Western Isles) offers some compensation for decline elsewhere. Fish farming is being taken very seriously, especially in the Highlands where there is plenty of water and considerable encouragement from the HIDB's financial incentives and the Oban Marine Laboratory's technical expertise.

Transport and power

Modernisation of transport is an inevitable and continuing process in any advanced economy. Change is very clear in the port rationalisation of the

Central Belt, including the naval installations.[60] Proposals for unification were made before the First World War but no progress was possible. During the Second World War the benefits of unified control were demonstrated by the activities of a regional port director appointed by the Admiralty. However, this did not prove a permanent arrangement and not even the need for cooperation to construct a large new dry dock on land between Greenock and Port Glasgow could create a unified harbour authority. A separate company was formed for the dry dock scheme. At the same time, in the 1960s John Brown & Co. envisaged a massive extension of their Clydebank yard including three huge dry docks for shipbuilding and repairs, using the existing channel of the Clyde. This plan was not realised and by the time the dock was ready (1964) the need for harbour reorganisation was being clearly spelt out by government (following the Rochdale Report). Important initiatives could be taken by a new Clyde authority in line with the growth of containerisation (and corresponding decline in general cargo) and the increase in the size of bulk carriers. The Greenock container terminal opened in 1969 while recommendations for bulk cargo handling at Ardmore or Hunterston led to development of the latter as an iron ore terminal opened in 1979. On the other hand several docks on the Upper Clyde have closed and considerable areas lie derelict despite some laying out of gardens in Glasgow between Custom House and Stobcross. Meanwhile the former naval base south of Ayr has been converted into Heads of Ayr holiday camp.

Turning to other modes of transport it is necessary to consider the record of rail closures balanced by the improvement of roads (including motorway construction) and the introduction of air services. The latter have an important inter-regional function but the insularity of Scotland's northern and western periphery and the great distances separating the main centres of population in the northern mainland gives air services an unusually high local importance. The efficiency of land and sea transport is not so limited as to require services on the 'flying doctor' model but inter-island flights in Orkney, Shetland and the Western Isles are now well-established and the infrastructure, which includes a considerable number of airstrips without regular landings, can certainly be used for emergency medical cases. At Stornoway, for example, an airport was developed on the former golf course of Melbost: an intermittent service to Inverness began in 1934, and the following year a route to Glasgow (Renfrew) was started. Flights to both Glasgow (now Abbotsinch) and Inverness continue today, along with local services to Benbecula (using a wartime RAF station at Balivanich) and Barra where aircraft land on the beach at Northbay. Long before this the remoter parts of Scotland in general were benefiting from motor bus services. For international traffic most interest attaches to Prestwick near Ayr (Kyle and Carrick), a major trans-Atlantic airport retained for civil use because of freedom from fog. A new terminal building was opened there in 1964.

The lack of any comprehensive rail system encouraged the railway companies at the beginning of the century to take advantage of new technology and introduce road services to complement their trains. The Great North of Scotland company operated buses out of Aberdeen to serve a rural section isolated from the Alford and Ballater branches, and rather than build a railway from Ballater through the Grampians to Speyside the same company found a bus service more easily reconcilable with the traffic potential. In the Highlands the steamer company David MacBrayne began to operate buses in 1907 with a Fort William–North Ballachulish (Lochaber) service which provided a more flexible alternative to a steamer along a section of the coast where a rail service was lacking. An Inverness–Glenurquhart service began in 1911, extended to Fort William in 1912, although services on the Caledonian Canal continued until 1929 when new bus services to Foyers and Fort Augustus started. There is very little duplication of railway routes by buses in the Highlands (apart from long distance coaches in summer) and it is remarkable how close is their integration when compared with their vigorous competition in other parts of Scotland, which has led to the elimination of rail services on the secondary routes. This is due to lack of profitability and the dependence of many operators on subsidies (including mail contracts) and the acceptance of financial losses by companies (employing the principle of cross subsidy).[61] Support by government and (since 1968) local authorities has enabled the variations in the quality of transport to be reduced during this century and especially since the Second World War.[62]

Equally, government regional policies have supported improvements in communications throughout Scotland. The most impressive changes have taken place in the Central Belt. The local contrasts in accessibility, already very considerable (Figure 11.4), have been increased by motorway building which provides an Edinburgh–Glasgow–Greenock axis and connections both northwards towards Stirling and Perth and southwards towards Carlisle. Development was rapid during the 1960s after the Toothill Report highlighted Scotland's accessibility problem and government responded with the plan for the Central Belt in 1963. Rail and air links with England have also improved: railway electrification has been completed between London and Glasgow (and also in the Glasgow suburbs) while reorganisation of rail terminals has reduced the number of principal stations in Edinburgh to one (Waverley) and in Glasgow to two (Central and Queen Street).[63] It is true that motorways and electrified railways have barely penetrated the north but there have been notable trunk road developments to Aberdeen and Inverness (including a crossing of the Beauly and Cromarty Firths to shorten the road distance between Inverness and

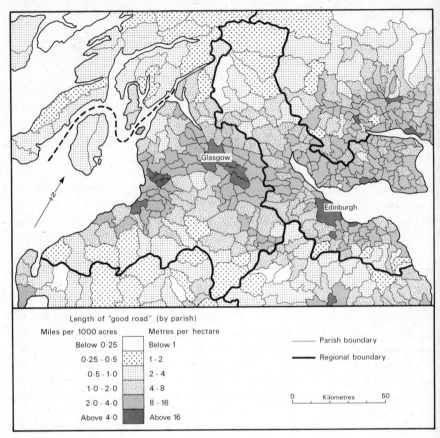

Figure 11.4. Road density in the Central Belt 1953
Source: Bartholomew's half inch map series 1951–3

Invergordon) and rail services have improved through restoration of double track sections between Perth and Inverness and the introduction of high speed trains to Aberdeen. The local roads in the Highlands have also seen many improvements, including surfacing, widening and realigning, not to mention some entirely new roads such as inter-island causeways which are mentioned in a study of island affairs (Chapter 14). These developments have exerted an effect commensurate with the more conspicuous projects in the Central Belt, especially in view of the simplified procedures for the operation of public bus services which have encouraged the Post Office to introduce post buses, while reduction of the railway system in the Highlands has been minimal. Of course, the north is still disadvantaged in terms of cost and travel time, especially with steamer services for which the principle of 'road equivalent tariff' remains contentious. But transport has been integrated into the regional planning exercise and this offers promise of further movement towards equality.

Electrification has made a major difference to the industrial potential of the Outer Regions because one of the major constraints has been eliminated. Some of the optimism surrounding rural electrification has been misplaced, because a sound infrastructure is a precondition for industrial growth not an immediate cause of it. However, promotion of the rural areas for manufacturing has become more realistic and important progress has clearly been made. Although electricity supply does not tend to attract much historical enquiry the geography is hardly intelligible without regard to the details of the evolution process during the present century. Table 11.5 indicates a very great increase in capacity during the post-war period for which statistics are readily available and also a growth in the contribution made by the Outer Regions. However, the average capacity of stations in the Outer Regions tends to be relatively small and it may, therefore, appear anomalous that at a time when the grid system within Scotland has improved to the point where a single concentration of power stations could serve the entire country there has been a proliferation of plants in the remoter parts. However, there has been considerable change in four important areas: the administrative limits of supply areas, the layout and capacity of the supply system, the maximum size of individual generating units and the relative costs of alternative fuels. Some dispersal of stations is desirable so that, provided that economies of scale are not sacrificed and selected sites confer advantages over fuel supply and cooling, dispersed regional markets may be served with relatively low transmission losses. Thus Dundee has its thermal station of Carolina Port with 307 MW and the Grampian region now has 1,320 MW oil-fired plant at Boddam near Peterhead (which followed the closure of the 57 MW coal-fired plant in Aberdeen in 1969). The existence of separate electricity boards for the North of Scotland (roughly the northern Outer Regions) and South of Scotland emphasises the logic of placing stations beside the two main urban markets in this area. In the Central Belt the eastward shift of coal mining has resulted in the building of the largest coal-fired stations on the Forth estuary at Cockenzie and Longannet but the preference for oil manifest at a time of falling coal output (before the steep price increases of the past decade) brought a 2,100 MW station to the Clyde at Inverkip, while nuclear stations have outflanked this cluster on both the Clyde (Hunterston) and Forth (Torness, under construction).[64] There are also nuclear stations at the north and south extremities of Scotland: the prototype fast reactor at Dounreay near Thurso (situated away from heavily settled areas for safety reasons) and a second 'conventional' UKAEA reactor at Chapelcross (Dumfries and Galloway) close to the main 275 kV transmission line from the Central Belt to England.

Table 11.5. *Electricity power station capacities 1948–78*

Region		Number of stations and total capacity (MW) for each type of power station						MW per thousand of population
		A.	B.	C.	D.	E.	F.	
Islands	1948				3 5.1		3 5.1	*
	1978	3 4.4		1 3.3	4 111.7		8 119.4	1.9
Highlands	1948	7 3.9		1 0.5	14 11.5		22 15.9	*
	1978	56 547.7	2 700.0		2 8.7	1 250.0	61 1,506.4	6.2
Grampian	1948			1 54.5	5 1.9		6 56.4	0.1
	1978			1 1,320.0			1 1,320.0	3.0
Tayside	1948	2 82.0		3 79.9			5 161.9	0.5
	1978	21 365.5		1 240.0			22 605.5	1.5
North	1948	9 85.9		5 134.9	22 18.5		36 239.3	0.2
	1978	80 917.6	2 700.0	3 1,563.3	6 120.4	1 250.0	92 3,551.3	3.1
Borders	1948			1 5.6			1 5.6	*
	1978							0.0
Dumfries & G'way	1948	5 104.4					5 104.4	0.7
	1978	5 107.0				1 200.0	6 307.0	2.1

		A		B		C		D		E		F		
		No.	MW	No.	MW	No.	MW	No.	MW	No.	MW	No.	MW	%
South	1948	5	104.4					1	5.6			6	110.0	0.4
	1978	5	107.0							1	200.0	6	307.0	1.3
Outer Regions	1948	14	190.3			6	140.5	22	18.5			42	349.3	0.2
	1978	85	1,024.6	2	700.0	3	1,563.3	6	120.4	2	450.0	98	3,858.3	2.8
East-Central	1948					4	216.0					4	216.0	0.2
	1978					5	3,560.0			1	1,250.0	6	4,810.0	3.6
West-Central	1948	2	15.5			6	605.7	2	0.7			10	621.9	0.3
	1978	4	145.8			4	1,718.0			2	1,422.0	10	3,285.8	1.3
Central Belt	1948	2	15.5			10	821.7	2	0.7			14	837.9	0.2
	1978	4	145.8			9	5,278.0			3	2,672.0	16	8,095.8	2.1
Scotland	1948	16	205.8			16	962.2	24	19.2			56	1,187.2	0.2
	1978	89	1,170.4	2	700.0	12	6,841.3	6	120.4	5	3,122.0	114	11,954.1	2.3

A. Conventional hydro
B. Pumped storage hydro (pumping capacity 741.0 MW)
C. Conventional thermal and gas turbine
D. Diesel generators (includes 8.7 MW standby capacity on Islay 1978)
E. Nuclear (includes Torness project) F. Total

* less than 0.1

Source: North of Scotland Hydro Electric Board and South of Scotland Electricity Board

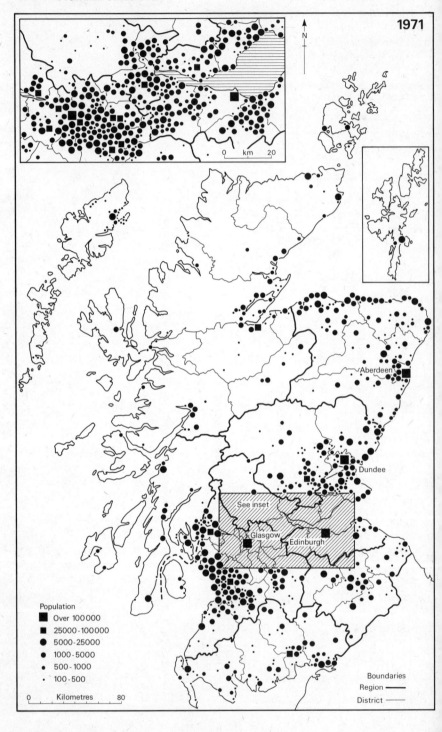

1971

Population
- ■ Over 100 000
- ▪ 25 000 - 100 000
- ● 5 000 - 25 000
- • 1 000 - 5 000
- · 500 - 1 000
- · 100 - 500

Boundaries
Region ———
District ———

0   Kilometres   80

0   km   20

See inset

Glasgow   Edinburgh

Aberdeen

Dundee

The majority of power stations in the Outer Regions are generating hydro-electricity and it has become difficult to reconcile the modest capacities of individual water catchments with the large scale of national demand made accessible by the grid system.[65] There are many places where it is technically feasible to build small plants of one megawatt or less in order to supply a village but the cost of each unit of electricity is high compared with a large plant and the first generation hydro plants have all been closed, though a few small plants built since the Second World War by the North of Scotland Hydro-Electric Board remain in operation in the West Highlands and Islands. Larger stations of up to thirty megawatts for public supply have multiplied since the schemes of Loch Luichart (Ross & Cromarty) 1926–34, Tummel–Rannoch (Perth & Kinross) 1928–33 and Galloway (Stewartry) 1935–36 and are attractive when transmission lines (usually 132 kV) are available for regional distribution. However, as the optimum size of generating stations has increased it has been impossible for hydro-electric plants to keep pace because catchment areas are too small and elaborate water works to increase potential would be too costly. Conventional hydro stations are no longer being built, though part of the explanation lies in the small number of significant catchments that remain undeveloped and the growing opposition from the environmentalists.[66] Nevertheless it should be noted that the existing hydro plants are retained, despite their relatively small outputs, because of low operating costs. And new construction will continue through pumped storage schemes which consume about 10 per cent more power than they produce, but utilise off peak power to build up a useful capacity that can be harnessed at time of peak demand. The physical potential for such schemes is almost limitless and development can be expected to keep pace with the growing disparity between the extremes of demand during each day. One final point in a confusing picture concerns the small diesel stations built in islands which have an inadequate hydro potential and yet have to generate their own supplies because of the lack of submarine cables to the mainland. Where these have been provided (as on Mull) the island plant can be downgraded to standby status.

Settlement patterns

The changes in the settlement pattern have been very far-reaching (Figure 11.5), and, fortunately, because of the restart of publication of census figures for all individual settlements (and not simply the former burghs) it

Figure 11.5. Distribution of population 1971
Source: Census of Scotland

Table 11.6. *Population change 1871–1971 by settlement size groups*

Region	Settlement size group: Below 300			300–499		
	A.	B.	C.	A.	B.	C.
Islands	—	39.4	−50.9	13	4.6	−8.0
Highlands	—	83.3	−58.6	19	8.1	−2.4
Grampian	—	82.8	−56.7	25	9.6	12.9
Tayside	—	51.2	−51.2	17	5.2	13.0
North	—	256.7	−55.6	74	27.5	4.2
Borders	—	27.5	−53.7	8	2.9	−21.6
Dumfries & Galloway	—	46.8	−47.8	20	6.8	33.3
South	—	74.3	−50.2	28	9.7	10.2
Outer Regions	—	331.0	−54.3	102	37.2	5.6
East-Central	—	64.2	−66.0	37	15.3	−6.1
West-Central	—	57.7	−61.3	34	12.5	−59.4
Central Belt	—	121.9	−63.9	71	27.8	−41.1
Scotland	—	452.9	−57.4	173	65.8	−20.0

A. Number of settlements (categories above 300 only)
B. Combined population 1971 (thousands)
C. Percentage population change 1871–1971
Source: Census of Scotland

is possible to make some comparison over settlement size groups with the late nineteenth century when similar information was available (Tables 11.6 and 11.7). If a settlement size of 1,000 is taken as indicating a break between urban and rural then in 1971 4.55 million out of a total of 5.23 million were urban dwellers. The balance between the regions has again shifted in favour of the Central Belt, though not as rapidly as before because the problems of the core have led to increased out-migration from Scotland as a whole.[67] Each region has experienced a considerable internal redistribution with growth in the largest settlements and decline in the lower categories and especially the dispersed population (Table 11.8). In a separate analysis it can be seen that the largest cities accounted for 51.6 per cent of Scotland's population in 1971 compared with 44.5 per cent in 1891, while the clustering of the largest cities in the Central Belt has also increased (Table 7.7). These trends are hardly surprising for the main towns have always provided a focus for surplus agricultural production and for the produce of rural industry. Rural dwellers can today have access to a wider range of services, by commuting to work, shops and entertainment, trends reinforced by labour shedding on farms and the reduction of local services in the countryside.[68] The new reality has been demonstrated in research on travel to work areas, some of which was carried out as a

Table 11.6 (*cont.*)

500–999			1,000–4,999			Over 4,999			Total		
A.	B.	C.	A.	B.	C.	A.	B.	C.	A.	B.	C.
4	2.6	−43.5	2	6.3	−49.2	2	11.1	*	21	64.3	−37.1
32	23.0	34.5	21	37.8	24.8	7	89.0	139.9	79	241.1	−18.0
32	23.7	14.5	34	73.7	50.7	8	248.8	122.7	99	438.6	15.1
25	16.5	70.1	12	26.1	−24.8	10	298.6	46.2	64	397.6	11.0
93	65.8	26.3	69	143.9	14.0	27	647.7	83.4	263	1,141.6	0.5
5	5.1	−30.0	10	22.4	−17.0	4	40.5	86.6	27	98.5	−17.3
9	6.6	−33.4	17	36.0	22.0	3	47.4	121.5	49	143.2	−7.9
14	11.7	−32.0	27	58.4	3.4	7	87.9	103.9	76	241.7	−12.0
107	77.5	11.8	96	202.3	10.7	34	735.6	85.1	339	1,383.3	− 1.0
64	47.8	112.4	93	208.5	78.2	45	1,000.0	191.0	239	1,335.8	94.0
49	37.4	−39.8	109	289.2	35.7	58	2,113.0	162.1	250	2,509.9	98.9
113	85.2	0.7	202	497.7	50.7	103	3,113.0	170.7	489	3,845.6	97.2
220	162.7	5.7	298	700.0	36.5	137	3,848.6	148.9	828	5,229.0	55.6

prelude to the integration of city and region in local government.[69] Small towns have suffered in the process of integration within individual city regions: this is revealed in lower rates of growth and relatively modest redevelopment of town centre properties.[70] By contrast the centres of large cities have been transformed to provide additional space for shopping, offices and entertainment and road systems have been remodelled to cope with more intense traffic flows.

Clearance of city centre sites has provided temporary scope for archaeological research but has generated conflict with conservation interests. The greatest conflicts have been encountered in Edinburgh where the protection of the classic Georgian architecture of New Town has been a high priority and a desire to retain open spaces has frustrated road developments.[71] Patrick Geddes was an advocate of conservation, seeking purchase, improvement and imaginative restoration of property rather than wholesale clearance. His work in Edinburgh was continued by the Marquess of Bute who carried out work in Canongate and Charlotte Square.[72] But Glasgow is coming to appreciate its Victorian heritage after a disastrous erosion of a valuable heritage in the early post-war period; Buchanan Street has become a focus for conservation work.[73] And smaller towns (notably Haddington in East Lothian) have proceeded with imaginative schemes which have done much to preserve a distinctly Scottish townscape.[74] A sensitive conservation plan in Ayr has ensured a continuity of development: the urban landscape is seen as a palimpsest since the

Table 11.7. *Growth of large settlements 1891–1971*

Region	1891				1971			
	A.	B.	C.	D.	A.	B.	C.	D.
Islands	9.8	2.6	12.4	11.9	17.6	0.0	17.5	27.2
Highlands	66.9	15.2	82.1	29.1	106.5	20.2	126.8	52.6
Grampian	192.0	29.8	221.8	52.6	287.3	35.3	322.6	73.6
Tayside	272.2	13.8	286.0	72.4	313.5	11.1	324.6	81.6
North	540.9	61.4	602.3	50.1	724.8	66.6	791.4	69.3
Borders	61.9	5.3	67.2	51.7	59.2	3.7	62.9	63.9
Dumfries & G'way	48.3	7.6	55.9	37.2	68.2	15.2	83.4	58.2
South	110.2	12.9	123.1	43.9	127.4	18.9	146.3	60.5
Outer Regions	651.1	74.3	725.4	48.9	852.2	85.5	937.7	67.8
East-Central	466.9	69.2	536.1	61.9	977.2	231.3	1,208.5	90.5
West-Central	803.9	205.5	1,009.4	60.2	1,943.2	459.0	2,402.2	95.7
Central Belt	1,270.8	274.7	1,545.5	60.8	2,920.4	690.3	3,610.7	93.9
Scotland	1,921.9	349.0	2,270.9	56.4	3,772.6	775.8	4,548.4	87.0

A. Population of burghs with over 1,000 inhabitants
B. Population of other settlements with more than 1,000 inhabitants
C. Total population of settlements with more than 1,000 inhabitants
D. Percentage of the total population
Source: Census of Scotland

features of each period have only been partially obliterated by subsequent development and the work of the thirteenth century land surveyor in laying out the burgage plots is still clearly visible.[75] But the cities have not simply experienced heavier pressure in their centres due to an increase in demand for services from their regions: their own populations have increased and the need to provide housing for the larger population and to relieve the slums has meant a substantial expansion of the built up area. Local authorities have dominated the urban housing programme since the First World War. Dundee made a rapid start with the Logie scheme commencing in 1919, a novel element being its district heating scheme. Rents at Logie and other contemporary municipal developments were too high for low income families and although philanthropism made some contribution (for Robert Fleming gave some of his fortune to build houses in his native town for letting at low rents) the burden of subsidy has again been assumed by the local authorities. Over the years the unrealistic level of council house rents has become a major political issue through heavy burdens on ratepayers and discouragement of owner occupation. Local authority involvement has reduced the polarisation between high status and low status areas but there are perceived differences within the public sector, well-demonstrated in Glasgow, where the inter-war projects of Knights-wood and Blackhill reflect similar contrasts to those generated in the nineteenth century as Blackhill has become progressively monopolised by problem families. Some studies of building form have been carried out to highlight the expansion of the cities but further work in planning history might provide insights into the working of the process as regards both urban form and status areas.

Out in the city regions it might be anticipated that better integration would stimulate country living and reduce the rate of growth in the main towns. Improved mobility (for many) together with interest in a better environment and avoidance of decongestion certainly stimulates rural living orientated to work in the cities. And some industrial spread is facilitated by improved infrastructure, available labour and government/local authority incentives. However, this seems to result in growth on a restricted basis up to the limits of acceptable daily commuting. Areas more distant from the main centres, which can be very extensive in the Outer Regions, may well be served by small towns but such local settlement patterns often lack the dynamism of the sub-regional systems focussing on towns such as Dumfries, Galashiels and Inverness.[76] Some attract substantial industrial employment, thanks in part to the oil industry, such as Invergordon and Peterhead. But others tend to provide bases for the centralisation of services without having a labour catchment and infrastructure attractive to large firms. Small country towns cannot provide a stimulating urban environment and young people living within their influence sense a degree of isolation that may be perceived as deprivation. The Highlands offer the classic case study – though attempts have been made to minimise depopulation by local society (in the crofting culture of the Hebrides) and by the nation through special remedial aid – but similar problems can be found in the other Outer Regions. The situation has been complicated, however, by the rise in 'second homes'.[77] Local authorities have sought to complement the main priority of accommodating growth in the core of each sub-region by developing outlying centres (including 'key villages') to the point where they can become attractive to industry.[78] But the policy, although logical enough, is often controversial because it accelerates rural depopulation (by withdrawal of services, and planning controls on new house building) without providing any guarantee of access to better employment opportunities.[79]

Conclusion

A conclusion to this section must avoid making final judgements on a process of adjustment which is still continuing. It is, however, quite evident that despite the failure of the Scots to support devolution proposals that

Table 11.8. *Population change 1961–71 by settlement size groups*

Region	Settlement size group: Below 100		100–199			200–499			500–999		
	B.	C.	A.	B.	C.	A.	B.	C.	A.	B.	C.
Islands	28.5	−12.6	53	7.2	−17.2	28	8.3	0.0	4	2.6	0.0
Highlands	62.9	−17.9	86	11.6	−7.9	56	16.9	23.4	32	23.0	12.7
Grampian	71.8	−20.2	53	7.3	−18.0	40	13.3	4.7	32	23.7	4.9
Tayside	42.7	−16.9	35	5.0	−7.4	31	8.7	−6.5	25	16.5	9.3
North	205.9	−17.8	227	31.1	−11.6	155	47.2	7.3	93	65.8	8.4
Borders	23.0	−19.3	19	2.8	7.7	15	4.6	−16.4	5	5.1	2.0
Dumfries & G'way	37.2	−15.6	41	5.8	−4.9	36	10.6	−5.4	9	6.6	0.0
South	60.2	−17.1	60	8.6	−1.1	51	15.2	−9.0	14	11.7	0.9
Outer Regions	266.1	−17.7	287	39.7	−9.6	206	62.4	2.8	107	77.5	7.2
East-Central	49.5	−12.9	60	8.2	−15.5	62	21.8	−5.2	64	47.8	13.3
West-Central	44.9	−9.7	50	7.4	−28.8	56	17.9	−9.6	49	37.4	4.8
Central Belt	94.4	−11.4	110	15.6	−23.2	118	39.7	−7.2	113	85.2	9.4
Scotland	360.5	−16.1	397	55.3	−13.9	324	102.1	−1.4	220	162.7	8.3

Table 11.8 (*cont.*)

Region	Settlement size group: 1,000–4,999			5,000–			Total		
	A.	B.	C.	A.	B.	C.	A.	B.	C.
Islands	2	6.3	8.6	2	11.1	1.8	89	64.3	−7.1
Highlands	21	37.8	17.0	7	89.0	17.7	202	241.1	4.6
Grampian	34	73.7	7.1	8	248.8	4.8	167	438.6	−0.4
Tayside	12	26.1	−6.1	10	298.6	5.4	113	397.6	−0.1
North	69	143.9	6.8	27	647.7	5.7	571	1,141.6	0.3
Borders	10	22.4	8.2	4	40.5	1.5	53	98.5	−3.6
Dumfries & G'way	17	36.0	4.0	3	47.4	8.2	106	143.2	−2.2
South	27	58.4	5.6	7	87.9	5.0	159	241.7	−2.8
Outer Regions	96	202.3	6.5	34	735.6	5.6	730	1,383.3	−0.2
East-Central	93	208.5	−10.1	45	1,000.0	9.7	324	1,335.8	4.7
West-Central	109	289.2	2.8	58	2,113.0	−0.2	322	2,509.9	−0.3
Central Belt	202	497.7	−3.1	103	3,113.0	2.8	646	3,845.6	1.4
Scotland	298	700.0	−0.5	137	3,848.6	3.3	1,376	5,229.0	1.0

A. Number of settlements 1971
B. Combined population (thousands)
C. Percentage change 1961–71

Source: Census of Scotland

231

might ultimately have led to a reassertion of independence, the sense of nationhood is expressed through a Scottish Office which is not only influential at Westminster (with cabinet rank for the Secretary of State) but effective in maintaining a coordinated regional approach to the various forms of planning which reflect the growth of state intervention in the economy during this century. A policy for the Central Belt should combine urban redevelopment with the creation of attractive sites for new industries to compensate for the much-diminished strength of the basic industries created in the Victorian period. But the vulnerability of new industries during recession (especially branch plants subject to external control) has been demonstrated, while the single-mindedness of new town development has led to acute problems in the heart of Glasgow (the greatest exporter of overspill population) that have recently called for drastic surgery. Appropriately, therefore, the first of the special studies related to this general review covers the planning of the Central Belt (Chapter 12). The other two studies are concerned with the Outer Regions. Forestry (dealt with in Chapter 13) has become a major preoccupation since the Second World War but mechanisation has prevented the large increase in employment in the rural areas that might have provided significant compensation for labour-shedding on hill farms. The migration to the towns, many of which have acquired an enhanced marketing and industrial role, has been sustained and in consequence rural districts have become heavily depopulated. The rapid decline in some rural areas has not attracted great attention from geographers who are preoccupied with the problems of urban–industrial renewal in the core of the region (the Central Belt) but the process is real enough. If the support for the non-governing Liberal and Scottish National Parties in the early 1970s is to be seen in any way as a protest against prevailing trends then the bias in seats towards the Outer Regions in seats held by members of these parties in the mid 1970s should surely be revealing.[80] One writer perceptibly saw a major spatial conflict as a likely outcome of further SNP success with 'traditional' Nationalist areas anticipating suitable recognition of their loyalty after independence.[81] The Highlands and Islands have certainly benefited from sustained government assistances and the study of the islands (Chapter 14) brings out the distinctive initiatives that have been taken. But in other rural regions it seems that the peripheral areas are too fragmented to attract adequate priority from regional planners.[82]

12

Planning for the Central Belt

The planning of urban development has been a theme running throughout this study but whereas previous attempts were related to the ideals of landowners and industrialists, there was a consensus emerging in the late nineteenth century that the cities and city regions of the time required not just efficient administration but also imaginative spatial organisation. It would be wrong to suppose that local authorities had previously lacked powers to control development: for centuries the Dean of Guild Court (an institution that existed right up until 1975) had the power of veto over building operations and could therefore establish codes of building practice to ensure reasonable precautions over fire hazards and smoke pollution. An overall view could be taken of town development and pressure exerted to maintain amenity and ensure the development of waste land. Some notable conservational decisions were taken such as the prevention of quarrying at Edinburgh's Salisbury Crags, immortalised in Walter Scott's *Heart of Midlothian*.[1] Before purchase of land for city parks become common, efforts were made to ensure that open spaces such as Perth Inch and Glasgow Green were not absorbed by residential or industrial development. However 'the available building and town planning powers which were widespread in the early modern period were gradually eroded in practice by the growth of municipal corporations who in their efforts to assert their own authority over burghal affairs, coincidentally dealt a death blow to precisely that agency which, in the rapidly industrialising environment of the early nineteenth century, had most to offer in terms of controlled urban development'.[2] Fortunately, the twelve courts that survived in 1868 did relate to the most important centres of population, although even in these cases they could not prevent the incidence of sanitary and other environmental problems.[3]

Development of modern town planning

Measures to create community management for water and sewage introduced a new strand into town planning. Glasgow brought water from Loch

Katrine in 1859 and a system of underground sewers had been built by 1860.[4] But much of the progress in the late nineteenth century came through renewed preoccupation with building regulations and street layouts and brought about the re-establishment of Dean of Guild Courts which numbered twenty in 1880 and 189 in 1912, by which time the 'adoptive' legislation of 1862 had been recast as a compulsory requirement. Models for street layouts were already to hand in the schemes of the eighteenth-century improvement era and they are perpetuated in the special improvement schemes of the late nineteenth century. They gave valuable experience in planning for better urban amenities and traffic circulation as well as revised minimum accommodation standards. The great failing was in displacing the poorest families into old properties already congested yet from which they could not escape because of the unpalatable truth that private enterprise could not provide new accommodation for poor families in such a way as to satisfy both building regulations and the rent-paying capacity of prospective tenants. This new discovery required a further revision of the early-nineteenth-century philosophy of freedom for the entrepreneur as an essential and indispensable driving force whose practical economic approach should be fettered only by a minimum of public scrutiny.

It has been pointed out that the selection of priorities in nineteenth-century planning (water, drainage and roads) determined that the engineer, rather than the architect, would be the first important technical officer of a local authority. But such people were concerned with systems and this may have helped broaden municipal thinking.[5] It may also have stimulated academic activity and generated the inspiring ideas put forward by Patrick Geddes who sought 'to comprehend the modern industrial and commercial city, in its totality, from the viewpoint of those living in it'.[6] While most observers were confused by the complexities of city life and the interaction of so many different factors Geddes offered a synthesis through a combination of history and geography. Since the Edinburgh he observed was not responding adequately to treatment prescribed by government legislation applied through the local authority and philanthropic organisations, a new approach was needed. 'Civics' should be based in urban and regional social surveys to comprehend the whole system and the perceptions of different social groups towards it. Only then could adequate plans be made to achieve a more equitable balance of economic and social forces that would usher in the 'Eutechnic' age and contrast with the laissez-faire of the 'Paleotechnic' and 'Neotechnic' eras.[7] The French sociologist F. Le Play was a source of stimulation through the trilogy of 'Place–Work–Folk', operationalised by Geddes through the Outlook Tower in Edinburgh which he acquired in 1892 as a prototype civic museum that would be a focus for scientific study of urban ecology and inspire a higher level of urban development. Unfortunately the approach proved too comprehensive for most professional people concerned with town planning and those with vested interests in the prevailing social structure were suspicious of the idea of social evolution (hence the rebuff suffered over recommendations for the layout of Pittencrieff Park in Dunfermline for which Geddes received a commission in 1903).[8] Yet his sociological conception has been vindicated over the years as an eminently logical and humane approach, regarding utopia as a city functioning efficiently in the eyes of its inhabitants. He stands in contrast to other visionaries who have idealised the escape from the normal conditions of the large industrial city. It is interesting to note that when Geddes presented his paper on 'Civics as applied sociology' in 1904 the first speaker from the floor was Ebenezer Howard of the Garden City Association who saw signs of the break-up of the 'great, closely-compacted, overcrowded city' with the twentieth century becoming known as 'the period of the great exodus' with continuing industrial decentralisation as firms escaped from the high cost and congestion of city centre locations.[9] Howard's vision in harnessing this process to create model cities in the country was potentially dangerous because it overlooked the areas that were already developed and would have to adjust to falling populations and rateable values. Arguably the twentieth-century urban development in Scotland, characterised by unprecedented dispersal, has been guided by planning policies that have failed to ensure the right balance of concern for the exporting and reception areas: expressed today in terms of new town and inner city.

Compulsory land use planning emerged only in 1909 in respect of new development on the margins of towns and cities. There would be controls over density and incompatible buildings would be separated. This did not involve any direction of developers to particular areas: trying to shape the whole of a town by planning was still thought impractical because it meant interference with constructive economic forces. However even this modest advance was undermined by war and depression which reduced the rate of development, while the great increase in road transport meant that development did not necessarily occur in concentrated form on the edge of the city. The period also marks a turning point over public responsibility for housing. State subsidies were available under the Housing and Town Planning (Scotland) Act of 1919, but it was hard to settle on a rate that would allow steady effort without leading to excessive state obligations. Overcrowding was dealt with by the laying down of maximum densities under the Housing (Scotland) Act of 1935. Council housing projects could of course be treated efficiently through the new planning system but private development proved difficult to control because building could not be ruled out in certain areas without liability to compensation. Yet development plans could not reasonably be produced for all areas and control could be exercised loosely through the sanction of demolition for unauthorised developments that were unacceptable.

Some further progress was made in the Town and Country Planning (Scotland) Act of 1932 when landowners could forgo the option of building in order to avoid land being assessed for death duty in terms of development value. In the 1930s, thinking evolved largely over a rural zone where non-agricultural development would not be allowed and although this concept was never formally applied (it reached the stage of a concrete recommendation in 1939) it did gradually create a consensus that a landowner did not automatically have the right to build, and generalised the notion of planning restriction beyond the specific case of ribbon development over which powers were granted in 1936. During the Second World War it was hardly a major extension of policy to apply statutory control to all unbuilt areas (1943) and the formalisation of this doctrine in peacetime along with the build-up of regional perspectives by local authorities paved the way for more effective and spatially discriminating development plans. Under the Town and Country Planning (Scotland) Act of 1947 each authority was to prepare a plan within four years and make subsequent revisions thereafter. All development would be controlled and planning authorities could now carry out public development of land. Further momentum came from the Barlow Report with its revelations over inter-regional as well as intra-regional balance.[10] Hence it was in the late 1940s that government first began to control the whole form of urban expansion half a century after the visionaries had looked into the crystal ball. Delay was inevitable while public opinion evolved and while new technology was assimilated but in the event progress was inspired too strongly by the 'new town' ideal, though this was understandable during an idealistic post-war reconstruction phase when it was easier to develop in new situations than improve existing built-up areas whose socio-economic problems were still barely understood – partly through failure to use the technique of regional survey that Geddes had advocated.

The conception of new towns

After the failure of his recommendations for Dunfermline, Geddes associated with Frank Mears in the scheme for a new suburb near Leven in Fife which also failed to materialise. But the naval base established at Rosyth (also in Fife) led to an Admiralty proposal for a new town on garden city lines. After a joint project with Dunfermline broke down (Rosyth is situated in Dunfermline parish) the Housing (Rosyth Dockyard) Act of 1915 allowed the Scottish National Housing Company to build at Westerton. In 1969 the stock was transferred to the Scottish Special Housing Association. However, another important project was started at Gretna

(Annandale & Eskdale) and it may be regarded as Britain's first government sponsored new town. Raymond Unwin, the doyen of early planning practice in Britain, was responsible for the layouts of the private ventures in England at Letchworth (garden city) and Hampstead (garden suburb) but during the First World War he worked for the Minister of Munitions in building a town to house workers at a new explosives factory. Gretna and Eastriggs were to house 13,500 people and construction went ahead quickly once the decision was taken in 1915. There was a shortage of timber despite the need for speed, so, brick construction was used in order to produce housing of long-term value. Brick hostels were built so that they could later be converted into terrace cottages. 'Permanent houses were also built, in terraces and as groups of semi-detatched and occasionally detatched units looking for all the world like a cheaper version of Hampstead Garden Suburb or a rather superior example of an inter-war housing estate.'[11] Indeed the townships, which still exist (though the cordite factory has gone), provided an obvious model for later council estates. There were hopes by the Garden City and Town Planning Association that Gretna could be adopted as the first of a programme of government sponsored new towns but it was only during the Second World War that this was seriously envisaged in Scottish regional planning.

The inevitability of a great expansion of activity on planning after the war led the Secretary of State for Scotland to commission various sub-regional studies to ensure that the Scottish Office would eventually be endowed with important responsibilities in this field. The most important study affected the Clyde Valley and it followed the establishment of a Clyde Valley Regional Planning Advisory Committee in 1927 (embracing Dunbartonshire, Lanarkshire and Renfrewshire) to coordinate development of roads and open spaces. Reconstituted in 1943 with representatives from the major burghs (including Glasgow) and two additional counties (Ayr and Bute) a large survey operation was mounted with the assistance of Patrick Abercrombie and the Clyde Valley Plan was produced in 1946.[12] The report recognised the decay of much of the housing stock especially in Glasgow and the overcrowding associated with it. It also recognised the economic problems of high unemployment and low productivity. Both problems could only be solved with a measure of decentralisation. The lack of suitable land for development around Glasgow, especially with Green Belt constraints, made overspill inevitable and as up to half a million people were displaced from the core of Glasgow a series of new towns would be required. Within the survey area new towns were recommended for Bishopton (Renfrew), Condorrat (Cumbernauld), East Kilbride and Houston (Renfrew), each with a population of 40,000–60,000. These new towns would provide an environment conducive to industrial diversification.

Yet there was an even broader conception of regional development in Scotland, for as many as 200,000 people might move eastwards mainly to East-Central Scotland where Frank Mears was in charge of a comparable study.[13] The expected growth of coal mining in the region (to counter the closures anticipated in the west) would create new jobs in the industry and in manufacturing associated with it. An orderly development by some 200,000 in thirty years would give rise to a series of settlement constellations in which the small mining village would give way to urban groupings large enough to offer a range of employments and services. The constellations would start at Port Seton in Lothian and extend through the coalfields south of the Forth to Blackburn and Bathgate (also Falkirk in Central Region) with a complementary chain north of the estuary from Tullibody (Central Region) to Kennoway/Leven, Kirkaldy and Markinch/Leslie (Fife). 'Not only do miners' families desire to live in mixed communities with varied social contacts and opportunities for alternative employment but the greater aggregate population is essential to yield recruits in sufficient numbers to balance the annual loss of men from the industry'.[14] In the new diversified communities miners would make up only ten per cent of the total labour force. Coal would initially be exported to other regions but some of it would go to industry attracted by the availability of fuel nearby, and the long-term danger of 'progressive deterioration towards black country conditions' would require the setting of limits and the eventual diversion of development to the Borders or Tayside where another regional survey drew attention to the potential of the Strathmore towns that were to be endowed with industrial estates of a size commensurate with their position in the central place hierarchy.[15] New towns would play a fundamental role in a regional development programme that would integrate the Central Belt and place a new industrial system on the transformed geography of coalmining.

The idea of new towns was supported by the Labour Party in Scotland in 1941 and eight locations were being widely canvassed by the end of the war: the four listed in the Abercrombie Plan and four in the east: Woodside (being developed in connection with the Rosyth base) along with Cardenden (Fife), Dalkeith (Midlothian) and Kennoway (Fife) which fitted in with the Mears constellation concept. Such thinking reflected the most urgent message of the Barlow Report, that the great cities were congested and that decentralisation was needed on a massive scale. The Clyde Valley Plan suggested a way in which the process could operate and since it was clearly inspired by a philosophy which the governing party in the immediate post-war period also embraced, its recommendations were taken very seriously.[16] The first new town of East Kilbride was designated in 1947, with a green zone on its northern flank to separate it physically from Cambuslang and Rutherglen.[17] The plan was based on a series of neighbourhoods and industrial areas were segregated. The initial target population was set at 45,000 but raised to 70,000 in 1960: it now stands at 82,500 a figure which will then be exceeded gradually through natural increase to an ultimate level of 100,000. In East-Central Scotland there was an early designation for Glenrothes, endorsing the idea of an urban constellation in the Markinch–Leslie area of Fife. The target population was 32,000 and there was only limited provision of industrial sites because it was assumed that the Rothes colliery would provide more than ten per cent of the employment. Unfortunately financial stringency prevented further designations. It is worth adding that proposals for the reorganisation of settlement on the Ayrshire coalfield envisaged a new town scheme for Colyton. Drongan was preferred in 1946 but although the community expanded through resettlement from outlying villages and provision of accommodation for miners at the new Killoch Colliery (opened 1953) enlargement of Cumnock has limited the population growth to 4,000.

The return of a Conservative government in 1951 indicated a lower priority for planning programmes but such was the gravity of the situation in Glasgow that a further new town, at Cumbernauld, was agreed with some of the financial support coming from Glasgow in terms of annual contribution (for ten years) in respect of those tenants nominated for accommodation in the new town.[18] About eighty per cent of the inhabitants would be Glaswegians forced out of the city by the overspill programme and plans were made to develop an elevated site to accommodate 50,000 people in residential areas grouped around a hill-top centre easily accessible by roads and walkways.[19] Target population was increased and the eventual ceiling is now to be 100,000. Once again financial considerations inhibited further progress and the Town Development (Scotland) Act of 1957 sought to provide alternative arrangements for Glasgow overspill by enabling local authorities to make agreements with Glasgow. Glasgow would make the same financial contribution as applied at Cumbernauld but government expenditure would be moderated since existing communities were being developed and the building of multi-storey blocks would, it was thought, provide significant economies while simultaneously allowing a rapid provision of new accommodation. With simultaneous building of multi-storey blocks in Glasgow the whole rehousing problem might have beeen solved without further new town designation.[20]

However, this thinking proved unrealistic and a fourth new town was designated at Livingston in Lothian in 1962. It was quickly built into a system of growth areas scattered across the Central Belt: centres that could accommodate the new manufacturing industries on which Scotland's economic development was to be based.[21] By this time regional planning had grown in scale and the whole Central Belt was considered as one integrated urban–industrial region. Although the movement of Glaswegians eastwards was anticipated in the Clyde Valley Plan it was now made explicit in the Livingston scheme which would generate a large community in an area of small towns and mining villages between Edinburgh and Falkirk.[22] The growth in the optimum size of new towns at this time is important. It means the growth of a large new town, with a distinctive grid-iron structure, across the Almond Valley. Interestingly the site had not been singled out for development in the Mears constellation plan which had thought in terms of a modest scale growth at Bathgate, Broxburn, East Calder and West Calder which now form the four 'corners' of the Livingston region. The last new town in Scotland was designated in 1966 and involves a substantial growth of the existing town of Irvine, to reach 100,000 eventually. It represents a further 'stretching' of Clyde Valley principles to support the physical conception of a Central Belt extending from Ayr to Dundee (where a large expansion programme was mapped out as part of estuarine strategy to cope with part of the population growth in Britain anticipated by the end of the century).[23]

Some implications of new town development

But while new towns were designated in sympathy with the recommendation of the Clyde Valley Plan there was little progress over the administrative regions.[24] For the study area was heavily fragmented: not only were there several different counties but numerous burghs each of which had considerable autonomy and the County of the City of Glasgow which was completely independent of the rural shires. Only after the Royal Commission report of 1969 was local government placed on a regional basis (1975) and a large Strathclyde region emerged which brought the whole of the Clyde Valley survey area together for the first time. The importance of this point does not rest on mere administrative efficiency but on fundamental differences of opinion with the principle of overspill being highly contentious to the potential exporting authorities.[25] Glasgow had withdrawn from the Clyde Valley Planning Advisory Committee in 1946 because of disagreement over overspill and in the six year period before it was reconstituted the city evolved plans that sought to rehouse slum dwellers within the city limits.[26] Glasgow was not alone in its opposition to overspill. The proposal for a new town at Houston to take overspill from Greenock and Port Glasgow was strongly opposed by the local authorities that stood to lose population and the project was quietly dropped in 1951. Eventually this was accepted as a physical impossibility and during the late 1950s and early 1960s there was growing convergence between Glasgow and the Scottish Office, with the latter showing such consistent support for Barlow principles that a Scottish regional plan was able to evolve without significant interruption through changes of government.[27] There was also little progress in the implementation of a package of measures prescribed in the Clyde Valley Plan for the integrated development of the region. The roads have been belatedly improved by motorway building within Glasgow and also across the Central Belt but the construction which paralleled the Greater Glasgow Transportation studies of the late 1960s follows a long delay during which key elements in the Clyde Valley plan were overlooked.

Similarly, important recreational projects such as Hamilton Low Parks and the Clyde/Muirshield Park were slow to get off the ground and the proposal for a national recreation centre at Balloch (Loch Lomond) has yet to be implemented. The failure to follow all the details of a controversial advisory plan is not in itself surprising although it was inevitable in view of the great priority that was understandably given to the housing situation. In Glasgow a strategy of comprehensive development evolved in the late 1950s with 29 areas where clearance and redevelopment would produce new accommodation at densities of 160 per acre (400 per hectare) on average, compared with 450 (1,125) previously.[28] Building on virgin sites on the edge of the city inevitably involved tenants in a more expensive journey to work and this is evident in the latest developments of Darnley and Summerston. But the early post-war housing schemes at Castlemilk and Easterhouse generated serious social problems because they were conceived as dormitories without local services or employment. Only in 1973 was the Easterhouse Centre opened. Difficulties also arose in slum areas that were redeveloped. Apart from the undue haste with which the tenement was dismissed as an acceptable housing form, and the expensive embrace of the multi-storey tower, with their acute social problems and illusory space-saving capacities, there has been an unsympathetic attitude to small industries that were swept away by the comprehensive approach. Also, because of the priority of slum clearance no explicit central area plan was formulated. There was little direct involvement by the local authority in redevelopment, and planning applications, it is argued, have been considered without regard to their effect in prejudicing future development or compromising an architecturally unique city.[29]

Clearly it can be seen in retrospect that there has been a failure to appreciate the financial costs involved in the package of five elements: overspill, green belt, new towns, Comprehensive Development Area (CDA) and motorway. By 1975 the general state of the economy imposed a pause but 'partly this was because of the exhaustion of their potential or disillusionment with their product'.[30] The overspill programme with heavy exports of Glasgow families by agreement between authorities, in addition to a substantial voluntary migration, left inner city areas to face a re-run of the late-nineteenth-century problems with decaying urban fabric, limited choice of employment and a high proportion of poor families.[31] Of course this condition was exacerbated by the transformation of the Scottish economy, something that the wartime planners totally failed to foresee. The grandiose plans for the coal industry proved totally unrealistic: the 1940 'Plan for Coal' anticipated an annual output of 30.6 million tons in the early 1960s and despite downward revision in the 1956 plan for 'Investing in Coal' (26.5 million tons) and the 1959 'Revised Plan for Coal' (18.2 million tons) the actual figure for 1961 was still lower than planned at 17.2 million tons (12.6 by the end of the decade). Thus all the plans were 'guilty of persistent over-optimism about the potential of the coal mining industry in Scotland'.[32] Mining difficulties resulted in heavy losses not only in the central coalfields but elsewhere, while changing fuel technology called for cuts in production and a close relationship between large mines and power stations, notably the Cockenzie and Longannet projects.

Particularly traumatic were the events at Glenrothes where the new Rothes Colliery opened in 1957. Yet within a few years the high costs of mining under the difficult geological conditions of the Limestone Coal had caused the mine to close and the function of the new town had to be reappraised. It was fortunate that although coal mining was seen as the main element in the town's economy the site was chosen for development because of good communications (given the Forth Road Bridge, and a projected east–west road from Clydeside through Fife which has not been built) and potential for a regrouping of settlements in central Fife. In the year the colliery opened an electronics firm opened in the town. A new industrial potential was found and a total of 28 factories opened between 1957 and 1967 providing the base for an impressive growth of population which has justified the late 1950s revision of the target population upwards to 70,000.[33] The success of Glenrothes with its new function as a town based on light industry, coupled with a similar record at East Kilbride, meant that government had little option but to do all in its power to stimulate firms to move into Scotland when the failure of the coal industry was repeated in other important sectors of the Scottish economy.[34] Glasgow's reputation over poor urban environment and bad labour relations (a product of the 'Red Clyde' myth) discouraged outside firms but the new towns, rendered accessible by improved communications, did prove effective and to this extent the 'growth area' approach of 1963 was logical and justified: the growth areas were basically the new towns along with Falkirk–Grangemouth (chosen because of the growth of the petrochemical complex). West-Central Scotland was appeased by inclusion of the old industrial towns of North Lanarkshire and also the Vale of Leven, where land reclamation would offer a better environment suitable for industry. But there was little recognition of the danger of having so much

Table 12.1. *Central Clydeside Conurbation 1801–1971*

Area	Population (000s) in:					
	1801	1851	1901	1951	1961	1971
City of Glasgow	73.5	345.0	761.7	1,089.8	1,055.0	897.5
Other Burghs	77.7	104.4	435.6	430.3	494.9	561.3
Non-burghal population		109.7	201.5	223.9	234.0	247.4
Total	151.2	559.1	1,398.8	1,744.0	1,783.9	1,706.2
Percentage of West-Central	44.3	59.2	70.0	71.2	70.9	68.0
Percentage of Scotland	9.4	19.3	31.1	34.2	34.4	32.6

a As far as possible modern administrative divisions (pre-1974) have been extended back into the nineteenth century. But population living within burgh boundaries is treated as non-burghal for years prior to the acquisition of burgh status. Problems arise in parishes where only burghal sections are included in the Central Clydeside conurbation. Population in the relevant sections of Cambusnethan, East Kilbride, Hamilton, Kirkintilloch, New Kilpatrick and Old Kilpatrick are not included in the table prior to the formation of the burghs.

Source: Census of Scotland.

industry subject to external control and the need for a positive plan for Glasgow industry was overlooked.[35]

Glasgow's disappointment with the growth area approach of 1963 was reflected in a modification of the CDA strategy to make more allowance for industry in the Springburn plan, which was much more diverse than its predecessors.[36] The city also began to show very stiff opposition to a further run-down of industry and population (Table 12.1). Considerable support was given to retain a shipbuilding industry in the city.[37] Upper Clyde Shipbuilders was formed in 1968 and replaced by Govan Shipbuilders in 1971 (when Yarrows resumed their independence) with the two yards, Govan (Fairfield) and Linthouse (Stephen). More than a hundred million pounds had been committed to the Upper Clyde by the end of 1975 to the point where Govan Shipbuilders became known locally as 'Treasure Island'. A new yard might have been built lower down the Clyde 'but so great was the power of continuity expressed in workers' attitudes and in the outlook of governments as they sought to maintain their standing and to avoid unrest that this element of industry could still draw to itself immense resources'.[38] The seriousness of Glasgow's problems eventually brought about a clear shift in regional development policy with the cancellation of the plan for Stonehouse (Lanark) new town and a transfer of resources (£120 million) to the Glasgow Eastern Area Renewal scheme (GEAR). The eight-year programme is a unique experiment in reconstruction that brings the Scottish Development Agency (SDA), a body set up by government to deal with serious urban–industrial problems following on from the success of the Highlands & Islands Development Board. The SDA is associated with the Scottish Special Housing Association in partnership with the regional (Strathclyde) and district (Glasgow) levels of local government.[39] In this project there is a close link between environmental improvements and industrial development, with the SDA playing a crucial role through advance factory building and massive land clearance, especially at Cambuslang where old metallurgical works will give way to new industrial estates. The scheme marked the conviction of many civil servants that their success in sponsoring the new towns could be transported to Glasgow and other of Scotland's urban problems in which local authorities had failed to show the flair of the Development Corporations; yet it should be noted that the district council was sufficiently impressed to cede to government and its agencies 'an influence over a sector of Glasgow such as no other city in Britain has hitherto yielded up'.[40]

Conclusion

The setting up of a kind of 'new town development corporation' for an inner city area, along with the cancellation of Stonehouse and the winding up of Irvine, brings Scottish regional planning into a post-Barlow phase. Although the Barlow Report may be blamed for not considering the long-term consequences of decentralisation (part of a general lack of expertise in regional economics) the main difficulties lie in the partial implementation of the Clyde Valley Plan and the lack of any regional authority to coordinate a new town programme with aid to the inner areas of cities, with appropriate emphasis on the balance of housing, community facilities and industry that the new towns fostered. New towns can hardly be regarded as mistakes.[41] That would be too excessive a reappraisal, especially since Glenrothes and Livingston still attract much political support in their respective regions (Lothian and Fife) while the Falkirk–Grangemouth expansion provides a focus for large scale industrial development in the Central region.[42] It may still be argued that there is substantial continuity in Scottish regional planning and reappraisal is inevitable in a rapidly changing society.[43] Certainly the scale of Glasgow's problems means that West-Central Scotland must take a leading role in any planning era be it the Improvement Trusts of the late nineteenth century, peripheral council estates between the wars, the Barlow philosophy of the early post-war period or the post-Barlow period now under way. The power of the authorities to control the form of settlement has increased as each period has revealed short-comings in what was seen at the time as the final solution. The shortcomings have meant considerable frustration of high ideals partly through lack of foresight and partly through inadequate expertise and administrative machinery. Perhaps there would have been greater success if Patrick Geddes had been heeded. Cities must be planned but with more regard for form that harmonises with the community's perception of its identify than patterns generated by a transient concept of utopia.

13

Forestry

The planting of private and state forests over the last half century has radically altered the landscape of Scotland, especially in the Outer Regions. Although environmental purists have deplored the invasion of open moorland country and some sensitive local feeling has misgivings about the 'colonialism' implicit in conifer monoculture, the regular patterns of commercial plantations represents no more than an extension of the planned landscape introduced during the improving movement.[1] Rightly, however, the aesthetic appeal of woodlands is being treated as a highly relevant factor now that recreation and amenity are being included in the cost–benefit analysis. But the significance of the forests goes much further. The stands of homegrown timber have lost some of their strategic importance but they can save valuable foreign exchange at a time of rising world prices. And for remote rural areas the woodlands have often been seen as great community assets because of the employment offered and the prospect of processing industries in the future.[2] Unfortunately these benefits are no longer substantial. Mechanisation of much of the forest work means fewer jobs and the impact of this contraction in remote areas has been strengthened by reorganisation of forest management and the centralisation of labour, with the result that outlying plantations, which may have displaced a farm-based population, have no permanent staff. The local depopulation thereby created by forestry has been much resented in some areas, notably Mull (Argyll & Bute), where the high costs of farming under island conditions make it difficult for indigenous interests to compete with the Forestry Commission.[3] At the same time the growing scale of the wood processing industry means more emphasis on large sawmilling and pulping enterprises which must be located at the major central points: only the small industries and the craft activities display a more scattered distribution pattern. But despite centralisation, and the low wages in the industry, arising from the low opportunity costs, forestry offers useful employment in rural areas and makes a positive contribution to the restructuring of settlement patterns.

Table 13.1. *Afforestation 1920–79*
(all figures are 000 ha per annum)

Period	Forestry Commission Planting		Forestry Commission Land Acquisition		Private planting	
	Scotland	Britain	Scotland	Britain	Scotland	Britain
1920–9	1.82	5.60	5.27	12.55	n.a.	0.36
1930–9	4.07	9.33	5.88	13.95	n.a.	0.45
1940–9	3.33	8.79	5.32	10.35	n.a.	0.54
1950–4	12.22	25.14	11.32	24.39	2.98	6.48
1955–9	11.41	23.94	10.08	21.32	5.31	11.71
1960–5	13.09	24.05	9.52	16.46	5.85	14.12
1965–9	12.68	20.55	14.34	16.21	6.61	12.96
1970–4	18.26	25.48	18.86	22.04	23.38	34.88
1975–9	13.50	15.64	10.16	10.42	8.14	10.08

Source: Forestry Commission annual reports.

Evolution of modern forestry

The present upsurge of interest in forestry follows a long period of neglect. Climatic change has been a potent factor in the erosion of woodlands but various types of human activity have also contributed.[4] Some interest in conservation is evident in the fifteenth century, for by 1460 the monks of Coupar Angus Abbey were fencing in the forest of Glenisla (Angus). Even in the Highlands where the need to clear woodland to create wintering grounds for livestock made a policy of protection difficult to justify there are cases of restrained exploitation. There were still some extensive forests in Scotland in 1914 (Figure 13.1) but the rapid depletion of these remaining domestic woodlands in Britain during the First World War gave rise to the idea of a strategic reserve (2.0 million ha).[5] But because forestry skills in the private sector were very scarce a state agency was needed. The Forestry Commission, formed in 1919, went ahead with great energy and planting was continued right through the inter-war period despite attempts by the Treasury to restrict its activities during the depression. The Second World War experience supported the logic of the state policy although very little of the woodland planted after 1919 was of much direct benefit to the renewed war effort. After the war the planting programme accelerated (Table 13.1) and following the Scottish Plan it was expected that planting in Scotland would expand from 14,400 ha in 1969, to 20,000 ha in 1976 (24,300 ha for Great Britain as a whole).[6] But in the light of a Treasury investigation into forestry economies, the combined planting and replanting efforts are limited to 22,000 ha per annum, of which approximately 75 per cent will be in Scotland with the greatest emphasis on the Highlands.

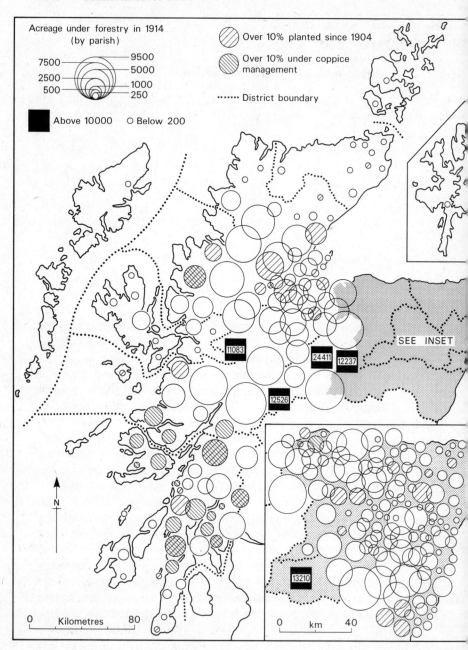

Figure 13.1. Woodlands in the Grampian and Highland regions in 1914 by parishes

Source: Agricultural returns

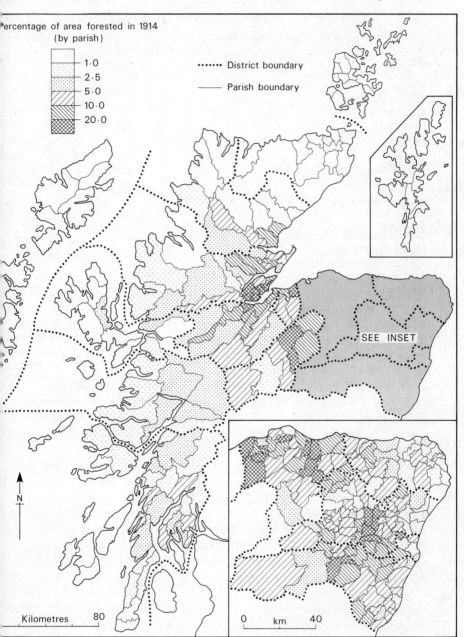

Percentage of area forested in 1914
(by parish)

- 1·0
- 2·5
- 5·0
- 10·0
- 20·0

••••••• District boundary

——— Parish boundary

SEE INSET

N

Kilometres   80

0   km   40

Table 13.2. *Forestry Commission activity in Scotland 1945–73*

Region	1945 Planted area	A.	B.	1973 Planted area	A.	B.	Land not planted	A.	B.
Highlands & Islands	33.71	46.9	16.9	219.35	48.7	25.8	194.17	73.9	58.8
Grampian	14.90	20.8	7.5	58.11	12.9	6.8	6.88	2.6	2.1
Tayside	4.64	6.5	2.3	32.95	7.3	3.9	10.24	3.9	3.1
North	53.25	74.2	26.7	310.42	68.8	36.5	211.29	80.4	64.0
Borders	2.92	3.4	1.5	29.21	6.5	3.4	3.39	1.3	1.0
Dumfries & G'way	7.31	10.2	3.7	52.83	11.7	6.2	22.90	8.7	6.9
South	10.22	14.2	5.1	82.04	18.2	9.6	26.29	10.0	8.0
Outer Regions	63.47	88.5	31.8	392.46	87.0	46.1	237.58	90.4	72.0
Central Belt	8.28	11.5	4.2	58.33	13.0	6.8	25.25	9.6	7.7
Scotland	71.75		36.0	450.79		53.0	262.83		79.7

Figures in 000 ha.
A. Percentage of Scottish total.
B. Percentage of Great Britain total.
Source: Forestry Commission Annual Reports.

Reduced targets are partly related to difficulties over land acquisition and now even the limited programme may be difficult to achieve because not enough land is being acquired.[7] However, it should not be overlooked that a substantial effort is made privately. Estates receive assistance for managing woodlands in an approved manner: planting and maintenance grants, in addition to favourable taxation procedures, give private forestry a higher return than that accruing to the state from the Forestry Commission plantations.[8]

Forestry must be seen as merely one of several legitimate rural land users all of which may well be interested in the same piece of land. The special urgency of the strategic reserve argument, coupled with the low land values of the 1920s and 1930s, enabled the Forestry Commission to acquire large properties which they were then obliged to manage as plantations and not as integrated estates. Although the strategic reserve idea is still relevant it is no longer the sole motive for planting: 'defence considerations have faded but an expanding and vigorous private and national forest estate is important to home industry, especially in view of the forecast of world shortage of timber by the turn of the century'.[9] But agriculture emerged from the Second World War with considerable growth potential arising from state subsidies and improvement grants. Not only has land been less easy to acquire for forestry but the consultation between the Commission and the Department of Agriculture and Fisheries for Scotland that is now necessary before any planting can be undertaken prevents the wholesale breakup of farms by large unbroken plantations. However, the role of forestry in rural development continues to receive great emphasis. The geography of state forests, determined from annual reports of the Forestry Commission, shows a pronounced clustering in Dumfries & Galloway as well as a strong axis of afforestation in the Highlands from Argyll & Bute to the Great Glen (Table 13.2). These areas are very suitable for tree growth and since land was available at relatively low cost there was a natural tendency to concentrate effort in them, but it is characteristic of forests in the Highlands that much of the land is unplantable and remains in hill farming (often with sporting interests superimposed).[10] The present policy of acquiring small blocks is, however, tending to reduce this problem and nowadays relatively little unplantable land is acquired. However the existing concentrations tend to be perpetuated because the new blocks must be managed from an existing forest base and they tend to be grouped close to existing woodland.

Scotland is becoming increasingly important for Forestry Commission planting (Figure 13.2).[11] The Scottish share of total Forestry Commission planted land in Great Britain rose from 36.0 per cent in 1945 to 53.0 in 1973, in which single year Scotland accounted for 76.7 per cent of the land planted. Since the mid 1960s, Scotland has accounted for more than three quarters of all new land acquired. In recognition of its central importance the Forestry Commission headquarters were transferred to Edinburgh during 1974–5. It is a matter for speculation whether the geography of forestry will maintain its 'growth areas' in preference to a more even spread. Although the pressure of other interests may inhibit much further development in the main areas and force a greater dispersal of effort there are experts who advocate a policy of 'forestry development areas' to 'concentrate the nation's afforestation effort and thereby meet modern industrial and social requirements'.[12] Although in each such area forestry would be closely integrated with agriculture, sports and tourism with joint fence lines to meet the needs of all users it would be the main land use, covering as much as 20,000 ha, and with a planting programme 'sustained for a sufficient period to permit adjustment of housing, schooling and other social services to create a permanent force of skilled labour for forestry'.[13] The Dee and Don valleys (Grampian), Moray Firth (Highland) and the Moffat area of Dumfries & Galloway have been suggested as possible sites. The South is a particularly promising area, physically suitable for spruce and well served by main roads. Hence both the Forestry Commission and private agencies have been very active. By contrast the Highland forests involve high planting and road building costs (with strong pressures from the amenity lobby) and although the Grampian and Tayside regions are very suitable for pine and larch, competition from both farming and grouse-shooting interests is strong (Figure 13.3).

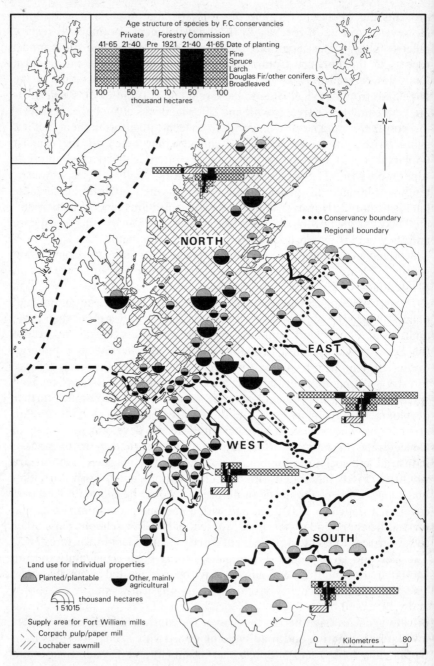

Figure 13.2. Forestry Commission plantations in the Outer Regions 1975
Source: Forestry Commission Annual Reports

Ancillary activities: smallholdings and tourism

One advantage of the early policy of the Forestry Commission in buying up large estates for their plantations was the availability of land for smallholdings which could be offered to supplement limited employment available in the forest. When the Forestry Commission was uncertain of its ability to keep workers fully occupied and when smallholdings were economically and socially acceptable there were clear merits in the scheme. Families would become rooted in the land with interests balanced between farming and forestry and the dispersal of the smallholdings, often based on the old farmhouses and cottages, would mean a built-in fire protection service. However, despite the depression which brought smallholdings to the height of their popularity there were limits to the acceptability of smallholdings by the workers and to their availability from the Forestry Commission. Since a proliferation of worthwhile part-time farms would have left little land for the plantations the holdings tended to be small and were not a central issue in a land use plan which was forced by Treasury pressure to use all resources for the main task in hand. However some of the Argyll & Bute forests made relatively generous provision with more than a dozen smallholdings at Ardgarten, Glenbranter and Glenfinart. But gradually the contradictions in the smallholding policy as well as falling interest by forestry workers tended to place more emphasis on the village community. Particularly after the Second World War, employees in forests which were not adjacent to existing communities were housed in new settlements. Thus the new village of Dalavich (Argyll) was built on the shore of Loch Awe to look after Inverliever forest and a community arose at Ae (Nithsdale) to serve the forest of that name. The villages, like the smallholdings system which preceded them, met with mixed fortunes. The houses were well planned and formed cosy terraces in the heart of the woodlands. Where they were close to other settlements and to public transport a strong community life developed. But the remoter settlements have not always proved attractive because the services are too limited and poor or nonexistent public transport makes it difficult for younger members of families to attend school or employment outside the forest service. The empty houses at Dalavich and Polloch (Lochaber), a phenomenon that arises partly from the decline in employment in forestry as a whole, underline the failure of the Commission's idealistic drive to repopulate the empty glens. It is fortunate that the boom in tourism should create a demand for accommodation at any rate during the summer, but the future of the forest settlement pattern would seem to lie with the main villages where a complex of rural activities may together support a community large and viable enough to support an acceptable range of local authority services.

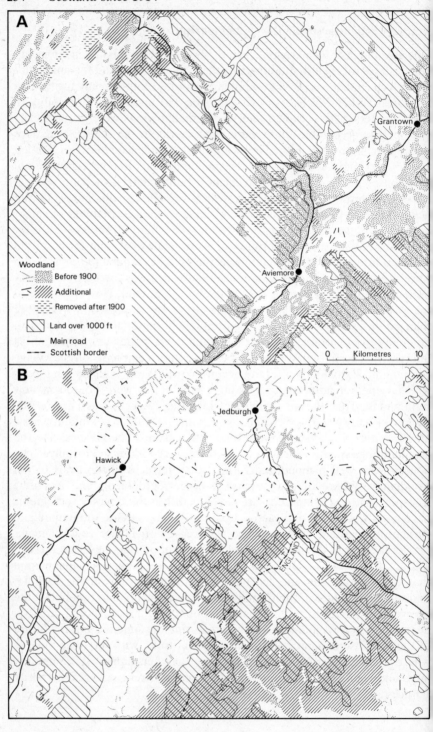

A

Woodland

Before 1900

Additional

Removed after 1900

Land over 1000 ft

Main road

Scottish border

0   Kilometres   10

Grantown

Aviemore

B

Jedburgh

Hawick

ENGLAND

Besides the basic silvicultural activities tourist interest arises from the origins of the forest. Visitors to Reelig Glen near Beauly (Inverness) can see the stands laid out beside the Moniack Burn by James Baillie Fraser in the early nineteenth century. The pathways and bridges of the old estate lead through the exotic plantations of Douglas fir, Oregon cedar, Spanish chestnut and Western hemlock. The stands of Douglas fir, planted about 1880, have been left because of their fine appearance although these fast growing trees would normally be felled after about fifty years. Although rather less lavish, European and Japanese larch at Craig Phadrig, Douglas fir and Sitka spruce at Culloden and Scots pine at Inchnacardoch, all within reach of Inverness, originate in the decade before the First World War. At Glenmore natural pinewoods remain, some four centuries old, and isolated remnants of the old pine forest will be seen at Morangie and Torrachility (Ross & Cromarty). The property recently acquired at Corrour (Lochaber) on Rannoch Moor (part of Strathmashie Forest) bears the stamp of the pioneering work of the late Sir John Stirling Maxwell who planted the slopes around Loch Ossian and Loch Treig and made the first attempts to drain and plough part of the moor itself. But there can be few woodlands as dramatic as Drumtochty (Deeside & Kincardine), part of Mearns Forest, covering the former heather moor on the slopes of Goyle Hill and Strathfinella Hill in the lee of the Cairn o'Mounth. Much of forestry work by the Gammell family was destroyed by the First World War fellings but a core of 80 ha of beech, larch and spruce and other ornamental trees remains on the sheltered lower slopes of the Drumtochty Glen, setting off both the small chapel and the early nineteenth century castellated mansion house built in the warm sandstone so characteristic of the Howe o' the Mearns. Planting has since been taken up to heights of over 300 m with a preference for larch, continuing the private estate tradition, as well as Sitka spruce (though the latter is replaced by Norway spruce on sites where spring frosts are likely to be severe). This mixing of species makes a positive contribution to a forest landscape which all too often presents a monotonous uniformity. The diversified woodlands, the snugness of the glen drained by the headwaters of Luther Water and the rays of the late winter sunshine on the mansion house fix a clear identity that few other state forests can match. Among the private forestry estates of Tayside, Cortachy near Kirriemuir and Glamis near Forfar (Angus) are outstanding examples. In the Grampian region there is the fine prospect from the summit of the Bin of Cullen across the woodlands of the Seafield estate

---

Figure 13.3. Local forestry studies: changes in the woodland area since 1900
A. Aviemore area (Badenoch & Strathspey)
B. Hawick area (Roxburgh)
Source: Ordnance Survey maps

towards the Moray coast, and the old grove of European larch planted by Sir Frances Grant of Monymusk in 1741 to form a large landscape garden or 'paradise' in the gorge of the Don in the Gordon district.

Large units of forest imposed on depopulated hill farming terrain do not entirely obliterate the older economy. While the better accommodation is retained for housing forest workers and smallholders, many ruined cottages and crumbling dykes are left buried deep in the woodlands, such as Nether Knocknashang in the Forest of Ae (Nithsdale) and the old farms deep in the Braes of Gartly, now swamped by Huntly Forest (Gordon). From the recreational angle the forests have much to offer in terms of the wild life. Red deer can only be tolerated in very small numbers, but roedeer find their way into the best fenced woods. The dense stands of conifers are ideal for breeding and herds of only three to six animals may be seen in small glades. But since trees can be managed by 'fraying' (stripping of bark as the animals remove the velvet from their antlers) numbers have to be kept down, though the Forestry Commission trappers aim at maintaining a healthy breeding stock. Other mammals in the forest include badgers, foxes, red squirrels, pine marten and wildcats. Forests contain a multitude of small birds: chaffinches and willow warblers are common at Farigaig on the shores of Loch Ness (where a Forest and Wild Life Exhibition is open to visitors), while fieldfares and redwings are winter visitors to Reelig Glen (Inverness). The water habitat of Loch Morlich (Badenoch & Strathspey) is particularly diverse, with dippers, herons, mallards, oyster catchers and sandpipers. Such resources are being encouraged to develop in forests through the use of nesting baskets to attract birds to promising stretches of water. In the woods themselves the bird population is affected by the tree species. Scots pine is more conducive to wild life – and ground vegetation – than is Douglas fir or Norway spruce, trees which cut out so much light that the new ground is covered only by a layer of dead leaves. On the other hand, the light branching habit of European larch allows light to reach the ground and the space it occupies may be underplanted with shade tolerant trees. Interest for the visitor is also maintained by greater flexibility in management. Alder, ash, birch, rowan and willow are left in the forest in small amounts to complete naturally with pine and in general to relieve the monotony of conifers, the birch being particularly effective in breaking up the 'dark' aspect of a large mass of conifers while its annual leaf fall forms a mild humus to ameliorate the acid humus formed under conifers.

Apart from selected forests which make special arrangements for visitors through the marking out of forest walks and provision of picnic places and car parks there are a limited number of Forest Parks where large forest estates offer exceptional recreational facilities. In 1935 the Forestry Commission decided to exploit the forests to the west of Loch Long

(Argyll) as a Forest Park, with the cooperation of the Corporation of Glasgow. There are notable woodlands, including the Benmore plantations of the nineteenth century and some small conifer stands at Glenbranter and Glenfinart, with attractive lochside areas and extensive tracts of open hill country above the forests. The whole Forest Park of 25,000 ha is relatively close to Glasgow but there is accommodation locally since the former mansion houses of Loch Goil and Glenfinart are now hotels while Ardgartan is a youth hostel and Benmore an educational centre.[14] Smaller projects in Argyll include the walks and picnic spots laid out at Aros, Mull, the wildlife centres at Carradale, Inverinan, Strachur and Tighnabruaich. A forest centre has also been provided at Dalavich, a forest village offering a fine prospect along Loch Awe. The facilities, which include catering, information, and accommodation, have been grafted on to a declining forest community which the tourist centre – and social club – may revive. And Argyll is the location of two of the Forestry Commission's three Arboreta, or collections of rare specimen trees: Kilmun in Benmore Forest and Crarae House on Loch Fyne. In Badenoch and Strathspey, there is the Queen's Forest where the attractions of Cairngorm and pine-fringed Loch Morlich bring many visitors. Glen More was the scene of extensive felling by Canadian lumbermen during the First World War. This followed a period of some forty years during which the area had been used mainly for stalking, with the woodland expanding by natural seeding. The Commission acquired the land in 1923 and commenced replanting, though native pines were encouraged to continue their natural reseeding in certain areas. Plantable land was exhausted by 1960. It was in 1948 that the Glen More Forest Park (5,000 ha) was established and now, in addition to the marking out of forest walks and longer treks, the Commission has installed an information centre and a large camping and caravan site. And over the years the development has been functionally incorporated into a much wider scheme for tourism and recreation with the opening of the new lodge by the Scottish Council of Physical Recreation (the old lodge is now a youth hostel) and the development of winter sports, linked with the improvement of the road right through to Coire Cas by 1967. Much of the land beyond the main forestry perimeter fence was sold to the HIDB in 1971 but, along with neighbouring private estates such as Glenavon and Rothiemurchus, the Forestry Commission remains deeply involved in the Cairngorm tourist industry.[15]

Provision of recreation facilities is a relatively recent innovation. Initially required to restrict all activities which did not contribute directly to timber production the Commission could not begin to realise the potential until the social benefits of forestry were explicitly recognised. Mature woodlands were now seen not only as an economic asset but also as 'a source of pleasure to the eye and spirit'.[16] The emphasis on 'magnificent scenery and the great variety of wildlife' was increased in 1963 by the requirements that the Commission should take account of public access and recreation in its planning and again in 1967 when the Countryside (Scotland) Act gave the Commission authority to cater for recreation to the point of providing accommodation and tourist facilities.[17] The 1972 White Paper recognised that forests can make an important contribution to recreation and accepted 'that it will in appropriate cases be right for the Commission to seek to enhance the appearance and attraction of its woodlands despite some resulting reduction in profitability'.[18] The need for a close interest in forestry planning by local authorities was also granted. Although it appears that few people entering forests see timber production as being inherently antagonistic to their recreation it obviously contributes to the ideal of multiple use if there is a graded age structure, variation in density and imaginative laying out of rides and clearings. Thus proposals for the designation of areas with high landscape value often include references to 'unsympathetic forestry' with long vertical lines marking the fire breaks or plantation boundaries. More specifically it has been suggested that recreational needs should influence land acquisition policy, especially near to urban areas, and that the Commission should take the initiative in seeking liaison with adjacent property owners to the point where local or subregional recreational plans might be worked out.

Some impression of the potential emerges from the surveys by I. P. Mitchell.[19] At some of the forests in Argyll and Bute, especially at Loch Awe, Tighnabruaich and Argyll Forest Park, boating offers distinct possibilities. This also applies to the Tummel (Tayside) group of Allean, Fascally and Glenerrochty. The Highland forests, however, offer the finest scenic attractions with Farigaig overlooking Loch Ness, Lael covering the Corrieshalloch Gorge and Slattadale standing beside Loch Marree. There are forests which although lacking in major arboricultural or scenic appeal do have positional advantages which would be exploited for tourist transit camps: Barcaldine stands on the main road between Oban and Fort William while the South Laggan section of Glengarry Forest is adjacent to the Fort William to Inverness road and the Caledonian Canal. Exceptional opportunities arise in Glen Affric where expansion of facilities along the roads leading to Loch Beneveian and Loch Mullardoch could be complemented by 'buffer' and 'wilderness' zones further inland. And Torrachilty Forest is well placed for water sports on Loch Achilty and for the proposed development of winter sports on the slopes of Ben Wyvis which could be exploited by a new road and 'Forest Park' style development adjacent to the existing community of Garve. It is urged by local interests concerned with the Ben Wyvis Ski Development Association that the skiing, especially short runs on the south facing Coire na Fareiach, could be better than the Cairngorms with good possibilities on the smooth slopes even with a minimal snow cover. No doubt present requirements need only modest exploitation but tourist pressure on rural Scotland is likely to increase and it is important that the Forestry Commission as a major landowner with interests in all the areas discussed by the National Parks Committee should be ready to take a positive lead.

Integration of farming and forestry

The integration of forestry with other activities has assumed importance because the concept of multiple use offers a solution to conflicts of interest involved in rural land use. Several studies have underlined the point.[20] Unless these are economic or political considerations which demand an exclusive land use policy, of the sort which drove sheep from the hills in the interests of deer in the late nineteenth century and forestry in the early twentieth, it is clearly desirable that planning should seek a solution whereby integration may offer positive benefits to all concerned. Forestry and farming may well combine on land with a high 'elasticity', since a small plantation may shelter the remaining farm land and justify intensification on the smaller area.[21] There are basic antagonisms: foxes are useful to the forester in controlling pests in the woodlands but to the hill farmer they are a menace, especially at lambing time and in some districts, notably Lochaber, local farmers have made great efforts to control the threat. In the case of muirburn there is again a division of interest between the farmer and sportsman who find the burning off of old heather and the encouragement of new growth virtually essential and the forester who is concerned about the safety of his trees, and will only burn heather before planting. Again, the forester is obliged to erect and maintain fencing to exclude deer: not only do these barriers drive the deer on to the sheltered grazings of adjacent farms but sheep on the rough ground above the plantations may be driven into pockets in the fencing in the course of their instinctive search for low ground in bad weather. With local consultation, problems may be minimised and an atmosphere created in which the fuller mixing of land uses could be considered. In this context reference may be made to the desirability of small blocks of forestry which will provide shelter for the intervening grazings and justify reseeding to the point where the increased carrying capacity more than compensates for the loss of land to the plantations.[22] This is a laudable ideal but the forest blocks may be uneconomic to fence and plant if they are too small and too scattered. Shelter belts are particularly marginal from the forestry viewpoint unless they have sufficient depth to justify the fencing and are accessible without heavy investment in road building.

Wood processing

The expansion of woodland in the last half century has generated optimism in the processing sector and indeed one important argument in favour of forestry in rural areas relates to the possibility of the raw material attracting local processing. For many years after the Forestry Commission was formed the output of timber was small and consisted solely of thinnings which were sawn up locally for pit-props, fencing stobs and firewood. A declining market for pit-props, combined with increasing timber output, led to a search for new processes. The result was the construction of a sawmill at Strachur by a firm of industrial timber merchants interested in the production of planks suitable for building and box-making. The mill was conveniently located in relation to the relatively heavily forested area of south Argyll and thinnings from some 1,200 ha. of forest are taken, providing work for 40 men. This Cowal-Ari Sawmilling Company proved to be a successful pioneer in the processing and marketing of fast-growing Sitka spruce, with especial concern for small-sized timber and the processing of waste products.[23] Over the years the growth in timber output has called for further processing facilities. The wider acceptance of home grown timber, now available at suitable collecting centres in large quantities, has resulted in a new geography of sawmilling in which large units at convenient central points within large catchment areas are replacing the small local (and sometimes temporary) mill. Several chipboard mills have been opened but the greatest investment was made at Fort William where a £15 million pulp and paper mill was opened in 1966 by Wiggins Teape. Fort William enjoyed a convenient location for the collection of timber from expanding forests in the North but unfortunately the economies of pulp production at Fort William, gravely undermined by rising transport costs, caused a closedown of that section of the mill in 1980. Nevertheless the strategic position of the area led to a further large project, the Kilmallie sawmill, opened in 1974 by the Elgin-based timber firm, Riddoch of Rothiemay. And further development of wood processing in Scotland should be feasible as more timber becomes available. In the South the Economic Forestry Group have urged that selection of areas for planting should be made with access to future processing centres in mind: their Eskdalemuir/Carsphairn project aims at concentrating forestry as part of a wider strategy of 'timber industry regions', each with its own processing unit or complex. As well as reducing the Fort William pulp mill hinterland and allowing separate developments round the inner Moray Firth and in south Argyll, Dumfries and Galloway might support a chain of mills extending from Langholm to Stranraer. At present however much of the wood from the South is processed in England, apart from the Annan chipboard mill and it is felt that for the foreseeable future existing mills will be able to take the increase in yield. Any completely new installations are likely to be sawmills, with lower capital and raw material requirements than pulp mills and an absence of the water supply and effluent problems which limit the choice of pulp mill location.[24]

14

Island perspectives

Small offshore islands are more prominent in Scotland than in any other part of the British Isles and the fact that they are particularly numerous off the north and west coasts has led to close parallels being drawn between Scotland and Scandinavian lands such as the Faeroes, Iceland and Norway.[1] It is very difficult to decide how many islands there are altogether because they range in size from Lewis & Harris with some 200,000 ha down to the most insignificant dimensions. The census of 1861 recognised 787 islands and all but 31 lay in the Highland counties extending from Bute to Shetland. Even then only 185 of these islands were inhabited: in 1971 the figure was down to 105. The story of island depopulation is quite as emotive as the saga of the clearances and even though the details are too fragmentary to permit a comprehensive study of desertion going far back in time there is a sufficient number of well documented cases to reveal community failure and landlord oppression on a scale that disturbs the social conscience of any one who is orientated by the ethos of the welfare state.[2] Yet sympathy for people who find it necessary to transfer to a new environment should not obscure the normality of this process, for a farmer who decides to farm an island by commuting from an external base, rather than by living permanently on the holding, is really behaving no differently from a mainland colleague who enlarges his holding by amalgamation and takes over a formerly separate holding where the farm house may then fall into disuse. Rural depopulation on the mainland has been just as dramatic as in the islands though it may be obscured in the official statistics because growth in urban areas may be set against rural decline. Furthermore, trends may not be immediately obvious to travellers because the depopulation is selective and emphasises settlements and individual houses that are not closely tied to the surfaced roads.

Yet in certain respects islands are different. Except where bridges and causeways have been built they are separated from other communities by a stretch of water that may vary from a short sheltered 'sound' as at Scalpay

(Harris) to several kilometres of open sea, as is the case with the Shetland islands of Fair Isle, Foula and the Skerries. Given a subsistence economy of the kind formerly practised on St Kilda regular intercourse with the outside world was not necessary and the annual visits of the factor from Harris were sufficient to handle the trade and other business.[3] Such economies could persist well into the nineteenth century given a landlord who would forgo the extra income that a perceived alternative organisation might yield and a community where sufficient numbers were prepared to deny themselves access to the higher living standards that migration might permit. Choices are stark because there was little scope for any intermediate situation whereby islanders might commute daily or weekly to work outside the community, in view of transport difficulties, and any seasonal or permanent migration would be inhibited by perceived culture shock in leaving a closely knit and self-contained community. But while the timing of change is impossible to determine with accuracy it is evident that the twentieth century has introduced a new perception of island life in which the remoteness that was once seen as a protection for a vigorous local culture becomes a constraint inhibiting access to the various innovations that are diffused down the central place hierarchy.[4] Even if local authorities are prepared to make concessions over thresholds and allow small communities to have certain services which in a normal situation would almost certainly be centralised there will be perceived isolation costs: partly financial (through limited choice of employment and increased prices for goods) and partly social (access to higher education and special recreational/cultural facilities); in the island as in Scotland as a whole it is the degree of integration into a continuous hierarchy of settlements and economic activity that is all important.

Variations in population trends

Today it is possible to claim that all islands are well integrated with the rest of the country in terms both of values and perceptions on the one hand and access to services on the other. Given the present commitment to welfare with basic services assured to the smallest communities it is likely that the number of future desertions will be relatively small. But the transition to the present pattern has been highly variable. The largest islands may be taken out of the reckoning because they have the resources to maintain relatively large populations, generate service centres at the intermediate level and attract investment in efficient transport links to the mainland (Figure 14.1 and Table 14.1). Largely through the growth of their leading towns (Kirkwall, Lerwick and Stornoway), Orkney Mainland, Shetland Mainland and Lewis–Harris have shown greater stability in population than have their satellite islands and account for a much higher proportion

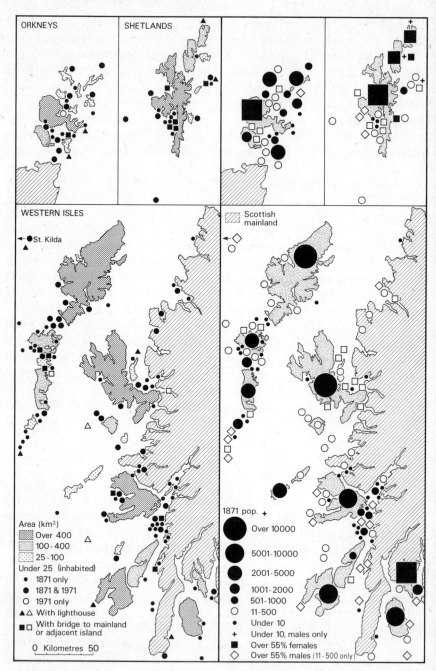

Figure 14.1. Island population 1871–1971 (Highlands & Islands only)
Source: Census of Scotland

Table 14.1. *Island population 1871–1971*

Group[a]	Category	1871			1921			1971		
		A.	B.	C.	A.	B.	C.	A.	B.	C.
Shetland	I	1	21.7	41.3	1	18.3	44.7	1	12.9	47.7
	II	2	6.4	48.7	2	3.9	48.4	2	2.3	51.7
	III	3	2.0	42.7	3	1.7	46.1	3	1.2	50.5
	IV	24	2.2	45.2	18	1.7	46.0	13	0.9	52.5
	Total	30	32.5	43.1	24	25.5	45.5	19	17.3	48.7
Orkney	I	1	16.5	44.5	1	14.1	46.4	1	12.7	48.4
	II	1	1.4	45.9	1	1.0	49.6	1	0.4	49.7
	III	7	10.5	48.0	7	7.1	48.6	7	3.2	51.7
	IV	21	3.1	46.7	21	2.3	51.0	14	0.6	53.3
	Total	30	31.6	45.9	30	24.4	47.6	23	17.0	49.3
Western Isles	I	1	25.9	47.7	1	31.7	46.8	1	22.2	48.1
	II	2	6.9	46.6	2	5.8	48.8	2	3.7	53.8
	III	3	3.9	48.4	3	3.9	49.9	3	2.6	53.5
	IV	31	2.8	47.8	26	2.8	47.4	12	1.4	55.6
	Total	37	39.5	47.6	32	44.2	47.3	18	30.0	49.6
Skye	I	1	17.3	46.0	1	11.0	47.3	1	7.2	48.6
	II	1	0.1	54.3	1	0.1	63.1	1	*	40.0
	III	2	0.7	46.5	2	0.6	51.0	2	0.2	44.4
	IV	17	0.8	47.4	18	0.5	53.1	9	*	56.8
	Total	21	18.9	46.1	22	12.3	47.9	13	7.5	48.4
Argyll & Bute	I	3	19.3	48.8	3	17.4	45.2	3	9.4	48.9
	II	2	10.8	42.8	2	19.9	41.4	2	8.6	43.9
	III	4	4.7	49.7	4	2.7	50.7	4	1.3	50.3
	IV	48	5.3	51.8	37	5.7	41.7	22	2.0	49.9
	Total	58	40.2	47.7	49	45.8	43.4	31	21.4	47.1
Others	I	—	—	—	—	—	—	—	—	—
	II	—	—	—	—	—	—	—	—	—
	III	—	—	—	—	—	—	—	—	—
	IV	11	0.3	52.0	16	0.4	53.1	1	0.5	46.9
	Total	11	0.3	52.0	16	0.4	53.1	1	0.5	46.9
Scotland	I	7	100.8	45.7	7	92.5	46.1	7	64.5	48.2
	II	8	25.6	45.5	8	30.8	44.1	8	15.1	47.7
	III	19	22.0	47.9	19	15.9	49.1	19	8.6	51.7
	IV	152	14.5	48.7	139	13.4	45.8	71	5.4	52.0
	Total	186	162.9	46.2	173	152.1	46.1	105	93.7	48.7

A. Number of inhabited islands
B. Total population (thousands)
C. Male population as a percentage of the total
* Less than 0.1
Category 1 has area over 400 km², Category 2 has area 100–400 km², Category 3 has area 25–100 km² and Category 4 is below 25 km²
[a] Stroma (Caithness) is grouped with Orkney; Skye includes Small Isles and islands off the west mainland of Ross & Cromarty and Sutherland; Argyll & Bute includes Eilean Shona, the whole of Firth of Clyde and Loch Lomond; Others covers the Solway and the whole east coast from Ness Islands (Inverness).

Source: Census of Scotland

of the total population of Orkney, Shetland and the Western Isles than a century ago.[5] The Inner Hebrides do not form distinct clusters clearly separate from the mainland and, significantly, they do not comprise discrete districts in the present administrative systems (in contrast to the three areas already mentioned which are each administered by independent 'island authorities'). While some of them, such as Islay, Mull and Skye, are sufficiently well endowed to support large populations their leading centres are relatively small. In 1971 Bowmore, Portree and Tobermory (total population 3,000) together accounted for only 22.8 per cent of the total population of their islands, compared with 33.2 per cent for Kirkwall, Lerwick and Stornoway (total population 15,900). Greater mainland dependence for the higher levels of servicing has made it relatively difficult to establish island growth points in the Inner Hebrides and it is particularly unfortunate that concentration on the leading settlement is constrained by the fact that under present transport arrangements they are not the points most accessible to the mainland.[6] The Clyde islands, especially Arran, Bute and Cumbrae, do have congruence between their main settlements and steamer terminals. Indeed the growth of Brodick, Millport and Rothesay (total population 8,500) has been quite astonishing in relation to their total island populations: in 1971 these settlements accounted for 63.8 per cent of their totals.[7] But the process of centralisation within each island has been greatly overshadowed by migration from the mainland, particularly to Millport and Rothesay. Some of this migration is related to retirement, inducing an ageing of the island population which is rather disturbing, and some to commuting to work in the Glasgow area.

The satellite islands are in a rather different category. Their resources are in general relatively modest and would normally support only a small community enjoying a limited range of services. The relatively high cost of maintaining these services means that small islands become particularly vulnerable to reorganisation which can greatly affect community morale. But generalisation is particularly difficult at this level because local circumstances are so variable. Differences in community size, island history, local resources, age structure and accessibility mean that the small island category gives a bewildering range of unique cases.[8] But leaving aside the islands with non-permanent populations (lighthouse keepers or service personnel, who will be mentioned more fully later) there appear to be five basic patterns. First, islands with subsistence economies that failed to adapt and decayed by migration to the point where evacuation was inevitable, as in the Western Isles with Mingulay in 1909 (one family remained until 1934) and St Kilda in 1930. Second, islands with subsistence economies which have been able to maintain a community and attract local services, with various ancillary occupations resting on a crofting base, as on

Barra and Tiree.[9] Third, islands on which crofting communities were re-established during the land settlement era: land agitation over Vatersay (Western Isles) began in 1902 when people from Castlebay (Barra) applied to the Congested Districts Board (CDB) for potato ground on the island. Allocation of some 25 ha to fifty applicants in 1903 was followed by squatting on the island (although the intention was that people would commute to their holdings from Barra and not live on Vatersay permanently). Eventually the whole of Vatersay was then taken over (1909) and sixty holdings for crofter–fishermen were staked out; the CDB also provided some basic infrastructure including roads and fencing, water and drainage. Vatersay is thus one of few islands that has actually increased its population between 1871 and 1971, although there has been a considerable reduction since the peak recorded after the land settlement.

It is difficult to find any close parallel to Vatersay but certain islands are known to have been settled as refuges at the time of the clearances: an example is Scarp in Harris which is still inhabited although the last of the indigenous population left in 1971. In the post-war period it has exemplified the common Hebridean problem of maintaining a viable community on a very limited resource base. The school closed in 1967, by which time the little community had dwindled to seven households, and the post office followed in 1969. Then, fourthly, come the islands where agriculture was thoroughly reorganised on commercial lines to give rise to a basically non-crofting community. In 1852 the laird of Coll cleared the island because it could not support its congested population and the land was redistributed into larger holdings with new houses and steadings suitable for dairy farming. Tenants with the necessary skills came in from Ayrshire and Kintyre and their descendants formed the core of the population when the *West Highland Survey* made its study of the island in 1947, though there were also a minority of true Highlanders of crofting-fishing stock.[10] Coll may be linked with such Orkney islands as Westray (Figure 14.2) where reorganisation of holdings has created a base for commercial farming but without any significant eviction of the native population.[11] Finally there are farming islands where instead of a genuine community there is basically a single household, as on Gometra in Mull and Eilean Shona in Lochaber. In such situations it is common to find that links with the island are not traditional and that the island is farmed from an appreciation of island life despite the inconveniences, rather than being used for escape proof sheep grazing from a mainland base.

The role of fishing

It would appear therefore that the impact of the clearances on the mainland in displacing small tenants to remote places with no previous

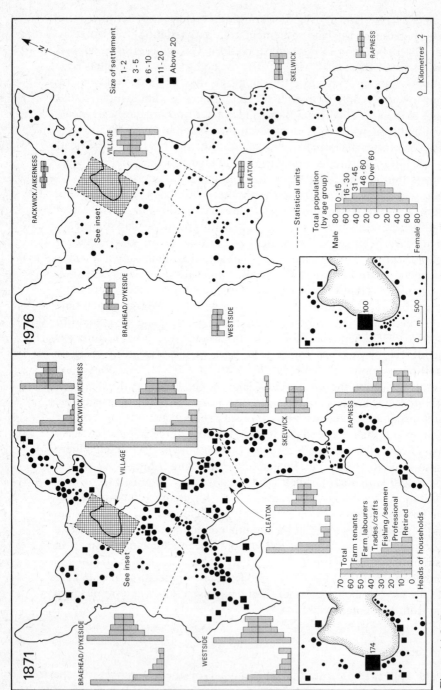

Figure 14.2. Population of Westray (Orkney) 1871–1976
Source: Census of Scotland and field work by Mr H. A. Scott

history of colonisation was seen also in the islands, especially in the Outer Hebrides, and resulted in remarkable contrasts in the relationship between population and resources. In both mainland and island situations the refuges have invariably lost population heavily in recent years but some small islands retain astonishingly large populations thanks to success with ancillary industries (fishing and textiles) and the development of a good infrastructure. Anomalies in island fortunes are highlighted most dramatically by small islands such as Eriskay (Western Isles) with a large population in relation to the land resources and others such as Mingulay that are now deserted. The Hebridean island of Scalpay and the Shetland islands of Burra and Whalsay are particularly impressive for their commitment to fishing and it is rather anomalous that so much of the fishing in the islands should be based in small communities well away from the main ports and continue to thrive in such places. Explanations remain incomplete but for Shetland H. D. Smith claims that 'a combination of boat ownership and enterprise by fishermen was necessary to maintain these communities', once momentum had been built up through opportunity for a combination of white fishing and herring fishing in adjacent waters.[12] With the ability to catch and sell fish all the year round fishermen were ready to accept a full-time involvement in the industry and to change from older regimes of subservience to landlord initiatives, through fishing tenures, or to the truck system of the merchants, to ownership of their own equipment and marketing agreements with merchants and curers. Herring boats might be laid up during the winter and small open boats used for the white fishing but activity can be virtually continuous.

Over the years circumstances have changed but there has been a readiness to innovate.[13] With assistance from fishery authorities and the HIDB the fleets have been modernised, with flexibility still the key to success, and harbours improved.[14] In the early 1970s there was a significant expansion of output in the islands, and processing of white fish and shell fish (to meet a rising Continental and American demand) became established in any number of localities, including Burra, Yell and Northmavine. However stimulation of development and use of new technology has not been accompanied by an adequate programme of rational resource management. Currently the situation in Shetland is difficult because of various conservation measures that have limited catches and led to some closure of processing units while the expansion of the oil industry has imposed some constraints on fishing in the vicinity of pipelines and presented the threat of pollution.[15] But the local authority believe that fishing will in future become Shetland's most important industry again, especially if new forms of regulation can ensure that local boats can enjoy special rights to access to their home waters, and some processing stations are being kept 'in mothballs' pending a future growth in catches. However, the drastic reduction of the former open-sea freedom of fishing has already brought important benefits to the Outer Hebrides.[16] Fishery limits have improved prospects for fishing off the Atlantic coast of Lewis for high quality white fish, which once supported a flourishing community at Loch Roag, and also for blue whiting that is eminently suitable for reduction to fish meal. The combination has been made viable by the provision of an assured market for ling and saithe through a Norwegian firm which was anxious to increase its capacity for production of dried fish (stokfisk) to satisfy a rising European demand. The new harbour and factory at Breasclete on Loch Roag (Lewis), completed in 1978, represents an important diversification of the fishing industry, and although the boats using the new pier are not necessarily local, or even Hebridean, the shore jobs do benefit the Breasclete community and further growth of trade may come through the landing of mixed catches, part for the factory and part for freezing in Stornoway and transfer to the mainland. Provided prices compare adequately with those offered at mainland ports, Lewis could become an important base for fish landing, offering boats an opportunity to spend more time at the grounds owing to the shorter journey to port.

Island manufactures

This last remark highlights a fundamental difficulty that has constrained island development over the last hundred years. Because the home market is very small it becomes increasingly difficult to generate local industries to serve the community: even for commodities like bread the optimum scale of production has grown too large to allow many local bakeries to survive against imports from the Scottish mainland. Island manufacturing for a wider market is a theoretical possibility but one that must take account of the relatively high transport costs for both raw materials and finished products, remoteness from customers that increases the problems of marketing, and limited access to highly specialised services that can assure the highest efficiency in both labour and management. There is a further difficulty in the cyclical nature of business which can result in outside industrialists establishing branch factories in island locations to make use of local labour at times of high demand, only to close such outlying factories during recession. These difficulties are not insuperable. Where local raw materials are available for processing as in the case of fish an enterprise may be viable provided that there is sufficient quantity landed to allow steady work at an acceptable scale, that management is efficient and transport costs for the finished product are reflected in a realistic differential in raw material prices between mainland and island landing points that fishermen will accept. Islands can also develop manufactures based on local skills: promotion that emphasises island production can give additional emphasis to any intrinsic distinctiveness in a product and stimulate purchase in preference to a lower-priced mass-produced item. But the crucial issue is whether, having identified a suitable product, it is possible to combine a high quality 'craft' approach with a scale of production that will support a marketing infrastructure and make a significant contribution to island employment. A related question is whether island producers will work rigidly to uniform procedures without which it may be difficult to achieve effective promotion. There are a good many craft workshops in the islands but their contribution to the viability of whole communities can only be modest. The most successful industries with a significant labour force are in the wool textile sector.

The Harris Tweed industry shows how a domestic tradition can be modernised successfully without losing all contact with its origins as a rural craft. Cloth was made on Harris crofts in the last century on a 'home industry' basis, but the Earl of Dunmore, who bought Harris in 1834, promoted the island tweed in London and tried to encourage weaving in other parts of the Outer Hebrides. By the 1870s weaving had taken root in Uist and Barra and the following decade it spread to Lewis. The industry was an excellent ancillary to crofting, especially welcome at a time when part-time fishing was declining. With support from proprietors (and from the Congested Districts Board during its short existence) machinery was installed in Harris (Tarbert and Geocrab) and Lewis (Stornoway) to handle the carding and spinning of island wool, thereby restricting the domestic activity to weaving. This compromise gradually won almost universal acceptance and the 'Orb' stamp can be applied only to cloth woven on crofts in the Outer Hebrides from wool processed in island mills. The wool now comes from the mainland but the standard combination of factory and domestic work in the islands has created an eminently marketable product and one that provides a fundamental role in the economy of Lewis. However, although backed by legal judgement the success of the industry will ultimately depend on how well it can adjust to changing conditions. A wider cloth that would find access to new markets calls for extensive re-equipment and the expensive new looms that have been developed for this purpose would have to be installed in central workshops and operated on a shift basis. But Lewis crofters are reluctant to give up their independence, as owners of their looms, and are concerned about the lack of flexibility that would arise under a shift system necessary to make the fullest use of the new equipment.

However the new technology has been introduced with HIDB support in the old Geocrab factory which turns out a material that is in fact 'Harris Tweed' but which cannot be stamped as such because it does not satisfy the legal requirements which the majority of Lewis weavers still support through the Harris Tweed Association.[17] There are also Harris people producing cloth in the traditional manner, entirely as a domestic industry, but the best prospects would appear to lie in the small integrated mill, or weaving shed using imported yarn, such as have multiplied in the post-war period. The success of hosiery and knitwear in Shetland has been constrained by failure to evolve a standard method of work and by the confusion that exists between the Shetland wool and Shetland manufactures (for the fine local wool is in fact mixed to achieve a blend that can be used in manufacture outside Shetland) but high demand for quality knitwear has led to several small cooperatives enabling the women folk to turn out socks and sweaters (sometimes using local wool) and complement the crofting and fishing of their husbands.[18] The peat resources of the islands offer a potential base for development but since the failure of the experiments in Lewis to produce tar, wax and lubricants just before the First World War and lack of success with peat fired power stations (after experiments at Altnabraec in Sutherland after the Second World War) it seems that domestic fuel will continue the only outlet.[19]

Distilling is well established on Islay, with additional units in Jura, Orkney and Skye.[20] The seaweed that gave rise to an important kelp industry at the turn of the eighteenth century was subsequently appreciated for the production of iodine, but after encountering high costs in importing fuel the extraction works set up on Tiree, at Bailemeadhonach, in 1863, was quickly transferred to Clydebank. All the processing units were located in the Central Belt in 1900 when foreign competition in potash salts had reduced the number to four (situated at Bonnybridge, Clydebank, Falkirk and Kilwinning).[21] Further uses were found in fertiliser production (Moray Firth Seaweed Company) and most recently in alginates: mainland processing at Barcaldine (Argyll & Bute) and Girvan (Kyle & Carrick) follows from drying and milling in the Outer Hebrides at Keose, Lochboisdale and Sponish.[22] Small engineering units have appeared in Barra (spectacle frames) and Sanday, Orkney (electronic components) under HIDB incentives but a much larger scale of activity has been achieved in Stornoway through construction of modules for North Sea Oil installations. This shift in the geography of the oil industry gives islands a new importance as service centres and stimulates a widening of perspectives usually restricted to the local community. The North Isles have been most affected: most of the servicing of the exploration work has been based on Shetland (Lerwick and Sandwick) while the handling of crude oil, with storage at pipeline landfalls pending transfer to tankers, will be concentrated on Flotta (Orkney) and Sullom Voe (Shetland). In both islands there is concern that a short-term influx of outside businessmen and technicians, coupled with short-term availability of high-wage employment to islanders, will disrupt normal community life and reduce commitment to traditional industries which may prove to be of greater benefit in the longer term. However, perception of 'conflict' is not a harbinger of impending crisis but a rational preparation for a thoughtful accommodation that could accelerate modernisation through improved infrastructure and greater exposure to innovation. New accommodation at Sullom Voe and additional capacity in transport services will be a permanent benefit while contact with an immigrant community must inevitably broaden experience and perceptions.[23]

The strategic factor

It is perhaps worth reflecting on the fact that while in the normal course of events the peripheral location of the Scottish islands means that they do not normally provide services for others there have been notable exceptions in history. Viking raiding and trading made the North Isles, and especially Jarlshof in Shetland a focal point in a maritime network covering the north Atlantic, and island society still bears the imprint of this temporary reversal of the normal pattern of movement along the Western Seaways.[24] Tourism is now much discussed as an area for development.[25] And the lighting of the seaways is based to a large extent on island lighthouses (Figure 14.3), some of which provide the sole reason for the continued inhabitation of certain tiny islands (at any rate until the recent demanning programme was implemented).[26] Again the islands have an important strategic significance and, while at present the radar station on the Shetland island of Unst is the only tangible sign, there are many remnants of wartime installations concerned with naval (and more recently aerial) activity. Northern routes to Scandinavia and the Baltic (important for naval stores) have been important in wartime as an alternative to the English Channel, with Orkney's Scapa Flow an excellent sheltered anchorage for the marshalling of convoys. The Napoleonic Wars eventually brought hostilities between Britain and the USA and it was to provide protection from privateers that a battery was installed at Longhope (Hoy) along with the Martello Towers of Crockness and Hackness in 1813–15.[27] Deteriorating relations with Russia led to some further scrutiny of northern defences but the reconstruction of the battery in 1866 was actually brought about by the threat of the Fenian Brotherhood attempting to force political change in Ireland through sea raiding. The battery was occupied only until the 1880s and has played no part in the world wars of the present century.

But in both of these Scapa Flow has been the scene of great activity concerned with the distant blockade of Germany: there are remains of shore installations including reinforced concrete forts built to protect the entrances in 1915, but most significant is the causeway connecting the Orkney Mainland with South Ronaldsay: the 'Churchill Barriers' were

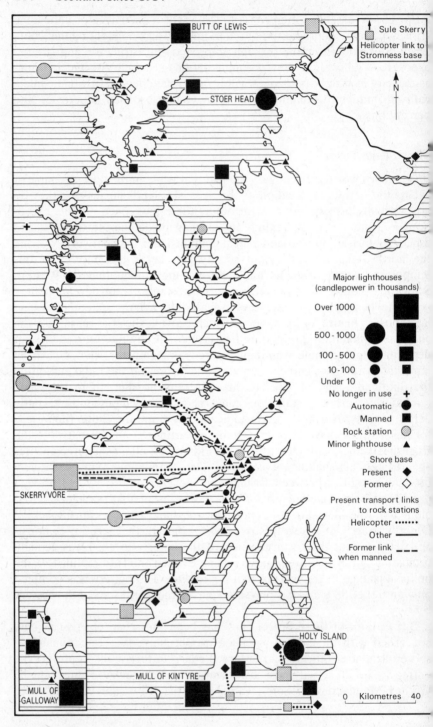

Sule Skerry
Helicopter link to
Stromness base

N

Major lighthouses
(candlepower in thousands)

Over 1000

500 - 1000

100 - 500

10 - 100
Under 10

No longer in use   +
Automatic   ●
Manned   ■
Rock station   ●
Minor lighthouse   ▲

Shore base
Present   ◆
Former   ◇

Present transport links
to rock stations
Helicopter   ••••••
Other   ———
Former link   — — —
when manned

BUTT OF LEWIS

STOER HEAD

SKERRYVORE

HOLY ISLAND

MULL OF KINTYRE

MULL OF
GALLOWAY

0   Kilometres   40

built during the Second World War to close the eastern entrances to Scapa Flow, after a German submarine had penetrated the defences and sunk a British warship, but the massive installations have an important peacetime role as a key element in the Orkney transport system.[28] Close by the causeway on the island of Lambholm stands the remarkable chapel created out of a Nissen Hut by Italian prisoners. The armed services made a significant wartime contribution to the development of South Uist and Benbecula: an RAF station opened at Balivanich (Benbecula) during the Second World War and to ensure that the base would be efficiently supplied from the Lochboisdale (South Uist) steamer terminal a causeway was built between Creagorry and Carnan to link the two islands. This eliminated the traditional (and potentially dangerous) practice of negotiating the sands of the South Ford at low tide. Balivanich airfield has been converted to civilian use and, with the building of a second causeway in 1960 from Benbecula and North Uist (crossing Grimsay en route) the whole of Uist has been integrated, with services in Benbecula accessible to the whole chain. Today the army has a connection with the Outer Hebrides through the rocket range on South Uist opened in 1961 and the island of St Kilda has been resettled as an observation·post.

The transport problem

The causeways of Orkney and Uist were anticipated by some earlier road connections such as the famous 'Atlantic Bridge' linking the Argyll & Bute mainland with Seil and the private bridge that connects Geometra and Ulva in Mull. Since the Second World War, however, the number of bridges and causeways has increased considerably with Burra Isle in Shetland the most recent addition. Shetland also has a link from mainland and Muckle Roe and between the major islands in the Skerries group, while Lewis is connected by bridge with Bernera. This represents a new stage in the development of island roads, where work started around the middle of the last century.[29] Local roads had rather limited priority when steamers called at many different places, but the introduction of car ferries, which have gradually stimulated a build up of the tourist trade, and the containerisation of freight traffic have required better roads and port facilities. Where bridges and causeways are not yet feasible, local ferry services are provided using the shortest sea crossings: links in Shetland between Lerwick and the islands of Unst and Yell now follow this 'overland' principle rather than the traditional all-sea routes. Skye is a land

Figure 14.3. Lighthouses in the west Highlands and Islands 1978
Source: Commission for Northern Lighthouses

bridge on one of the routes to the Outer Hebrides although it is not yet feasible to use Jura as a stepping stone to Islay.[30]

The switch from sea to road for local distribution has broken down the once complex steamer itineraries and given more frequent and reliable services. But some communities have found themselves becoming relatively less accessible, such as Park in Lewis where the ferry crossing of Loch Erisort has been replaced by an all-land route that continues the original Lemreway–Cromore road to a junction with the Stornoway–Tarbert road south of Balallan. And the landscape is strewn with reminders of the former patterns, such as the harbour of Peter Port which provided for a steamer call at Benbecula before the causeways were built. The island problem is thus being solved by the reduction or elimination of 'insularity'. The revolution in transport, emphasised again by the opening of two-tier air services, is paralleled by comprehensive power supplies by the North of Scotland Hydro Electric Board, which has opened island generators and gradually connected the local systems by submarine cable with the grid: only a few districts remain as 'recalcitrant areas' not yet enjoying this innovation which removes one of the major impediments to manufacturing. The progress in education, medical services and retailing makes an interesting geographical topic although the impression of greater equality must be tempered by a realisation that many prices are relatively high: postal charges may not reflect distance or the mode of transport but for passengers and freight sea crossings are relatively expensive and although government is prepared to provide subsidies the principle of a 'road equivalent tariff' (holding steamer fares to the levels prevailing for road journeys over similar distances) is not yet accepted.[31] Transport costs are thus a key element in island politics although it has been demonstrated that they are not the only constraint to development.[32]

Conclusion

In an age of welfare and planning there is growing sensitivity over the island phenomenon and through the Secretary of State for Scotland's Advisory Panel and later through the HIDB special measures have been taken to stimulate local initiative: after considerable success with fisheries, community cooperatives offer good prospects for intensifying agriculture and expanding ancillary industries.[33] This in turn reflects an acknowledgement that for the majority of island *communities* crofting must be the base of any strategy for development, and follows the thinking of Arthur Geddes in his plea for social surveys to discover the links between environment and society as a base for constructive planning.[34] Small holdings have been perceived as the only basis for survival in environments where stable non-agricultural employment is not widely available yet where emigration from the homeland is unacceptable to the majority. The modern island culture has therefore built up around the croft and the instinct derived from hard experience has consistently sought to strengthen the system, as was made clear at the turn of the nineteenth century when security of tenure for crofters was followed by a resettlement process 'led' to no small degree by illegal squatting on farm and deer forest land.[35] Modernisation may eventually eliminate the croft, which has declined quite sharply as a socio-economic institution on the Highland mainland, but for the present it remains as a remarkable product of the continuing adjustment by peripheral economic adversity, and acts as a filter through which innovations must pass.[36] The value of this mechanism was demonstrated immediately after the First World War when Lord Leverhulme became laird of Lewis and Harris and offered a package of proposals to separate agricultural and non-agricultural work. The scheme was economically ruinous (hence the halt to all development after Leverhulme's death) and the protection of crofting was shown to be providential.[37] While greater integration seems to bring greater dangers of 'internal colonialism' for peripheral areas it is reassuring that late Victorian legislators were farsighted enough to underpin island defences.[38]

15

Conclusion

The story of Scotland's changing geography must be seen as a continuing narrative, yet it is necessary to draw an arbitrary line and take stock of the experiences already dealt with. It is time to reconsider the general ideas discussed in the introduction to see how the Scottish case relates to them. It is evident that Scotland achieved both modernisation and development after the union. As the study of the improving movement demonstrates (Chapter 4), this growth did not take place as a sudden discontinuous spurt in which agriculture played only a passive role. The fact that Scotland was not as wealthy as England should not be construed as backwardness that would spawn a superficial modernisation rather than comprehensive development.[1] At the same time the rise of industry during the eighteenth and nineteenth centuries was not inevitable. Textiles provided the base for eighteenth-century expansion, for there was only a hint of the role that minerals (coal and iron ore) were destined to play in the future. A crop of iron furnaces emerged over a period of three decades between 1727 (Invergarry) and 1755 (Furnace), but although these works were outstanding for the Highland locations selected they used iron ore imported from England and consumed timber as fuel rather than coal. They appeared as a threat to Scotland's economic integrity, opening a prospect of Scottish resources being exploited by English business. Although the union gave the Scots unhindered access to the domestic and colonial markets of England and Wales there was no guarantee that this would allow a strong regional economy to emerge. There were certainly moves towards a new order in the seventeenth century 'but without union the new order could never have been brought to function properly'.[2] Equally, however, there was no guarantee of success with the precondition of union satisfied and for a time prosperity seemed highly unlikely, thanks to the French War and Jacobite Rebellion, a sluggish movement of private and public money north of the border and the poor quality of Scottish manufactures. A long period of adjustment was needed and, as R. H. Campbell observes, the buoyant overseas markets revealed several limitations in Scottish commercial practice, particularly challenging at a time of capital shortage and shortcomings in agriculture.[3] There was a considerable time lag before Glasgow achieved supremacy over Bristol, Liverpool and Whitehaven but eventually the 'port city' of Scotland emerged, as Chapter 8 has shown. The Scottish merchants became more efficient, notably in adopting a store system of trading with the colonies (rather than a consignment system) which may have helped them to provide a more efficient network of credit and avoid the more damaging consequences of the Revolutionary Wars. Wealth was generated and finance provided for both agricultural improvement and industrial growth. It has been shown how the mineral riches were unlocked, and a highly potent association of coal and iron in Lanarkshire produced a mid-nineteenth-century growth industry that allowed Scotland some share in the dynamism of take-off fostered by the English cotton industry in the late eighteenth century (Chapter 9). The progression extended to steel, heavy engineering and shipbuilding: *specialist* industries emerging out of the *generalist* industries sustained by the raw material base.[4]

How was it possible for Scotland to become such a fully active participant in Britain's industrial revolution? Rostow considers that the preconditions for take-off were being fulfilled quite widely in Western Europe during the late seventeenth and early eighteenth centuries, but Britain was the first to develop the preconditions fully thanks to trading possibilities and natural resources, along with a favourable social and political structure: 'the idea spreads not merely that economic progress is possible but that economic progress is a necessary condition for some other purpose'.[5] Yet in view of Scotland's well developed sense of nationhood there was no guarantee that English values would be embraced as a matter of course. Would an elite in Scotland 'regard modernisation as a possible task, serving some end they judged to be ethically good or otherwise advantageous' and would the population at large be prepared 'for a life of change and specialised function'?[6] In fact the Scots initially took an independent course in reforming their institutions and in some respects were more constructively innovative than the English. Max Weber's thesis of the protestant ethic is well known.[7] R. H. Tawney has pointed out the association between 'the storm and fury of the Puritan revolution' and 'a dazzling outburst of economic enterprise', as economic aims become a discrete area for human endeavour no longer shackled by the dictates of Christianity.[8] A clear causal connection between Protestantism and economic take-off may be rejected, yet S. N. Eisenstadt argues that it is difficult to deny some connection in view of the emphasis on individual responsibility: with its strong 'this-worldly' impulses Protestantism was caught up from the very beginning in the socio-economic and political changes that

European society was undergoing from the end of the seventeenth century.[9] He goes on to assert that scope for reform is greatest where a leading role is played by a cohesive elite which can overhaul institutions without disrupting the whole fabric of the old order. Evidently, in much of Europe, innovative religious groups were closely associated with a strong autonomous middle class. Scotland played a leading role in this process and became a Calvinist society *par excellence*. It seems that Calvinism took root as an extension of the 'togetherness' nurtured under the feudal system in Scotland. Hence S. A. Burrell argues that 'nowhere was the Calvinist–Presbyterian system more thoroughly rooted in popular feeling or more pervasive in its influence'.[10] And the Scottish boast that the Presbyterian system of church government underpinned the best reformed church in Christendom was fortified by a strong political will to preserve Scottish national identity against Charles I's attempts in 1637–8 to anglicise the northern kingdom. We are therefore dealing with a national ideology and not one that was narrowly based in a particular class interest. And with a finely balanced constitution between church and state which provided for self-government through complementary assemblies, for ethics and faith on the one hand and politics and law on the other, the Scots could dream of redressing the balance of economic success between themselves and their fellow Presbyterians, the Dutch. For the economy at the time was backward and the small merchant class was a long way from becoming a large and diversified class of capitalist entrepreneurs. Scotland seemed destined for greatness if only something could be done to stimulate trade. Hence the tremendous enthusiasm for the Darien scheme, the sense of bitter frustration at its dismal failure and not least the distinct ambivalence to the union agreement which the English offered as an alternative stimulus to economic growth.

Scotland's Presbyterian church was therefore a potent and yet disciplined force for change. Reform of the universities gave access to less-affluent students and the bias in education to a scientific method implied an acceptance of change and an encouragement of industrial skills to enable the Scots to gain a technical lead. Yet while progressive attitudes were fostered in the nation at large, intellectuals did not advance a case for drastic social change. The landowners embraced the reformist consensus while their monopoly of political power was not disputed. There was social stability for the economic improvements which they initiated. But at the same time it is clear that the political ascendancy of the landowners did not lead them to develop their properties for purely personal gain. The accelerating pace of agricultural change in the late eighteenth century, when the benefits of union became fully evident, attracted a large measure of cooperation from the peasantry in return for which the landowners showed due sensitivity over the crucial issue of resettlement. It must not be supposed that the process of change was entirely painless. Initial euphoria over the Glorious Revolution was followed by considerable scepticism and a measure of conflict between church and state. Andrew Fletcher's philosophical politics invoked the Platonic 'small is beautiful' principle and argued for a state based on fundamental principles (not pragmatic considerations). Any union with England would need to have a federal basis to preserve autonomy, not least so as to permit a highly authoritarian economic strategy modelled on the *dirigiste* policy of ancient city states (with forced labour and public works) to contain the individualism of the modern Christian world.[11] And Alexander Moncrieff condemned the whole notion of economic growth unless it was guided by a faith-inspired general assembly.[12] Fortunately, however, the Scottish Enlightenment adjusted positively to union and moderate counsels prevailed, expressed most effectively by David Hume and Adam Smith commending the union for facilitating a combination of English technology and Scottish philosophy. This paved the way for a remarkable degree of late-eighteenth-century harmony between solid economic advance and social progress. Whereas the closing years of the seventeenth century had nurtured the illusion that Scotland could be a great state on her own, with protection for infant industries supplying the home market in preference to imports, there was now an appreciation of Scotland's need to produce goods of quality that could succeed in overseas markets. And as the first fruits of this union-based strategy were harvested around 1750, philosophical circles in Edinburgh (notably the Select Society) began to adopt a clear deterministic slant as if success under the landowners, as natural leaders of society, was inevitable; whereas for the earlier 'polite societies' (like the Rankenian Club) the emphasis had been very much on free will with an improvement of society possible through education and the emulation of suitably progressive models.[13] There were to be some protests against unregulated individualism and the rich rewards for capital. Robert Owen's ideas of cooperation for village communities provided inspiration for the working-class activities of the 1830s: his belief that happiness could only be attained by conduct that would promote the happiness of the community was a 'generalised challenge to the whole competitive ethic'.[14] Capitalism, however, became more assertive in the nineteenth century and through her specialist industries Scotland contributed even more to the maturing of the British economy than to the take-off.

Yet whereas Scotland was an innovative region during the nineteenth-century drive for economic maturity in Britain, more so than during take-off when the textile industry of West-Central Scotland absorbed English technology, the twentieth century has found Scottish industry hard-pressed to maintain its competitive position. The stage of high mass consumption has seen Scotland once again become an importer of capital and technology. The decline of Scotland's basic industries has been dramatic and it is reasonable to look back and ask why this change was not foreseen more clearly and balanced by effective measures to create a new industrial structure. The advantages of Scotland in terms of accessible minerals (coal and iron ore) and relatively cheap labour had been heavily eroded by the end of the nineteenth century. However, while the position of the coal and iron industries deteriorated steadily, the specialist industries of locomotives and shipbuilding experienced extreme difficulties through the 1920s. Some attempts were made to diversify through production of cars and aircraft, and prospects seemed bright during the boom period immediately after the First World War. Yet the structural change in Scottish industry during the 1920s and 1930s was negligible. Shipbuilding and mechanical engineering employed 29.2 per cent of the industrial workforce in the UK in 1924 but 54.1 in Scotland. In 1935 the figures were 26.5 and 53.7 respectively, reflecting a decline in the number of jobs of 9.2 per cent in the UK but only 0.3 per cent in Scotland. For cars and electrical engineering the employment share in Scotland increased over the same period more rapidly than in the UK: 42.4 per cent as against 38.1, but the actual shares in 1935, with 7.0 in Scotland and 33.4 in the UK highlight the disparity. It was clear by the 1930s that there was overcapacity in Scottish industry, given the long-term fall in demand and the erosion of Scotland's competitive position, but rationalisation did not proceed quickly enough, due in part to resistance from some individual firms fearful of the effects of radical change. Furthermore this tentative and hesitant attitude, inspired by managerial attitudes moulded by the pre-1914 years which saw decline as an inevitable short-term cyclical pattern, was amply justified by the policy of rearmament which brought a marked upswing in the fortunes of the basic industries in the late 1930s. The need for change was no longer so pressing: the likely decline of the great industries was accepted but the process then appeared a sufficiently long-term contraction for adaptation to be envisaged with equanimity. The heavy orders of the war years certainly provided an answer to the charge that Scottish industry was overcommitted to the basic industries, although the normal peacetime demands were far less reassuring.

R. H. Campbell, however, considers that there was inadequate appreciation of the greatly reduced potency of those 'determinants of industrial success' which had been so crucial in the past and the implications that this would have for any rejuvenation of Scottish industry.[15] Thus unrealistic perception of the resource base for the traditional industries in the middle of the twentieth century continued to feature in the thinking of the 1950s. As the study of the modern planning of the Central Belt brings out (Chapter 12), only with the White Paper on Central Scotland in 1963 was there a clear appreciation of the need to switch emphasis dramatically to light industry based in the New Towns. This in turn underlines the prevailing assumption that it was for the government to produce a new industrial system. The growth of state intervention in the economy, projected north of the border by the Scottish Office (which was formed in 1885 and based largely in Edinburgh just before the Second World War), has been pressured by a devolution movement which successive governments have sought to appease by various forms of aid. It is for future historians to judge how far the home rule movement has assisted Scotland's industrial reconstruction. It would appear that the problems are deep-seated and would not be immediately moderated, let alone eliminated, by some new political arrangement. The issue lies in the benefits of initiatives extracted from government, such as support for specific industries, elaboration of development area policies and formation of the Scottish Development Agency, against the weaknesses arising from conservative attitudes in labour and management: the reservations of outside firms about the adaptability of labour and the effect of restrictive practices on productivity. There is little doubt about the benefits of government action as W. Ferguson explains how the wartime Secretary of State for Scotland T. Johnston would impress on cabinet committees that there was a strong nationalist movement in Scotland which could be dangerous if Scottish interests were not given adequate attention.[16] A number of important initiatives were taken in Scotland during the Second World War of which the establishment of the North of Scotland Hydro Electric Board in 1943 is perhaps best remembered. The latter is more debateable because it is complicated by the geographical position of Scotland on the edge of the UK economy and the consequence that in the absence of powerful incentives to draw industry out to the periphery there will be a natural consolidation in the centre of the home market. To many Scots the 'southward drift of industry' occurred in the 1920s and 1930s in spite of rather than because of their labour reserves and, in the post-war period, assessment of the role of the labour market has been complemented by discussion of other location factors such as transport costs and the local environment.[17]

To recap, the regional development model may be reconsidered with a view to relating the three stages of development to the periods adopted for this study. It is evident that to consider coal and iron as primary resource industries would unreasonably force the area's eighteenth- and nineteenth-century geography into a lowly position on the model scale. Furthermore, the boom in coal and iron in the early nineteenth century followed a half century of incredible activity in the Glasgow area that saw the rise of the tobacco trade and the expansion of textiles based very largely on imported cotton. Such was the growth of Glasgow, and the importance of both manufacturing and services, that Scotland could be seen as entering the second (industrial) stage well before the end of the eighteenth century. The first (pre-industrial) stage in Scotland certainly covers the period up to 1707. The years 1707–1821 witness a gradual commercialisation of the primary industries and attempts to strengthen settlement patterns and local industry in the context of expansion of overseas trade and access to the English market. The textile industry made great advances with cotton in West-Central Scotland complemented by linen in the East-Central region. Grampian also shared in the growth of linen with locally-grown flax supplemented by imported material. In the Outer Regions more generally there were improving landowners who sought to combine intensification of agriculture and fishing with manufacturing, the latter to be accommodated in planned villages that would act as service centres for the farm population as well as dormitories for industrial workers. Thus it may be argued that Scotland approached the second stage of development by the end of the eighteenth century, when many of the preconditions for rapid industrial growth had been satisfied. The second stage certainly covers the 1821–1914 period. For this period brings an intensification of urban–industrial development in the core region (the Central Belt) and further elaboration of the central place system, with limited industrial growth, in the Outer Regons. Trade intensifies and sub-regional specialisation increases with the completion of the railway system, and there is a consequent increase in employment in the service sector.

The years since 1914 fit best with the third (post-industrial) stage of the model. Massive adjustments have been needed but although they have produced even higher levels of urbanisation and services they have basically been achieved within a context of 'great cities' and a buoyant tertiary sector. Coal and iron stand out as basic industries which have contracted since the First World War and been replaced as employers by other manufactures and by services. The transition has been a painful one because the lag in the creation of new jobs has meant relatively high unemployment even in the post-war period, throughout which regional policies have been in force. There have also been spatial discontinuities with much of the new industry taking root in the New Towns in preference to the older industrial towns. The ethos of 'equality' in regional and sub-regional economic systems, expressed by the development area policies of successive governments, and the spread of electrification and motor vehicles have resulted in a more dispersed industrial geography. But this has not invalidated the central place system: indeed the application of 'growth pole' concepts in planning recognises the process of regional contagion, through which the city permeates the region.

The extensive Outer Regions, although they contain only 26.5 per cent of the population now (1971) compared with 63.6 in 1755, stand as an important area of primary production in terms of agriculture, forestry and fishing. These resources figured to some extent in medieval trade, and exploitation was largely on a commercial footing by the eighteenth century. The pattern does not really seem to have conformed to the dual economy model since diffusion from the Central Belt to the Outer Regions was largely uninhibited and since complementary specialisation patterns emerged. However the case of the Highlands requires some elaboration. Before the union there were sharp conflicts between the Highlands and Lowlands, and they hardly functioned as a political unit. Although the Lowlands constituted the political and economic heart of the country the Highlands remained distinct on account of their Gaelic culture and history of separatism dating back to the Scottish and Scandinavian colonisations. Resistance to the Reformation exacerbated friction by introducing the modernisation issue more explicitly. J. Prebble states that by 1690 'the Highlanders were already regarded by many Lowlanders as an obstacle to the complete political union of England and Scotland and their obstinate independence of spirit . . . had to be broken and humbled'.[18]

Given this reluctance to embrace Lowland values it is possible to see how the dangers of French support for the Jacobite movement should have led to the appalling blunder of the Glencoe massacre of 1698. As W. Ferguson explains, 'the mass of Lowlanders viewed the Highlanders with fear and hatred, and not least those who lived exposed to their depradations along the borders of the Highlands'.[19] Yet the manifest lack of sympathy meant that conflict was exacerbated rather than absorbed and Glencoe 'did more than any other single event to promote Jacobitism in the Highlands'.[20] The final suppression of Jacobitism in 1746 led to the abolition of hereditary jurisdictions and the introduction of a style of landownership on the southern model. The cultural base for separatism was largely eroded, completing the process begun in the seventeenth century when it had been the norm for Highland chiefs to have their sons educated in the Lowlands. The Highlands were now brought into a centrally planned political system. The peasantry were left to adapt to the new values of Highland proprietors and to the introduction of a number of capitalistic innovations. That they did so with difficulty is well-known but the reasons for their misgivings are less fully understood. Resistance to modernisation may be seen as conservatism, indicative of a preference for traditional practices that would exemplify the dual economy model. However, if opposition is seen as a product of misgivings about the potential of a capitalist system to employ the whole population then the instinctive desire for a smallholding base is an eminently logical and positive response. The emergence of a crofting system does not point to any rejection of capitalism in the Highlands but rather to a compromise with the Lowland model of agricultural improvement in the light of the physical and population resources of the region in the early nineteenth century.[21]

Such a willingness to evolve new values reflects a significant re-evaluation of the Highlands after the defeat of the Jacobites. The enlightenment generated a desire to extend development to the north and T. C. Smout writes how 'optimism was indeed the keynote of those in command of Highland society in the last three or four decades of the eighteenth century: there was an atmosphere of beneficient change about the place, a hopefulness without parallel in Highland experience'.[22] Adam Smith warmly applauded efforts in education and religious teaching. The public could facilitate 'the necessity of acquiring those most essential parts of education' by 'establishing in every parish or district a little school where children may be taught for a reward so moderate that even a common labourer can afford it',[23] while the Presbyterian clergy, with their modest incomes, lacked the 'contemptuous and arrogant airs' associated with well-endowed churches and were obliged to live near the people, thereby exerting 'more influence over the minds of the common people than perhaps the clergy of any other established church'.[24] An important stimulus to the prevailing atmosphere of goodwill came from the revival of thinking previously associated with Andrew Fletcher. Writing his *Discourse concerning the affairs of Scotland* in 1698, during the 'seven ill years', Fletcher had advocated stern measures to cope with the very serious social problems.[25] A Hellenic slavery system was seen as more humane in coping with unemployment than unregulated individualism: controlled servitude was better than vagabondage. More fundamental, however, was his classical view of city states showing considerable vitality given an independent existence compared with decadence under the parasitic rule of Rome. The same thinking was applied to Scotland, with a vigorous independent Scotland contrasted with the likelihood of grave compromise in the event of union. Although the analogy was seen as misleading given the economic liberty of the eighteenth century, a sense of nostalgia brought a yearning for Scottish values and it was in the Highlands where the search appeared most rewarding. Although Highland values had clashed with those of the lowlands throughout the medieval period, it seemed from the romantic standpoint of the late eighteenth century that the Highland way of life represented the Lowland pattern before English practices became widely adopted. This new perception of the Highlands was fostered by the migration of Highlanders to the Central Belt and by the increase in travel through the region by southerners. The fruits can be seen in the government's readiness to persevere with a special set of excise regulations to accommodate the special situation of the Highland distilleries and by the efforts of private landowners to establish planned villages on the Highland margins (see Chapters 5 and 6).

Yet while the perception of the Highland periphery has never fallen back to the sense of antagonism prevalent in the seventeenth century there has nevertheless been some ambivalence over the need for special effort to extend the penetration of capitalist forces without undermining the Gaelic culture now accepted as an essential part of the Scottish national heritage.[26] While crofting represents a compromise with the Lowland ideology of improvement it was a hard-won concession and one constantly threatened during the middle decades of the nineteenth century through unqualified government backing for property rights at a time when many estates had passed out of the hands of traditional owners and when the profits of sheep farming seemed infinitely more attractive than the liability of a peasantry prone to famine. However, as the study of crofting revealed (Chapter 10), government policy in the late nineteenth century moved strongly in the direction of protective measures for the Highlands and a regional development strategy was built around the smallholding ideal. Indeed, so great was the enthusiasm for small farms during the early decades of the twentieth century, and especially after the First World War, that it seemed as if crofting would be an effective solution to economic and social problems on a national as well as a regional scale. Fears were expressed that a 'crofterisation' of Scotland was taking place and that unrealistic notions of smallholding systems as nourishment for the towns were diverting attention from more fundamental problems.[27] The industrial towns needed much more direct assistance. Yet, as the study of forestry demonstrates (Chapter 13), the land settlement movement had important ramifications and there were serious expectations that smallholdings linked with part-time work in the new plantations would effect a repopulation of deserted glens. The Highlands offered the most obvious potential, though there were considerable possibilities elsewhere, and there was considerable agreement in the statements of both politicians and academics about the development prospects for forestry, tourism and hydro-electricity.[28]

The academic backing has become stronger with the powerful ecological study of F. F. Darling strengthening the consensus view that depopulation is the basic problem in contrast to the overpopulation that was diagnosed a century earlier.[29] This mounting pressure for a reappraisal of resources in Scotland in general and in the Highlands in particular has brought a considerable response. Although very few new smallholdings have been created since the Second World War there has been renewed support for Highland crofting since the 1950s. The hydro-electric programme has resulted in power supplies for virtually every Highland community while the increasingly complementary activities of forestry and tourism have seen great expansion. The improvement in infrastructure has been a factor in a significant industrialisation, although the special powers of the HIDB have been equally crucial in accounting for the industrial successes of the Highlands compared with other rural peripheral areas throughout

Britain.[30] Not that the growth in the Highlands has been entirely painless. Working on the assumption that industrial growth can occur most effectively in substantial concentrations the HIDB has placed considerable emphasis on major growth areas.[31] And the 'Scottish Plan' of 1966 suggested that the best future for the Highlands lay in adherence to national norms rather than advocacy of special treatment for a unique case.[32] However, while the economic argument cannot be discounted, for the Highlands must inevitably continue to integrate with the capitalist system of the country at large, there remains a case on social grounds that the new structures should rest more conformably on the essentially dispersed settlement geography of the west Highlands and Islands.[33] Such a compromise, involving a distinctive Highland response to the development process, is backed up by experience in developing counties over the deleterious 'backwash' effects on peripheral areas resulting from development concentrated on a growth pole. The growth of an urban–industrial centre may attract strong migration flows causing rural depopulation such that the rural districts cannot themselves develop.[34] As the study of Scottish islands indicated (Chapter 14), the viability of Highland communities has also been supported by the offshore oil activities which have brought a new industrial potential to some of the remotest parts, and by experience with community cooperatives which gives grounds for supposing that employment can be generated within individual communities. But it is also very much in keeping with two centuries of Highland development when central government has shown a readiness to absorb conflict and find a compromise between the basically irreconcilable objectives of integration and autonomy for a region with a distinctive set of cultural and resource attributes.

APPENDIX

Employment data from the 1851 and 1881 censuses

Regional totals are reached through county groupings – hence all Bute with
Highlands, Moray with Grampian, Midlothian and Stirling with East-Central and
Perthshire with Tayside
* below 0.1
totals may not add up exactly due to rounding

A. Employment 1851–81

Region	Sector: Agriculture				Manufacturing				Heavy industry				Light industry: textiles				Ratio 1		Ratio 2	
	1851		1881		1851		1881		1851		1881		1851		1881		1851	1881	1851	1881
	A.	B.	A.	B.	A.	B.	A.	B.	A.	B.	A.	B.	A.	B.	A.	B.				
Highlands & Islands	109.9	260.3	79.1	199.0	25.9	61.4	25.6	64.3	7.5	17.7	7.5	18.9	14.2	33.6	13.5	33.8	0.18	0.14	0.43	0.43
Grampian	79.1	232.7	56.6	138.5	31.9	93.9	38.9	95.1	9.2	27.2	15.8	38.6	16.8	49.6	15.5	37.9	0.29	0.29	0.51	0.59
Tayside	41.7	123.0	28.9	71.8	78.4	231.4	88.7	220.6	8.9	26.1	14.4	35.7	62.8	185.3	65.5	162.9	1.37	1.30	1.38	1.44
North	230.6	209.5	164.6	136.2	136.2	123.8	153.1	126.7	25.6	23.2	37.6	31.1	93.8	85.2	94.4	78.1	0.43	0.39	0.76	0.82
Borders	21.7	200.3	16.3	126.9	12.2	112.7	19.5	151.8	2.2	20.7	2.8	21.9	8.1	74.6	14.4	112.2	0.41	0.51	0.65	1.05
Dumfries & Galloway	32.5	197.2	20.8	132.9	16.6	101.0	13.9	88.3	3.9	23.6	3.9	25.0	10.0	60.8	6.9	44.3	0.37	0.28	0.58	0.54
South	54.2	198.5	37.1	130.2	28.8	105.6	33.3	116.8	6.1	22.4	6.7	23.6	18.1	66.3	21.3	74.8	0.39	0.38	0.61	0.75
Outer Regions	284.8	207.3	201.7	135.1	165.1	120.2	186.4	124.8	31.7	23.1	44.4	29.7	111.9	81.5	115.8	77.5	0.42	0.39	0.73	0.81
East-Central	48.9	83.1	35.8	45.8	109.3	185.7	128.9	165.0	39.4	66.9	61.8	79.2	54.3	92.2	46.6	59.6	1.62	1.53	0.80	0.83
West-Central	54.5	58.8	32.0	21.9	258.7	279.3	323.6	221.6	74.7	80.6	160.8	110.1	162.6	175.5	125.5	85.9	3.47	4.28	1.50	1.28
Central Belt	103.4	68.2	67.8	30.2	368.0	242.9	452.6	201.9	114.0	75.3	222.6	99.3	216.9	143.2	172.1	76.8	2.60	2.83	1.20	1.11
Scotland	388.2	134.4	269.5	72.2	533.1	184.5	639.0	171.1	145.7	50.4	267.0	71.5	328.8	113.8	287.9	77.1	1.00	1.00	1.00	1.00

Region	Light industry: food				Professional/commercial				Domestic			
	1851		1881		1851		1881		1851		1881	
	A.	B.	A.	B.	A.	B.	A.	B.	A.	B.	A.	B.
Highlands & Islands	4.3	10.0	4.6	11.6	26.2	62.0	34.5	86.7	18.9	44.8	20.6	51.7
Grampian	5.9	17.2	7.6	18.6	27.1	79.8	37.3	91.1	19.3	56.7	23.7	58.0
Tayside	6.8	20.0	8.9	22.0	29.5	86.9	39.7	98.9	13.4	39.4	17.2	42.8
North	16.9	15.3	21.1	17.4	82.7	75.2	111.5	92.2	51.5	49.5	61.5	50.9
Borders	1.9	17.4	2.3	17.6	8.8	80.7	10.3	80.2	5.3	49.2	7.0	54.7
Dumfries & Galloway	2.7	16.6	3.0	19.0	12.3	74.7	14.1	90.0	9.1	55.1	9.8	62.7
South	4.6	16.9	5.2	18.4	21.1	77.1	24.4	85.6	14.4	52.8	16.8	59.1
Outer Regions	21.5	15.6	26.3	17.6	103.8	75.5	135.9	91.0	66.0	48.0	78.3	52.4
East-Central	15.7	26.6	20.5	26.2	67.3	114.3	96.6	123.6	34.7	59.0	47.4	60.7
West-Central	21.5	23.2	37.3	25.6	93.6	101.0	175.0	119.8	35.6	38.4	59.5	40.7
Central Belt	37.1	24.5	57.8	25.8	160.8	106.2	271.6	121.1	70.3	46.4	106.9	47.7
Scotland	58.6	20.3	84.2	22.5	264.6	91.6	407.5	109.1	136.3	47.2	185.3	49.6

Ratio 1: Jobs in industry in relation to jobs in agriculture where Scotland is 1.00
Ratio 2: Jobs in industry in relation to jobs in professional/commercial and domestic sectors where Scotland is 1.00

A. Total employed (thousands)
B. Jobs per thousand of the total population

B. *Employment in primary activities 1851–81*

Region	Agriculture				Forestry				Fishing			
	1851		1881		1851		1881		1851		1881	
	A.	B.	A.	B.	A.	B.	A.	B.	A.	B.	A.	B.
Highlands & Islands	97.1	230.4	62.2	156.4	0.4	1.0	0.4	1.0	12.4	29.4	16.5	41.4
Grampian	75.4	221.9	48.9	119.6	0.2	0.5	0.3	0.8	3.5	10.3	7.4	18.1
Tayside	40.6	119.8	27.0	67.2	0.3	0.7	0.5	1.2	0.8	2.3	1.5	3.8
North	213.0	193.5	138.0	114.2	0.9	0.8	1.2	1.0	16.7	15.1	25.4	21.0
Borders	21.2	195.4	15.2	118.6	0.2	1.5	0.3	2.7	0.3	3.2	0.8	6.0
Dumfries & Galloway	31.9	193.8	20.0	127.5	0.3	1.8	0.4	2.5	0.3	1.6	0.4	2.6
South	53.1	194.4	35.2	123.5	0.5	1.7	0.7	2.6	0.6	2.2	1.2	4.1
Outer Regions	266.2	193.8	173.1	115.9	1.3	1.0	2.0	1.3	17.3	12.6	26.6	17.8
East-Central	46.7	79.3	31.0	39.7	0.4	0.7	0.6	0.7	1.8	3.1	4.2	5.3
West-Central	53.6	57.9	30.6	21.0	0.4	0.4	0.6	0.4	0.5	0.6	0.8	0.6
Central Belt	100.2	66.1	61.6	27.5	0.8	0.5	1.2	0.5	2.4	1.6	5.0	2.2
Scotland	366.5	126.9	234.9	62.9	2.1	0.7	3.1	0.8	19.6	6.8	31.5	8.4

A. Total employed (thousands)
B. Jobs per thousand of the total population

291

C. *Employment in Textiles 1851–81*

Region	Cotton 1851 A.	B.	1881 A.	B.	Linen 1881 A.	B.	Wool 1851 A.	B.	1881 A.	B.	Hosiery/Knitwear 1851 A.	B.	1881 A.	B.	Clothing/Tailoring 1851 A.	B.	1881 A.	B.	Silk 1851 A.	B.	1881 A.	B.
Highlands & Islands	2.9	7.0	0.2	0.5	0.1	0.3	3.5	8.3	1.7	4.2	1.0	2.3	4.6	11.6	6.8	16.0	5.8	14.7	*	*	*	*
Grampian	7.4	21.9	0.4	0.9	1.4	3.6	2.7	7.8	1.9	4.7	1.6	4.8	1.4	3.3	5.0	14.8	7.2	18.1	*	0.2	*	0.2
Tayside	53.5	158.0	1.3	3.3	28.0	69.7	1.8	5.3	1.9	5.8	0.4	1.1	0.1	0.3	7.0	20.5	7.6	19.0	0.1	3.1	*	*
North	63.9	58.1	1.9	1.6	29.6	24.5	8.0	7.2	5.6	4.6	3.0	2.7	6.1	5.0	18.7	17.0	20.7	17.1	0.2	0.2	0.1	*
Borders	0.6	55.3	*	*	*	*	3.1	28.4	10.1	78.5	2.3	21.0	1.3	10.1	2.2	19.9	2.6	19.9	*	*	*	*
Dumfries & Galloway	3.2	19.2	*	0.4	*	*	1.0	5.9	2.3	14.2	0.4	2.5	0.2	1.3	5.1	31.2	3.7	23.5	0.3	2.0	*	*
South	3.7	13.7	*	0.3	*	*	4.1	14.8	12.4	43.5	2.7	9.9	1.5	5.2	7.3	26.7	6.2	21.9	0.3	1.2	*	*
Outer Regions	67.7	49.2	2.0	1.3	29.6	19.8	12.0	8.8	18.0	12.0	5.6	4.1	7.6	5.1	26.1	19.0	26.9	18.0	0.5	0.4	0.1	*
East-Central	30.5	51.8	2.1	2.7	12.4	15.9	6.1	10.3	5.9	7.6	1.1	1.9	0.2	0.2	15.6	26.4	17.4	22.2	1.0	1.7	*	*
West-Central	121.4	131.1	40.6	27.8	4.2	2.9	5.6	6.1	7.4	5.0	4.3	4.7	0.5	0.3	27.5	29.7	36.7	25.1	3.7	4.0	3.0	2.0
Central Belt	152.0	100.3	42.7	19.0	16.6	7.4	11.7	7.7	13.3	5.9	5.4	3.6	0.7	0.3	43.0	28.4	54.1	26.5	4.7	3.1	3.0	1.3
Scotland	219.6	76.0	44.7	12.0	46.2	12.4	23.7	8.2	31.3	8.4	11.1	3.8	8.2	2.2	69.1	23.9	81.0	21.7	5.2	1.8	3.1	0.8

A. Number of Jobs (thousands)
B. Number of jobs per thousand of the population

Source: Census of Scotland

D. *Employment in heavy industry 1851–81*

Region	Sector 1 1851 A.	B.	1881 A.	B.	Sector 2 1851 A.	B.	1881 A.	B.	Sector 3 1851 A.	B.	1881 A.	B.	Sector 4 1851 A.	B.	1881 A.	B.
Highlands & Islands	*	*	*	0.2	0.4	0.8	0.5	1.2	1.8	4.2	1.8	4.6	0.2	0.5	0.5	1.3
Grampian	0.2	0.7	0.6	1.4	0.4	1.2	0.6	1.4	2.4	7.0	2.5	6.1	0.5	1.4	1.7	4.2
Tayside	0.4	1.2	1.4	3.4	0.6	1.8	0.8	2.1	2.3	6.9	2.4	5.9	1.0	3.0	3.6	9.0
North	0.7	0.6	2.0	1.7	1.3	1.2	1.9	1.6	6.5	5.9	6.7	5.5	1.7	1.6	5.8	4.8
Borders	*	0.2	*	0.4	*	0.8	*	0.7	0.8	7.6	0.7	5.5	0.1	1.0	0.7	5.4
Dumfries & Galloway	*	0.4	*	0.5	0.7	4.3	0.2	1.5	1.2	7.4	1.1	6.8	0.2	1.0	0.4	2.8
South	*	0.3	0.1	0.4	0.8	2.9	0.3	1.2	2.0	7.5	1.8	6.2	0.3	1.0	1.1	4.0
Outer Regions	0.8	0.6	2.2	1.5	2.1	1.6	2.2	1.5	8.5	6.2	8.5	5.7	2.0	1.5	7.0	4.7
East-Central	4.3	7.2	7.7	9.8	2.5	4.3	2.8	3.6	5.5	9.4	5.2	6.6	2.1	3.5	6.1	7.8
West-Central	15.8	17.1	39.0	26.7	3.0	3.3	8.0	5.5	8.3	9.0	10.5	7.2	5.2	5.7	25.5	17.4
Central Belt	20.1	13.3	46.6	20.8	5.6	3.7	10.8	4.8	13.9	9.1	15.7	7.0	7.3	4.8	31.6	14.1
Scotland	20.9	17.2	48.8	13.1	7.7	2.7	13.0	3.5	22.2	7.7	24.1	6.5	9.3	3.2	38.6	10.3

D. Employment in heavy industry 1851–81 (cont.)

Region	Sector 5				Sector 6				Sector 7			
	1851		1881		1851		1881		1851		1881	
	A.	B.	A.	B.	A.	B.	A.	B.	A.	B.	A.	B.
Highlands & Islands	2.9	6.9	2.1	5.2	0.5	1.3	0.7	1.8	0.1	0.3	*	0.2
Grampian	3.9	11.6	7.0	17.1	0.7	1.9	1.0	2.4	*	0.2	*	*
Tayside	2.6	7.7	4.0	10.0	0.7	2.0	1.1	2.7	0.2	0.6	0.1	0.3
North	9.5	8.6	13.1	10.8	1.9	1.7	2.7	2.3	0.4	0.4	0.2	0.1
Borders	0.8	7.8	1.1	8.2	*	*	*	0.2	*	0.8	*	*
Dumfries & Galloway	0.9	5.2	1.0	6.1	*	0.5	*	0.1	0.2	1.3	0.3	1.9
South	1.7	6.3	2.0	7.1	*	0.3	*	0.1	0.3	1.1	0.3	1.1
Outer Regions	11.2	8.1	15.1	10.1	2.0	1.4	2.8	1.9	0.7	0.5	0.5	0.3
East-Central	11.5	19.6	22.0	28.2	0.5	0.8	1.1	1.4	10.4	17.7	15.7	20.1
West-Central	13.0	14.1	28.5	19.5	1.9	2.1	14.6	10.0	24.1	26.0	37.5	25.7
Central Belt	24.5	16.2	50.5	22.5	2.4	1.6	15.7	7.0	34.5	22.8	53.2	23.7
Scotland	35.7	12.4	65.6	17.6	4.4	1.5	18.5	4.9	35.2	12.2	53.7	14.4

Sector 1 Iron ore mining and iron production
Sector 2 Non-ferrous mining and manufacture; precious stones
Sector 3 Blacksmiths and ironmongers
Sector 4 Engineering
Sector 5 Chemicals including wood processing, paper and printing
Sector 6 Shipbuilding
Sector 7 Coal mining

A. Number of jobs (thousands)   B. Number of jobs per thousand of the total population

Source: Census of Scotland

E. Employment: commercial and professional 1851–81

Region	Railways				Roads				Canals/Shipping				Trades				Armed Services				Professions			
	1851		1881		1851		1881		1851		1881		1851		1881		1851		1881		1851		1881	
	A.	B.	A.	B.	A.	B.	A.	B.	A.	B.	A.	B.	A.	B.	A.	B.	A.	B.	A.	B.	A.	B.	A.	B.
Highlands & Islands	*	0.1	1.0	2.6	11.3	3.2	1.6	4.1	3.0	7.1	3.8	9.6	13.6	32.2	13.7	34.6	1.3	3.2	1.4	3.5	6.9	16.3	12.8	32.3
Grampian	0.3	0.8	1.7	4.2	1.7	5.0	2.3	5.6	1.9	5.6	2.0	4.9	14.8	43.4	15.5	37.8	1.1	3.3	0.7	1.6	7.4	21.8	15.2	37.0
Tayside	1.1	3.3	3.2	7.9	1.9	5.7	2.8	7.1	2.3	6.7	1.7	4.3	16.2	47.7	17.3	43.1	0.8	2.4	0.6	1.4	7.2	21.2	14.1	35.0
North	1.4	1.3	5.9	4.9	4.9	4.5	6.8	5.6	7.2	6.5	7.6	6.2	44.5	40.4	46.5	38.5	3.3	3.0	2.6	2.2	21.4	19.5	42.1	34.8
Borders	0.4	4.0	0.7	5.7	0.8	8.4	0.9	6.6	*	0.2	*	0.3	5.2	47.7	5.5	42.6	0.2	1.7	*	0.8	2.1	19.5	3.1	24.2
Dumfries & Galloway	0.5	3.2	1.2	7.9	1.1	6.7	1.0	6.3	0.6	3.9	0.4	2.8	6.4	39.1	6.7	42.6	0.3	1.6	0.2	1.0	3.3	20.2	4.6	29.4
South	1.0	3.5	2.0	6.9	1.9	7.1	1.8	6.5	0.7	2.4	0.5	1.7	11.6	42.5	12.1	42.6	0.5	1.7	0.2	0.9	5.4	19.9	7.7	27.1
Outer Regions	2.4	1.7	7.9	5.3	6.9	5.0	8.6	5.8	7.8	5.7	8.0	5.4	56.1	40.9	58.7	39.3	3.7	2.7	2.9	1.9	26.9	19.6	49.8	33.3
East-Central	3.2	5.5	6.0	7.6	4.6	7.9	6.3	8.1	3.3	5.6	5.0	6.4	32.1	54.5	37.5	48.0	2.5	4.3	2.9	3.7	21.5	36.5	38.9	49.8
West-Central	3.2	3.4	12.1	8.3	7.3	7.8	12.9	8.8	6.6	7.1	9.4	6.5	45.8	49.4	73.0	50.0	2.4	2.6	2.5	1.7	28.4	30.6	65.0	44.5
Central Belt	6.4	4.2	18.0	8.0	11.9	7.8	19.2	8.6	9.9	6.5	14.4	6.4	77.9	51.4	110.5	49.3	4.9	3.2	5.4	2.4	49.8	32.9	104.0	46.4
Scotland	8.8	3.0	25.9	6.9	18.8	6.5	27.9	7.5	17.7	6.1	22.4	6.0	134.0	46.4	169.2	45.3	8.6	3.0	8.3	2.2	76.7	26.6	153.7	41.2

Notes

Notes to Chapter 1

1 I. D. Whyte (1978) 13. See also the slightly modified version that forms the antecedent to this article: Scottish historical geography: survey and prospect, *Edinburgh University Department of Geography Discussion Paper* 8 (1976). I. D. Whyte & K. A. Whyte. Sources for Scottish historical geography: an introductory guide, *Institute of British Geographers Historical Geography Research Series* 6 (1981).

2 G. Neilson, The cathedral and its bishopric (Glasgow) *Scottish Geographical Magazine* 37 21–6 (1921); A. C. O'Dell, A geographical interpretation of the development of Scottish railways, *Ibid.* 55 129–47 (1939); W. Power, Glasgow: the rise of trade and industry, *Ibid.* 37 37–42 (1921). See also A. G. Ogilvie, Our ignorance of Scotland with some suggestions, *Scottish Geographical Magazine* 53 387–94 (1937) for a perception of the limited scope for historical geography.

3 Economic histories have multiplied since the pioneer work of H. Hamilton (1932) and include B. Lenman (1977), S. G. E. Lythe (1960) and T. C. Smout (1969).

4 W. R. Kermack, *Historical geography of Scotland*, Edinburgh, W. A. & A. R. Johnston (1913). See also W. R. Kermack (1912).

5 A. C. O'Dell (1939). See also I. D. Duff, The human geography of S. W. Ross-shire 1800–1920, *Scottish Geographical Magazine* 45 277–95 (1929); T. M. Steven, A geographical description of the county of Ayr, *Ibid.* 28 393–412 (1912).

6 A. G. Ogilvie, Our ignorance of Scotland with some suggestions, *Scottish Geographical Magazine* 53 387–94 (1937).

7 S. J. Jones (1968); R. Miller & J. Tivy (1958); A. C. O'Dell & J. Mackintosh (1963).

8 A. C. O'Dell & K. Walton (1962).

9 R. Millman, *The making of the Scottish landscape*, London, Batsford (1975).

10 I. H. Adams (1978); M. L. Parry & T. R. Slater (1980).

11 I. D. Whyte (1978) 5.

12 M. Weber, *The theory of social and economic organisation*, New York, Free Press (1964).

295

13 K. W. Deutsch, Social mobilization and political development, *American Political Science Review* **55** 493–575 (1961). See also S. N. Eisenstadt, *Modernization: protest and change*, Englewood Cliffs NJ: Prentice Hall (1966).

14 S. I. Abumere, The geography of modernisation: some unresolved issues, *Geo Journal* **5** 67–76 (1981).

15 For example, D. Chirot, *Social change in a peripheral society: the creation of a Balkan colony*, New York, Academic Press (1976) 119–21.

16 W. W. Rostow, *The stages of economic growth: a non-communist manifesto*, Cambridge, University Press (1971).

17 *Ibid.* **8.**

18 *Ibid.* **10.**

19 S. N. Eisenstadt, *Tradition change and modernity*, New York, Wiley (1973) 16. See also B. F. Hozelitz, Noneconomic factors in economic development, *American Economic Review* **47** 28–71 (1957); D. Lerner, *The passing of traditional society*, New York, Free Press of Glencoe (1958).

20 S. Kuznets, The state as a unit in a study of economic growth, *Journal of Economic History* **11** 25–41.

21 E. A. Wrigley, Parasite or stimulus: the town in a pre-industrial economy: P. Abrams & E. A. Wrigley (eds.), *Towns in societies: essays in economic history and historical sociology*, Cambridge, University Press (1978) 295–309.

22 E. A. Wrigley, A simple model of London's importance in changing English society and economy 1650–1750: P. Abrams & E. A. Wrigley, *op. cit.*, 215–43.

23 E. A. Wrigley, *London*, Weidenfeld & Nicolson (1969) 148.

24 N. H. Lithwick & G. Pacquet, Urban growth and regional contagion: Idem (eds.), *Urban studies: a Canadian perspective*, Toronto, Methuen (1968) 18–39.

25 G. Humphrys, A simple regional evaluation model illustrated by a case study of South Wales: P. Compton & M. Pecsi (eds.), *Regional development and planning*, Budapest, Hungarian Academy of Sciences (1976) 159–70.

26 H. W. Richardson, *Regional growth theory*, London, Macmillan (1973) 133–50. See also J. Friedman & W. Alonso, *Regional development and planning*, Cambridge Mass., MIT Press (1964); E. L. Ullman, Regional development and the geography of concentration, *Proceedings and Papers Regional Science Association* **4** 179–98 (1958).

27 P. O'Sullivan, *Geographical economics*, London, Macmillan (1981) 170.

28 *Ibid.* 170.

29 E. Shils, *Centre–periphery: essays in macrosociology*, Chicago: University of Chicago Press (1975) 3–16.

30 P. Kothari, The confrontation of theories with national realities: S. N. Eisenstadt & S. Rokkan (eds.), *Building states and nations*, Beverly Hills: Sage Publications (1973) 99–116.

31 S. N. Eisenstadt (ed.), *Readings in social evolution and development*, Oxford, Pergamon (1970) 29.

32 M. Hechter, *Internal colonialism: the Celtic fringe in British national development 1536–1966*, London, Routledge & Kegan Paul (1975). See also S. W. Williams, Internal colonialism, core–periphery contrasts and devolution, *Area* **9** 272–8 (1977).

33 D. Turnock (1979) 7–11.

Notes to Chapter 2

1 I. M. Henderson, *The Picts*, London, Thames & Hudson (1967); F. T. Wainwright (ed.), *The problem of the Picts*, Edinburgh, Nelson (1955).
2 E. G. Bowen, *Britain and the western seaways*, London, Thames & Hudson (1972); W. Kirk, The primary agricultural colonisation of Scotland, *Scottish Geographical Magazine* **73** 65–90 (1957).
3 E. W. MacKie, The Scottish Iron Age, *Scottish Historical Review* **49** 1–32 (1970); E. W. MacKie, Continuity in Iron Age fort building traditions in Caithness: E. M. Meldrum (ed.), *The Dark Ages in the Highlands*, Inverness, Inverness Field Club (1971) 5.
4 F. T. Wainwright, *The Northern Isles*, Edinburgh, Nelson (1962) 82–3. See also J. R. C. Hamilton, *Excavations at Clickhimin*, London, HMSO (1968); L. Laing, *Orkney and Shetland: an archaeological guide*, Newton Abbot, David & Charles (1974).
5 J. Bannerman, *Studies in the history of Dalriada*, Edinburgh, Scottish Academic Press (1974).
6 M. O. Anderson, The Pictish region: Idem (ed.), *Kings and Kingship in Scotland*, Edinburgh, Scottish Academic Press (1973) 139; I. Henderson, Inverness: a Pictish capital: L. Maclean of Dochgarroch (ed.) (1975) 91.
7 A. Small, Historical geography of the Norse Viking colonisation of the Scottish Highlands, *Norsk Geografisk Tijdsshrift* **22** 1–16 (1968).
8 W. R. Kermack (1912) 295.
9 W. R. Kermack (1912) 301.
10 H. J. Mackinder, *Britain and the British seas*, Oxford, Clarendon Press (1922) 282–96. See also D. P. Kirby, The evolution of the frontier: P. MacNeill and R. Nicholson (eds.) (1975) 52–4.
11 J. D. Mackie, *A history of Scotland*, Harmondsworth, Penguin Books (1964) 38.
12 A. Small, Shetland: location the key to historical geography, *Scottish Geographical Magazine* **85** 155–61 (1969).
13 B. F. Crawford, The pawning of Orkney and Shetland, *Scottish Historical Review* **48** 35–53 (1969); B. E. Crawford, *The Earls of Orkney and Caithness and their relations with Norway and Scotland 1158–1470*, University of St Andrews PhD thesis (1971).
14 G. Donaldson (1974) 23–4.
15 N. P. Brooks & G. Whittington, Planning and growth in the medieval Scottish burgh: the example of St Andrews, *Transactions Institute of British Geographers* **2** 278–95 (1977).
16 Information on Edinburgh's changing role in trade and burgh taxation is shown in P. MacNeill and R. Nicholson (eds.) (1975) 63–5; 74–6; 94–5.
17 G. W. S. Barrow, The beginnings of feudalism in Scotland, *Bulletin of the Institute of Historical Research* **29** 1–31 (1956); R. L. G. Ritchie, *The Normans in Scotland*, Edinburgh University Press (1954).
18 W. R. Kermack (1912) 303.
19 I. B. Cowan, *The parishes of medieval Scotland*, Edinburgh, Scottish Record Society (1967); W. D. Simpson, The province of Mar, *Aberdeen University Studies* **121** (1944); W. D. Simpson, The earldom of Mar, *Ibid.* **124** (1949).

20 J. M. Houston, The Scottish burgh, *Town Planning Review* **25** 114–27 (1954). See also I. H. Adams (1978); A. A. M. Duncan, Burghs before 1296: P. MacNeill and R. Nicholson (eds.) (1975) 31–2; W. M. Mackenzie, *The Scottish burghs*, Edinburgh, Oliver & Boyd (1949).

21 A. Ballard, The theory of the Scottish burgh, *Scottish Historical Review* **13** 16–29 (1915); G. Neilson, On some Scottish burghal origins, *Juridical Review* **14** 129–40 (1902).

22 A. H. Forbes, *Forres: a royal burgh 1150–1975*, Elgin, Moray & Nairn County Library (1975).

23 R. Muir, Development of sheriffdoms: P. MacNeill and R. Nicholson (eds.) (1975) 30.

24 I. F. Grant (1934) 38. See also I. D. Whyte, The growth of periodic market centres in Scotland 1600–1707, *Scottish Geographical Magazine* **95** 13–26 (1979).

25 R. Cant, The Middle Ages: D. Omand (ed.) (1976) 125–40. See also H. L. Brereton, *Gordonstoun: ancient estate and modern school*, Edinburgh, W. & R. Chambers (1968); P. MacNeill & R. Nicholson (eds.) (1975) 20–7.

26 G. S. Barrow, Macbeth and other mormaers in Moray: L. Maclean of Dochgarroch (ed.) (1975) 109.

27 R. Cant, *op. cit.*, 132.

28 G. M. Fraser, The Mounth passes over the Grampians, *Scottish Geographical Magazine* **36** 116–22; 169–80 (1920).

29 R. Nicholson, The Highlands in the fourteenth and fifteenth centuries: P. MacNeill and R. Nicholson (eds.) (1975) 67–8; G. W. S. Barrow, The Highlands in the lifetime of Robert the Bruce: Idem, *The Kingdom of the Scots*, London, Arnold (1973) 362–83.

30 P. MacNeill and R. Nicholson (eds.) (1975) 55–62; E. M. Barron, *The Scottish War of Independence: a critical study*, London, Nisbet (1914); G. W. S. Barrow, *Robert Bruce and the community of the realm in Scotland*, London, Eyre and Spottiswoode (1965).

31 D. Daiches, *Scotland and the union*, London, John Murray (1977) 10.

32 T. I. Tae, *The administration of the Scottish frontier 1513–1603*, Edinburgh University Press (1966).

33 R. W. and J. M. Munro, The Lordship of the Isles: P. MacNeill and R. Nicholson (eds.) (1975) 65–7; W. R. Kermack, *The Scottish Highlands: a short history*, Edinburgh, Johnston-Bacon (1957); J. M. Munro, The Lordship of the Isles: L. Maclean of Dochgarroch ed., *The Middle Ages in the Highlands*, Inverness, Inverness Field Club (1981) 25–37; R. Nicholson, *Scotland: the later Middle Ages*, Edinburgh University Press (1974).

34 S. G. E. Lythe (1960) 38–45; J. R. Coull, Fisheries in Scotland: evidence in Macfarlane's Geographical Collections, *Scottish Geographical Magazine* **93** 5–16 (1977).

35 S. G. E. Lythe, Origin and development of Dundee, *Scottish Geographical Magazine* **54** 344–57 (1938).

36 I. C. M. Barnes, The Aberdeen stocking trade, *Textile History* **8** 77–98 (1977); I. F. Grant, An old Scottish handicraft industry, *Scottish History Review* **18** 277–89 (1921).

37 W. R. Scott, Scottish industrial undertakings before the union, *Scottish Historical Review* **2** 407–15; **3** 53–60; 287–97; 406–11 (1904–5).

38 I. H. Adams, The salt industry of the Forth basin, *Scottish Geographical Magazine* **81** 153–62 (1965).

39 E. G. R. Taylor, John Taylor and the transport problems of the early Stuart period, *Scottish Geographical Magazine* **49** 129–38 (1933). For the importance of Culross in customs revenue see A. Murray, Customs revenue and ports: P. MacNeill & R. Nicholson (eds.) (1975) 94.

40 W. Scott, *Heart of Midlothian*, London, A. & C. Black (1901) 19. See also N. P. Brooks, Urban archaeology in Scotland: N. W. Barley (ed.), *Archaeology and history of the European town*, London, Council for British Archaeology (1977) 19–33; J. P. Whitehead & K. Alauddin, The town plans of Scotland: some preliminary considerations, *Scottish Geographical Magazine* **85** 109–21 (1969).

41 S. G. E. Lythe, *The economy of Scotland in its European setting 1560–1625*, Edinburgh, Oliver & Boyd (1960). See also J. Davidson and A. Gray, *The Scottish staple at Veere*, London, Longmans Green (1909); M. P. Rooseboom, *The Scottish staple in the Netherlands*, The Hague, M. Nijhoff (1910).

42 T. C. Smout, Timber supply in later seventeenth century Scotland, *Scottish Forestry* **14** 3–13 (1961).

43 W. W. Straka, Emigration to the Baltic region: P. McNeill & R. Nicholson (eds.) (1975) 95–6. See also T. L. Christiansen, Scots in Denmark in the sixteenth century, *Scottish Historical Review* **49** 125–45 (1970); T. A. Fischer, *The Scots in Germany*, Edinburgh, O. Schulze (1902) (reprinted Edinburgh, Donald, 1974).

44 R. Miller & J. Tivy (eds.) (1958) 5.

45 I. B. Cowan, Regional aspects of the Scottish Reformation, *Historical Association Pamphlets: General Series* **92** (1978); G. Donaldson, *The Scottish Reformation*, Cambridge, University Press (1960); W. S. Reid, The coming of the reformation: P. MacNeill and R. Nicholson (eds.) (1975) 83–5.

46 J. H. G. Lebon, The development of the Ayrshire coalfield, *Scottish Geographical Magazine* **49** 138–54 (1933); See also: W. Dodd, Ayr: a study of urban growth, *Ayrshire Archeological and Natural History Society Collections* **10** 308–82 (1972).

47 F. V. Emery, The geography of Sir Robert Gordon 1580–1661 and Sir Robert Sibbald 1641–1722, *Scottish Geographical Magazine* **74** 3–12 (1958); F. V. Emery. A 'Geographical Description' of Scotland prior to the Statistical Account, *Scottish Studies* **3** 1–16 (1959); B. M. W. Third, Changing landscape and social structure in the Scottish lowlands as revealed by eighteenth century estate plans, *Scottish Geographical Magazine* **71** 83–93 (1955).

48 I. D. Whyte (1979) 258.

49 G. Whittington, Was there a Scottish agricultural revolution? *Area* **7** 204–6 (1975).

50 R. A. Gailey, The evolution of Highland rural settlement, *Scottish Studies* **6** 155–77 (1962).

51 M. B. Cottam & A. Small, The distribution of settlement in southern Pictland, *Medieval Archaeology* **18** 43–65 (1974).

52 G. Whittington & J. A. Soulsby, A preliminary report on an investigation into

Pit-place names, *Scottish Geographical Magazine* **84** 117–25 (1968); G. Whittington, Place-names and the settlement pattern of Dark Age Scotland, *Proceedings of the Society of Antiquaries for Scotland* **106** 99–110 (1974–5). See also W. F. H. Nicolaisen, *Scottish place-names: their study and significance*, London, Batsford (1976).

53 G. W. S. Barrow, Rural settlement in central and eastern Scotland, *Scottish Studies* **6** 123–44 (1962); A. Geddes & J. Forbes, Rural communities of fermtoun and baile in the lowlands and highlands of Aberdeenshire 1696, *Aberdeen University Review* **32** 98–104 (1947).

54 R. A. Dodgshon, Scotland: landscape in need of improvement, *Geographical Magazine* **51** 479–85 (1979).

55 R. A. Dodgshon, Scandinavian 'solskifte' and the sunwise division of land in eastern Scotland, *Scottish Studies* **19** 1–14 (1975); V. Gaffney, Where east is north, *Scots Magazine* **72** 229–31 (1959).

56 R. A. Dodgshon, Changes in Scottish township organization during the medieval and early modern periods, *Geografiska Annaler* **58B** 51–65 (1977).

57 A. Fenton, Scottish agriculture and the Union: an example of indigenous development: T. I. Rae (ed.), *The union of 1707: its impact on Scotland*, Glasgow, Blackie (1974) 75–93.

58 I. F. Grant, The Highland openfield system *Geographical Teacher* **13** 480–8 (1926); I. M. Matley, The origins of infield–outfield agriculture in Scotland: the linguistic evidence, *Professional Geographer* **18** 275–9 (1966).

59 R. A. Dodgshon, The nature and development of infield–outfield in Scotland, *Transactions, Institute of British Geographers* **59** 1–23 (1973); R. A. Dodgshon, Towards an understanding and definition of run-rig: the evidence for Roxburghshire and Berwickshire, *Ibid.* **64** 15–33.

60 I. M. L. Robertson, The head dyke: a fundamental line in Scottish geography, *Scottish Geographical Magazine* **65** 6–19 (1949).

61 G. Whittington, Scotland: A. R. H. Baker and R. A. Butlin (eds.) *Studies of field systems in the British Isles*, Cambridge University Press (1973) 530–79.

62 G. Whittington & D. U. Brett, Locational decision making on a Scottish estate prior to enclosure, *Journal of Historical Geography* **5** 33–43 (1979).

63 M. M. McArthur (ed.), *Survey of Lochtayside 1769*, Edinburgh, Scottish History Society (1936).

64 A. Fenton, *op. cit.*, 77.

65 R. A. Butlin, The runrig system, *Area* **1** 44–6 (1969); I. F. Grant, Everyday life on an old Highland farm 1769–82, London. Longmans Green (1924) 102; A. N. L. Hood, Runrig on the eve of the agricultural revolution in Scotland, *Scottish Geographical Magazine* **90** 130–4 (1974).

66 I. M. L. Robertson, *op. cit.*

67 G. Donaldson, *Scotland James V to James VII*, Edinburgh, Oliver & Boyd (1971) 401.

68 D. Nobbs, *England and Scotland 1560–1707*, London, Hutchinson (1952) 158–9. See also S. A. Burrell, Calvinism capitalism and the middle classes: S. N. Eisenstadt (ed.), *The protestant ethic and modernisation: a comparative view*, New York, Basic Books (1968) 135–54.

69 B. Lenman & G. Parker, Crime and control in Scotland 1500–1800, *History Today* **30** (Jan) 13–17 (1980).
70 J. McFaulds, Aspects of Scottish economic policy 1660–1707, Strathclyde University M.A. Thesis (1974).
71 Some speculations are offered by T. M. Devine & S. G. E. Lythe, The economy of Scotland under James VI, *Scottish Historical Review* **50** 91–106 (1971).
72 B. Webster, *Scotland from the eleventh century to 1603*, London, Sources of History (1975) 231.
73 I. D. Whyte (1979) 261–2.

Notes to Chapter 3

1 See D. Stevenson, Professor Trevor-Roper and the Scottish revolution, *History Today* **30** 34–40 (Feb. 1980).
2 P. H. Brown, *The legislative union of England and Scotland*, Oxford, Clarendon Press (1914); A. V. Dicey & R. S. Rait, *Thoughts on the union between England and Scotland*, London, Macmillan (1920).
3 J. Prebble, *The Darien disaster*, London, Secker & Warburg (1968). See also J. H. Burton ed. *The Darien Papers*, Edinburgh, Bannatyne Club (1849); G. P. Insh, *The Company of Scotland Trading to Africa and the Indies*, London, Scribner (1932); G. P. Insh, *Scottish colonial schemes 1620–1686*, Glasgow Maclehose (1922).
4 T. C. Smout, *Scottish trade on the eve of union 1660–1707*, Edinburgh, Oliver & Boyd (1963) 279. See also T. Keith, *Commercial relations of England and Scotland*, Cambridge University Press (1910).
5 P. W. J. Riley, *The union of England and Scotland*, Manchester University Press (1978).
6 L. M. Cullen & T. C. Smout, Economic growth in Scotland and Ireland: Idem (eds.) (1977) 3–18.
7 J. D. Mackie, *History of Scotland*, Harmondsworth, Pelican (1964) 264–310. See also R. H. Campbell, The Anglo-Scottish union of 1707: the economic consequences, *Economic History Review* **16** 468–77 (1963–4).
8 T. C. Smout, Development and enterprise in Glasgow 1556–1707, *Scottish Journal of Political Economy* **7** 194–212 (1960); T. C. Smout, The Glasgow merchant community in the seventeenth century, *Scottish Historical Review* **47** 53–71 (1968); W. I. Stevenson, Geography of the Clyde tobacco trade in the eighteenth century, *Scottish Geographical Magazine* **89** 36–43 (1973).
9 T. M. Devine, *The Tobacco Lords*, Edinburgh, Donald (1975) 172. See also J. M. Payne, The rise of Glasgow in the Chesapeake tobacco trade 1707–1775: P. L. Payne (ed.), *Studies in Scottish business history*, London, Cass (1967) 299–318.
10 T. M. Devine, The colonial trades and industrial investment in Scotland 1770–1815, *Economic History Review* **29** 1–13 (1976); T. M. Devine, Colonial commerce and the Scottish economy c. 1730–1815: L. M. Cullen & T. C. Smout (eds.) (1977) 177–90; T. M. Devine, An eighteenth century business elite: Glasgow–West India merchants c. 1750–1815, *Scottish Historical Review* **57** 40–67 (1978).

11 T. M. Devine, *The Tobacco Lords*, 171.

12 S. G. E. Lythe & J. Butt (1975) 166–7.

13 J. C. Logan, Dumbarton Glass Works Company, *Business History* **14** 67–81 (1972). See also R. H. Campbell, The industrial revolution: a revision article, *Scottish Historical Review* **46** 37–55 (1967).

14 C. A. Whatley, The processes of industrialisation in Ayrshire 1707–1871, University of Strathclyde PhD thesis (1975).

15 T. C. Smout (1964) 219.

16 J. Mackinnon, *The social and industrial history of Scotland*, London, Longmans Green (1921).

17 A. Smith, *The theory of moral sentiments*, New York, Kelley (1966). See also T. D. Campbell, *Adam Smith's science of morals*, London, Allen & Unwin (1971); D. Winch, *Adam Smith's politics: an essay in historiographical revision*, Cambridge, Cambridge University Press (1978).

18 T. Berry, *James Dunbar 1742–1798: a study of his thought and of his contribution to and place in the Scottish Enlightenment*, University of London PhD thesis (1970). See also A. C. Chitnis, *The Scottish Enlightenment: a social history*, London, Croom Helm (1976); B. Lenman, *The new history of Scotland: integration enlightenment and industrialization – Scotland 1746–1832*, London, Arnold (1981).

19 W. C. Lehmann, *Henry Home, Lord Kames, and the Scottish Enlightenment*, The Hague, Nijhoff (1971); D. Daiches, *The paradox of Scottish culture: the eighteenth century experience*, Oxford University Press (1964); E. J. Hobsbawm, Scottish reformers of the eighteenth century and capitalist agriculture: E. J. Hobsbawm et al eds., *Peasants in history*, Calcutta, Oxford University Press (1980) 3–29; I. S. Ross, *Lord Kames and the Scotland of his day*, Oxford, Clarendon Press (1972).

20 B. C. Skinner, The archaeology of the lime industry in Scotland, *Post Medieval Archaeology* **9** 225–30 (1975).

21 Old Statistical Account (henceforth abbreviated OSA) Grange IX 562–3.

22 R. O. Forsyth, *The beauties of Scotland*, Edinburgh, A. Constable & J. Brown (1805–8) V 314.

23 OSA Newmachar VI 470.

24 OSA Cambuslang V 252.

25 OSA Pitsligo V 97.

26 OSA Nigg XIX 199.

27 R. Miller, Major General William Roy, *Scottish Geographical Magazine* **72** 97–100 (1956); R. A. Skelton, The military survey of Scotland 1747–55, *Ibid.* **83** 5–16 (1967).

28 F. F. Darling, History of Scottish forests, *Scottish Geographical Magazine* **65** 132–7 (1949).

29 OSA Strachan V 377.

30 H. Hamilton (ed.), *Selections from the Monymusk Papers*, Edinburgh, Scottish History Society (1945) 160.

31 OSA Keith I 415.

32 T. R. Slater, The mansion and policy: M. L. Parry & T. R. Slater (1980) 223–47; J. D. Wood, The geography of the Nithsdale–Annandale region

1813–6, Edinburgh University PhD thesis (1962).

33 J. M. Lindsay, The use of woodland in Argyllshire and Perthshire 1650–1850, University of Edinburgh PhD thesis (1974).

34 H. L. Edlin, Coppice-with-standards and the oak tanning bark trade in the Scottish Highlands, *Scottish Forestry* 9 145–8 (1955). See also J. M. Lindsay, The commercial use of Highland woodland 1750–1870, *Scottish Geographical Magazine* 93 30–40 (1976); J. M. Lindsay, Forestry and agriculture in the Scottish Highlands 1750–1850, *Agricultural History Review* 25 23–36 (1977).

35 G. R. Taylor, John Taylor the water poet and the transport problems of the early Stuart period, *Scottish Geographical Magazine* 49 129–38 (1933) 132.

36 A. Fenton, The curragh in Scotland with notes on the floating of timber, *Scottish Studies* 16 61–81 (1972).

37 M. L. Anderson, *A history of Scottish forestry*, London, Nelson (1967) II 61. See also D. Murray, *The York Buildings Company*, Edinburgh, Brattan Pub. Co. (1973).

38 OSA XX xix.

39 *Ibid.* xxxv.

40 *Ibid.* xiii.

41 *Ibid.* xxx.

42 V. Morgan, The first statistical account for studying the agrarian geography of late eighteenth century Scotland, University of Cambridge PhD thesis (1968). See also A. Geddes, Scotland's statistical accounts of parish, county and nation, *Scottish Studies* 3 17–29 (1959).

43 A. Geddes, Burghs of laich and brae, *Scottish Geographical Magazine* 61 38–45 (1945).

44 *Ibid.*

45 OSA Stow VII 135.

46 OSA Blackford III 208.

47 OSA Auchterhouse XIV 525. See also A. A. Anderson, Development of the road system in the Stewarty of Kirkcudbright, *Transactions of the Dumfries & Galloway Natural History & Archaeological Society* 44 205–22; 45 211–27 (1967–8); G. M. Fraser, *The old Deeside road*, Finzean, R. Callander (1980); D. G. Moir, The roads of Scotland, *Scottish Geographical Magazine* 73 101–10; 167–75 (1957); J. R. Stephen, The history of roads in the Highlands and Islands of Scotland in the eighteenth and nineteenth centuries, Aberdeen University PhD thesis (1936).

48 J. Mathieson, General Wade and his military roads in the Highlands, *Scottish Geographical Magazine* 40 193–213 (1924). See also A. Graham, The military road from Braemar to Spittal of Glenshee, *Proceedings of the Society of Antiquaries of Scotland* 97 226–36 (1963–4); D. G. Moir, The roads of Scotland, *Scottish Geographical Magazine* 73 101–10; 167–75 (1957); J. Richmond, Ruthven in Badenoch, *Scots Magazine* 102 302–8 (1974); J. B. Salmond, *Wade in Scotland*, Edinburgh, Moray Press (1934).

49 A. Smith, *Wealth of nations*, London, Methuen (1904) I 20.

50 I. D. Whyte (1979) 222–45.

51 Quoted by S. W. E. Vince (ed.) (1944) 582.

52 A. C. O'Dell, A century of coal transport: L. D. Stamp and S. W. Wooldridge (eds.) *London essays in geography*, London, Longmans (1951) 229–40.
53 A. Fenton & J. J. Lawrenson, Peat in Fetlar (Shetland), *Folk Life* 2 3–26 (1964).
54 J. E. Coull, Salmon fishing in the northeast of Scotland before 1800, *Aberdeen University Review* **42** 31–8 (1967); A. Murray, *Peterhead a century ago*. Peterhead, P. Scrogie (1910) 405.
55 B. Lenman (1975) 181. See also G. Jackson, Scottish shipping 1775–1805: P. L. Cottrell & D. H. Aldcroft (eds.), *Shipping trade and commerce 1450–1914 – essays in honour of Ralph Davis*, Leicester, Leicester University Press (1981) 117–36.
56 OSA Delting I 5.
57 A. A. Graham, *Two canals in Aberdeenshire Proceedings of the Society of Antiquaries for Scotland* **100** 170–8 (1967–8); J. Lindsay, Aberdeenshire Canal 1805–54, *Journal of Transport History* **6** 158–65 (1963–4). See also H. M. Cadell, Scottish canals and waterways, *Scottish Geographical Magazine* **39** 73–98 (1923).
58 P. H. Brown, *History of Scotland*, Cambridge University Press (1911) III 256.
59 W. H. K. Turner, Flax cultivation in Scotland, *Transactions Institute of British Geographers* **55** 127–44 (1972).
60 A. J. Durie (1979) 158–62; See also A. J. Durie, The markets for Scottish linen 1730–1775, *Scottish Historical Review* **52** 30–49 (1973); A. J. Durie, The Scottish linen industry in the eighteenth century: L. M. Cullen & T. C. Smout (eds.) (1977) 88–99.
61 D. Bremner, *The industries of Scotland*, Edinburgh, Black (1869) 224.
62 A. S. Cowper, Linen in the Highlands 1753–1762, *Edinburgh College of Commerce Occasional Paper 1* (1969).
63 A. J. Durie, Linen spinning in the north of Scotland 1746–1773, *Northern Scotland* **2** 13–36 (1974).
64 N. E. McLain, Scottish lintmills 1729–70, *Textile History* **1** 293–308 (1973).
65 E. E. Gauldie, Scottish bleachfields 1718–1862, University of St Andrews BPhil, thesis (1967).
66 W. Cramond, *The annals of Cullen*, Buckie, Johnston (1888).
67 R. H. Campbell, *States of the annual progress of the linen manufacture 1727–1754*, Edinburgh, Scottish Record Office (1964) viii.
68 OSA Erskine IX 76.
69 *Ibid.*
70 OSA Paisley VIII 65. See also M. Blair, *The Paisley Shawl*, Paisley, Alexander Gardner (1904); M. Blair, *Paisley thread industry*, Paisley, Alexander Gardner (1907).
71 A. J. Durie, The fine linen industry in Scotland 1707–1822, *Textile History* **7** 173–85 (1976).
72 H. Hamilton (1932) 123. See also N. McClain, Aspects of the Scottish economy during the American War of Independence, University of Strathclyde MLitt thesis (1968); W. H. Marwick, The cotton industry and the industrial revolution in Scotland, *Scottish Historical Review* **21** 207–18 (1924); M. L. Robertson, Commerce and the American War of Independence, *Economic History Review* **9** 123–31 (1956–7).

73 J. Ferrie et al., Robert Thom's water-cuts, *Transactions of the Glasgow Archaeological Society* **15** 129–38 (1966).
74 OSA Paisley VIII 65.
75 J. Butt, Industrial archaeology of Gatehouse of Fleet, *Industrial Archaeology* **3** 127–37 (1966).
76 J. Butt, The Scottish cotton industry during the Industrial Revolution 1780–1840: L. M. Cullen & T. C. Smout (eds.) (1977) 116–28.
77 OSA Anstruther Wester III 88.
78 B. Gaskin, The decline of the handloom weaving industry in Scotland, Edinburgh University PhD thesis (1955); N. Murray, *The Scottish handloom weavers 1790–1850*, Edinburgh, Donald (1978).
79 OSA Prestonpans XVII 65.
80 OSA Saltcoats VII 9. See also N. M. Scott, Documents relating to coal mining in the Saltcoats district in the first quarter of the eighteenth century, *Scottish History Review* **19** (1922).
81 OSA Saltcoats VII 18.
82 B. F. Duckham, *A history of the Scottish coal industry* Newton Abbot, David & Charles (1970) 2 vols.; B. F. Duckham, Life and labour in a Scottish colliery 1698–1755, *Scottish Historical Review* **47** 109–28 (1968).
83 J. A. Hassan, The supply of coal to Edinburgh 1790–1850, *Transport History* **5** 125–51 (1972). See also R. Douglas, Coal mining in Fife in the second half of the eighteenth century: G. W. S. Barrow (ed.), *The Scottish tradition: essays in honour of R. G. Cant*, Edinburgh, Scottish Academic Press (1974) 211–22.
84 P. L. Payne, The Govan Collieries 1804–5, *Business History* **3** 75–96 (1961).
85 R. H. Campbell, The financing of Carron Company, *Business History* **1** 28–33 (1958); R. H. Campbell (1961).
86 P. Cadell, *The iron mills of Cramond*, Edinburgh University, Dept. of Extra-Mural Studies (1973) 5.
87 J. R. Hume & J. Butt, Muirkirk 1786–1802: the creation of a Scottish industrial community, *Scottish Historical Review* **45** 161–83 (1966).
88 J. Butt and I. Donnachie, The Wilsons of Wilsontown Ironworks: a study in entrepreneurial failure, *Explorations in Entrepreneurial History* 150–68 (1967).
89 D. Steel, The linen industry in East-Central Scotland 1750–1900, St Andrews University PhD thesis (1975).
90 D. Bremner (1869) 233.
91 D. Bremner (1869) 248.
92 S. J. Jones, Historical geography of Dundee: S. J. Jones (ed.) (1968) 271–2.
93 W. H. K. Turner (1953) 20. See also W. H. K. Turner (1957).
94 A. J. Durie (1979) 163. See also C. Gulvin, The union and the Scottish woollen industry 1707–1760, *Scottish Historical Review* **50** 121–37 (1971).
95 I. L. Donnachie & N. K. Stewart, Scottish windmills: an outline and inventory, *Proceedings of the Society of Antiquaries for Scotland* **98** 276–99 (1964–6).
96 OSA Holme V 411.
97 C. Rampini, *Shetland and the Shetlanders*, Kirkwall, Wm Peace (1884) 60.
98 D. F. Macdonald, *Scotland's shifting population 1770–1850*, Glasgow, Jackson & Son; K. Walton, Population changes in Northeast Scotland 1696–1951, *Scottish Studies* **5** 149–80 (1961). A. J. Youngson, Alexander Webster and his

'Account of the Number of People in Scotland', *Scottish Studies* **15** 198–200 (1961–2).

99 M. L. Parry, Changes in the extent of improved land: M. L. Parry & T. R. Slater (eds.) (1980) 177–99.

100 M. L. Parry, Secular climatic change and marginal agriculture, *Transactions, Institute of British Geographers* **64** 1–13 (1975).

101 R. D. Lobban, The migration of Highlanders into Lowland Scotland c. 1750–1890, Edinburgh University PhD thesis (1969); W. C. A. Ross, Highland emigration, *Scottish Geographical Magazine* **50** 155–66 (1934).

102 OSA Fodderty VII 414; Daviot & Dunlichty XIV 76.

103 I. H. Adams, The changing face of Scotland and the role of emigration: B. S. Osborne (ed.), *The settlement of Canada: origins and transfer*, Kingston Ont.: Queens University (1976) 2–11; V. R. Cameron, *Emigrants from Scotland to America 1774–5*, Baltimore, Genealogical Pub. Co. (1965).

104 A. C. Chitnis (1976) 240. See also J. P. Shaw, The new rural industries: M. L. Parry & T. R. Slater (eds.) (1980) 291–317.

Notes to Chapter 4

1 G. Whittington, Was there a Scottish agricultural revolution?, *Area* **7** 204–6 (1975). See also J. E. Handley (1963).

2 A. Smith, *Wealth of nations*, London, Methuen (1904) I 219–20.

3 J. B. Caird (1964).

4 T. C. Smout and A. Fenton, Scottish agriculture before the improvers: an exploration, *Agricultural History Review* **13** 73–93 (1965). See also A. Fenton, The rural economy of East Lothian in the seventeenth and eighteenth centuries, *Transactions of the East Lothian Antiquarian Society* **9** 1–23 (1963).

5 T. C. Smout (1964) 229.

6 I. H. Adams, The land surveyor and his influence on the Scottish rural landscape, *Scottish Geographical Magazine* **84** 248–55 (1968); I. H. Adams, *The mapping of a Scottish estate*, University of Edinburgh, Department of Educational Studies (1971); I. H. Adams, Economic process and the Scottish land surveyor, *Imago Mundi* **27** 13–18 (1975); I. H. Adams, *Bruce May: land surveyor 1749–93*, Edinburgh, Scottish History Society 1979; H. Fairhurst, The surveys for the Sutherland clearances 1813–20, *Scottish Studies* **8** 1–18 (1964); B. M. W. Third, The significance of Scottish estate plans and associated documents, *Scottish Studies* **1** 39–64 (1957).

7 M. C. Storrie, William Bald's plan of Ardnamurchan & Sunart in 1807, *Scottish Studies* **5** 112–16 (1961).

8 I. H. Adams, Division of commonty in Scotland, Edinburgh University PhD thesis (1967); L. R. Timperley (ed.), *Directory of landownership in Scotland c. 1770*, Edinburgh, Scottish Record Society (1976).

9 J. B. Caird (1964) 73.

10 OSA. Innerwick I 125.

11 OSA Duthil & Rothiemurchus IV 311.

12 R. Mitchison, The movement of Scottish corn prices, *Economic History Review* **18** 278–91 (1964).

13 OSA Urquhart XV 95–6.

14 H. Hamilton (ed.), *Selections from the Monymusk Papers 1713–1755*, Edinburgh, Scottish History Society (1945); H. Hamilton, *Life and labour on an Aberdeenshire estate*, Aberdeen Third Spalding Club (1946).

15 R. A. Dodgshon, The economics of sheep farming in the Southern Uplands during the age of improvement 1750–1833, *Economic History Review* **29** 551–69 (1976).

16 J. R. Allan (1952) 75.

17 H. Hamilton (ed.), *op. cit.*, lxxii.

18 *Ibid.*, lxx.

19 J. Black (1870–1) 7.

20 OSA Deskford IV 360.

21 OSA Stronsay & Eday SV 400.

22 J. E. Donaldson, *Caithness in the eighteenth century*, Edinburgh, Moray Press (1938) 181–3.

23 A. Geddes, Changing landscape of the Lothians 1600–1800, *Scottish Geographical Magazine* **54** 129–43 (1938). See also G. East, Land utilisation in Lanarkshire at the end of the eighteenth century, *Scottish Geographical Magazine* **33** 89–110 (1937); G. Whittington, Land utilisation in Fife at the close of the eighteenth century, *Scottish Geographical Magazine* **82** 184–93 (1966).

24 A. Fenton, Scottish agriculture and the union – an example of indigenous development: T. I. Rae (ed.), *The union of 1707 – its impact on Scotland*, Glasgow, Blackie (1974) 87.

25 A. C. Cameron, *History of Fettercairn*, Paisley; Parlane (1899).

26 OSA Alvah IV 395.

27 W. P. L. Thomson, Funzie Fetlar: a Shetland run-rig township in the nineteenth century, *Scottish Geographical Magazine* **86** 170–85 (1970).

28 OSA Firth & Stenness XIV 132.

29 OSA Dollar XV 160.

30 R. A. Dodgshon, Removal of run-rig in Roxburghshire and Berwickshire, *Scottish Studies* **16** 121–37 (1972). See also M. Gray, Abolition of run-rig in the Scottish Highlands, *Economic History Review* **1** 46–57 (1952).

31 OSA Dalserf II 374.

32 OSA Fraserbrugh VI 6.

33 OSA Tullynessle IV 30.

34 OSA Wiston & Roberton VI 307.

35 OSA West Kilbride XII 410; Girvan XII 336.

36 OSA Newmachar XVI 475.

37 OSA St Fergus XV 154.

38 OSA Rayne XV 111–5.

39 OSA Monquitter VI 128–9.

40 OSA Stronsay & Eday XV 403–4.

41 OSA Erskine IX 63–5.

42 OSA Beith VIII 315.

43 R. H. Campbell, The Scottish improvers and the course of agrarian change in the eighteenth century: L. M. Cullen & T. C. Smout (eds.) (1977) 204–15.

44 See also R. Mitchison, *Agricultural Sir John*, London, Bles (1962).

45 M. C. Storrie (1965).
46 M. Gray, The kelp industry in the Highlands and Islands, *Economic History Review* **4** 197–209 (1951); A. J. Youngson, *After the Forty Five*, Edinburgh University Press (1963) 134–9.
47 M. I. Adam, Eighteenth century Highland landlords and the poverty problem, *Scottish Historical Review* **19** 1–20; 161–79 (1921).
48 P. Gaskell (1968); J. Prebble, *The Highland clearances*, London Secker & Warburg (1963).
49 Scottish Record Office GD50/2/1.
50 *Ibid.*
51 *Ibid.*
52 Quoted by A. J. Youngson (1974) 109.
53 E. R. Cregeen, Tacksmen and their successors, *Scottish Studies* **13** 93–144 (1969).
54 I. Carter, Economic models and the recent history of the Highlands, *Scottish Studies* **15** 99–120 (1971).
55 OSA Garvald XIII 195.
56 OSA Dalmeny I 230.
57 M. M. McArthur (ed.), *Survey of Lochtayside 1769*, Edinburgh, Scottish History Society (1936).
58 M. C. Storrie, Landholdings and population in Arran from the late eighteenth century, *Scottish Studies* **11** 49–74 (1967).
59 J. G. Dunbar, Auchindrain: a multiple tenancy in Mid Argyll, *Folk Life* **3** 61–7 (1965); H. Fairhurst, An old estate plan of Auchindrain, *Scottish Studies* **12** 183–7 (1968); J. W. Watson (ed.), Auchindrain, *Ibid.* **7** 230–4 (1963). See also H. Fairhurst et al., Scottish clachans, *Scottish Geographical Magazine* **76** 67–76; **80** 160–83 (1960–4); H. Fairhurst, Rural settlement pattern of Scotland: R. W. Steel & R. Lawton (eds.), *Liverpool Essays in Geography*, London, Longmans (1967) 193–209; H. Fairhurst, Rosal: a deserted township in Strathnaver, *Proceedings of the Society of Antiquaries for Scotland* **100** 135–69 (1967–8). H. Fairhurst, The deserted settlement at Lix, West Perthshire, *Ibid.* **101** 160–99 (1968–9).

Notes to Chapter 5

1 OSA Houston I 319.
2 OSA Cambuslang V 251.
3 OSA Galston II 75; East Kilbride III 423.
4 OSA Dalziel III 461.
5 OSA Anstruther III 88.
6 OSA Kilmacolm IV 276; OSA Muirkirk VII 603.
7 OSA Old Cumnock VI 413; OSA Kilmacolm IV 276.
8 OSA Lanark XV 17.
9 D. Lockhart, The evolution of the planned village in north east Scotland, University of Dundee PhD thesis (1975). See also J. M. Houston, Village planning in Scotland 1845–1945, *Advancement of Science* **5** 129–32 (1948).
10 J. Butt (ed.), *Robert Owen; prince of cotton spinners*, Newton Abbot, David & Charles (1971). M. Cole, *Robert Owen of New Lanark*, London, Batchworth

Press (1953). See also F. Podmore, *Robert Owen: a biography*, London Allen & Unwin (1906) – reprint New York, A. M. Kelley 1968.
11 T. C. Smout (1969) 403–11.
12 A. M. Smith, The forfeited annexed estates 1752–1784, Dundee University PhD thesis (1975); A. M. Smith, The forfeited annexed estates 1752–1784: G. W. S. Barrow (ed.), *The Scottish tradition: essays in honour of R. G. Cant*, Edinburgh, Scottish Academic Press (1974) 198–211.
13 Scottish Record Office GD50/2/1.
14 J. Anderson (1785).
15 OSA Alvah IV 397.
16 OSA Nairn IV 116.
17 OSA Kettle I 379.
18 OSA Sorn XX 167–8.
19 OSA Cross & Burness 487.
20 R. O. Forsyth, *The beauties of Scotland*, Edinburgh, A. Constable & J. Brown IV 524.
21 OSA Inchinnan III 533.
22 OSA Callander XI 594.
23 OSA Kirkpatrick Durham II 255.
24 OSA Borgue XI 42.
25 OSA Alford XV 468.
26 OSA Monquitter VI 129.
27 K. Walton, Regional Settlement: A. C. O'Dell & K. Walton (eds.) (1963) 87–99. H. Woolmer, Grantown on Spey: an eighteenth century new town, *Town Planning Review* 41 237–49 (1970).
28 V. Gaffney (1960); V. Gaffney, *Tomintoul: its glens and its people*, Golspie, Sutherland Press (1976).
29 I. G. Lindsay & M. Cosh, *Inveraray and the Dukes of Argyll*, Edinburgh University Press (1973) 258.
30 J. Knox, *Discourse on the expediency of establishing fishing stations or small towns in the Highlands of Scotland*, London, J. Walker (1786).
31 J. Dunlop, The British Fisheries Society 1786–1893, Edinburgh University PhD thesis (1952), J. Dunlop, The British Fisheries Society 1786 questionnaire, *Northern Scotland* 2 37–55 (1974–5); E. D. Hyde, British Fisheries Society 175–1850, University of Strathclyde PhD thesis (1974).
32 E. Richards, *The Leviathan of Wealth: the Sutherland fortune in the Industrial Revolution*, London, Routledge & Kegan Paul (1973); E. Richards, The Sutherland clearances: new evidence from Dunrobin, *Northern Scotland* 2 57–74 (1974–5).
33 OSA Urray VII 256–7; Creich VIII 375–83; Invergordon II 564; Dingwall III 18.
34 OSA Aberlady VI 547.
35 OSA Creich VIII 381.
36 T. C. Smout, The landowners and the planned village: N. T. Phillipson & N. Mitchison (eds.) (1970) 74–106.
37 J. D. Wood, Planning intentions for nineteenth century estate village, *Scottish Studies* 15 39–52 (1971).

38 J. Anderson (1785) viii.

Notes to Chapter 6

1 R. B. Weir, The distilling industry in Scotland in the nineteenth and early twentieth centuries, Edinburgh University PhD thesis (1974). See also D. Daiches, *Scotch whisky*, London, Deutsch (1969).
2 I. C. Taylor, *Highland whisky*, Inverness, An Comunn Gaidhealach (1968) 2.
3 C. Tovey, *British and foreign spirits*, London, Whittaker & Co. (1864) 129.
4 A. J. Youngson (1973) 111.
5 A. J. Youngson (1974) 164.
6 OSA Mortlach XVII 438–9.
7 OSA Urquhart V 208.
8 *Ibid.* 211.
9 *Ibid.* 211.
10 OSA Urray VII 252.
11 OSA Urquhart V 211.
12 H. Hamilton (1932) 103–10.
13 Resentment over high duties is mentioned by P. Hume Brown, *The legislative union of England and Scotland*, Oxford, Clarendon Press (1914) 137–41. It is also a prominent theme in the novels of Sir Walter Scott: derogatory references to 'English gaugers and supervisers' in *Rob Roy*, Boston, Houghton-Mifflin (1956) 30.
14 OSA Clackmannan XIV 624.
15 *Resolution of the landed interest of Scotland respecting the distillery*, Edinburgh, n.p. (1786).
16 T. M. Devine, The rise and fall of illicit whisky working in North Scotland 1780–1840, *Scottish Historical Review* **54** 155–77 (1975).
17 OSA Draine IV 479.
18 Lord Teignmouth, *Sketches of the coasts and islands of Scotland*, London: J. W. Parker (1836) I 203–9.
19 NSA Aberdeenshire XII 793.
20 T. M. Devine, *op. cit.* 167.
21 I. A. Glen, A maker of illicit stills, *Scottish Studies* **14** 67–83 (1970).
22 C. Tovey, *op. cit.* 140.
23 T. M. Devine, *op. cit.* 177.
24 S. Sillett, *Illicit Scotch*, Aberdeen, Impulse Publications (1965).
25 C. Tovey, *op. cit.* xxi–xxii.
26 I. Donnachie, *A history of the brewing industry in Scotland*, Edinburgh, Donald (1979) 120–1.
27 NSA Perthshire X 328.
28 R. B. Weir, Patent still distillers and the role of competition: L. M. Cullen and T. C. Smout (eds.) (1977) 129–44.
29 The role of physical factors is discussed by A. MacPherson, Scotch whisky, *Scottish Geographical Magazine* **80** 99–106 (1964); M. C. Storrie, Scotch whisky industry, *Transactions Institute of British Geographers* **31** 97–114 (1962).
30 For details of later developments see D. Turnock (1979) 68–92.

31 H. Hamilton (ed.), *The county of Banff*, Edinburgh, Collins (1961) 105–22; Idem, *The county of Moray and Nairn*, Edinburgh, Collins (1965) 160–7.

Notes to Chapter 7

1 R. H. Campbell, *Scotland since 1707*, Oxford, Blackwell (1965); J. Mackinnon, W. H. Marwick, *Scotland in modern times*, London, Frank Cass & Co. (1964).
2 S. G. E. Lythe, Shipbuilding at Dundee down to 1914, *Scottish Journal of Political Economy* **9** 219–32 (1964); S. G. E. Lythe, Gourlays of Dundee, *Abertay Historical Society Publication* **10** (1964).
3 J. Butt, *The industrial archaeology of Scotland*, Newton Abbot, David & Charles (1967); S. B. Calder, *Industrial archaeology of Sutherland*, Strathclyde University MA thesis (1974); I. Donnachie, *Industrial archaeology of Galloway*, Newton Abbot, David & Charles (1971); I. L. Donnachie, Lime industry in southwest Scotland, *Transactions Dumfries & Galloway Natural History & Archaeological Society* **8** 146–52 (1971).
4 E. R. Cregeen, *Argyll estate instructions 1771–1805*, Edinburgh, Constable (1964); E. R. Cregeen, The changing role of the House of Argyll: N. T. Phillipson & N. Mitchison (eds.) (1970) 5–23; R. A. Gailey, Agrarian improvement and the development of enclosure in the southwest Highlands, *Scottish Historical Review* **42** 105–25 (1963).
5 W. E. Dodd, Telford's churches, *Scots Magazine* **95** (1971) 113–18.
6 G. Anderson & P. Anderson, *Guide to the Highlands and Islands of Scotland*, Edinburgh, Tait (1842) 51–2.
7 J. Thomson, *An account of the pleasure tours of Scotland*, Edinburgh, n.p. (1824) 16.
8 *Ibid*. 103.
9 L. J. Evenden, The settlement hierarchy of southeast Scotland, Edinburgh University PhD thesis (1969).
10 R. Paddison, The evolution and present structure of central places in North East Scotland, Aberdeen University PhD thesis (1969).
11 J. A. Hassan, The development of the coal industry in Lothian 1815–73, Strathclyde University PhD thesis (1976). See also J. Brown, *The history of Sanquhar*, Dumfries, J. Anderson (1891); J. L. Carvel & J. C. George, *New Cumnock coalfield*, Edinburgh, Constable (1946); B. F. Duckham (1970); R. Goodwin, Some physical and social factors in the evolution of a mining landscape: a study of the eastern area of the Fife coalfield, *Scottish Geographical Magazine* **75** 3–17 (1959); J. H. G. Lebon, The development of the Ayrshire coalfield *Scottish Geographical Magazine* **49** 138–54 (1933); J. Strawhorn, *New history of Cumnock*, Cumnock, Cumnock Town Council (1966); A. J. Youngson Brown, The Scottish coal industry 1854–1886, Aberdeen University DLitt thesis (1952).
12 J. Mackinnon (1921) 120–2. See also H. Matthew, The geography of the early synthetic alkali industry in Great Britain, *Scottish Geographical Magazine* **96** 26–38 (1980); K. Warren, *Chemical industry foundations: the alkali industry in Britain to 1926*, Oxford, Clarendon Press (1980).
13 J. Butt, James Young: Scottish industrialist and philanthropist, Glasgow

University PhD thesis (1964); J. Butt, Technical change and the growth of the British oil shale industry 1680–1870, *Economic History Review* **17** 511–21 (1964–5); J. Butt, Scottish oil mania of 1864–6, *Scottish Journal of Political Economy* **12** 195–209 (1965); H. M. Cadell, *The story of the Forth*, Glasgow, J. Maclehose (1913); H. M. Cadell, Industrial possibilities of the Forth estuary, *Scottish Geographical Magazine* **34** 177–89 (1918).

14 M. S. Cotterill, Scottish gas industry to 1914, Strathclyde University PhD thesis (1976); J. A. Hassan, The gas market and the coal industry of the Lothians in the nineteenth century, *Industrial Archaeology* **12** 49–73 (1977).

15 E. Gauldie, *The Dundee textile industry 1790–1885*, Edinburgh, Scottish History Society (1969) xx. See also B. Lenman et al., Dundee and its textile industry 1850–1914, *Abertay Historical Society Publication* **14** (1969); W. H. K. Turner, The evolution of the pattern of the textile industry within Dundee, *Transactions Institute of British Geographers* **18** 107–19 (1952); W. H. K. Turner (1966).

16 E. Gauldie, *op. cit.*, xx.

17 D. Chapman, The establishment of the jute industry: a problem in location theory, *Review of Economic Studies* **6** 33–55 (1938–9); W. M. Walker, *Juteopolis: Dundee and its textile workers 1885–1923*, Edinburgh, Scottish Academic Press (1979).

18 W. H. K. Turner (1957).

19 W. H. K. Turner, Textile industry of Perth and district, *Transactions Institute of British Geographers* **23** 123–40 (1957).

20 A. G. Thomson, *The paper industry in Scotland 1590–1861*, Edinburgh, Scottish Academic Press (1974).

21 A. J. Robertson, The decline of the Scottish cotton industry 1860–1914, *Business History* **12** 116–28 (1970). See also T. W. Leavitt, Fashion commerce and technology in the nineteenth century: the shawl trade, *Textile History* **3** 51–63 (1972).

22 For a general review see D. Turnock, *The new Scotland*, Newton Abbot, David & Charles (1979) 53–66. See also C. Gulvin, *The Tweedmakers: a history of the Scottish fancy woollen industry 1600–1914*, Newton Abbot, David & Charles (1974); N. Hood, A geography of competition: the Scottish woollen textile industry, *Scottish Geographical Magazine* **89** 74–80 (1973); J. G. Martindale, The rise and growth of the tweed industry in Scotland: J. G. Jenkins (ed.), *The wool textile industry in Great Britain*, London, Routledge & Kegan Paul (1972) 269–80.

23 J. T. Coppock (1976); T. B. Franklin (1952); J. A. Symon (1959).

24 B. Walker, The influence of fixed farm machinery on farm building design in east Scotland, *Scottish Archaeological Forum* **8** 52–74 (1976).

25 D. Turnock, Glimpses of Orkney's agrarian history, *Country Life* **164** 410–11 (1978).

26 C. P. Snodgrass, Influences of physical environment on agricultural practice in Scotland, University of Edinburgh PhD thesis (1931).

27 J. Black (1870–1) 15.

28 J. Black (1870–1) 15.

29 A. R. B. Haldane (1952); J. G. Kyde, *The drove roads and bridle paths around Braemar*, Edinburgh, Oliver & Boyd (1958).

30 J. Black (1870–1) 21. See also W. McCombie, *Cattle and cattle breeders*, London, n.p. (1867).

31 J. Black (1870–1) 13.

32 J. Milne, On the agriculture of Aberdeenshire and Banffshire, *Transactions of the Highland and Agricultural Society of Scotland* 3 378–401 (1870–1) 400.

33 C. P. Snodgrass, Lanarkshire: agricultural geography of a Scottish county, *Scottish Geographical Magazine* 53 176–99 (1937). See also W. G. East, Land utilisation in Lanarkshire at the end of the eighteenth century, *Ibid.*, 53 89–110 (1937).

34 P. E. O'Sullivan, Land use changes in the forest of Abernethy, *Scottish Geographical Magazine* 89 95–106 (1973).

35 M. L. Anderson (1967) 155. See also J. M. Lindsay, Some aspects of timber supply in the Highlands 1700–1850, *Scottish Studies* 19 39–53 (1975); J. M. Lindsay, Commercial use of Highland woodlands: a reconsideration, *Scottish Geographical Magazine* 82 30–40 (1976).

36 N. MacLeod, *Reminiscences of a Highland parish*, London, A. Strahan (1867) 323.

37 J. Hunter, Sheep and deer: Highland sheep farming 1850–1900, *Northern Scotland* 1 199–222 (1973).

38 P. Stack, *Island quest*, London, Collins & Harvill Press (1979) 100. G. Bain, *The river Findhorn from source to sea*, Nairn, Nairnshire Telegraph (1911); I. D. Duff, The human geography of Southwest Ross-shire 1800–1920, *Scottish Geographical Magazine* 45 277–95 (1929); P. Gaskell (1968).

39 B. Lenman (1975) 200–87; See also S. G. E. Lythe, The Dundee whale fishery, *Scottish Journal of Political Economy* 3 158–69 (1964).

40 H. D. Smith, The Scandinavian influence in the making of modern Shetland: J. R. Baldwin (ed.) (1978) 29.

41 A. Fenton, Craig fishing in the North Isles of Scotland, *Scottish Studies* 17 71–80 (1973).

42 J. R. Coull, Fisheries in northeast Scotland before 1800, *Scottish Studies* 13 17–32.

43 M. Gray, Organisation and growth in the east coast herring fishing 1800–85: P. L. Payne (ed.), *Studies in Scottish business history*, London, Cass (1967) 187–216.

44 M. Gray, Fishing industries of Scotland 1790–1914, *Aberdeen University Studies* 55 (1978) 211.

45 H. D. Smith, The historical geography of trade in the Shetland Islands, Aberdeen University PhD thesis (1972).

46 A. J. S. Paterson, *The Victorian Summer of the Clyde steamers 1865–88*, Newton Abbot, David & Charles (1972).

47 G. Donaldson, *Northwards by sea*, Edinburgh, private publication (1966) 15; A. C. O'Dell (1939) 176–87.

48 P. T. Wheeler, Shipping services to the east coast of Sutherland, *Journal of Transport History* 6 110–17 (1963–4).

49 K. Brown, The first railway in Scotland: The Tranent–Cockenzie waggonway, *Railway Magazine* 82 1–4 (1938).

50 C. F. D. Marshall, *A history of British railways down to 1830*, Oxford

University Press (1937); J. Thomas, *Regional history of the railways of Great Britain: Scotland – Lowlands and Borders*, Newton Abbot, David & Charles (1971); W. Vamplew, Railways and the Scottish transport system in the nineteenth century, *Transport History* **1** 133–45 (1968).

51 S. G. E. Lythe & C. E. Lee, The Dundee & Newtyle Railway, *Railway Magazine* **97** 546–50; 689–94; 847–51 (1951).

52 S. G. E. Lythe, The Arbroath & Forfar Railway, *Railway Magazine* **99** 53–8; 128–32 (1953).

53 J. Butt & J. T. Ward, The promotion of the Caledonian Railway, *Transport History* **3** 164–92; 225–54 (1970).

54 J. Hyslop & R. Hyslop, *Langholm as it was*, Sunderland, Hills & Co. (1912). See also D. R. MacGregor, Town Development and transport: North Berwick and Haddington, *Scottish Geographical Magazine* **65** 81–92 (1949).

55 I. H. Adams, The historical geography of the Gifford & Garvald light railway, *Transactions of the East Lothian Antiquarian Society* **13** 77–96 (1972).

56 J. Thomas, *Forgotten railways: Scotland*, Newton Abbot, David & Charles (1976) 40–5.

57 A. C. O'Dell, Transport of Aberdeen, *Scottish Geographical Magazine* **79** 108–13 (1963).

58 I. Brodie, *Steamers of the Forth*, Newton Abbot, David & Charles (1976); J. Prebble, *The High Girders*, London, Secker & Warburg (1956).

59 W. Vamplew, Railway investment in the Scottish Highlands, *Transport History* **3** 141–53 (1970).

60 H. A. Vallance, *The Highland Railway*, Newton Abbot, David & Charles (1969).

61 J. Thomas, *West Highland Railway*, Newton Abbot, David & Charles (1969).

62 A. R. B. Haldane, *Three centuries of Scottish posts*, Edinburgh University Press (1971).

63 W. Vamplew, Railways and the transformation of the Scottish economy, *Economic History Review* **24** 37–54 (1971); A. S. Morris, The nineteenth century Scottish carrier trade: patterns of decline, *Scottish Geographical Magazine* **96** 74–82 (1980).

64 W. Vamplew, The railways and the iron industry: a study of their relationship in Scotland: M. C. Reed (ed.), *Railways in the Victorian economy: studies in finance and economic growth*, Newton Abbot, David & Charles 33–73 (1969).

65 T. M. Aitken, A palace in the sandhills, *Scots Magazine* **93** 548–59 (1970). For urban tramways see for example D. L. G. Hunter, The Edinburgh cable tramways, *Journal of Transport History* **1** 170–84 (1953–4).

66 J. R. Kellett, *The impact of railways on Victorian cities*, London, Routledge & Kegan Paul (1969) 208–43.

67 N. I. Beckles, The development of the port and trade of Dundee 1815–1967, Dundee University PhD thesis (1969).

68 B. Lenman (1975) 111. See also A. R. Buchan, The engineers of a minor port: Peterhead 1772–1872, *Industrial Archaeology Review* **3** 243–57 (1979).

69 S. Luther-Davies, Urban and historical geography of Kirkwall and Stromness, Glasgow University PhD thesis (1974); A. C. O'Dell, Lerwick: a port study,

Scottish Geographical Magazine **50** 27–35 (1934); J. R. Nicolson, *Lerwick Harbour*, Lerwick, Lerwick Harbour Trust (1976).

70 J. Veitch, The Talla Railway, *Scots Magazine* **102** 140–9 (1974).

71 T. C. Smout, Lead mining in Scotland 1650–1850: P. L. Payne (ed.), *Studies in Scottish business history*, London, Frank Cass (1967) 103–35. See also T. C. Smout, The lead mines of Wanlockhead, *Transactions Dumfries & Galloway Natural History & Archaeological Society* **39** 144–58 (1962); P. Swinbank, Wanlockhead, *Scottish Archaeological Forum* **8** 23–36 (1976). See also the useful series of publications by the Wanlockhead. Museum Trust.

72 N. S. C. Macmillan, *Campbeltown and Machrihanish Light Railway*, Newton Abbot, David & Charles (1970); N. S. C. Macmillan, Coal mining and associated transport in Kintyre 1750–1967, University of Strathclyde MSc thesis (1972). See also C. L. D. Duckworth & G. E. Langmuir, *Clyde river and other steamers*, Glasgow, Brown & Ferguson (1937).

73 D. L. Smith, *The Dalmellington Iron Company: its engines and men*, Newton Abbot, David & Charles (1967).

74 N. L. Tranter, The demographic impact of economic growth and decline: Portpatrick 1820–91; *Scottish Historical Review* **57** 87–105 (1978).

75 A. J. Youngson, *The making of classical Edinburgh 1750–1840*, Edinburgh University Press (1966).

76 J. R. Coull, The historical geography of Aberdeen, *Scottish Geographical Magazine* **79** 80–93 (1963); T. Donnelly, Rubislaw granite quarries 1750–1939, *Industrial Archaeology* **11** 225–38 (1974).

77 S. J. Jones, Historical geography of Dundee: S. J. Jones (ed.) (1968) 259–77; S. J. Jones, The 1841 Census of Dundee, *University of Dundee Department of Geography Occasional Papers* **3** (1975).

78 I. H. Adams (1978): G. Gordon: The status areas of early to mid-Victorian Edinburgh, *Transactions Institute of British Geographers* **4** 168–91 (1979); G. Gordon & J. Robb, Small-scale residential segregation in the nineteenth century Scottish cities, *Scottish Geographical Magazine* **97** 77–84 (1981); F. W. Green, Urban centres of the Moray Firth Lowlands, *Scottish Geographical Magazine* **52** 157–81 (1936); D. C. D. Pocock, The fair city of Perth, *Scottish Geographical Magazine* **85** 2–8 (1969).

79 J. E. Handley, *The Irish in modern Scotland*, Cork, Cork University Press (1947).

80 M. W. Flinn et al. (1977) 20.

81 S. G. Checkland (1977) 20.

82 G. Best, Scottish Victorian city, *Victorian Studies* **12** 329–58.

83 P. J. Smith, Planning as environmental improvement: slum clearance in Victorian Edinburgh: A. Sutcliffe (ed.), *The rise of modern urban planning 1800–1914*, London, Mansell (1980) 99. See also F. McKichen, A burgh's response to the problems of urban growth: Stirling 1780–1880, *Scottish Historical Review* **57** 68–86 (1978).

84 *Ibid.* 84.

85 *Ibid.* 102.

86 N. A. McIntosh, Changing population distribution in the Cart Basin in the eighteenth and nineteenth centuries, *Transactions Institute of British Geo-*

graphers **22** 39–59 (1956); J. C. Dewdney, Changes of population density in the county of Fife, *Scottish Geographical Magazine* **71** 27–42 (1955).

87 J. Cossar, The distribution of towns and villages of Scotland, *Scottish Geographical Magazine* **26** 298–318 (1910): F. H. Green, Rural and coastal settlement in the Moray Firth Lowlands, *Scottish Geographical Magazine* **52** 97–117 (1936); I. M. L. Robertson, Changing form and function of settlement in southwest Argyll 1841–1961, *Scottish Geographical Magazine* **83** 29–45 (1967).

88 R. H. Osborne, The movements of people in Scotland 1851–1951, *Scottish Studies* **1** 21–46 (1958).

89 M. W. Flinn et al. (1977) 478. See also R. D. Lobban, Migration of Highlanders into Lowland Scotland 1750–1890, Edinburgh University PhD thesis (1969).

90 M. W. Flinn, Malthus emigration and potatoes in the Scottish northwest 1770–1870: L. M. Cullen & T. C. Smout (eds.) (1977) 47–64.

91 M. Gray, The Highland potato famine of the 1840s, *Economic History Review* **7** 357–68 (1954–5); M. Gray, Economic welfare and money income in the Highlands 1750–1850, *Scottish Journal of Political Economy* **2** 47–63 (1955); J. McIntyre, Dearth and harvest failure, Edinburgh University MA thesis (1973); R. N. McMichael, The potato famine of the 1840s in the West Highlands and Islands, Edinburgh University MA thesis (1974); R. N. Salaman, *History and social influence of the potato*, Cambridge University Press (1949). See also M. W. Flinn et al. (1977) 421–38.

92 J. M. Cameron, A study of the factors that assisted and directed Scottish emigration to Upper Canada 1815–55, University of Glasgow PhD thesis (1970). See also I. C. C. Graham, *Colonists from Scotland: emigration to North America 1707–1783*, Ithaca, NY, Cornell University Press (1956). M. L. Hansen, *The Atlantic migration 1607–1860*, Cambridge Mass., Harvard U.P. (1940); D. L. Jones, The background and motives of Scottish emigration to the U.S.A. in the period 1815–61, Edinburgh PhD thesis (1970).

Notes to Chapter 8

1 J. D. Marwick, *River Clyde and harbour of Glasgow*, Glasgow (1898); J. D. Marwick, *The River Clyde and the Clyde Burghs*, Glasgow, Maclehose (1909).

2 J. B. S. Gilfillan & H. A. Moisley, Industrial and commercial developments to 1914: R. Miller & J. Tivy (eds.) (1958) 150.

3 W. F. Macarthur, *History of Port Glasgow*, Glasgow, Jackson Wylie & Co. (1932).

4 R. Miller & J. Tivy (eds.) (1958) 157.

5 D. M. Macintyre, The port and its development: J. Gunn & M. I. Newbigin (eds.) (1921) 43.

6 OSA Dumbarton IV 23.

7 I. A. G. Kinniburgh, Greenock: growth and change in the harbours of the town, *Scottish Geographical Magazine* **76** 89–98 (1960).

8 J. F. Riddell, *Clyde navigation: a history of the development and deepening of the river Clyde*, Edinburgh, Donald (1979) 46.

9 W. F. Macarthur, *op. cit.*, 93.

10 J. F. Riddell, *op. cit.*, 327.

11 *Ibid.*, 167–88.
12 W. Robertson, A history of the river Clyde and the development of the port of Glasgow, *Transactions, Institute of Engineers & Shipbuilders in Scotland* **92** 237–59 (1949).
13 J. M. Desbarats, Some geographical aspects of port modernisation: the case of Clydeport, *Scottish Geographical Magazine* **88** 182–95 (1972); I. A. G. Kinniburgh, New developments at Clydesport, *Scottish Geographical Magazine* **82** 144–53 (1966).
14 A. Slaven (1975) 125.
15 J. L. Carvel, *Stephen of Linthouse: a record of two hundred years of shipbuilding*, Glasgow, Alexander Stephen (1950).
16 D. R. MacGregor, *The tea clippers*, London, Conway Martime Press (1972).
17 J. Clelland, *Annals of Glasgow*, Glasgow, J. Hedderwick (1916); J. Cleland, *Rise and progress of the city of Glasgow*, Glasgow, J. Brash (1820); J. Cleland, *Description of the city of Glasgow*, Glasgow, J. Smith (1840); J. D. Marwick, *Early Glasgow*, Glasgow, Maclehose (1911); R. Renwick et al., *History of Glasgow*, Glasgow, Maclehose (1921–34) 3 vols.
18 J. H. Kellett (1969) 2; J. R. Kellett, *Glasgow: a concise history*, London, Blond (1962).
19 J. O. Mitchell, quoted by J. H. Kellett (1969) 10.
20 *Ibid.*, 10. See also G. S. Pryde, The city and burgh of Glasgow 1100–1750: R. Miller & J. Tivy (eds.) (1958) 134–49; T. C. Smout, The development and enterprise of Glasgow 1556–1707, *Scottish Journal of Political Economy* **7** 194–212 (1960).
21 J. H. Kellett, Property speculators and the building of Glasgow 1780–1830, *Scottish Journal of Political Economy* **8** 211–32 (1961).
22 J. R. Kellett (1969) 12.
23 J. W. Gregory, Glasgow and its geographical history: J. Gunn & M. I. Newbigin (eds.) (1921) 5.
24 J. Orr & S. C. Orr, The growth of the engineering industries: R. Miller & J. Tivy (eds.) (1958) 190–200; J. Thomas, *Springburn story*, Newton Abbot, David & Charles (1964); W. Vamplew, Scottish railways and the development of Scottish locomotive building in the nineteenth century, *Business History Review* **46** 320–38 (1972).
25 J. W. Whitehand, Building cycles and the spatial patterns of urban growth, *Transactions Institute of British Geographers* **56** 39–55 (1972). See also M. Simpson, Middle class housing and suburban communities in the west end of Glasgow 1830–1914, Glasgow University BLitt thesis (1970).
26 J. Lindsay, Municipal history and activities: J. Gunn & M. I. Newbigin (eds.) (1921) 31–2.
27 J. R. Kellett, Glasgow railways 1830–1880: a study in natural growth, *Economic History Review* **17** 354–68 (1964); J. Thomas, *Scotland: Lowlands and Borders*, Newton Abbot, David & Charles (1971).
28 J. R. Kellett, Urban and transport history from local records: an example from Glasgow solicitors' papers. *Journal of Transport History* **6** 222–40 (1963–4); J. R. Kellett, *The impact of railways on Victorian cities*, London, Routledge & Kegan Paul (1969); M. Simpson, Urban transport and the development of

Glasgow's West End 1830–1914, *Journal of Transport History* **1** 146–60 (1971–2).

29 A. J. S. Paterson, *The golden years of the Clyde steamers 1889–1914*, Newton Abbot, David & Charles (1969).

30 D. W. Lamont, Population migration and social area change in Central Glasgow 1871–1891. Glasgow University PhD thesis (1976). See also F. Worsdall, *The tenement – a way of life: a social historical and architectural study of housing in Glasgow*, Edinburgh, W. & R. Chambers (1979).

31 J. Butt, Working class housing in Glasgow 1851–1914: S. D. Chapman (ed.) *The history of working class housing*, Newton Abbot, David & Charles (1971). See also C. M. Allan, The genesis of British urban redevelopment with regard to Glasgow, *Economic History Review* **18** 598–613 (1965); R. Rodger, Scottish urban housebuilding 1870–1914, University of Edinburgh PhD thesis (1976); J. N. Tarn, Housing in Liverpool and Glasgow: growth of civic responsibility, *Town Planning Review* **39** 319–34 (1969). For events in Edinburgh see P. J. Smith, Planning as environmental improvement – slum clearance in Victorian Edinburgh: A. Sutcliffe (ed.), *The rise of modern urban planning 1800–1914*, London, Mansell (1980) 128–33.

32 H. J. Mackinder, L'envoi: J. Gunn & M. I. Newbigin (eds.) (1921) 77–8.

33 S. G. Checkland, *The Upas tree: Glasgow 1875–1975*, Glasgow, University of Glasgow Press (1977).

Notes to Chapter 9

1 J. Butt, *The industrial archaeology of Scotland*, Newton Abbot, David & Charles (1967) 106.

2 R. H. Campbell (1961).

3 W. D. Campbell, Locational factors in the development of the Scottish iron and steel industry 1760–1970, Edinburgh University MSc thesis (1970).

4 J. G. A. Baird, *Muirkirk in byegone days*, Muirkirk, W. S. Smith (1910).

5 J. Butt, Glenbuck ironworks, *Ayrshire Collections* **8** 68–75 (1967–9); I. L. Donnachie & J. Butt, Three eighteenth century Scottish ironworks, *Journal of Industrial Archaeology* **1** 213–21 (1964–5).

6 J. Butt, Scottish iron and steel industry before the hot blast, *Papers of the Iron and Steel Institute* **580** (1966–7).

7 R. D. Corrins, The great hot blast affair, *Industrial Archaeology* **7** 233–63 (1970).

8 A. M. Macgeorge, *The Bairds of Gartsherrie*, Glasgow, University Press (1875). See also J. Macarthur, *New Monkland parish*, Glasgow, C. L. Wright (1890); T. R. Miller, *The Monkland tradition*, London, Nelson (1958); G. Thomson, *The growth of the Monklands*, Airdrie, Airdrie Advertiser (1947); A. Miller, *The rise and progress of Coatbridge*, Glasgow, Robertson (1864).

9 J. L. Carvel, *The Coltness Iron Company*, Edinburgh, T. & A. Constable (1948).

10 A. M. C. MacEwan, The Shotts Iron Company 1800–1850, Strathclyde University MLitt thesis (1972). See also A. Muir, *The story of Shotts*, Edinburgh, Shotts Iron Co. (c. 1954).

11 R. D. Corrins, William Baird and Company: coal and iron masters, Strathclyde University PhD thesis (1974).

12 See also J. J. Byres, Entrepreneurship in the Scottish heavy industries 1870–1900: P. L. Payne (ed.), *Studies in Scottish business history*, London, Cass (1967) 250–96.

13 I. F. Gibson, The economic history of the Scottish iron and steel industry, London University PhD thesis (1955); J. H. G. Lebon, The agrarian and industrial revolutions in Ayrshire: L. D. Stamp & S. W. Wooldridge (eds.), *London essays in geography*, London, Longmans (1951), 175–97; C. A. Whatley, The process of industrialisation in Ayrshire 1707–1871, Strathclyde University PhD thesis (1975).

14 R. H. Campbell, The growth and fluctuations of the Scottish pig iron trade 1828–1873, Aberdeen University PhD thesis (1956). See also R. H. Campbell, Developments in the Scottish pig iron trade 1844–8, *Journal of Economic History* **15** 209–26 (1955).

15 M. W. Flinn, British overseas investment in iron ore mining 1870–1914, Manchester University MA thesis (1952–3).

16 J. H. G. Lebon, The development of the Ayrshire coalfields, *Scottish Geographical Magazine* **49** 138–54 (1933).

17 K. Warren (1965).

18 B. C. Skinner, *The Cramond iron works*, Edinburgh University Dept of Extra-Mural Studies (1965) 14. See also P. Cadell, *The iron mills of Cramond*, Edinburgh University Dept of Extra-Mural Studies (1973).

19 G. Thomson, Dalnottar Iron Company, *Scottish Historical Review* **35** 10–20 (1956).

20 R. H. Campbell (1961) 33.

21 K. Warren (1965) 23.

22 P. L. Payne (1979) 17.

23 I. F. Gibson, The establishment of the Scottish steel industry, *Scottish Journal of Political Economy* **5** 22–39 (1958); J. Riley, The rise and progress of the Scottish steel industry, *Journal of the Iron and Steel Institute* **2** 394–5 (1885).

24 S. G. Checkland, *The mines of Tharsis*, London, Allen & Unwin (1967).

25 P. L. Payne (1979) 54. See also R. H. Campbell, *The rise and fall of Scottish industry 1707–1939*, Edinburgh, Donald (1980) 118–30.

Notes to Chapter 10

1 O. Mackenzie, *A hundred years in the Highlands*, London, Arnold (1921).

2 E. Richards, How tame were the Highlanders during the clearances? *Scottish Studies* **17** 35–59 (1973) 43. See also E. Richards, *The Leviathan of Wealth*, London, Routledge & Kegan Paul (1973).

3 J. R. Coull, Crofters' common grazings in Scotland, *Agricultural History Review* **16** 142–54 (1968).

4 D. Campbell, Highland shielings in the olden times, *Transactions of the Inverness Scientific Society and Field Club* **5** 62–90 (1895–9).

5 H. Fairhurst (1967). See also J. Stewart, Old Monachyle, Balquidder *Medieval Village Research Group Report* **25** 17–9 (1977).

6 J. MacCulloch (1824) 130.

7 *Ibid.*, 119.

8 Anon, *A critical examination of Dr MacCulloch's work*, Edinburgh, n.p. (1826) 269–74.

9 D. Stewart, *Sketches of the Highlanders of Scotland*, Edinburgh, n.p. (1822) 189.

10 D. J. MacCuish, Ninety years of crofting legislation, *Transactions, Gaelic Society of Inverness* **50** 296–326 (1976–8).

11 M. I. Adam (1922) 166.

12 J. S. Keltie, *A history of the Scottish Highlands*, Edinburgh, Fullarton (1879) 8.

13 P. Gaskell (1968) 13.

14 E. Richards, The Sutherland clearances: new evidence from Dunrobin *Northern Scotland* **2** 57–74 (1974–5); P. T. Wheeler, Landownership and the crofting system in Sutherland since 1800 *Agricultural History Review* **14** 45–56 (1966). See also J. R. Coull, Melness: a crofting community on the north coast of Sutherland, *Scottish Studies* **7** 80–98 (1963).

15 E. Richards (1970) 170.

16 D. Turnock (1977) 49–54.

17 M. C. Storrie, Landholdings and settlement evolution in West Highland Scotland, *Geografiska Annaler* **74B** 138–61 (1965).

18 J. R. Hunter (1976).

19 D. Turnock, North Morar: the improving movement on a West Highland estate, *Scottish Geographical Magazine* **85** 17–30 (1969).

20 J. Hunter, The emergence of the crofting community: the religious contribution 1798–1843, *Scottish Studies* **18** 94–116 (1974) 112.

21 E. Richards, Problems on the Cromartie Estate 1851–3, *Scottish Historical Review* **52** 149–64 (1973).

22 H. J. Hanham (1969) 64. See also D. W. Crowley, The 'Crofters Party' 1885–1892, *Scottish Historical Review* **35** 110–26 (1956); J. Hunter, Politics of Highland land reform 1873–1895, *Scottish Historical Review* **53** 45–68 (1974); J. Hunter, Gaelic connections: the Highlands and Islands, *Scottish Historical Review* **54** 178–204 (1975); J. G. Kellas, The Crofters' War 1882–1888 *History Today* **12** 281–8 (1962), E. Richards, Patterns of Highland discontent 1790–1860: R. Quinault & J. Stevenson (eds.), *Popular protest and public order*, London, George Allen & Unwin (1974) 75–114.

23 J. Pennell & E. Pennell, *Our journey to the Hebrides*, London, T. Fisher Unwin (1890) 72–3.

24 D. Turnock (1977) 55.

25 M. Gray (1973) 89.

26 E. Buckland et al., *Report on the herring fisheries of Scotland* (C 1979), London, HMSO (1878) xx.

27 *Ibid.*, xxi.

28 M. Gray (1973) 113.

29 G. Kay, The landscape of improvement, *Scottish Geographical Magazine* **78** 100–11 (1962). See also M. L. Parry, Changes in the upper limit of cultivation in southeast Scotland 1750–1950, Edinburgh University PhD thesis (1973); M. L. Parry, The abandonment of upland settlement in South Scotland, *Scottish Geographical Magazine* **92** 50–60 (1976).

30 OSA Kilmuir Easter VI 187.
31 J. R. Allan (1952) 78.
32 I. Carter (1979) 160–84. See also I. Carter, Peasantry of Northeast Scotland, *Journal of Peasant Studies* **3** 151–91 (1976); I. Carter, Social differentiation in the Aberdeenshire peasantry 1696–1870, *Journal of Peasant Studies* **5** 48–65 (1977); M. Gray, North East agriculture and the labour force 1790–1875: A. A. MacLaren (ed.), *Social class in Scotland*, Edinburgh, Donald (1976) 86–104.

Notes to Chapter 11

1 N. H. Lithwick and G. Pacquet, Urban growth and regional contagion: Idem (eds.), *Urban studies: a Canadian perspective*, Toronto, Methuen (1968) 32.
2 I. M. L. Robertson, Scottish population distribution: implications for location decisions, *Transactions Institute of British Geographers* **63** 111–24 (1974); D. C. Rich, Accessibility and economic activity: a study of locational disadvantage in Scotland, Cambridge University PhD thesis (1975).
3 N. MacCormick, *The Scottish debate: essays on Scottish nationalism*, London, Oxford University Press (1970); T. Nairn, The three dreams of Scottish nationalism: K. Miller (ed.), *Memoirs of a modern Scotland*, London, Faber (1970) 34–54.
4 G. McCrone, *Scotland's future: the economics of nationalism*, Oxford, Blackwell (1969). See also G. McCrone, *Scotland's economic progress 1951–1960*, University of Glasgow (1965).
5 G. C. Cameron and B. D. Clark, Industrial movement and the regional problem, *University of Glasgow Social and Economic Studies Occasional Paper* (1966); G. C. Cameron & G. L. Reid, Scottish economic planning and the attraction of industry, *Ibid.* **6** (1966); G. McDonald, Social and geographical mobility in Scottish new towns, *Scottish Geographical Magazine* **91** 38–51 (1975).
6 Scottish Development Department Central Planning Research Unit, Aspects of Population change in the city of Glasgow, *C.P.R.U. Paper* **1** (1972).
7 C. A. Oakley, *Scottish industry today: a survey of recent developments*, Edinburgh, Moray Press (1937).
8 Scottish Economic Committee, *Scotland's industrial future: the case for planned development*, Glasgow, SEC Publication (1939).
9 Scottish Home Department, *A programme for Highland development*, Edinburgh, HMSO (Cmd 7976) (1950). See also Scottish Office, *Review of Highland policy*, London HMSO (Cmnd 785) (1959); Scottish Economic Committee, *Highlands and Islands of Scotland: a review of economic conditions and recommendations for improvement*, Edinburgh, SEC Publication (1938). A. Geddes and F. D. M. Spaven, The Highlands and Isles: G. H. J. Daysh et al., *Studies in regional planning*, London, Philip (1949) 3–53. See also C. M. Law, *British regional development since World War One* Newton Abbot, David & Charles (1981).
10 H. M. Begg et al., Special regional assistance in Scotland, *Fraser of Allander Institute Research Monograph* **3** (1976). For proposed changes to development areas see A. R. Townsend, Unemployment geography and the new government's 'regional' policy *Area* **12** 9–18 (1980).

11 J. Toothill et al., *Inquiry into the Scottish economy 1960–1961*, Edinburgh, Scottish Council (Development and Industry) (1961).

12 Scottish Development Department, *Central Scotland: a programme for development*, Edinburgh, HMSO (Cmnd 2188) (1963).

13 Scottish Office, *The Scottish economy 1965–1970: a plan for expansion*, Edinburgh, HMSO (Cmnd 2864) (1966). An unofficial updating has been provided by R. E. Nicoll et al., *A future for Scotland: a study of the key factors associated with growth in Scotland*, Edinburgh, Scottish Council (Development & Industry) (1973).

14 M. Gaskin et al., *North east Scotland: a survey of its development potential*, Edinburgh, HMSO (1969); Scottish Development Department, *The Central Borders*, Edinburgh, HMSO (1968). Scottish Development Department, *A strategy for Southwest Scotland*, Edinburgh, HMSO (1970).

15 J. G. Kellas, *The Scottish political system*, Cambridge University Press (1973).

16 P. J. Bull, The spatial components of intra-urban manufacturing change: suburbanisation in Clydeside 1958–68, *Transactions Institute of British Geographers* **3** 91–100 (1978).

17 W. Lithgow et al., *Oceanspan: a maritime based development strategy for a European Scotland 1970–2000*, Edinburgh, Scottish Council (Development & Industry) (1970); see also A. Hargrave, Whatever happened to Oceanspan? *Business Scotland* **20** 80–1 (1976); R. E. Nicoll, Crisis on Clydeside, *Town & Country Planning* **39** 465–7 (1971).

18 S. G. Checkland (1977) 13.

19 H. R. Jones & D. C. D. Pocock, Some economic and social implications of the Tay Road Bridge, *Scottish Geographical Magazine* **82** 93–110 (1966); M. Pacione, Traditional and new industries in Dundee, *Ibid.* **88** 53–60 (1972).

20 W. R. Scott & J. Cunnison, *The industries of the Clyde valley during the war*, Oxford, Clarendon Press (1924). P. L. Payne, *Colvilles and the Scottish steel industry*, Oxford, Clarendon Press (1979).

21 K. Warren (1965).

22 H. D. Watts, The locations of aluminium reduction plant in the UK, *Tijdschrift voor Econ. en Soc. Geografie* **61** 148–56 (1970). See also G. A. Mackay, A study of the economic impact of the Invergordon aluminium smelter, *H.I.D.B. Special Report* **15** (1978); J. S. Smith, Development and rural conservation in Easter Ross, *Scottish Geographical Magazine* **90** 42–56 (1974).

23 L. V. Chilton, The aluminium industry in Scotland, *Scottish Geographical Magazine* **6** 153–62 (1950); M. J. F. Gregor & R. M. Crichton, *From croft to factory: the evolution of an industrial community in the Highlands*, Edinburgh, Nelson (1946).

24 K. Chapman, The structure and development of the oil-based complex at Grangemouth, *Scottish Geographical Magazine* **90** 98–109 (1974).

25 K. Chapman, *North Sea Oil and gas: a geographical perspective*, Newton Abbot, David & Charles (1976); M. Gaskin et al., *Economic impact of North Sea oil on Scotland*, Edinburgh, HMSO (1978).

26 J. P. Day, The jute industry in Scotland during the war: D. T. L. Jones et al., *Rural Scotland during the war*, London, Oxford University Press (1926) 265–307.

27 C. P. Snodgrass, Map of economic regions of Scotland, *Scottish Geographical Magazine* **59** 14–18 (1943). See also C. P. Snodgrass, The influence of physical environment on the principal cultivated crops of Scotland, *Scottish Geographical Magazine* **48** 329–47 (1932); C. P. Snodgrass, Stock farming in Scotland and its relations to environment, *Ibid.* **49** 24–34 (1933).

28 W. J. Carlyle, The away wintering of ewe hoggs from Scottish hill farms, *Scottish Geographical Magazine* **88** 100–14 (1972); W. J. Carlyle, Breeds of hill cattle in Scotland, *Ibid.* **90** 27–41 (1974); W. J. Carlyle, The movements of Irish cattle in Scotland, *Journal of Agricultural Economics* **24** 331–51 (1973); W. J. Carlyle, Some geographical aspects of the movements of Scottish store cattle, *Edinburgh University Department of Geography Occasional Paper* **3** (1973); H. M. Leppard, Scottish carse agriculture: the Carse of Gowrie, *Economic Geography* **10** 217–38 (1934).

29 I. R. Bowler, Regional variations in Scottish agricultural trends, *Scottish Geographical Magazine* **91** 114–22 (1975). J. T. Coppock (1976).

30 A. Rathore, The role of agricultural labour in the depopulation trends in rural Scotland 1945–6, University of Glasgow BLitt thesis (1968); H. R. Wagstaff, The rural economy of Scotland in a period of rapid decline in agricultural population, *Scottish Agricultural Economics* **22** 103–12 (1972). T. P. Russell, The size and structure of Scottish agriculture, *Scottish Agricultural Economics* **20** 299–325 (1970).

31 G. Clark, Farm amalgamation in Scotland, *Scottish Geographical Magazine* **95** 93–107 (1979); G. A. Urquhart, The amalgamation of agricultural holdings, *Journal of Agricultural Economics* **16** 405–12 (1964–5).

32 S. W. E. Vince (ed.), *Land of Britain: Highlands of Scotland*, London, Geographical Publications (1944) 639.

33 H. M. Cadell, Land reclamation in the Forth valley, *Scottish Geographical Magazine* **45** 7–22; 81–9 (1929). A. G. Ogilvie, Debatable land in Scotland, *Scottish Geographical Magazine* **61** 42–5 (1945). See also L. Symons, The economic conquest of the hills, *Scottish Geographical Magazine* **75** 18–29 (1959).

34 F. Beavington, A brown forest soil at high altitudes in Aberdeenshire, *Scottish Geographical Magazine* **88** 134–40 (1972).

35 D. Howat et al., Drainage of soils of low permeability: the Slammanan project, *West of Scotland Agricultural College Research & Development Publication* **8** (1978). J. R. Raeburn, The economics of upland farming: J. Ashton & W. H. Long (eds.), *The remoter rural areas of Britain*, Edinburgh, Oliver & Boyd (1972) 3–24.

36 W. J. Carlyle, Store stock marketing by small farmers in the Crofting Counties, *Scottish Geographical Magazine* **94** 113–23 (1978).

37 H. A. Moisley, The Highlands and Islands: a crofting region? *Transactions Institute of British Geographers* **31** 83–95 (1962).

38 D. J. MacCuish, The origin and development of crofting law, *Transactions of the Gaelic Society of Inverness* **43** 181–96 (1962).

39 P. Mewett, Occupational pluralism in crofting, *Scottish Journal of Sociology* **2** 31–49 (1977).

40 J. S. Grant, The importance of the part-time holding: P. G. Sadler & G. A.

Mackay (eds.), *The changing fortunes of marginal regions*, Aberdeen, Institute for the Study of Sparsely Populated Areas (n.d.) 150. See also J. S. Grant, The crofting problem, *Scottish Agriculture* **44** 12–7 (1964).

41 J. S. Grant n.d., *op. cit.*, 150.

42 J. MacCuish, The case for converting crofting tenure to ownership, *Transactions of the Gaelic Society of Inverness* **43** 181–96 (1962). See also A. Collier, *The crofting problem*, Cambridge University Press (1953).

43 J. Tivy, Easter Ross: a residual crofting area, *Scottish Studies* **9** 64–84 (1965).

44 A. S. Mather, State aided land settlement in Scotland, *Aberdeen University O'Dell Memorial Monograph* **6** (1978).

45 A. Geddes, *The isle of Lewis and Harris*, Edinburgh University Press (1955).

46 J. L. Blake. Pasture improvement schemes in the Isle of Lewis, *Scottish Studies* **6** 108–13 (1962); C. F. MacDonald, Agricultural cooperation in Lewis, *Scottish Agriculture* **42** 69–72 (1962).

47 Advisory Panel on the Highlands and Islands, *Report on land use*, Edinburgh, HMSO (1964); M. A. M. Dickie, The Crofting Counties: problems and prospects, *Transactions of the Royal Highland & Agricultural Society of Scotland* **5** 7–22 (1961); R. Grieve, Problems and objectives in the Highlands and Islands: J. Ashton & W. H. Long (eds.), *The remoter rural areas of Britain*, Edinburgh, Oliver & Boyd (1972) 130–45. D. I. Mackay, Regional planning for the north of Scotland, *Aberdeen University Review* **41** 75–83 (1965); D. I. Mackay & N. K. Buxton, The north of Scotland economy: a case for redevelopment, *Scottish Journal of Political Economy* **12** 23–49 (1965); D. C. Thomson & I. Grimble (eds.), *The future of the Highlands*, London, Routledge & Kegan Paul (1968) 93–150.

48 J. M. Bryden & G. Houston, *Agrarian change in the Scottish Highlands*, London, Martin Robertson (1976).

49 J. Anderson, Letter respecting the prevention of emigration: R. Fraser, *Inquiry into the most effectual means of improvement of the coasts and western isles of Scotland*, London, G. & W. Nicol (1803) 81–98.

50 D. N. McVean & J. D. Lockie, *Ecology and land use in upland Scotland*, Edinburgh University Press (1969): L. D. Stamp (ed.), Land use in the Highlands and Islands, *Advancement of Science* **21** 141–90 (1964–5).

51 HIDB, Strath of Kildonan, *H.I.D.B. Special Report 5* (1970); HIDB, Island of Mull: survey and proposals for development, *H.I.D.B. Special Report, 10* (1973).

52 A. S. Mather, Red deer land use in the northern Highlands, *Scottish Geographical Magazine* **88** 36–47; 86–99 (1972).

53 Scottish Development Department, *Cairngorm area*, Edinburgh, HMSO (1967).

54 R. Aitken, Wilderness areas in Scotland, Aberdeen University PhD thesis (1977); G. F. Ballantine, Planning for remoteness, *Journal of the Town Planning Institute* **57** 60–4 (1971); W. H. Murray, *Highland landscape: a survey*, Edinburgh, National Trust for Scotland (1962).

55 R. Millman, Outdoor recreation in the Highland countryside, University of Aberdeen PhD thesis (1970).

56 Scotland, *National parks: a Scottish survey*, Edinburgh, HMSO (Cmd 6631) (1945); Scotland, *National parks and the conservation of nature in Scotland*, Edinburgh, HMSO (Cmd 7235) (1947).

57 J. I. Stewart, The Scottish herring fishing, *Scottish Geographical Magazine* **47** 219–27 (1931).

58 J. R. Coull, Modern trends in Scottish fisheries, *Scottish Geographical Magazine* **84** 15–28 (1968); M. Gray, The fishing industry: D. Omand (ed.) (1976) 196–209.

59 J. R. Coull, The mobile Scottish fisherman, *Aberdeen University Review* **41** 175–8 (1966).

60 J. A. Fleming, Gareloch: ancient and modern, *Scottish Geographical Magazine* **63** 20–5 (1947); M. W. Flinn, The overseas trade of Scottish ports 1900–1960, *Scottish Journal of Political Economy* **13** 220–37 (1969).

61 J. Mathieson, The tragedy of the Scottish Highlands, *Scottish Geographical Magazine* **54** 257–63 (1938).

62 D. M. Christie, Freight transport in the Highlands, Dundee University PhD thesis (1972); F. T. Wilkin, *Transportation in a sparsely populated area: a study of transport in the Highland region of Scotland*, Portsmouth Polytechnic Department of Civil Engineering (1976).

63 R. Moira, A comment of the new plan for Edinburgh, *Scottish Geographical Magazine* **63** 116–28 (1947).

64 J. H. Jones and C. B. Marshall, The Longannet power project, *Geography* **53** 410–12 (1968); D. R. Diamond, Electricity and petroleum: R. Miller and J. Tivy (eds.) (1958) 212–18.

65 K. J. Lea, Hydroelectricity in Scotland, *Transactions Institute of British Geographers* **46** 155–65 (1961). See also F. G. Baily, Water Resources of Scotland, *Scottish Geographical Magazine* **47** 129–44 (1931); G. D. Banks, Hydroelectric development in the Highlands, *Ibid.* **66** 65–76 (1950).

66 A. Arthur, The conservation of certain glens in Scotland, *Scottish Geographical Magazine* **61** 16–18 (1945); K. J. Lea, Hydroelectric power developments and the landscape in the Highlands, *Ibid.* **84** 239–55 (1965).

67 T. R. Hollingsworth, *Migration: a study based on Scottish experience 1931–1964*, Edinburgh, Oliver & Boyd (1970); H. R. Jones, Recent migration from and within Scotland, *Tijdschrift voor Econ. en Soc. Geografie* **58** 135–45 (1967); H. R. Jones, Migration to and from Scotland since 1960, *Transactions Institute of British Geographers* **49** 145–59 (1970); H. R. Jones, A spatial analysis of human fertility in Scotland, *Scottish Geographical Magazine* **91** 102–13 (1975); R. Lumb, A community based approach to the analysis of migration in the Highlands & Islands of Scotland, *Sociological Review* **28** 611–27 (1980); R. Ng, Internal migration regions in Scotland, *Geografiska Annaler* **51B** 139–47 (1969).

68 E. M. Soulsby, An analysis of selected aspects of demographic change in the Border counties of Scotland 1755–1961, St Andrews University PhD thesis (1971). See also D. R. Macgregor, On the importance of regions to Scotland: J. N. Wolfe (ed.), *Government and nationalism in Scotland*, Edinburgh University Press (1969) 153–64.

69 F. H. W. Green, Some relations between town and country in Scotland, *Scottish Geographical Magazine* **68** 2–12 (1952); H. A. Moisley, Glasgow's sphere of

influence: R. Miller & J. Tivy (eds.) (1958) 285–301; Royal Commission on Local Government in Scotland, *Report*, Edinburgh, HMSO (Cmnd 4150) (1969).

70 J. W. R. Whitehand, The study of variations in the building of town centres, *Transactions Institute of British Geographers* **4** 559–75 (1979).

71 A. MacEwan, Edinburgh: an experiment in positive conservation, *Town Planning Review* **4** 395–406 (1975); D. Smith, The conservation of a Georgian new town, *Town & Country Planning* **38** 398–400 (1970).

72 P. Geddes, *Civic survey of Edinburgh*, Edinburgh, Outlook Tower Association (1910).

73 Lord Esher, *Conservation in Glasgow*, Glasgow Corporation (1971).

74 C. McWilliam (1975) 206–15.

75 W. Dodd (1970–2) 360–73.

76 D. Harris, The idea of the growth area, *Official Architecture and Planning* **29** 577–81. Holmes Planning Group, *The Moray Firth: a plan for growth in a sub-region of the Scottish Highlands*, Inverness, HIDB (1968); W. D. C. Lyddon, North Sea oil and its consequences for housing and planning, *Planning and Administration* **3** 71–84 (1976).

77 Dartington Amenity Research Trust, *Second Homes in Scotland*, Totnes, Dartington Trust (1977).

78 T. Sprott, *Advance factories and rural action*, Aberdeen, Grampian Regional Council (1976). An alternative approach is outlined by E. T. Parham, *Speyside study*, Aberdeen, North East Scotland Development Authority (1973). See also R. M. Gorrie, Shelter belts and cottage industry in Scottish planning, *Scottish Geographical Magazine* **63** 11–16 (1947).

79 D. Turnock, Depopulation in northeast Scotland with reference to the country-side, *Scottish Geographical Magazine* **84** 256–68 (1968).

80 A. H. Taylor, The electoral geography of Welsh and Scottish nationalism, *Scottish Geographical Magazine* **89** 44–52 (1973).

81 G. Harvie, *Scotland and nationalism*, London, George Allen & Unwin (1977) 278.

82 M. Gaskin, The remoter rural areas in the national context: J. Ashton & W. H. Long (eds.), *The remoter rural areas of Britain*, Edinburgh, Oliver and Boyd (1972) 165–85. F. R. Stevenson, Planning and development in Scotland, *Town Planning Review* **26** 5–18 (1955).

Notes to Chapter 12

1 W. F. Gray, The quarrying of Salisbury Crags, *Book of the Old Edinburgh Club* **18** (1932) 181–210.

2 R. Rodger, *The origins of Scottish town planning*, Edinburgh, Planning History Group Conference Paper (1978) 11–12.

3 P. J. Smith, The foul burns of Edinburgh, *Scottish Geographical Magazine* **91** 25–37 (1975).

4 J. Gunn & M. I. Newbigin (eds.) (1921) 31.

5 B. Gillie, *Problems of historiography of British town and regional planning*, Edinburgh, Planning History Group Conference Paper (1978). B. Gillie, Landmarks in the history of British town and country planning 1909–1939,

Planning History Bulletin **2** 5–11 (1980); See also G. E. Cherry, *The evolution of British town planning*, Leighton Buzzard, Leonard Hill (1974).

6 H. E. Mellor (ed.), *The ideal city*, Leicester University Press (1979). See also P. Geddes, Edinburgh and its region, *Scottish Geographical Magazine* **18** 302–12 (1902); W. I. Stevenson, Patrick Geddes 1854–1932: T. W. Freeman & P. Pinchemel (eds.), *Geographers: Bibliographical studies 2*, London, Mansell (1978) 53–65; H. E. Mellor, Cities and evolution – Patrick Geddes as an international prophet of town planning before 1914: A. Sutcliffe (ed.), *The rise of modern urban planning 1800–1914*, London, Mansell (1980) 199–223.

7 H. E. Mellor (1979) *op. cit.*, 24.

8 P. Geddes, *City development: a study of parks gardens and culture-institutes*, Edinburgh, Carnegie-Dunfermline Trust (1904).

9 H. E. Mellor (1979) *op. cit.*, 92.

10 Royal Commission on the Distribution of the Industrial Population, *Report*, London, HMSO (Cmd 6153) (1940).

11 J. Minett, *Gretna: Britain's first government sponsored new town*, Edinburgh, Planning History Group Conference Paper (1978). See also W. L. Creese, *The legacy of Raymond Unwin*, Harvard, MIT Press (1967).

12 L. P. Abercrombie & R. H. Matthew, *Clyde Valley regional plan*, Glasgow. Clyde Valley Regional Planning Advisory Committee (1946).

13 F. C. Mears, *A regional survey and plan for central and southeast Scotland*, Edinburgh Central & Southeast Scotland Regional Planning Advisory Committee (1948) 63.

14 *Ibid.* 66.

15 G. Payne, *The Tay valley plan: a physical social and economic survey and plan for the future development of East Central Scotland*, HMSO.

16 R. Smith, *The impact of the Clyde Valley plan*, Edinburgh, History of Planning Group Conference Paper (1978).

17 R. Gardner Medwin & F. J. Connell, New towns in Scotland, *Town Planning Review* **20** 305–14 (1949); R. Smith, The origin of Scottish new town policy and the founding of East Kilbride, *Public Administration* **52** 143–59 (1974).

18 L. H. Wilson, Cumbernauld new town; R. G. Putnam et al. (eds.), *A geography of urban places*, London, Methuen (1970) 453–62.

19 J. Retter, *Drongan the story of a mining village*, Lugar, Cumnock & Doon Valley District Council (1978).

20 C. W. Miney, Town development and regional planning in Scotland, *Journal of the Town Planning Institute* **51** 13–19 (1965).

21 Scottish Development Department, *Central Scotland: a programme for development and growth*, Edinburgh, HMSO (Cmnd 2188) (1963).

22 Scottish Development Department et al., *Lothians regional survey and plan* Edinburgh, HMSO (1966) 2 vols. See also D. A. Bull, New town and town expansion schemes: urban form and structure, *Town Planning Review* **38** 165–86 (1967); D. Field, New town and town expansion schemes, *Town Planning Review* **38** 196–216 (1968–9).

23 A. D. Campbell & W. D. C. Lyddon, *Tayside: potential for development*, Edinburgh, HMSO (1970); I. Masser, Three estuarine studies, *Town Planning Review* **43** 117–28 (1973); S. J. Jones (ed.), *Dundee and district*, Dundee, British

Association (1968). See also Scottish Office, *The Scottish economy 1965–70: a plan for expansion*, Edinburgh, HMSO (Cmnd 2864) (1966).

24 See, however, Glasgow Corporation, *Greater Glasgow Transportation Study*, Glasgow, Glasgow Corporation (1967–8) 2 vols.

25 R. Smith, The politics of an overspill policy: Glasgow Cumbernauld and the Town Development (Scotland) Act, *University of Glasgow Discussion Papers in planning* **2** (1975).

26 Glasgow Corporation, *First and second planning reports of the city engineer*, Glasgow Corporation (1945–6). See also J. Forbes, A map analysis of potentially developable land, *Regional Studies* **3** 179–95 (1969).

27 R. Grieve, The region, *Advancement of Science* **20** 516–26 (1963–4); R. Grieve and D. J. Robertson, The city and the region, *University of Glasgow Social and Economic Studies Occasional Paper* **2** (1964); R. Grieve, Regional planning in Scotland, *The Planner* **59** 411–16 (1974); J. H. McGuiness, Regional economic development: progress in Scotland, *Journal of the Town Planning Institute* **54** 103–12 (1968).

28 T. Hart, The comprehensive development area, *University of Glasgow Social and Economic Studies Occasional Papers* **9** (1968); See also J. B. Cullingworth, A profile of Glasgow housing, *op. cit.* **8** (1968); J. Forbes & I. M. L. Robertson, Patterns of residential movement in Greater Glasgow, *Scottish Geographical Magazine* **97** 85–97 (1981); K. J. Lea, Greater Glasgow, *Scottish Geographical Magazine* **96** 1–18 (1980); R. Miller, The new face of Glasgow, *op. cit.* **86** 5–15 (1970).

29 D. F. Sim, Building adaptation and redevelopment in the central business district of Glasgow, Glasgow University PhD thesis (1976). See also D. R. Diamond et al., The central business district of Glasgow: K. Norborg (ed.), Proceedings of the I.G.U. symposium in urban geography, *Lund Studies in Geography* **24B** 525–34 (1962).

30 S. G. Checkland (1977) 76. See also S. G. Checkland, The British industrial city as history: the Glasgow case, *Urban Studies* **1** 34–54 (1964).

31 M. Barke, Some aspects of population and social change in Glasgow 1961–71, *Professional Geographer* **30** 20–9 (1978).

32 H. Murray, Coalmining: Scottish Development Department et al., *Lothians Regional Survey and plan*, Edinburgh, HMSO (1966) **I** 65–8. See also P. R. Crowe, The Scottish coalfields, *Scottish Geographical Magazine* **45** 321–37 (1929); R. A. Moore, Scottish coal, *Scottish Geographical Magazine* **66** 26–36 (1950); Scottish Office, *Report of the Scottish Coalfields Committee*, Edinburgh HMSO (Cmd 6575) (1944).

33 P. J. Smith, Changing conjectives in Scottish new town policy, *Annals, Association of American Geographers* **56** 192–507 (1966); P. J. Smith, Glenrothes: some geographical aspects of new town development, *Scottish Geographical Magazine* **83** 17–28 (1967); See also J. McNeil, The Fife coal industry 1947–67, *Scottish Geographical Magazine* **89** 81–94 (1973); J. McNeil, Factors in industrial location: the Fife case 1958–1970, *Scottish Geographical Magazine* **90** 185–97 (1974); D. C. D. Pocock, Urban renewal the example of Fife, *Scottish Geographical Magazine* **86** 123–33 (1970).

34 C. J. Robertson, New industries and new towns in Scotland's industrial growth, *Scottish Geographical Magazine* **80** 114–23 (1964). See also J. D. McCallum, A

history of British regional policy to 1964, *University of Glasgow Discussion Papers in Planning* **5** (1976); P. D. McGovern, The new towns of Scotland, *Scottish Geographical Magazine* **84** 29–44 (1968).

35 D. R. Diamond, Urban change in mid-Scotland, *Scottish Geographical Magazine* **78** 150–1 (1962); J. Firn, External control and regional development: the case of Scotland, *Environment & Planning* **7** 393–414 (1975); C. J. Robertson, The economic geography of central Scotland: J. A. Steers (ed.), *Field studies in the British Isles*, London, Nelson (1964) 344–59. I. M. L. Robertson, Population distribution and locational problems: an approach by grid squares in central Scotland, *Regional Studies* **6** 237–45 (1972).

36 Glasgow Corporation, *The Springburn study: urban renewal in a regional context*, Glasgow Corporation (1967). See also E. Anderson, The effect of planning on inner city commercial areas and small firms with special reference to Glasgow, University of Strathclyde MSc thesis (1974); G. C. Cameron & K. M. Johnson, Comprehensive urban renewal and industrial relocation: The Glasgow case: J. B. Cullingworth & S. C. Orr (eds.), *Regional and urban studies: a social science approach*, London, Allen & Unwin (1969); R. McKean, The impact of C.D.A. policies on industry in Glasgow, *University of Glasgow Urban & Regional Studies Discussion Paper* **15** (1975).

37 C. J. Carter, Some post-war changes in the industrial geography of the Clydeside conurbation, *Scottish Geographical Magazine* **90** 14–26 (1974); R. N. Davidson, The pattern of employment densities in Glasgow, *Urban Studies* **7** 69–75 (1970); R. A. Henderson, Industrial overspill from Glasgow *Urban Studies* **11** 61–79 (1974).

38 S. G. Checkland (1977) 51.

39 J. G. Carney & R. Hudson, The Scottish Development Agency, *Town & Country Planning* **46** 507–9 (1978). See also V. Cable, Glasgow: area of need: G. Brown (ed.), *Red paper on Scotland*, Edinburgh University Student Publications Board (1975) 232–46; M. Day, Environmental improvement in Glasgow, *Town & Country Planning* **43** 317–20 (1975).

40 R. Grieve et al., Planning in Scotland, *The Planner* **66** (1980) 62–76.

41 M. Horne, *A reappraisal of the new towns*, Summer School Report London, RTPI (1978) 22–5.

42 Scottish Development Department et al., *The Grangemouth/Falkirk regional survey and plan*, Edinburgh, HMSO (1968) 2 vols. See also M. Barke, Urban change: Falkirk 1800–1961, University of Glasgow PhD thesis (1974); M. Barke, The changing urban fringe of Falkirk, *Scottish Geographical Magazine* **90** 85–97 (1974); D. Semple, The growth of Grangemouth, *Scottish Geographical Magazine* **74** 78–85 (1958).

43 D. Diamond, New towns in their regional context: H. Evans (ed.), *New towns: the British experience*, London: Town & Country Planning Association (1972) 54–65.

Notes to Chapter 13

 1 J. Cruickshank, The Black Isle Ross-shire: a land use study, *Scottish Geographical Magazine* **77** 5–14 (1961); H. L. Edlin, *Forestry in Scotland*, Edinburgh, Forestry Commission (1973).

2 T. Claxton, Afforestation in the Western Highlands and its effect on repopulation, *Geography* **17** 193–203 (1932).
3 The Mull situation is discussed in D. Turnock, *Patterns of Highland development*, London, Macmillan (1970).
4 E. W. Fenton, Some aspects of man's influence on the vegetation of Scotland, *Scottish Geographical Magazine* **53** 16–24 (1937).
5 Ministry of Reconstruction, *Final report of the sub-committee on forestry* (Cd 8881), London, HMSO (1918).
6 Forestry Commission, *Postwar forest policy* (Cmd 6447), London, HMSO (1943).
7 A. S. Mather, Patterns of afforestation in Britain since 1945, *Geography* **63** 157–66 (1978).
8 Forestry Commission, *Post-war forest policy: private woodlands* (Cmd 6500), London, HMSO (1944).
9 Department of Education and Science: Land Use Study Group, *Forestry agriculture and the multiple use of rural land*, London, HMSO (1966).
10 A. S. Mather, Problems of afforestation in north Scotland, *Transactions Institute of British Geographers* **54** 19–32 (1971); A. S. Mather, Land use changes in the Highlands and Islands 1946–75: a statistical review, *Scottish Geographical Magazine* **95** 114–22 (1979).
11 H. L. Edlin, The Forestry Commission in Scotland 1919–69, *Scottish Geographical Magazine* **85** 84–95 (1969).
12 J. D. Matthews et al., Forestry and the forest industries: J. Ashton and W. H. Long (eds.), *The remoter rural area of Britain*, Edinburgh, Oliver & Boyd (1972) 45.
13 *Ibid.* 47.
14 J. Walton, *National Forest Park Guides: Argyll*, Edinburgh, HMSO (1949). See also Forestry Commission, *Guide map to your forests*, London, HMSO (n.d.).
15 J. Walton, *National Forest Park Guides: Glen More*, Edinburgh, HMSO (1956).
16 Forestry Commission, *40th Annual Report (1958–59)*, London, HMSO (1960) 9. A context for Britain as a whole is provided by J. Sheail, *Rural conservation in inter-war Britain*, Oxford, Clarendon Press (1981) 170–92.
17 Forestry Commission, *46th Annual Report (1964–65)*, London, HMSO (1966) 9.
18 *Forest Policy*, London, HMSO (1972) 13.
19 I. P. Mitchell, Planning for recreation in state forests in Scotland, MSc thesis, Heriot-Watt University (1970).
20 D. R. Chaffey, The relative economics of forestry and agriculture on hill land in Scotland, University of Edinburgh, MSc thesis (1967); J. A. Dickson and R. A. Innes, Forestry in north Scotland *Forestry* **32** 65–100 (1959); G. A. Pearson, Multiple use in forestry, *Journal of Forestry* **42** 243–9 (1944).
21 Natural Resources (Technical) Committee, *Forestry agriculture and marginal land*, London, HMSO (1957).
22 R. J. G. Horne, An account of the integration of agriculture forestry and grouse shooting on the Glenlivet estates, *Scottish Forestry* **18** 77–82 (1964); T. B. Macdonald, The Strathoykell plan, *Journal of the Forestry Commission* **35**

115–18 (1966–7); W. F. S. Mutch & A. R. Hutchison, The integration of forestry and farming, *East of Scotland College of Agriculture Economics and Management Series 2* (1980).

23 B. Holtam, Forestry and its dependent industries in Scotland, *Scottish Forestry* **24** 173–85 (1970); J. Macdonald, Future trends in Scottish forestry: L. A. Elgood et al., *Natural resources in Scotland*, Edinburgh, Scottish Council Development and Industry (1961) 345.

24 J. A. Dickson, Utilisation of Britain's timber resources, *Commonwealth Forestry Review* **46** 112–24 (1967).

Notes to Chapter 14

1 J. R. Coull, A comparison of demographic trends in the Faroe and Shetland islands, *Transactions, Institute of British Geographers* **41** 159–66 (1967); J. R. Coull, Crofter fishermen in Norway and Scotland, *Aberdeen University Geography Department O'Dell Memorial Monograph* **2** (1972).

2 S. Jaatinen, *The Human geography of the Outer Hebrides*, Helsinki, Acta Geographica (1957); H. A. Moisley, The deserted Hebrides, *Scottish Studies* **10** 44–68 (1966); T. M. Murchison, Deserted Hebridean isles, *Transactions of the Gaelic Society of Inverness* **42** 283–344 (1953–9); P. T. Wheeler, *The island of Unst, Shetland*, Nottingham, Geographical Field Group (1964). See also, A. C. O'Dell & K. Walton, *Highlands & Islands of Scotland*, London, Nelson (1962) 296–325; W. H. Murray, *The islands of Western Scotland*, London, Eyre-Methuen (1973).

3 K. Macaulay, *St. Kilda*, Edinburgh, Thin (1974) reprint of original 1764; A. Small (ed.), *A St. Kilda handbook*, Edinburgh, National Trust for Scotland 1979; T. Steel, *The life and death of St. Kilda*, Edinburgh, National Trust for Scotland (1965). See also, I. A. S. Holburn, *The Isle of Foula*, Lerwick (n.d.); D. P. Willis, Population and economy of Fair Isle, *Scottish Geographical Magazine* **83** 113–17 (1967).

4 J. W. Shepherd et al., *Personality and attitudinal factors affecting migration from the Hebrides*, Aberdeen University Psychology Department (n.d.).

5 A. Geddes, The development of Stornoway, *Scottish Geographical Magazine* **63** 57–63 (1947); A. C. O'Dell, The urbanisation of the Shetland Islands, *Geographical Journal* **81** 501–18 (1933); A. C. O'Dell, Lerwick: a port study, *Scottish Geographical Magazine* **50** 27–35 (1934).

6 A. T. A. Learmonth, The population of Skye, *Scottish Geographical Magazine* **66** 77–103 (1950).

7 I. M. L. Robertson, Population trends of Great Cumbrae island, *Scottish Geographical Magazine* **89** 53–62 (1973); M. C. Storrie & C. L. Jackson, *Arran 1980–81: 2021?*, Edinburgh, Scottish Council for Social Service (1967).

8 M. C. Storrie, The census of Scotland as a source for the historical geography of Islay, *Scottish Geographical Magazine* **78** 152–65 (1962).

9 J. R. Coull, The island of Tiree, *Scottish Geographical Magazine* **78** 17–32 (1962).

10 F. F. Darling (ed.), *West Highland Survey*, Oxford University Press (1955) 377–405.

11 J. R. Coull, The economic development of the island of Westray, *Scottish Geographical Magazine* **82** 154–68 (1966); J. R. Coull, Population trends and structures on the island of Westray, *Scottish Studies* **10** 69–77 (1966). See also: H. Marwick, *Orkney*, London, Batsford (1976); R. Miller, Orkney: a land of increment: R. Miller & J. W. Watson (eds.), *Geographical essays in memory of A. G. Ogilvie*, Edinburgh, Nelson (1959) 7–15; R. Miller, *Orkney*, London, Batsford (1976); A. C. O'Dell, The geographical controls of agriculture in Orkney and Shetland, *Economic Geography* **11** 1–19 (1935).

12 H. D. Smith, The development of Shetland fisheries and fishing communities: P. H. Fricke (ed.), *Seafarer and community: towards a social understanding of seafaring*, London, Croom Helm (1973) 25. See also H. D. Smith, *The making of modern Shetland*, Lerwick, Shetland Times (1977).

13 R. F. Byron, Burra fishermen: the social organisation of work in a Shetland community, University College London PhD thesis (1974); C. A. Goodlad, Old and trusted, new and unknown: technological confrontation in the Shetland herring industry: P. Andersen & C. Wadel (eds.), *North Atlantic fishermen: anthropological essays on modern fishing*, St John's Newfoundland (1972) 61–81. See also C. A. Goodlad, *Shetland fishing saga*, Lerwick, Shetland Times (1971).

14 J. L. Blake, The Outer Hebrides fisheries training scheme, *Scottish Studies* **8** 113–31 (1964); W. Russell, *In great waters: a study of the social and economic impact of investment in the fisheries of the Highlands and Islands*, Inverness, HIDB (1972).

15 J. R. Coull et al., *The fisheries in the Shetland area: a study in conservation and development*, Aberdeen University Geography Department (1979).

16 J. I. Prattis, Discontinuities in priorities and policies in the development of a regional fishery in Scotland, *Maritime Studies & Management* **3** 27–32 (1975); J. I. Prattis, Competing technologies and conservation in the Barra lobster fishery, *Economic Development & Cultural Change* **26** 561–75 (1978). See also F. Carré, Le paysans–pecheurs Ecossais, *Norois* **71** 451–76 (1971).

17 H. A. Moisley, Harris Tweed: a growing Highland industry, *Economic Geography* **37** 353–70 (1961). See also F. Thompson, *Harris Tweed: the story of a Hebridean industry*, Newton Abbot, David & Charles (1969).

18 J. M. Macaskill et al., Planning for progress: Shetland woollen industry, *H.I.D.B. Special Report* **4** (n.d.).

19 F. Thompson, Candles from peat: the Lewis chemical works in the 1860s, *Scots Magazine* **92** 434–8 (1969). See also R. H. Campbell et al., *Scottish industrial history: a miscellany*, Edinburgh, Scottish Historical Society (1978) 181–212.

20 M. C. Storrie, Islay: a Hebridean exception, *Geographical Review* **51** (1961) 87–108.

21 R. Miller & J. Tivy (eds.) (1958) 182–4.

22 V. Rampton, The brown seaweed industries in the British Isles: R. H. Osborne et al. (eds.), *Geographical essays in honour of K. C. Edwards*, University of Nottingham Department of Geography (1970) 233–41.

23 I. H. McNicoll, The impact of local government activity on a small rural economy, *Urban Studies* **14** 339–45 (1977); J. R. Nicolson, *Shetland and oil*, London, Wm Luscombe (1975).

24 I. A. Morrison, Orkneying a Saga Jarlshof and the Viking sea routes, *Northern Studies* 2 22–5 (1973); A. Small, The historical geography of the Norse Viking colonisation of the Scottish Highlands, *Norsk Geografisk Tidsskrift* 22 1–16 (1968); A. Small, Shetland; Location the key to historical geography, *Scottish Geographical Magazine* 85 155–61 (1969). See also E. Balneaves, *The windswept isles: Shetland and its people*, London, Gifford (1977); E. Linklater, *Orkney and Shetland*, London, Hale (1975).

25 M. Brownrigg & M. A. Greig, The economic impact of tourist spending in Skye, *H.I.D.B. Special Report* 13 (1974).

26 C. Mair, *A star for seamen: the Stevenson family of engineers*, London, John Murray (1978); R. W. Munro, *Scottish Lighthouse*, Stornoway, Thule Press (1979); B. Wilson, *The lighthouses of Orkney*, Stromness, Museum (1975).

27 R. P. Fereday, *The Longhope battery and towers*, Stromness, Rendall (1971).

28 F. Ruge, *Scapa Flow 1919*, London, Ian Allan (1973). See also D. Howarth, *The Shetland Bus*, Edinburgh, Nelson (1951).

29 A. C. O'Dell, *Historical geography of the Shetland islands*, Lerwick, Manson (1939).

30 Highland Transport Board, *Highland transport services*, Edinburgh, HMSO (1967). S. D. Nutley, Transport and accessibility in the northwest Highlands and Islands, Aberdeen University PhD thesis (1978); W. I. Skewis, *Transport in the Highlands and Islands*, Glasgow University Geography Department (1962); S. D. Nutley, Patterns of regional accessibility in the northwest Highlands and Islands, *Scottish Geographical Magazine* 95 142–54 (1979).

31 M. L. Crosgill, The Lewis Hospital Stornoway: some aspects of the development of medical care in an island community, *Medical History* 17 49–60 (1974). See also the various contributions to the 'islands' series of David & Charles: P. Bailey (*Orkney*, 1970); N. Banks (*Six Inner Hebrides*, 1977); P. MacNab (*Mull*, 1970); J. R. Nicolson (*Shetland*, 1972); F. Thompson (*St. Kilda and other Hebridean outliers*, 1970; *Harris and Lewis*, 1973; *Uists and Barra*, 1974). F. C. Sillar & R. Meyer (*Skye*, 1973).

32 M. Gaskin, *Freight rates and prices in the islands*, Inverness, HIDB (1971).

33 J. B. Caird & H. A. Moisley, Leadership and innovation in the crofting communities of the Outer Hebrides, *Sociological Review* 9 85–102 (1961).

34 A. Geddes, *The isle of Lewis and Harris*, Edinburgh, Edinburgh University Press (1955) 296–300.

35 J. B. Caird & H. A. Moisley, The Outer Hebrides: J. A. Steers (ed.) *Field studies in the British Isles*, Edinburgh, Edinburgh University Press (1964) 374–90. See also J. B. Caird, *Park: a geographical study of a Lewis crofting district*, Nottingham, Geographical Field Group (1959); A. Fenton, *The Northern Isles*, Edinburgh, Donald (1978); E. W. Marwick, The folklore of Orkney and Shetland, London, Batsford (1975); H. A. Moisley, *Uig: a Hebridean parish*, Nottingham, Geographical Field Group (1962).

36 J. L. Blake, Pasture improvement schemes in the isle of Lewis, *Scottish Studies* 6 108–13 (1962); R. H. W. Bruce, Crofting progress in Shetland, *Scottish Agriculture* 47 174–80 (1968); J. B. Caird, Changes in the Highlands of Scotland, *Geoforum* 12 5–36 (1972); J. B. Caird, Problems of transformation of agri-

culture in the crofting settlements of the Outer Hebrides: B. Sarfalvi (ed.) *Urbanization in Europe*, Budapest, Academy of Sciences (1975) 279–94.
37 M. MacLeod, Did the people of Lewis refuse Lord Leverhulme's schemes? *Transactions of the Gaelic Society of Inverness* **42** 257–70 (1953–9). See also W. P. Jolly, *Lord Leverhulme: a biography*, London, Constable (1976); N. Nicolson, *Lord of the Isles: Lord Leverhulme in the Hebrides*, London Weidenfeld & Nicolson (1960).
38 For a modern anthropological assessment see J. Ennew *Changing cultures: the Western Isles today*, Cambridge University Press (1980); A. P. Cohen, The Whalsay croft: traditional work and customary identity in modern times: L. S. Wallman (ed.), *Social anthropology of work*, London, Academic Press (1979) 250–67.

Notes to Chapter 15

1 E. Gershenkron, *Economic backwardness in historical perspective*, Cambridge Mass., Harvard UP (1966) 6–11.
2 T. C. Smout, *Scottish trade on the eve of the union 1660–1707*, Edinburgh, Oliver & Boyd (1963) 280.
3 R. H. Campbell, *The rise and fall of Scottish industry 1707–1939*, Edinburgh, Donald (1980) 12.
4 R. H. Campbell, *op. cit.* 6–22.
5 W. W. Rostow, *The stages of economic growth: a non-communist manifesto*, Cambridge, University Press (1971) 6.
6 *Ibid.* 26.
7 M. Weber, *The protestant ethic and the spirit of capitalism*, New York, Charles Scribner & Sons (1958).
8 R. H. Tawney, *Religion and the rise of capitalism*, Harmondsworth, Penguin (1938) 274.
9 S. N. Eisenstadt, The protestant ethic thesis in an analytical and comparative framework: S. N. Eisenstadt (ed.), *The protestant ethic and modernisation: a comparative view*, New York, Basic Books (1968) 3–45.
10 S. A. Burrell, Calvinism capitalism and the middle classes: some after-thoughts on an old problem: S. N. Eisenstadt (ed.), *op. cit.* 142. See also G. Marshall, *Presbyteries and profits*, Oxford, Clarendon Press (1980); G. Marshall, *Presbyteries and profits: Calvinism and the development of capitalism in Scotland 1560–1707*, Oxford, Clarendon Press (1980).
11 G. E. Davie, *The Scottish enlightenment*, London, Historical Association (1981) 7–11. See also D. Daiches (ed.), *Andrew Fletcher of Saltoun: selected writings and speeches*, Edinburgh, Scottish Academic Press (1979).
12 G. E. Davie, *op. cit.* 21–8.
13 N. Phillipson, The enlightenment: social structures: P. Fritz and D. Williams (eds.), *City and society in the eighteenth century*, Toronto, Hakkert (1973) 99–147. See also N. Phillipson, Culture and society in the eighteenth century province: the case of Edinburgh and the Scottish enlightenment: L. Stone (ed.),

The university in society, Princeton NJ, Princeton University Press (1974) 407–48; N. T. Phillipson, Nationalism and ideology: J. N. Wolfe (ed.), *Government and nationalism in Scotland*, Edinburgh, University Press (1969) 167–88.

14 J. H. Treble, The social and economic thought of Robert Owen: J. Butt (ed.), *Robert Owen: prince of cotton spinners*, Newton Abbot, David & Charles (1971) 37.

15 R. H. Campbell, *op. cit.* 133.

16 W. Ferguson, *Scotland: 1689 to the present*, Edinburgh, Oliver & Boyd (1968) 384.

17 G. M. Thomson, *Scotland that distressed area*, Edinburgh, Porpoise Press (1937) 3; C. Harvie, *The new history of Scotland: no gods and precious few heroes – Scotland 1914–1980*, London, Arnold (1981).

18 J. Prebble, *Glencoe*, London, Secker & Warburg (1966) 11.

19 W. Ferguson, *op. cit.*, 16.

20 *Ibid.* 25.

21 I. Carter, Economic models and a recent history of the Highlands, *Scottish Studies* **15** 99–120 (1971).

22 T. C. Smout (1969) 346.

23 A. Smith, *An inquiry into the nature and causes of the wealth of nations*, London, Methuen (1904) II 270.

24 *Ibid.* II 295.

25 D. Daiches (ed.), *op. cit.*

26 D. Turnock, The Highlands: changing approaches to regional development: G. Whittington and I. Whyte (eds.), *Historical geography of Scotland*, London, Academic Press (forthcoming).

27 D. T. Jones et al., *Rural Scotland during the war*, London, Oxford University Press (1926) 233.

28 For example, H. F. Campbell, *Highland reconstruction*, Glasgow, Alex. MacLaren & Sons (1920); J. Gollan, *Scottish prospect: an economic administrative and social survey*, Glasgow, Caledonian Books (1948); A. Lamont, *Scotland: the wealthy nation*, Glasgow, Secretariat Ltd (1954).

29 F. F. Darling, *West Highland survey: an essay in human ecology*, London, Oxford University Press (1955).

30 D. J. Spooner, Industrial movement, rural areas and regional policy: P. A. Compton & M. Pecsi (eds.), *Regional development and planning*, Budapest, Hungarian Academy of Sciences (1976) 140.

31 The role of towns in the development process and the need for a specific settlement hierarchy to accord with a particular phase of expansion have been touched on by D. V. Glass, *The town in a changing civilisation*, London, John Lane (1935); B. Hoselitz, Generative and parasitic cities, *Economic Development & Cultural Change* **3** 278–95 (1955).

32 Scottish Office, *The Scottish economy 1965–1970: a plan for expansion*, Edinburgh, HMSO (Cmnd 2864) (1966) 52.

33 I. Carter, The Highlands of Scotland as an underdeveloped area: E. de Kadt & G. Williams (eds.), *Sociology and development*, London, Tavistock Pubs. (1974) 279–311; I. Carter, A. socialist strategy for the Highlands: G. Brown

(ed.), *Red paper on Scotland*, Edinburgh, Edinburgh University Student Publications Board (1975) 247–53.

34 E. Brutzkus, Centralized versus decentralized urbanization in developing countries, *Economic Development & Cultural Change* **23** 633–52 (1975).

Bibliography

Adam, M. I., (1922). Eighteenth century Highland landlords and the poverty problem, *Scottish Historical Review* **19**, 161–79.

Adams, I. H. (1978), *The making of urban Scotland*, London, Croom Helm.

Allan, J. R. (1952), *North East Lowlands of Scotland*, London, Hale.

Anderson, J. (1785), *Account of the present state of the Hebrides and western coast of Scotland*, Edinburgh, G. G. J. & R. Robinson.

Anderson, M. L. (1967), *A history of Scottish forestry*, London, Nelson.

Baldwin, J. R. (ed.) (1978), *Scandinavian Shetland: an ongoing tradition*, Edinburgh, Scottish Society for Northern Studies.

Black, J. (1870–1), On the agriculture of Aberdeen and Banff, *Transactions of the Highland and Agricultural Society of Scotland* **3**, 1–36.

Bremner, D. (1869), *The industries of Scotland: their rise progress and current condition*, Edinburgh, A. & C. Black.

Caird, J. B. (1964), The making of the Scottish rural landscape, *Scottish Geographical Magazine* **80**, 72–80.

Campbell, R. H. (1961), *Carron Company*, Edinburgh, Oliver & Boyd.

Carter, I. (1979), *Farmlife in northeast Scotland 1840–1914: the poor man's country*, Edinburgh, Donald.

Checkland, S. G. (1977). *The Upas Tree: Glasgow 1876–1975*, University of Glasgow Press.

Chitnis, A. C. (1976), *The Scottish enlightenment*, London, Croom Helm.

Coppock, J. T. (1976), *An agricultural atlas of Scotland*, Edinburgh, Donald.

Cullen, L. M. & Smout, T. C. (eds) (1977), *Comparative aspects of Scottish and Irish social and economic history*, Edinburgh, Donald.

Dodd, W. (1970–2), Ayr: a study of urban growth, *Ayrshire Archaeological & Natural History Collections* **10**, 301–79.

Donaldson, G. (1974), *Scotland: the shaping of a nation*, Newton Abbot, David & Charles.

Duckham, B. F. (1970), *A history of the Scottish coal industry*, Newton Abbot, David & Charles, 2 vols.

Durie, A. J. (1979), *The Scottish linen industry in the eighteenth century*, Edinburgh, Donald.

Fairhurst, H. (1967), The rural settlement pattern in Scotland with special

337

reference to the west and north: R. W. Steel & R. Lawton (eds), *Liverpool essays in geography*, London, Longmans. 193–209.

Fenton, A. (1976), *Scottish country life*, Edinburgh, Donald.

Flinn, M. W. et al. (1977), *Scottish population history*, Cambridge University Press.

Franklin, T. B. (1952), *A history of Scottish farming*, London, Nelson.

Gaffney, V. (1960), *Lordship of Strathavon*, Aberdeen, Third Spalding Club.

Gaskell, P. (1968), *Morvern transformed*, Cambridge University Press.

Grant, I. F. (1934), *The economic history of Scotland*, London, Longmans Green.

Gray, M. (1973), Crofting and fishing in the north West Highlands, *Northern Scotland* **1**, 89–114.

Gunn, J. & Newbigin, M. I. (eds) (1921), *City of Glasgow: its origin and development* Edinburgh, Royal Scottish Geographical Society.

Haldane, A. R. B. (1952), *Drove roads of Scotland*, Edinburgh, Nelson.

(1962), *New ways through the glens*, Edinburgh, Nelson.

Hamilton, H. (1932), *The industrial revolution in Scotland*, Oxford. Clarendon Press.

Handley, J. E. (1953), *Scottish farming in the eighteenth century*, London, Faber.

(1963), *The Agricultural revolution in Scotland*, Glasgow, Burns.

Hanham, H. J. (1969), The problem of Highland discontent 1880–1885, *Transactions of the Royal Historical Society* **19**, 21–65

Hume, J. R. (1974), *Industrial archaeology of Glasgow*, Glasgow, Blackie.

Hunter, J. R. (1976), *The making of the crofting community*, Edinburgh, Donald.

Jones, S. J. (ed.) (1968), *Dundee and district*, Dundee, British Association.

Kellas, J. G. (1968), *Modern Scotland: the nation since 1870*, London, Pall Mall.

Kellett, J. H. (1969), Glasgow: M. D. Lovel (ed.), *Historic towns*, London, Lovell Johns.

Kermack, W. R. (1912), The making of Scotland: an essay in historical geography, *Scottish Geographical Magazine* **28**, 195–305.

Lenman, B. (1975) *From Esk to Tweed: harbours ships and men of the east coast of Scotland*, Glasgow, Blackie.

(1977), *An economic history of modern Scotland*, London, Batsford.

Lythe, S. G. E. (1960), *The economy of Scotland*, Edinburgh, Oliver & Boyd.

Lythe, S. G. E. & Butt, J. (1975), *An economic history of Scotland 1100–1939*, Glasgow, Blackie.

MacCulloch, J. (1824), *The Higlands and Western Isles of Scotland*, London.

Mackinnon, J. (1921), *The social and industrial history of Scotland*, London, Longmans Green.

Maclean, I., of Dochgarroch (ed.) (1975), *The hub of the Highlands the book of Inverness and district*, Inverness, Inverness Field Club.

MacNeill, P. & Nicholson, R. (eds) (1975), *Historical atlas of Scotland 400–1600*, St Andrews, Conference of Scottish Medievalists.

McWilliam, C. (1975), *Scottish townscape*, Glasgow, Collins.

Miller, R. & Tivy, J. (eds) (1958), *The Glasgow region*, Glasgow British Association.

Millman, R. (1975), *The making of the Scottish landscape*, London, Batsford.

O'Dell, A. C. (1939), *The historical geography of the Shetland Islands*, Lerwick, Manson.

O'Dell, A. C. & Mackintosh, J. (eds) (1963), *The North-East of Scotland*, Aberdeen, British Association.

O'Dell, A. C. & Walton, K. (1962), *Highlands and Islands of Scotland*, Edinburgh, Nelson.

Omand, D. (ed.) (1976), *The Moray book*, Edinburgh, Paul Harris.

Parry, M. L. & Slater, T. R. (eds) (1980), *The making of the Scottish countryside*, London, Croom Helm.

Payne, P. L. (1979), *Colvilles and the Scottish steel industry*, Oxford, Clarendon Press.

Phillipson, N. T. & Mitchison, N. (eds) (1970), *Scotland in the age of improvement*, Edinburgh, Edinburgh University Press.

Richards, E. (1970), The prospects for economic growth in Sutherland at the time of the clearances, *Scottish Historical Review* **49**, 154–71.

Slaven, A. (1975), *The development of the West of Scotland 1750–1960*, London, Routledge & Kegan Paul.

Smout, T. C. (1964), Scottish landowners and economic growth, *Scottish Journal of Political Economy* **11**, 218–31.

(1969) *A history of the Scottish people 1560–1830*, London, Collins.

Storrie, M. C. (1965), Landholdings and settlement evolution in West Highland Scotland, *Geografiska Annaler* **47B**, 138–61.

Symon, J. A. (1959), *Scottish farming past and present*, Edinburgh, Oliver & Boyd.

Turner, W. H. K. (1953), Eighteenth century developments in the textile region of east central Scotland, *Scottish Geographical Magazine* **69**, 10–21.

(1957), The textile industry of Dunfermline and Kirkaldy 1700–1900, *Scottish Geographical Magazine* **73**, 129–45.

(1966), The concentration of jute and heavy linen manufactures in east central Scotland, *Scottish Geographical Magazine* **82**, 29–145.

Turnock, D. (1977), *The Lochaber area: a case study of changing rural land use in the West Highlands of Scotland*, Nottingham, Geographical Field Group.

(1979), *The new Scotland*, Newton Abbot, David & Charles.

Vince, S. W. E. (ed.) (1944), *Land of Britain: Highlands of Scotland*, London, Geographical Publications.

Warren, K. (1965), Locational problems in the Scottish iron and steel industry since 1760, *Scottish Geographical Magazine* **81**, 18–37; 87–103.

Whyte, I. D. (1978), Scottish historical geography: a review, *Scottish Geographical Magazine* **94**, 4–23.

(1979), *Agriculture and society in seventeenth century Scotland*, Edinburgh Donald.

Youngson, A. J. (1973), *After the Forty Five*, Edinburgh University Press.

(1974), *Beyond the Highland line*, London, Collins.

Index

Administrative districts are given for all placenames except where these relate to former burghs

Abbeys *see* Religious Houses
Aberchirder, 140
Abercrombie, P., 237–8
Aberdeen, 2, 13, 15, 18–19, 23, 25, 120, 131, 146, 215, 221
  Industry in, 57, 118, 159
  Transport in, 51–2, 135, 140, 143, 219–20
Aberdour (Dumfermline), 135
Aberfoyle (Stirling), 44
Aberlady (East Lothian), 95
Abernethy (Badenoch & Strathspey), 59, 128–9
Abernethy (Perth & Kinross), 14
Abington (Lanark), 127
Accessibility, 50, 170, 187, 195, 209, 229, 246
Administration, 16, 18, 30, 87 *see also* Local Government
Ae (Nithsdale), 253, 256
Agricultural Machinery, 124
Agricultural Regions, 124–5
Agricultural Revolution, 27, 41, 66–7
Agriculture, 4, 22, 26–31, 40, 62–3, 66–84, 94, 123–8, 133, 207–14, 277
Aircraft, 202–3, 282
Airdrie, 51, 171
Air Services, 218, 276
Alba, 14–15
Alford (Gordon), 90, 124–5
Alginates, 272
Alloa, 50, 96, 143
Allotment *see* Smallholding
Alexander II, 20, 23
Altnabraec (Caithness), 272
Alumina, 205–6
Aluminium, 119, 205–6
Alvah (Banff & Buchan), 71, 89

Alyth, 60
Amalgamation, 191, 209, 212
America, 38–9, 56–7, 79, 93, 155
Angus, 15, 55, 59
Annan, 56, 138, 260
Annexed Estates, 42, 53, 79, 87–9, 183
Anstruther, 83
Arbroath, 20, 60, 138, 143
Ardeer (Cunninghame), 171
Ardnamurchan (Lochaber), 21, 180, 182, 184
Ardrossan, 51, 64, 92, 138–9, 176
Ardtornish-Westminster, Treaty of, 20
Ardyne Point (Argyll & Bute), 202
Argyll, 15, 21, 79, 164, 182, 251, 253, 256–8, 260, 275
Argyll, Duke/Earl of, 21–2, 82, 92–3, 104, 119, 183
Army *see* Military
Arran (Cunninghame), 81, 93, 266
Artisan *see* Craftsman
Assessment *see* Taxes
Atholl (Perth & Kinross), 45
Atlantic, 25, 51, 153, 183, 218, 270
Auchindrain (Argyll & Bute), 81
Auchtermuchty, 60
Auliston (Lochaber), 183
Aviemore (Badenoch & Strathspey), 214
Ayr, 19, 22, 25, 83, 145, 227, 240
Ayrshire, 9, 39, 170–3, 176, 237, 239, 267
Ayton (Berwickshire), 54

Badenoch & Strathspey, 53
Bairds of Gartsherrie, 169–73, 175, 178
Balgonie (Kirkaldy), 168
Ballachulish (Lochaber), 206, 219

Ballater, 140, 219
Ballindalloch (Stirling), 57
Baltic, 23, 273
Banavie (Lochaber), 183
Banff, 18–19, 54
Bannockburn (Stirling), 20
Barcaldine (Argyll & Bute), 272
Barley, 61
Baronage, 19–22
Barra (Western Isles), 21, 218, 267, 271–2
Barrhead, 56, 139, 164
Barrisdale (Lochaber), 79, 88
Bathgate, 121, 139, 203, 238, 240
Baulk, 30, 43
Beardmore, W. & Co., 177, 202–3
Beattock (Annandale & Eskdale), 138
Beauly (Inverness), 87, 255
Beauly Firth, 49, 136, 213
Beef, 50
Beer, 22
Beith (Cunninghame), 76
Bellshill (Motherwell), 139
Benbecula (Western Isles), 218, 275–6
Ben Wyvis (Ross & Cromarty), 258
Bervie (Kincardine & Deeside), 61
Berwick, 14
Berwickshire, 74
Bessemer Converter, 176–7
Birsay (Orkney), 16
Birse (Kincardine & Deeside), 105
Blackband, 168, 171–2
Blackburn (West Lothian), 238
Blackford (Perth & Kinross), 48
Bladnoch (Wigtown), 108
Blairgowrie, 60
Blantyre (Hamilton), 173
Blast Furnace *see* Iron Furnace
Bleaching, 54, 57, 61, 91
Blending, 108, 207
Board of Trustees for Manufactures, 42, 53–5
Boats *see* Fishing Boats
Boddam (Banff & Buchan), 141
Bog Ore *see* Iron Ore
Boiler Making *see* Engineering
Bo'ness, 26, 51, 64, 143
Bonnybridge (Falkirk), 272
Border, 14, 20–1, 25, 138
Borders, 61, 69, 238
Borgue (Stewarty), 90
Bothwell (Hamilton), 174
Bothy, 191
Bounty, 60, 93
Bowling (Dumbarton), 51, 133
Bowmore (Argyll & Bute), 266
Braemar (Kincardine & Deeside), 140
Branch Plant, 200

Breasclete (Western Isles), 270
Brechin, 60
Bressay (Shetland), 93, 136, 144
Brewing, 119
Bridges, 140, 262, 275–6
British Fisheries Society 93–4
British Linen Company, 53
Brodick (Cunninghame), 266
Broomielaw (Glasgow), 26, 52, 154, 156–7
Brora (Sutherland), 103, 105
Broxburn (West Lothian), 121, 240
Buccleuch, Duke of, 58, 92, 141
Buckie, 120, 140
Building Cycle, 162–3
Burghead, 107, 118, 136, 159
Burgh of Barony/Regality, 28, 82 *see also* Royal Burgh
Burra (Shetland), 133, 269, 275
Burntisland, 135, 140, 143, 205–6
Bus Services, 218–20
Bute (Argyll & Bute), 164, 262, 266
Butter, 50

Cabrach (Moray), 71
Cairngorms, 214, 257, 259
Caithness, 13, 16, 53, 70, 140, 171
Calders (West Lothian), 240
Caledonian Canal, 51, 135, 183, 215, 219, 258
Caledonian Railway, 138–40, 143, 157, 163–4, 175–6
Callander, 48, 87, 90
Cambuslang (Glasgow), 83, 204, 238
Cameron *see* Clan Cameron
Campbell *see* Clan Campbell
Campbeltown, 82, 104, 107, 145
Campsie Hills, 17
Canal, 50–1, 58–9, 121, 168, 173
Canmore, House of 16, 19
Capital/Capitalism, 26, 31, 39, 59, 68, 83, 90, 161, 170, 181, 188, 192, 281, 285, 287
Cardenden (Dunfermline), 238
Carham (Berwickshire), 12, 14
Carlisle, 138, 145
Carluke (Lanark), 83, 127
Carron (Falkirk), 50–1, 58–9, 121, 168, 173
Cars, 202, 282
Carse of Gowrie (Dundee), 27
Carse of Stirling (Stirling), 42
Castle, 19–20
Castlemilk (Glasgow), 241
Catrine (Cumnock & Doon Valley), 57, 83, 87
Cattle, 37, 67, 69–71, 76, 78, 124–5, 156, 186 *see also* Livestock
Causeway, 275–6
Cawdor (Nairn), 89

Celts, 17–19
Census, 117–18, 225–9
Central Belt, 8–10, 62–3, 69, 74, 151–2,
    225–9, 284–5
  Agriculture etc. in, 123–8
  Industry in, 54, 57, 61, 86, 98–108, 272
  Planning in, 232–45
  Transport in, 133–46, 218–19
Central Place *see* Service Centre
Centre *see* Core
Cereals, 27, 31, 43, 49, 70, 82, 97–108, 156
Chapelcross (Annandale & Eskdale), 221
Charcoal, 46, 58–9, 128, 167
Charlestown (Dunfermline), 49–50
Cheese, 83, 127–8
Chemical Industry, 58, 121, 161, 172, 176,
    205, 272
Chiefs *see* Baronage
Chipboard, 260
Christianity, 14
Church, 22, 24, 31, 41, 74, 83, 85, 91, 93,
    120, 160–1, 280, 286
Church of Scotland, 46, 97, 120 *see also*
    General Assembly
Churchill Barriers (Orkney), 273–5
Cistercians, 19
City *see* Town
City Region *see* Hinterland
Clachan, 180
Clan Cameron, 21, 183
Clan Campbell, 21, 119
Clan MacIan, 21
Clan MacKenzie, 21
Clan MacLean, 79
Clan MacNeil, 21
Clearances, 105, 182–5, 262, 267
Clergy, 22, 74, 76, 99, 286
Clover, 70–1, 80, 209, 212
Clyde, 12, 25–6, 51, 83, 85, 118, 125–7, 133,
    138, 153–66, 169, 201, 206, 218, 243
Clydebank, 139, 156, 160, 162, 164, 197, 201,
    218, 272
Clyde Valley Plan, 237–8, 240–1, 244
Coal, 6–7, 23–4, 26, 39, 50, 57–8, 68, 74,
    120–1, 143, 168–9, 173–4, 197, 238–9,
    242, 278, 282–4
Coast, 135 *see also* Tidewater
Coastal Shipping *see* Shipping
Coatbridge, 58, 121, 139, 164, 175, 177, 202
Cockenzie, 50, 121, 136, 221, 242
Coigach (Ross & Cromarty), 186
Coke, 59, 168–72, 178
Coll (Argyll & Bute), 267
Colonialism, 3, 48, 82, 93, 246, 277, 279, 285
Colonisation, 18, 21, 82, 120, 152–3, 269
Colony, 37–8, 116
Coltness (Motherwell), 170–1, 178

Columba, 14
Colville, D., 175
Colyton (Kyle & Carrick), 239
Common Grazing/Pasture, 73, 185, 212
Commerce *see* Trade
Commission for Highland Roads & Bridges,
    48
Commonty, 68
Commonwealth, 12
Communications *see* Transport
Community Cooperative, 288
Commuting, 226–7, 262, 266
Comprehensive Development Area, 241,
    243
Comrie (Perth & Kinross), 48
Congested Districts Board, 120, 185–8, 267,
    271
Conservation, 44–6, 85, 227–8, 247, 269
Conservative Party, 239
Consolidation, 27, 42, 73, 81, 91, 180
Consumption Dyke, 43, 70
Coppicing, 45
Core, 7–8, 15
Corn *see* Cereals
Corn Milling *see* Milling
Corpach (Lochaber), 183
Cottager *see* Croft *and* Smallholding
Cotton, 39, 56–7, 59, 83–7, 161–2, 170–1,
    284
Council Housing, 235–6
Countryside Commission for Scotland, 214
Coupar Angus, 23, 28, 91, 247
Counties, 27
Crafts/Craftsmen, 24–5, 93, 174, 180, 202,
    271
Cramond (Edinburgh), 39, 58–9, 173–4, 176
Crathie (Kincardine & Deeside), 87
Creamery *see* Milk Manufacture
Crianlarich (Stirling), 15
Crinan (Argyll & Bute), 15
Crinan Canal, 51, 135
Croft, 30, 62, 71, 76, 105, 119–20, 123,
    179–92, 211–13, 267, 271–2, 277, 285,
    287
Crofters' Commission, 211–3
Crofting Counties, 191
Cromarty, 18
Cromarty Firth, 49, 136, 206, 219
Crop Failure, 184
Cruden Bay (Banff & Buchan), 141, 206
Cullen, 54, 82
Culloden (Inverness), 97
Culross, 24
Culture, 20, 180, 287
Cumbernauld, 204, 237, 239
Cumbrae (Cunninghame), 266
Cumnock, 170, 172–3

Cupar, 60, 140
Curragh, 46

Dairsie (North East Fife), 60
Dairying, 82–3, 127–8, 267
Dalavich (Argyll & Bute), 253, 257
Dalkeith, 58, 238
Dalmally (Argyll & Bute), 15
Dalmellington (Cumnock & Doon Valley),
   133, 145–6, 170–2
Dalmeny (Edinburgh), 81, 121, 143, 206
Dalriada, 13
Dalserf (Hamilton), 74, 127
Dalzell (Motherwell), 175, 204
Dalziel (Motherwell), 83, 127
Darien, 37, 280
David I, 17
Davoch, 27
Dean of Guild Court, 233–4
Deanston (Stirling), 57
Debateable Land, 19, 209
Decentralisation, 196, 237
Dee, River, 15, 129, 214, 251
Deer, 256
Deer Forest, 129, 213, 277
Defence, 143
Denmark, 24
Depopulation, 184, 229, 262, 267, 287–8
Depression, 196
Deprivation, 105–6
Desertion, 262
Deskford (Moray), 70
Destitution, 93, 119
Destitution Road *see* Famine Road
Devolution, 196, 229, 283
Devon (Perth & Kinross), 168
Diffusion, 9, 48, 65
Distilling *see* Whisky
Distress *see* Destitution
Dollar, 73
Dolphinton (Lanark), 128
Don, River, 15, 57, 251, 256
Dornoch, 93
Dornoch Firth, 94, 136
Dornie (Skye & Lochalsh), 94
Dounreay (Caithness), 221
Draff, 61, 207
Drainage, 30, 42, 45, 209, 234
Dress, 74–6
Drimnin (Lochaber), 180–1, 183–4
Drongan (Cumnock & Doon Valley), 239
Drumlanrig (Nithsdale), 45
Drumtochty (Kincardine & Deeside), 255
Dual Economy, 195
Dufftown, 96, 107
Duffus (Moray), 19

Dumbarton, 25, 58, 69, 135, 153–4, 158–9,
   207, 237
Dumbuck (Renfrew), 26, 51, 153–5
Dumfries, 19, 229
Dumfries & Galloway, 108, 124, 128, 207,
   251, 260
Dunadd (Argyll & Bute), 13, 15
Dunbar, 129, 143
Dundee, 2, 22–3, 50, 52, 129, 147, 221, 240
   Industry in, 54, 60–1, 118, 197, 204
   Transport in, 135–6, 141, 143, 159
Dunfermline, 17, 23–4, 49, 54, 60, 175,
   235–6
Dunkeld (Perth & Kinross), 14
Dunlop (Kilmarnock & Loudoun), 83, 127
Dunrossness (Shetland), 133
Duns, 54
Dunvegan (Skye & Lochalsh), 93
Duthil (Badenoch & Strathspey), 69
Dyeing, 57, 161

Eaglesham (Eastwood), 96
Easterhouse (Glasgow), 241
East-Central Scotland, 58, 117, 121, 124,
   238, 284 *see also* Central Belt
East Kilbride, 56, 139, 164, 203, 237–8, 242
East Mathers (Kincardine & Deeside), 49
Economic Development *see* Modernisation
Eday (Orkney), 89
Edinburgh, 5, 17, 22, 24–5, 27, 49, 63, 121,
   146, 150, 213, 227, 234, 240, 251, 283
   Industry in, 54, 58, 196–7, 203
   Transport in, 51–2, 58, 82–3, 133–5,
   138–9, 219
Edinburgh & Glasgow Railway, 138, 163–4
Education, 4, 6–7, 22, 24, 41, 85, 120, 123,
   192, 263, 286 *see also* School *and*
   University
Eglinton (Cunninghame), 172–3
Eglinton, Earl of, 92, 155, 170–1
Eilean Donan (Skye & Lochalsh), 20
Electricity, 119, 221–5 *see also* Hydro
   Electricity
Electronics, 203–4, 242
Elgin, 18–19, 82, 260
Emigration, 25, 78, 80, 181, 183, 209, 277
Employment, 52, 207–9, 212, 229, 242, 246,
   253, 263, 272, 282, 284, 289–94 *see also*
   Labour
Enclosure, 67–74, 79, 91
Energy, 195 *see also* Coal, Electricity, Oil
   etc.
Engineering, 158–60, 175–6, 203, 272, 279,
   282
England, 15–16, 17, 20–1, 24, 27, 31–2, 37,
   145, 172, 221, 260, 278, 284
Enlightenment *see* Scottish Enlightenment

Entrepreneur, 39 *see also* Manager
Environment Problems, 233–6
Eriskay (Western Isles), 269
Erskine (Renfrew), 55–6, 76
Eskdalemuir (Annandale & Eskdale), 260
Estate, 42, 62, 66–96, 111, 166, 250, 255–6,
    287 *see also* Annexed/Forfeited Estates
Estate Maps, 28, 68
Europe, 24–5, 38, 152, 155
European Economic Community, 209, 215
Evacuation, 266
Eviction *see* Clearance
Excise Duties 98–108
External Control, 242–3, 270
Extractive Industries, 119, 145–6
Eyemouth, 61

Fair Isle (Shetland), 263
Fair Rents, 185–8
Falkirk, 59, 138, 171, 176, 238, 242, 272
Falkland, 60
Famine, 184, 287
Famine Road, 184
Farm, 78, 95, 119, 123–8, 179, 192, 209–13,
    259–60, 267, 277
Feed *see* Fodder
Ferintosh (Ross & Cromarty), 98
Ferry, 140, 146, 275–6
Feu, 25, 91, 161, 180
Feudalism, 16, 18–19, 21, 27, 31, 57, 82, 90
Field System, 29–30, 43, 72–6, 80–1, 190
Fife 17, 49, 55, 60, 83, 129, 135, 140, 143, 167
Fife Adventurers, 21
Findlater, Earl of, 54, 70
Finnart (Dumbarton), 206
Firth *see* Clyde, Forth, Tay etc.
Fishing, 21–2, 50–1, 53, 61–2, 73, 88, 93–4,
    105, 119, 129–33, 140, 144, 160, 180,
    187–8, 212, 215–7, 267–70, 272, 276
Fishing Boats, 131–3 *see also* Trawler
Fish Farming, 217
Fish Meal, 215, 270
Fish Processing, 61, 131–2
Flotta (Orkney), 272
Flax, 24, 40, 52–4, 61, 76, 92
Fochabers (Moray), 82, 91, 124
Fodder, 61, 67, 70, 108
Fodderty (Ross & Cromarty), 63
Food Processing, 206–7
Fordyce (Banff & Buchan), 54
Forest, 128–9, 213–14, 232, 246–61, 287
Forest Park, 256–7
Forestry Commission, 246–61
Foreign Ownership, 207
Forfar, 14, 23, 60, 138
Forfeited Estates, 38, 87, 136, 167
Forge, 173–6

Forres, 18–19
Fort *see* Castle
Fort Augustus (Inverness), 87, 219
Fort George (Inverness), 78, 91
Fort William (Lochaber), 87, 140, 205–6,
    219, 258, 260
Forth, 12, 17, 23–4, 49–51, 58–9, 133,
    135–6, 140, 143, 169, 206, 221, 242
Forth–Clyde Canal, 50–1, 64, 83, 158, 161,
    174, 176
Forties, 206
Foula (Shetland), 263
Foundry, 24, 158, 176
Foyers (Inverness), 119, 205, 219
Fragmentation, 30, 43
France, 21–2, 24, 31, 38
Fraserburgh, 74, 120, 132, 140, 217
Free Church, 186
Frontier *see* Border
Fruit, 127
Funzie (Shetland), 73
Furnace (Argyll & Bute), 278
Fuel, 44, 89, 128, 178

Gaelic, 16, 285
Gairloch (Ross & Cromarty), 188
Galashiels, 229
Galloway, 19, 69, 225 *see also* Dumfries &
    Galloway
Garden City Association, 235
Gardenstown (Banff & Buchan), 215
Garioch (Gordon), 51
Garmond (Banff & Buchan), 84
Garmouth (Moray), 107
Gartcosh (Monklands), 205
Gartsherrie (Monklands), 169, 171–3, 175,
    177
Garvald (East Lothian), 139
Gas, 121, 168
Gatehouse of Fleet, 56–7, 87
Geddes, P., 212, 227, 234–6, 245
General Assembly (Church of Scotland), 24,
    31, 47, 120
Geocrab (Western Isles), 271
Germany, 24–5, 62
Ghetto, 165
Girvan, 74, 272
Glamis (Angus), 60, 225
Glasgow, 2, 5, 25–6, 38, 125, 147–50,
    153–66, 200–1
  Industry in, 57, 59, 121, 174–8, 196–7,
    202–3
  Planning in, 213, 227, 229, 232–4, 237,
    239–40, 242–4, 283
  Trade/Transport in, 50–2, 56–7, 82–3,
    133–4, 145, 200, 205, 218–19, 279

Glasgow Eastern Area Renewal (GEAR), 204, 243–4
Glasgow & Garnkirk Railway, 136–8, 163, 169
Glasgow & South Western Railway, 138–40, 157, 164
Glass, 24
Glass House, 127
Glen Affric (Inverness), 258
Glenbuchat (Gordon), 71
Glencoe (Lochaber), 22, 214, 285
Glendessary (Lochaber), 183
Glenelg (Skye & Lochalsh), 87
Glen Feshie (Badenoch & Strathspey), 214
Glengarnock (Cunninghame), 139, 170–1, 173, 177–8
Glengarry (Lochaber), 59, 258
Glenisla (Angus), 247
Glenlivet (Moray), 72, 105, 107, 124–5, 207
Glen More (Badenoch & Strathspey), 257
Glenrothes, 197, 239, 242, 244
Golspie (Sutherland), 140
Gorbals (Glasgow), 162–3
Gordon, Duke/Earl of, 21, 91, 103, 124–5
Gordon Castle (Moray), 45, 124
Gourdon (Kincardine & Deeside), 217
Govan (Glasgow), 58, 139, 156, 159–60, 162, 170–1, 176, 202, 243
Government *see* Administration *and* Local Government
Government Intervention, 65, 100–3, 119–20, 140, 148, 150, 182, 185–8, 219, 232, 284, 287
Grain *see* Cereals
Grain Whisky, 207
Grampian Region, 2, 9, 53, 61, 70, 74
  Agriculture, Forestry etc. in, 124–5, 128–33, 188–92, 207, 251
  Industry in, 119
Grange (Moray), 43
Grangemouth, 51, 63–4, 118, 121, 133, 143, 175, 206, 242
Granite, 119
Grant, Sir A., 44, 67, 70
Granton (Edinburgh), 129, 135, 141, 215
Grantown-on-Spey, 43, 48
Grass *see* Clover
Grazing *see* Pasture
Great Glen, 20, 128, 251
Great North of Scotland Railway, 140–1, 219
Green Belt, 237, 241
Greenock, 26, 51–2, 63, 83, 139, 141, 151, 154–60, 204–5, 218–19, 240
Gretna (Annandale & Eskdale), 138, 236–7
Grid *see* Electricity
Growth *see* Modernisation
Growth Area/Point, 251, 266

Haddington, 23, 227
Hadrian's Wall, 13, 15
Haf, 62, 133
Hallside (Glasgow), 176–7
Hamilton, 127
Harbour *see* Port
Harris (Western Isles), 262–3, 271, 277
Harris Tweed, 271–2
Hawick, 138
Head Dyke, 29–30
Heads of Ayr (Kyle & Carrick), 218
Hebrides, 13–16, 21, 25, 62, 73, 94, 133, 180, 185, 187, 213, 218, 229, 262–77
Helensburgh, 138, 164
Helmsdale (Sutherland), 140
Hemp, 23
Herring, 23, 79, 93–4, 129, 132–3, 152, 188, 215, 269
Hides, 23–4, 50
Highland Railway, 140
Highland Society, 183
Highlands, 2, 8–9, 15, 17, 23, 30–2, 40–1, 48, 62–5, 232, 285–8
  Agriculture/Crofting in, 71, 74, 76–81, 124, 179–88, 207–13, 225
  Discontent in, 65
  Fishing in, 62, 132–3, 187
  Forestry in, 45, 246–61
  Industry in, 53–4, 97–108, 119, 186, 197, 205–6, 278
  Settlement in, 87–8
  Transport in, 48, 135–6, 140, 166–7, 218–21
Highlands & Islands Development Board (HIDB), 187, 200, 212–13, 217, 244, 269, 271, 276, 287–8
Hill Farm Research Organisation (HFRO), 209
Hillington (Glasgow), 197
Hinterland, 18, 23, 229, 233
Holdings *see* Farm
Holme (Orkney), 61
Hosiery, 23, 53, 76, 89, 272
Hotels, 141, 257
Houldsworth, H., 170
Housing, 148, 161–6, 235–6, 244 *see also* Council Housing
Houston (Renfrew), 82, 204, 237, 240
Hoy (Orkney), 273
Huntly, 43, 91, 124, 140, 256
Huntly, Earl of, 21
Hydro Electricity, 119, 205–6, 225, 287
Hunterston (Cuninghame), 201, 205, 218, 221

Illicit distillation *see* Smuggling
Import *see* Trade

Improving Movement, 1, 26, 54, 62, 66–96, 105, 111, 278
Inaccessibility *see* Accessibility
Inchinnan (Renfrew), 90
Industrial Estate, 197
Industrialisation/Industry, 4–7, 23–4, 31, 39, 41, 83, 87, 95, 120–3, 144–6, 186, 213, 221, 232, 244, 270–3, 278–9, 282–4
Industrial Location, 115, 141, 144–6, 167–76, 200–1
Infield *see* Field System
Infrastructure *see* Electricity, Transport etc.
Inner City, 201, 241, 244
Inner Hebrides *see* Hebrides
Innerwick (East Lothian), 69
Innovation, 116–17, 158–9
Inshore Fishing, 215–17
Integration, 140, 178, 204–5, 207, 227, 253–60, 263
Inveraray (Argyll & Bute), 91–2
Inveravon (Moray), 71
Inverbervie, 54
Invergarry (Lochaber), 278
Invergordon, 201, 205–6, 220
Inverie (Lochaber), 88
Inverkeithing, 50, 143
Inverkip (Inverclyde), 221
Inverlochy (Lochaber), 22
Inverness, 18, 52, 71, 136, 140, 197, 218–20, 229, 255
Inverurie, 51
Iodine, 272
Iona (Argyll & Bute), 22, 213
Ireland, 14, 16, 21, 25–6, 38, 83, 97, 100, 140, 155, 179, 205
Iron, 24, 39, 59, 118, 133–5, 141, 159, 162, 167–78, 196, 204–5, 284 *see also* Malleable Iron
Iron Furnace, 46, 58–9, 121, 169–72, 174, 178, 278
Iron Ore, 24, 58, 168–78, 218, 278, 282–3
Irvine, 240
Islands, 20, 32, 105, 262–77, 288
Islands Authorities, 9, 266
Islay (Argyll & Bute), 20, 29, 106, 108, 145, 272, 276
Isolation *see* Accessibility

Jacobites, 22, 38, 87, 278, 285–6
James II, 22
Jarlshof (Shetland), 273
John, 20
Johnstone, 51, 56, 155, 176
Jura (Argyll & Bute), 272, 276
Jute, 23, 129, 196

Kames, Lord, 42

Keith, 43–4, 54
Kelp, 50, 78, 184, 272
Kennoway (Kirkcaldy), 238
Kettle (North East Fife), 89
Kilbagie (Clackmannan), 61, 102
Kilbirnie, 139
Killoch Colliery (Cumnock & Doon Valley), 239
Kilmacolm (Inverclyde), 83, 139, 154
Kilmarnock, 136, 138, 170
Kilmaurs (Kilmarnock & Loudoun), 128
Kilsyth, 59
Kilwinning, 170–1, 175, 272
Kinghorn, 135, 143
Kinlochleven (Lochaber), 119, 205–6
Kinloch Rannoch (Perth & Kinross), 87
Kinloss (Moray), 19
Kintyre, 20, 22, 102–4, 106, 267
Kippen (Stirling), 87
Kirk *see* Church
Kirkcaldy, 60–1, 129, 135, 238
Kirkintilloch, 136
Kirkmichael (Moray), 71, 91
Kirknewton (Edinburgh), 49, 83
Kirkpatrick Durham (Stewartry), 90
Kirktoun *see* Township
Kirkwall, 25, 136, 143, 263–6
Kirriemuir, 60
Knoydart (Lochaber), 184
Kyleakin (Skye & Lochalsh), 94
Kyle of Lochalsh (Skye & Lochalsh), 140, 187

Labour, 6, 28, 32, 53–4, 56, 59, 63, 76, 88–9, 117, 131, 145, 175, 180–1, 192, 203, 242, 282–3
Labour Party, 196, 238
Labour Shedding, 6, 209, 226
Laird *see* Landowner
Lairg (Sutherland), 105
Lammermuir Hills (Berwickshire/East Lothian), 14, 17, 62
Lanark, 19, 25, 83, 127
Lanarkshire, 9, 55, 57, 162, 172–8, 237, 242, 279
Land Holding, 21, 26–31, *see also* Farm
Land Hunger, 191
Landowner/Landownership, 28, 31, 39, 41, 49, 62, 66–96, 103, 105, 107, 111, 124, 128, 152, 161, 179–92, 213, 280–1
Land Settlement, 21, 185, 212
Land Use, 66–81, 207–14, 235–6, 250–61
Langholm, 138, 260
Largs, 25
Laurencekirk, 54
Lead, 145–6
Lease, 27, 42, 79 *see also* Tenant

Leisure *see* Tourism
Leith, 21, 26, 50–1, 129, 135, 143, 145
Lenzie (Strathkelvin), 139, 164
Lerwick, 48, 133, 136, 143–4, 263–6, 272, 275
Letterewe (Ross & Cromarty), 24, 167
Levellers, 69
Leven, 54, 60–1, 143, 236, 238
Leverhulme, Lord, 186–7, 212, 277
Lighthouse, 136, 266, 273
Light Industry, 166
Lime/Lime Kiln, 27, 43, 49–50, 58, 74, 79, 119, 124, 183, 209
Linen, 23, 37, 39, 52–7, 59–61, 68, 88, 91–2, 118, 284
Lint Mill, 54, 91
Linwood (Renfrew), 203
Literacy, 31
Livestock, 31, 37 *see also* Cattle, Sheep etc.
Livingston, 196–7, 204, 239–40, 244
Local Government, 227–9, 233–4, 240, 244, 253, 266
Lochaber, 21–2, 69, 99
Lochaline (Lochaber), 184
Loch Arkaig (Lochaber), 183
Loch Awe (Argyll & Bute), 59, 258
Lochbay (Skye & Lochalsh), 94
Lochboisdale (Western Isles), 272, 275
Loch Broom (Ross & Cromarty), 53, 87
Loch Carron (Skye & Lochalsh), 53
Loch Erisort (Western Isles), 276
Loch Etive (Argyll & Bute), 46, 59, 167
Loch Fyne (Argyll & Bute), 46
Loch Horn (Lochaber/Skye & Lochalsh), 79
Lochiel Estate (Lochaber), 184
Loch Katrine (Stirling), 163, 234
Loch Laggan (Badenoch & Strathspey/Lochaber), 205
Loch Linnhe (Argyll & Bute/Lochaber), 183
Loch Lomond (Dumbarton/Stirling), 57, 241
Loch Long (Argyll & Bute/Dumbarton), 256–7
Loch Luichart (Ross & Cromarty), 225
Loch Marree (Ross & Cromarty), 257
Loch Morlich (Badenoch & Strathspey), 256–7
Loch Ness (Inverness), 168, 256, 258
Loch Ossian (Lochaber), 255
Loch Rannoch (Perth & Kinross), 46
Loch Roag (Western Isles), 270
Loch Spynie (Moray), 19
Loch Tay (Perth & Kinross/Stirling), 29, 81
Loch Treig (Lochaber), 205, 255
Lockerbie, 128
Locomotives, 136, 202
Logierait (Perth & Kinross), 43

London, 4–5, 12, 22, 51, 60, 63, 102, 271
Longannet (Dunfermline), 221, 242
Longside (Banff & Buchan), 51
Lord of the Isles, 20–1
Lords *see* Baronage
Lorn (Argyll & Bute), 20
Lossiemouth, 215
Lothian, 20, 23, 26, 58, 70–1, 121, 124, 173

Macbeth, 19
Machinery, 60–1, 176, 209, 246, 271
MacIan *see* Clan MacIan
MacKenzie *see* Clan MacKenzie
Mackinder, H. J., 165–6
MacLean *see* Clan MacLean
MacNeil *see* Clan MacNeil
Mailer *see* Croft *and* Smallholding
Malcolm III, 19–20
Malcolm IV, 19
Mallaig (Lochaber), 140, 187
Malleable Iron, 39, 174–7
Malting, 207
Management/Manager, 95, 108, 111, 269, 282–3
Manpower *see* Labour
Manufactures *see* Industry *and* Rural Industry
Mar (Gordon/Kincardine & Deeside), 18, 46
Marginal Land, 188–90, 209
Market, 27, 43, 48, 82–96, 111, 188, 207, 215, 269, 278–9, 283
Market Gardening, 82, 125–7
Markinch, 238–9
Marxism, 192
Mears, F., 238–40
Mechanisation *see* Machinery
Meigle (Angus), 48
Melrose, 19, 54, 61
Menteith (Stirling), 45
Mercantilism, 31–2
Merchandise/Merchant *see* Trade
Metallurgy, 118–19
Methil, 143
Migration, 32, 63, 118, 132, 146–52, 180–1, 191, 196, 211, 232, 241, 266, 288 *see also* Emigration
Military, 25, 78, 88, 93, 107, 143, 218, 266, 273–5
Military Road 48
Milk, 79, 83, 127–8
Milk Manufacture, 128
Milling, 61, 119, 124, 173
Millport, 266
Minch, 20, 94, 188
Ministers *see* Clergy
Mingulay (Western Isles), 266, 269

Modernisation, 3, 5, 31, 37–8, 277–8, 285
Moffat, 251
Molendinar Burn (Glasgow), 174
Monasteries *see* Religious Houses
Monck, Gen. G., 22
Monkland, 51, 59, 83, 121, 136, 168–78
Monkland Canal, 59, 138, 169
Monkland & Kirkintilloch Railway, 169
Monopolies, 18, 25, 29
Monquitter (Banff & Buchan), 76, 91
Monymusk (Gordon), 44, 67, 70, 84, 95,
    116–20, 256
Moorland, 209, 214, 246, 255
Moray, 15, 18–19, 48
Moray Firth, 15, 18, 49, 61, 94, 106–7, 132,
    251, 260
Mormaer, 19
Morvern (Lochaber), 21, 79, 182–4
Mossend (Motherwell), 175
Mossmorran (Dunfermline), 206
Motherwell, 139, 175–8, 197
Motor Vehicles, 202 *see also* Cars
Motorway, 218–19, 241
Motte, 19
Muir/Muirland *see* Moorland
Muirkirk (Cumnock & Doon Valley), 59, 83,
    168, 171, 173–4, 176
Mull (Argyll & Bute), 79, 93, 186, 225, 246,
    267, 275
Muthill (Perth & Kinross), 108

Nail/Nailer, 173
Nairn, 18–19, 82
Napier Commission, 186–8, 191
Napoleonic Wars, 41, 61, 76, 78, 85, 93, 104,
    106, 179, 183, 273
National Trust for Scotland, 24, 214
Nation State, 14–15, 20, 30–1
Natural Gas Liquids (NGL), 206
Navigation Act, 26, 37, 62
Navy *see* Military
Neilson, J. B., 168, 175
Neilston (Renfrew), 56
Netherlands, 24, 31
Nethy Bridge (Badenoch & Strathspey), 128
Newbattle (Midlothian), 23
Newburgh (Gordon), 140
Newcastle, 138
Newcastleton (Roxburgh), 92, 138
New Cumnock *see* Cumnock
Newhaven (Edinburgh), 24
New Lanark (Lanark), 57, 84–7, 95–6
Newmachar (Gordon), 74
New Monkland *see* Monkland
New Statistical Account *see* Statistical
    Account
Newton Stewart, 82

Nigg (Aberdeen), 44
Nigg (Ross & Cromarty), 206
Nith, River (Nithsdale), 138
North America *see* America
North British Railway, 138–40, 143, 164
North Isles *see* Orkney *and* Shetland
Northmavine (Shetland), 269
North Morar (Lochabar), 184
North of Scotland Hydro Electric Board,
    221–5, 276, 283
North Sea Oil, 206
North Uist *see* Uist
Nuclear Power, 221–5

Oats, 73, 83
Oban, 140, 258
Ochil Hills (Perth & Kinross), 17, 48
O'Dell, A. C., 2, 50
Oil, 121, 196, 206, 269, 272, 288
Oil Refinery, 206
Oil Shale, 121
Old Deer (Banff & Buchan), 51
Old Statistical Account *see* Statistical
    Account
Open Hearth Furnace, 176–8
Ormiston (East Lothian), 54, 67
Outer Hebrides *see* Hebrides
Outer Regions, 9–10, 40, 50, 64–5, 74, 120,
    151–2, 232, 284–5
    Agriculture Forestry & Fishing in, 123–33,
        207–17, 246–61
    Industry in, 59–62, 91–3, 95–6, 117–23,
        141, 204–7, 221
    Power in 221–5
Outfield *see* Field System
Overpopulation, 69, 184–5
Overspill Population, 196, 232, 241
Owen, R., 85

Paisley, 25, 55–6, 57, 90, 138, 155, 164, 173
Park (Western Isles), 276
Parish, 46–52, 116, 120, 129–30, 191–2, 286
Parks, 163, 233, 241
Parliament, 24, 31, 100
Pasture, 45, 80 *see also* Common
    Grazing/Pasture
Peat, 49, 89, 212, 272
Peebles, 140
Pendicle *see* Croft *and* Smallholding
Pentland Hills (Edinburgh), 49
Pentland Firth (Caithness/Orkney), 25
Peripheral Regions, 7–8 *see also* Outer
    Regions
Perth, 17–18, 23, 51, 54–5, 60–1, 88, 135,
    140, 143, 219–20, 233
Perth & Kinross, 14, 69
Perthshire, 29

Peterhead, 51, 120, 129, 132, 215, 221, 229
Petrochemicals, 206
Picts, 13–15, 27
Pier *see* Port
Pigs, 83
Pipeline, 206, 272
Pitsligo (Banff & Buchan), 43, 54
Placenames, 28
Plague, 22
Plaiding *see* Wool
Planned Village, 40, 43–4, 48, 82–96, 180–1, 286
Planning *see* Regional Planning
Plantation *see* Colonisation
Plockton (Skye & Lochalsh), 94
Poland, 24
Police, 90
Pollution, 129
Poor Law, 148, 152, 181
Population, 8–9, 32, 40, 78, 87, 111–15, 117–18, 146–52, 179, 181, 263–7, 284
Port, 6, 22, 25, 31, 48, 50–2, 94, 115, 131–2, 141–4, 187–8, 201, 205–6, 218, 269–70, 276
Port Dundas (Glasgow), 161, 169
Port Elphinstone (Gordon), 61
Port Glasgow 26, 52, 83, 154–8, 202, 218, 240
Portpatrick (Wigtown), 145–6
Port Seton (Edinburgh), 238
Portsoy, 43
Portree (Skye & Lochalsh), 266
Potato, 79, 183
Poverty, 32, 147–50
Power *see* Energy
Power Station, 221–5, 242, 272
Presbyterianism, 22, 25, 30–1, 87, 279–80, 286
Prestongrange (East Lothian), 24
Prestonpans, 24, 57–8, 121, 136
Prestwick (Kyle & Carrick), 218
Prices, 67, 69, 74, 76, 106, 129, 145, 163, 174, 192, 263, 276
Proletariat *see* Labour
Protection, 31
Protestant Ethic, 279
Protestantism *see* Presbyterianism
Public Works *see* Infrastructure
Pulp, 260–1
Pumped Storage, 225
Pumpherston (West Lothian), 121

Quarrying, 188
Quoy, 29

Raasay (Skye & Lochalsh), 129
Radicalism, 186

Rafting, 46
Raiding, 20–1, 25–6
Railway, 50–1, 135–46, 163–4, 166, 174, 187, 200, 205–6, 218–20, 284
Rannoch Moor (Lochaber/Perth & Kinross), 46, 257
Ravenscraig (Motherwell), 204–5
Rayne (Gordon), 76
Reclamation, 81, 84, 125, 141, 191, 212–13, 242
Recreation *see* Tourism
Reformation, 25
Regional Adjustment, 40–1, 64–5, 88, 103–6, 151–2, 277
Regional Development, 2, 6–7, 32–3, 62–5, 211, 238, 283
Regional Planning, 195, 229, 232–45, 282
Regional Protection, 196
Regional Specialisation, 69–71
Religious Houses, 23
Renfrew, 22, 25, 127, 153–4, 156, 159
Renfrewshire, 55, 57
Reservoir, 23
Resettlement, 105, 183–4, 277, 280
Retirement, 266
Rhynie (Gordon), 91
Roads, 23, 48–9, 53, 74, 91, 111, 135, 140, 200, 206, 214, 218–20, 227, 234–5, 242, 275–6
Rogart (Sutherland), 105
Rolling Mill, 205
Roman Catholicism, 22
Run-rig, 30, 73–4, 80
Rural Development, 46–52, 251
Rural Settlement, 1, 13, 26–30, 80–1, 111–15, 225–9, 284 *see also* Village
Rural Industry, 41, 53–4, 60, 69, 91–3
Russia, 39
Rostow, W. W., 3, 7, 279
Rosyth (Dunfermline), 143, 236, 238
Rotation, 70, 74
Rothesay, 39, 56, 266
Rothiermurchus (Badenoch & Strathspey), 46, 257
Roxburghshire, 74
Roy, Gen., 1
Royal Burgh, 16–19, 25, 28–9, 31–2, 82, 84
Rutherglen, 26, 139, 152, 164, 238

St Andrews, 17
St Fergus (Banff & Buchan), 51, 74
St Kilda (Western Isles), 263–6, 269
Salmon, 23, 153, 213
Salt, 24, 57–8
Saltcoats, 27, 58, 175
Sanday (Orkney), 272
Sandwick (Shetland), 272

Sanquhar, 145
Scalloway (Shetland), 144
Scalpay (Western Isles), 262–3, 269
Scandinavians *see* Vikings
Scapa Flow (Orkney), 273–5
Scarp (Western Isles), 267
Scattald, 73
School, 53, 83, 85, 91–2, 120, 163
Scone (Perth & Kinross), 14
Scotia *see* Alba
Scots, 13–15
Scots Pine, 45, 128, 255
Scott, Sir. W., 24, 129, 233
Scottish Council (Development & Industry),
     201, 203
Scottish Development Agency, 197, 243–4,
     283
Scottish Enlightenment, 39–44, 68, 84, 281
Scottish Industrial Estates Commission, 197
Scottish Malt Distillers, 207
Scottish Milk Marketing Board, 128
Scottish National Party, 196, 232
Scottish Office, 197, 232, 237, 240, 283
Scottish Plan, 197, 247, 288
Scottish Special Housing Association, 236,
     244
Scrabster (Caithness), 140
Scrap Iron, 177–8, 204
Seafield, Earl of, 82
Seaweed, 272
Secretary of State for Scotland, 200, 232,
     237, 276, 283
Seine Net Fishing, 215
Serfdom *see* Feudalism
Service Centre, 43, 82–96, 111, 213, 266, 276
Servicemen *see* Military
Services, 195 *see also* Service Centre
Settlement *see* Rural Settlement *and* Town
Sheep, 45, 78, 93, 124, 179–84, 207, 259,
     267, 287
Shell Fish, 269
Shelter Belt, 45, 259
Sheriffdom, 18, 20
Shetland, 13, 16, 49–50, 53, 62, 129–31, 133,
     136, 140, 181, 218, 262–6, 272, 275
Shieling, 180
Shipbuilding, 31, 118, 141–3, 156, 158–60,
     175–7, 201–2, 218, 243, 279, 282
Shipping, 23, 26, 43, 50, 135–6, 139, 153–7
Shires *see* Counties
Shotts (Motherwell), 59, 133–5, 171, 178
Shooting, 91
Sibbald, R., 27
Sidlaw Hills (Angus/Perth & Kinross), 23
Silk, 56
Sinclair, Sir J., 46–52, 78
Skara Brae (Orkney), 13

Skiary (Lochaber), 79
Skill *see* Labour
Skins *see* Hides
Skye (Skye & Lochalsh), 20, 99, 272, 275
Slamannan (Falkirk), 138, 171
Slum Clearance, 165, 178
Smallholding, 80, 84, 89–90, 94, 105, 123,
     129, 185, 188–92, 211–13, 253, 276–7,
     285, 287, *see also* Croft
Smith, A., 41, 49, 67, 81, 281, 286
Smuggling, 100–8
Social Mobilisation, 3
Social Overhead Capital *see* Infrastructure
Social Problems, 42, 165, 186–7, 195, 272–3
Society of Improvers, 67
Soft Fruit *see* Fruit
Sorn (Cumnock & Doon Valley), 89
Sound of Mull (Argyll & Bute/Lochaber),
     15
South of Scotland Electricity Board, 221–5
South Ronaldsay (Orkney), 50, 273
South Uist *see* Uist
Specialisation, 69–71, 116–20, 123–8, 141
Spey, 17, 108, 118, 140, 205, 207, 214, 219
Spinning *see* Linen, Wool etc.
Spinningdale (Sutherland), 56
Splint Coal, 168, 178
Springburn (Glasgow), 139, 162, 165, 202,
     243
Strome Ferry (Skye & Lochalsh), 140
Strontian (Lochaber), 145, 182
Squatting, 267, 277
Stanley (Perth & Kinross), 57, 87
State, 119
Statistical Account: New, 47, 128
     Old, 43, 46–52, 63, 74–81, 89–90, 96
     Third, 47
Steam Power, 57, 124, 147, 156
Steamship, 133, 135–6, 139–40, 166, 187,
     220, 276
Steel, 118, 128, 173, 176–8, 204–5, 279
Stirling, 15, 17, 51, 219
Stockings *see* Hosiery
Stonehouse (Lanark), 243–4
Stornoway, 48, 82, 94, 140, 218, 263–6, 272
Stow (Ettrick & Lauderdale), 48
Strachan (Kincardine & Deeside), 44
Strachur (Argyll & Bute), 257–60
Stranraer, 260
Strathclyde, 14, 125–8, 240
Strathconon (Ross & Cromarty), 105
Strathdon (Gordon), 71, 107
Strathmiglo (North East Fife), 60
Strathmore (Angus/Kincardine & Deeside),
     23, 51, 136
Strelitz (Perth & Kinross), 88
Stevenston, 26, 58

Stromness, 25, 143
Stronsay (Orkney), 70, 76
Subsidies, 276
Subsistence, 7, 73, 81, 89, 93
Sugar, 52
Sullom Voe (Shetland), 206, 272–3
Sutherland, 16, 69, 180
Sutherland, Duke of, 103, 140
Sweden, 24, 39
Symbister (Shetland), 62

Tacksman, 42, 57, 79–80, 179, 182
Tain, 18
Tan Bark, 45, 128
Tanera (Ross & Cromarty, 93
Taxes, 18, 25, 28, 50, 100, 153
Tay, 14, 23, 43, 49, 140, 143
Taynuilt (Argyll & Bute), 46, 167–8
Tayport, 140
Tayside, 9, 27, 57, 206, 238, 251, 255
Technology, 4–6, 41–4, 51, 68–9, 81, 111,
    136, 178, 271, 281–2
Tenant, 30, 42–3, 70, 73, 76, 79–81, 124,
    179–92, 211, 267
Tenement, 85, 162–6
Textiles, 5, 24, 53, 99, 117–18, 206, 278,
    283–4 *see also* Linen, Wool etc.
Thanage, 27
Thankerton (Lanark), 128
Third Statistical Account *see* Statistical
    Account
Thurso, 140
Tidewater, 175, 204–6
Tighnabruaich (Argyll & Bute), 257–8
Timber *see* Wood
Tiree (Argyll & Bute), 79, 104, 119, 267, 272
Tobacco, 37–9, 52, 56, 283
Tobermory, 94, 266
Tomintoul (Moray), 91, 95
Toothill Report, 197, 219
Torness (East Lothian), 221
Tourism, 129–30, 209, 211, 213–14, 253–9,
    273, 275, 287
Toun *see* Township
Town, 2, 4, 24, 63–5, 141, 146–52, 191–2,
    195–204, 225–9, 232, 284, 287
Town & Country Planning (Scotland) Act,
    236
Township, 27–9, 80, 84, 96
Trade, 5, 7, 18, 22–7, 29, 31, 37–9, 41, 115,
    153–66, 181, 263, 269, 284
Tradesman, 89, 160
Tranent, 50, 136
Transport, 6, 31–2, 40, 48–9, 115, 148, 169,
    174, 217–21, 241, 270, 275–6
Trawler, 129–31, 188, 215
Troon, 136

Truck System, 269
Tullibody (Clackmannan), 238
Tullynessle (Gordon), 74
Tummel (Perth & Kinross), 225, 258
Turnips, 70–1, 74, 76, 125
Turnpike *see* Road
Turriff, 61
Tweed, River, 14–15
Tyne, 15
Tynninghame (East Lothian), 67

Uist (Western Isles), 213, 271, 275
Ullapool (Ross & Cromarty), 88, 94
Unemployment, 197
Union, 5, 32, 37–8, 58, 62, 67, 278, 281
Union Canal, 51, 100, 133, 138
University, 17, 280
Unst (Shetland), 273, 275
Uphall (West Lothian), 83
Upper Clyde Shipbuilders, 202, 243
Urban Settlement *see* Town
Urquhart (Moray), 69
Urquhart (Ross & Cromarty), 98–9
Urray (Ross & Cromarty), 99

Vale of Leven (Dumbarton) 57, 162, 202,
    242
Vatersay (Western Isles), 267
Village, 119, 131, 190, 225, 229, 253 *see also*
    Planned Village
Vikings, 14, 16, 20, 25, 273
Voe, 133

Wales, 6, 168–70, 175
Wanlockhead (Nithsdale), 84, 133, 145–6
Wars of Independence, 18, 20
Water, 23–4, 233–4
Water Power, 40, 56–7, 60, 85, 124, 145,
    168, 173–4
Water Transport, 133–6
Waulkmill, 28
Weaver/Weaving, 92, 96 *see also* Linen,
    Wool etc.
West-Central Scotland, 54–9, 117–23, 242,
    244, 281, 284 *see also* Central Belt
Western Isles *see* Hebrides
West Highlands *see* Highlands
West Kilbride (Cunninghame), 74
West Linton (Tweedale), 43, 49
Westray (Orkney), 50, 267–8
Whaling, 73, 129–31
Whalsay (Shetland), 269
Whisky, 22, 40, 61, 96–108, 118, 124, 140,
    207, 272, 286
White Fishing, 61–2, 94, 132–3, 187–8,
    215–17
Wick, 94, 132, 136

Wigtown, 22
Wilderness, 214, 258
Wild Life, 256–8
William the Conquerer, 20
William the Lion, 20
Wilsontown (Lanark), 59, 133, 168, 171, 174
Wind Power, 61
Winter Sports, 258–9
Wishaw *see* Motherwell

Wiston & Roberton (Lanark), 74
Wood, 24, 156, 168, 246–61
Woodland, 44–6, 128–9
Wood Processing, 246, 260–1
Wool, 23, 61, 89, 272 *see also* Hosiery

Yell (Shetland), 269, 275
York Buildings Company, 46, 50, 136, 167